STUTTGARTER ARBEITEN ZUR GERMANISTIK

herausgegeben von

Ulrich Müller, Franz Hundsnurscher und Cornelius Sommer

Nr. 67

MAX FRISCH

His Work and Its Swiss Background

by

Malcolm Pender

AKADEMISCHER VERLAG HANS-DIETER HEINZ

Stuttgart 1979

Die Reihe „STUTTGARTER ARBEITEN ZUR GERMANISTIK"
ist die **neugermanistische** Fortsetzung der Reihe
„GÖPPINGER ARBEITEN ZUR GERMANISTIK".
Verlag Alfred Kümmerle, Göppingen.
In den „GÖPPINGER ARBEITEN ZUR GERMANISTIK"
erscheinen ab Band 160 ausschließlich Veröffentlichungen aus
dem Gebiet der Altgermanistik und der Sprachwissenschaft.

Verlag Hans-Dieter Heinz, Stuttgart 1979
Druck: Sprint-Druck GmbH, Stuttgart 30
ISBN 3-88099-068-9
Printed in Germany

For

Mary, Ute and Elizabeth

Acknowledgements

I wish to record my thanks to everyone who helped me to complete this study. I owe special debts to Professor W. W. Chambers, Glasgow, for his invaluable advice and support in the preparation of the material, and to Professor E. O. McInnes, Hull, for tirelessly furthering the project. I should also like to thank Professor J. M. Ritchie, Sheffield, for his help and encouragement.

The editors of German Life and Letters allowed me to reprint sections of my article in vol. 32, 1979, and the editors of Quinquereme allowed me to include from a forthcoming article a paragraph on pages 194-195. I thank them for this permission.

The University of Strathclyde   October 1979
Glasgow.

CONTENTS

I   <u>THE SWISS SITUATION AND MAX FRISCH</u>

1. The Swiss Situation

Introduction

Few countries can be said to excite the intellectual attention of
its nationals as much as Switzerland. An assessment of Swiss
peculiarities has well-nigh become a requirement if a Swiss is to
merit serious consideration within the country. The matter is not
restricted to the public domain, but has ramifications which extend
into the sphere of the individual personality. The nature of the
individual's attitude to Switzerland is regarded as a projection of
his attitude towards himself [1]. A definition of Switzerland thus
forms part of the individual's progress towards a valid definition of
his own personality. If one aspect of the attempt to define the Swiss
situation is its scope, another is its spirit, which is characterised
by the belief that Switzerland is 'ein besonderes Wesen' [2]. This is
reflected not only in creative writing, but also in a long tradition
of essay-writing. It is especially in this latter genre that arguments
are put forward and writers' personal definitions are found [3].

It is important that the factors which inspire this examination of
background and origins should be enumerated, as they inevitably colour
the conclusions which writers reach. This study is concerned with the
conclusions of a notable contemporary, Max Frisch. It will be shown
that Frisch's attitudes have been derived from the same basic situation
as that confronting Swiss writers in his own and in previous generations.
Because of the special experience of his generation, however, these
attitudes acquire a less optimistic and more sombre cast than those of
his predecessors.

The Swiss situation and its definition

A characteristic of the history of Switzerland is the marked
difference in its development from that of her neighbours. Indeed,
Hermann Weilenmann sees this development as running counter in all its
stages to the general pattern of European historical development.
Weilenmann cites four instances of this contrary movement: the break
with feudalism in 1291, the federative nature of the cantonal alliances
at the beginning of the modern era when the greater part of Europe was
under absolute monarchical rule, the relative lack of upheaval caused
by religious differences after the Reformation, and fourthly, as a
consequence of the French Revolution, the creation of a multi-lingual
confederation [1]. The manifestations of 1848 across Europe were also

to have a unique outcome in Switzerland, 'the one country in which the progressives had achieved an enduring triumph' [2]. These differences and the fact that the composition of the modern confederation can be said to reflect more directly its origin than the political structure of her neighbours, nourish the idea of the sturdy independence of the Swiss people. It has not always been realised that this has been an independence which Switzerland's powerful neighbours have found convenient to accept.

The favour and protection accorded to the country by the French kings from the end of the fifteenth century did much to buttress the relatively frail confederation against serious assault. Despite its plentiful supplies of troops to both sides, the confederation did not become involved in the Thirty Years War. Instead, it emerged from the Peace of Westphalia in 1648 with its neutrality recognised by the major European powers. This recognition was disregarded by Napoleon in 1798, and the French invasion emphasised the vulnerability of the country to resolute and determined attack. This vulnerability was tacitly admitted one hundred and fifty years later during the Second World War in the concept of the 'Reduit', whereby the Swiss army planned to sacrifice a large part of Swiss territory in order to hold out in the country's most inaccessible terrain, should the country's neutrality again be violated.

The uneasy position which reality occupies between the Swiss assertion of independence on the one hand and toleration by others of this independence is ironically highlighted by the letter which Napoleon sent in 1802 to the member cantons of the Helvetic Republic which he had created from the old confederation [3]. The letter acknowledged the uniqueness of Switzerland, but at the same time implicitly underlined her defencelessness since it constituted the first step which Napoleon took towards imposing on the powerless cantons the Act of Mediation two months later. Yet benefits accrued to Switzerland from the French intervention, the most fundamental being a change in the political status of the individual [4]. Thus the only serious breach of Swiss neutrality in modern times had positive consequences in that the confederation acquired through it a dimension which it did not up until then possess.

The paradoxical relationship between the avowed Swiss desire for independence and its practical implementation by others is further emphasised by the undignified squabbling amongst the cantons at the Vienna peace conference of 1815, where the fabric of Switzerland was preserved by the Allies and not by the Swiss themselves [5]. Whether in

fact the emergence of Switzerland intact from two world wars in the
course of the twentieth century is due to respect on the part of the
participants for this independence or more to the economic and
geographical usefulness to them of Switzerland during the hostilities
is a very involved question which precludes all simple answers. Moreover, the particular development of Swiss history and the country's
geographical position render the country unique. Despite many assertions
to the contrary, no generalisations can profitably be drawn from the
interaction of geography and history in the Swiss case.

It is perhaps in the nature of things that the Swiss should seek
to make this random historical development, over which they have been
able to exercise at best only partial control, appear to be the product
of a conscious act of will. The legend of Wilhelm Tell and the rejection
of Habsburg overlordship by the three forest cantons provides, firstly,
an explicable focal point for the various subsequent cantonal alliances.
It is an explanation of the sheer obscurity which surrounds the
alliance of 1291. In the second place, this explanation accounts for
the differences of Swiss history from that of her neighbours in that the
rejection of the Habsburgs can be portrayed as the first triumph of the
innate Swiss penchant for democracy. Increasing use of original
documents as the basis for historical judgements helped, in the course
of the nineteenth and twentieth centuries, to present a more sober
interpretation of the facts of Swiss history, and so went some way to
dispelling popular misconceptions [6].

If the difference of development, its random nature, and control by
foreign interests present the facts of Switzerland as opposed to an
idealised interpretation, then an accommodation with these facts is
rendered more difficult, especially in this century, by Switzerland's
neutrality. At the start of the First World War, Carl Spitteler, in
his well-known address Unser Schweizer Standpunkt, appeals for strict
observance of that neutrality, although well aware of the difficulties
which it implies:

> Wir müssen uns eben die Tatsache vor Augen halten, dass im
> Grunde kein Angehöriger einer kriegführenden Nation eine
> neutrale Gesinnung als berechtigt empfindet. [7]

The Second World War, so much more destructive and so much more
comprehensive in its involvement, was to strain this neutrality to its
utmost. It cast a harsh light on the problems of those living within
the framework of this neutrality, and the questions which they faced
were formulated by Edgar Bonjour after the War:

> What ardour or energy can it (neutrality) inspire? Is it
> not too cool for hot-blooded youth, too many-facetted for an
> age which loves clear-cut issues?...Does neutrality not lead
> to a deadening of moral feeling, does it not, when consistently
> maintained, end in the abominable condition of a resigned and [8]
> cowardly indifference?

The 'Bedürfnis nach Rechtfertigung' [9] which runs through the attitude
of the Swiss to their country derives in large part from these questions.
It arises from a feeling that the political entity which is Switzerland
must be justified since it is not apparently viable in terms which are
normally accepted as defining a country. Switzerland has 'no continuous
natural boundaries, no common language, no common race, no common
religion, not even a common history' [10]. In these circumstances, it is
not surprising that the tone of some of the comments of those who are
involved in the situation and attempting to come to terms with it is so
anguished.

The one single factor which would appear to militate most against
political unity is the lack of a common language. This lack causes two
difficulties for the Swiss. Firstly, a multi-lingual state runs counter
to the modern acceptance of the idea that language and nation are
co-extensive terms. Thus the Swiss do not have the focus for national
identity usually provided by a single language within the state. As
the original German-speaking nucleus of cantons was gradually widened to
include other language groups, it developed from a 'Nationalstaat' to
a 'Nationalitätenstaat' [11]. The special development of Switzerland
thus runs counter to the rise elsewhere of nationalism as a political
force. Because this development was not in any way organic, the country
has been subjected to severe internal strains in time of national
crisis, such as during the First and Second World Wars [12].

The other difficulty deriving from a lack of common language
arises from the fact that three of the country's four official
languages are those of three major European cultures, each with a powerful national identity. Gottfried Keller's famous objection to the idea
that Switzerland constitutes a mere collection of appendages to those
cultures [13] was formulated seven years before the existence of official
languages was guaranteed by the Swiss constitution in 1848. The
substance of the objection was still applicable a century later, when
precisely the assertion refuted by Keller formed the basis of Nazi
propaganda which sought to reinforce unexamined assumptions about those
who share a common language. Yet language does create ties: in 1968
J.R. von Salis was able to claim that the German-Swiss are better informed

about the Germans than about their countrymen in other parts of
Switzerland [14]. The belief that this ease of linguistic communication
across the frontier had to be resisted if the political fabric of
Switzerland was to be sustained was one of the motivations behind
Unser Schweizer Standpunkt.

The second major feature of Switzerland which evokes comment is
its size. On the one hand, there is the recognition that the country
is small, which results 'in a certain mauvaise honte' [15]. On the other
hand, the very size of neighbouring countries introduces a qualitative
distinction: not only does the physical protection afforded by the
state to the citizen appear to be narrowly circumscribed by the
territorial limitations of that state, but these limitations give rise
to feelings of inadequacy since the psyche of the nation must apparently
be related to that size. C.-F. Ramuz, in a well-known question, asks
despairingly:

> Un petit pays est-il condamné par sa petitesse à ne [16]
> pas connaître la grandeur?

Max Frisch combines the problem of language with the problem of size;
he writes of a journey in Germany when he responded to the vastness of
the country with its single language:

> Wie schön, dass man tagelang fahren kann, und das Feld, das
> vorbeizieht, heisst immer noch Feld, nicht champ, nicht campo.
> (II 525)

The extent of territory over which the language is spoken accords it a
dimension absent from the same language in Switzerland. The intellect
is haunted by a vision of Switzerland as 'eine vergraste Provinz
abseits der Geschichte' [17]. The precision of the most perspicacious
writing on Switzerland springs from a desire to differentiate that which
is held to be Swiss while at the same time acknowledging honestly the
validity and extent of the cultures which surround the country, and on
which it can and does draw.

The two difficulties of language and size encountered by the Swiss
in coming to terms with their country are increased by a third factor –
its permanent neutrality. There are strains in maintaining a posture
of attentive and armed inaction, and these are symbolised in the figure
of Felix Moeschlin's soldier who wished to fight with the Germans in the
First World War, not from any particular wish to espouse the German
cause, but 'bloss um dabei zu sein' [18]. In times of crisis, when there
are calls for clear commitment to one side or the other, the difficulties
in maintaining a foreign policy of non-alignment are highlighted. On
the one hand, there is the assumption that action is morally superior

6.

to inaction. To the German-Swiss soldier the idea that he is 'nicht zum Heldentum berufen' [19] is a concept contrary to much traditional military thinking. On the other hand, the assumption that inaction is superior to action must be resisted. This was Spitteler's urgent message:

> Dass wir als Unbeteiligte manches klarer sehen, richtiger beurteilen als die in Kampfleidenschaft Befangenen, versteht sich von selber. Das ist ein Vorteil der Stellung, nicht ein geistiger Vorzug. [20]

Yet the attitude attacked by Spitteler felt itself vindicated when Switzerland emerged intact and prosperous, not only at the end of the First World War, but also at the end of the Second. Walter Muschg felt that the Swiss ought then to have regarded their being spared as an opportunity to assume a moral obligation to those who had suffered; but the opportunity to show generosity was lost, inertia was stronger than any move towards combatting self-satisfaction [21]. Max Frisch also sees Switzerland's escape as being quite fortuitous and in no way attributable to superior moral qualities (II 589). Smallness and weakness must not absolve Switzerland from all responsibility. Jörg Steiner's line 'Hiroshima ist ein Dorf in der Schweiz' [22] is an attempt to emphasise this. If neutrality implies physical withdrawal, it should not also imply moral evasion of the problems of the world.

The difficulty of moving towards a national self-awareness is not of course confined to Switzerland, but Albin Zollinger nonetheless considers that there are special impediments placed in modern Switzerland's way to a proper understanding of herself by her 'Relativitäten und Differenzierungen' [23], which arise from the complex composition of the country and which it is increasingly difficult to respect in a world which tends to standardisation. In addition, the national of a small country harbours not merely unexamined attitudes towards his nationality, but also the psychological need to assert the quality of that nationality [24]. In the case of Switzerland this feeling of superiority is reflected in her nationals' praise of the political and linguistic composition of the country. Co-existence of the language groups in Switzerland in the heart of a Europe whose modern history has been characterised by war and dissension, the basis of which has resided largely in the conflict between language groups, can be used to proclaim Switzerland as a 'Vorbild Europas' [25]. The fact that the country remained unharmed amid the devastation of the Second World War appeared to be the final and irrefutable proof of the moral worth inherent in the political structure of the country, of the moral reward which justly accrued to the Swiss nation. The false assessment at the basis of this

belief persists as an 'Existenzlüge' [26] in a manner deleterious to the
country. This unfounded self-assurance, which prompts notions of moral
superiority, militates against that which, despite its age, is 'ein
höchst delikates und gefährdetes Gebilde' [27]. It would appear that, far
from offering its citizens permanent moral asylum, Switzerland imposes
on them a heavy burden of obligation to achieve self-definition.

The apparent lack of elements traditionally accepted as cohesive in
a nation, the smallness of that nation and its sustained neutrality in
foreign policy all increase the difficulties encountered in defining the
essence of a nation. This has led to the view that the Swiss nation has
been formed by a 'Wille zum Staat' [28]. The disparate elements which
constitute the nation are posited as cohering by virtue of an ethos
under which they can be ordered. While not rejecting this view, Karl
Schmid has objected that it overlooks the cohesion afforded by the
dimension of time [29]. A third cohesive element has been suggested. A
character in Meinrad Inglin's novel Schweizerspiegel (1938), shortly
after he has witnessed the severe internal strains to which his country
has been subjected as a result of the First World War, claims that there
is a spiritual kinship between the groups which make up Switzerland [30].
The two cohesive factors of volition and time are seen to require a third,
more shadowy, dimension of spiritual affinity.

The dialectic thus set up in the attempt to establish an adequate
definition of Switzerland has been expressed in several forms. This
dialectic is implicit in Spitteler's Unser Schweizer Standpunkt (1914),
when he refers to his French-speaking countrymen and the obligation the
German-Swiss have towards them:

> Wir müssen uns bewusst werden, dass der politische Bruder [31]
> uns nähersteht als der beste Nachbar und Rassenverwandte.

Ramuz's Besoin de Grandeur (1937) is a full-length exploration of the
dialectic as he saw it; for him it can only be resolved in the moral
sphere:

> Nous sommes...tout petits...où trouver la grandeur qui [32]
> seule peut nous sauver?

Ramuz's argument was taken up at this point in 1963 by Manfred Gsteiger,
who differentiates the dilemma:

> Damit sind die zwei Pole genannt, zwischen denen unser
> geistiges Leben oszilliert. Aber sie heissen nicht nur Klein-
> heit und Grösse, sie heissen auch Vielheit und Einheit, Region
> und Nation, Heimat und Fremde, Individuum und Gesellschaft,
> Kunst und Moral, Mensch und Gott. [33]

The many spheres in which the impact of this dialectic is felt indicate
the width and complexity of the problem.

To this dialectical framework Karl Schmid has added two further
concepts, 'Doppelbürgertum' and 'Gegenläufigkeit'. 'Doppelbürgertum'
relates to the socio-cultural position of the Swiss citizen:

> Als Angehöriger einer die Grenzen unseres Landes weit über-
> spannenden Sprachgemeinschaft ist er dem deutschen, franzö-
> sischen, italienischen Kulturbereich verpflichtet. Als Glied
> der Eidgenossenschaft muss er aber überdies und gleichzeitig
> Träger einer ganz bestimmten staatlichen und genossenschaft-
> lichen Kultur sein, welche seine soziale und staatsbürger-
> liche Wertwelt bestimmt. [34]

Hans Bänziger, in his study of Jakob Schaffner, Robert Walser und Albin
Zollinger, indicates the conditions under which this 'Doppelbürgertum'
exists. Switzerland must be able to provide a political and intellectual
focus for its citizens. Failure to do so may give rise to the forms of
estrangement from the country exemplified by each of the three writers [35].

Schmid's second concept, 'Gegenläufigkeit', not only resolves the
historical and psychological contradictions of the country, but also
confers on her a role in the psychological composition of Europe as a
whole. The manifestations of 'Gegenläufigkeit' derive from a

> Gesetz der polaren Ergänzung, das offenbar alles Leben
> bestimmt...Und je wissentlicher und willentlicher ein indi-
> viduelles oder ein kollektives Bewusstsein - das Bewusstsein
> einer Nation oder einer Epoche zum Beispiel - es nur noch mit
> einem beschränkenden und beschränkten Ausschnitt des seelisch
> Möglichen zu tun haben will, um so dichter und zündkräftiger
> organisiert sich das Verbannte und das Verfemte anderswo als
> gegenläufiger Komplex. [36]

Building on ideas similar to those contained in Näf's historical
explanation of the structure of the Swiss state [37], and expanding
Weilenmann's brief outline of the development of Switzerland since the
Middle Ages [38], Schmid goes on to depict Switzerland as a country which
harbours these compensating forces. He concludes:

> Wir meinen, diese ganz unbewusste Bereitschaft, dem Wider-
> läufigen ein Ort zu sein, bestimme diese schweizerische
> Nationalität in ihrer Tiefe. [39]

This definition of function seeks to resolve the problem of relating the
differences of Switzerland to the generality of Europe.

The polarities expressed as 'Bruder' - 'Nachbar', 'petitesse' -
'grandeur', 'Wille' - 'Geschichte', 'Vielheit' - 'Einheit', and the
concepts of 'Doppelbürgertum' and 'Gegenläufigkeit' all represent
attempts at a delineation of the Swiss situation in terms of the social,
political and cultural role of the individual citizen, who requires to
recognise clearly the dialectic within which he is placed. For if the
cultural debt to the surrounding countries is acknowledged, it can the
more readily be so if the quite different and apparently durable

political structure of the debtor is stressed. The affirmation of
difference within a context of similarity creates an interplay between
that which is differentiated and that which is acknowledged. This
interplay gives rise to a situation which is peculiarly Swiss:

> Es ist für diesen Staat und für die seelische Struktur dieser
> Nation fundamental, dass 'das Politische' und 'das Kulturelle'
> praktisch ungeschiedene Bereiche sind. [40]

Yet ironically, the many syntheses of the country apparently prevent
Swiss achievements from having a sufficiently distinct character to make
them readily discernible to the rest of the world [41].

Perhaps for the very reason that there will never be a simple solution,
not only to the imprecise idea of Switzerland held by outsiders, but also
to the problems of definition of the insiders, Switzerland is, for those
born into it, 'unentrinnbar' [42]. In 1939 Albin Zollinger claimed that
the difficulties of being Swiss are increasing in the twentieth century [43].
Max Frisch, with his rigorous attention to his 'Zeitgenossenschaft'
(II 340), exemplifies the particular difficulties of that generation of
Swiss who lived through the Second World War and experienced the
radically changed world which emerged after it.

The predicament of the Swiss writer

If the creative writer possesses 'a vital capacity for experience' [1],
this will tend to come into conflict with the restrictive influence of
the institutions and traditions of his environment. Yet these
institutions and traditions tend to be viewed by the generality of men
as immutable [2]. Part of the writer's motivation must spring from his
perception of the limitations thus placed on self-realisation. The
writer can therefore be viewed as 'ein rätselhaftes Vitamin' [3] within
the body of society, without which that body would atrophy. This role
has been, and is often, withheld from the writer, so that his relationship
to the environment is characterised by complexities and tensions, which
are shaped and coloured by the political traditions in which he lives and
works. Although this relationship is always difficult, there are grounds
for believing that for the Swiss writer, and more particularly for the
German-Swiss writer, it is today unusually complex and fragile. Certainly
Kurt Guggenheim, in his significantly entitled study Heimat oder Domizil?
Die Stellung des deutschschweizerischen Schriftstellers in der Gegenwart,
believes these difficulties to be more marked in German-speaking
Switzerland than elsewhere [4]. Such a belief is worthy of examination.
It is necessary first of all to establish which difficulties encountered
by the German-Swiss writer have been considered specifically attributable

to the fact of his Swiss environment, what, in fact, the local and particular manifestations of the general problem have been held to be.

On the one hand, the contrast between the spirit of the environment and the process of artistic creation renders the artist at best dubious within the Swiss community [5]. The view is advanced that democracy is a political commitment to a specific environment, whereas art, because it is apparently at best an adjunct to the concern with everyday affairs which such a commitment implies, must contain leanings towards a dissociation from that environment. On the other hand, the artist sees that the nature of creative activity is prejudiced by this Swiss definition of commitment which inhibits the creation of artistic work [6]. A society whose ethos strongly promotes notions of direct involvement in government, commerce and industry, cannot but feel distrustful towards those of its members who wish to devote themselves to what is considered a peripheral activity [7]. Even literary history and criticism can subscribe to the view that writing should at all times be subordinate to the pursuit of everyday affairs [8]. In addition, the writer or artist encounters a strong tendency towards conformity, and an equally strong feeling that it is artistic endeavour above all else which opposes this tendency. Dora Gerber, in her important monograph Studien zum Problem des Künstlers in der modernen deutschschweizerischen Literatur, describes the differing goals which give rise to this conflict:

> Norm und Ideal wird...der Bürger, der seine Pflichten mit Verantwortungsbewusstsein erfüllt, daneben aber weder durch seine geistige Haltung noch durch seine Lebensführung aus dem Rahmen fällt. Künstler können sich in diesem Sinne unangenehm bemerkbar machen, weil gerade sie darauf Anspruch erheben, ihr Leben nach persönlichem Gutdünken zu gestalten. [9]

Peter Bichsel indicates the inhibitions of this Swiss conformity: 'Wir haben Angst, untypisch zu werden' [10].

Distrust of the artist is not, of course, a peculiarly Swiss phenomenon, but the size of Switzerland gives rise to two special circumstances. Firstly, this distrust is there more perceptible, even strident, since it appears to stem from a legitimate concern for the practical survival of the country. As a consequence art – and literature especially – has never established itself as a matter of great public interest. Secondly, the social group sympathetic to the artist is even smaller and less significant than elsewhere. The artist has little hope of positive encouragement, much less of financial support [11]. The sense of futility induced in the Swiss writer by this robust distrust and lack of regard has been well chronicled by C.-F. Ramuz (1878-1947). He had bitter personal experience of the emotional and financial strain of

being a writer in Switzerland. Frisch records, for example, that Ramuz
had to ask the Schweizer Schriftstellerverein for the money to pay for
his last operation (II 562). It is therefore understandable that Ramuz
should once have compared the writer in a small country to the socially
marginal figures of the criminal and the beggar [12]. The prevailing
attitude towards literature is reflected in the apparent refusal to
accord the writer a social function. The writer feels his isolation the
more keenly when he reflects that the country in which he lives has not
in the past sought accommodation with the artist, that it has viewed the
departure of the impossibly constrained creative mind with unconcern.
Yet if he perseveres with his work in such a milieu, the writer will
need to overcome his feelings as a member of that society which has after
all imbued him with its social values. It was Carl Spitteler, with his
strong sense of commitment to Switzerland and his equally strong antipathy
to many of her attitudes, who formulated this ambivalence most forcefully:

> Der Grundzug des schweizerischen Schriftstellers ist das
> Schamgefühl, so dass es den einzelnen grosse Überwindung
> kostet, sein Inneres der Öffentlichkeit blosszulegen...
> Wir schämen uns alle im Grunde unseres Dichternamens,
> wohlverstanden nicht etwa der Dichtertätigkeit oder gar
> der Dichtkunst, wohl aber der landläufigen Vorstellung, [13]
> die an dem Dichternamen haftet.

Within the Swiss ethos, only if the writer can show that he is socially
useful in that he exercises another profession can he be accepted. This
appears to be the extent to which the social function of the writer is
admitted by much of public opinion.

If the disapproval of what is held to be the artist's rejection of
a commitment to society concedes to him as an artist no function within
society, the question arises as to the nature of the reaction of society
to continuing manifestations of creative activity, and in turn, of the
impact which society's reaction has on that which is created. In Switzerland what has been created tends to be understood in terms of craftmanship [14]. Literature is envisaged in terms which derive from those
activities which are deemed to be socially useful. If this is also the
prevailing opinion about art in general, the main function of the printed
word will consequently be to convey information and therefore to instruct,
rather than to please and amuse [15]. For a society which regards
literature in terms of usefulness, didacticism must be its major
characteristic. This need not be mere pedantic didacticism. For Emil
Ermatinger the moral content of the writer's work enhances his status,
indeed it extends to him the possibility of a meaningful function in
society:

12.

> Die enge Verflochtenheit des dichterischen Schaffens mit dem
> beruflichen und politischen Tun des Bürgers bedingt weiter
> die moralisch-lehrhafte Art der schweizerischen Literatur.
> Der schweizerische Dichter, indem er unter dem Druck und
> Antrieb der Verantwortlichkeit schafft, kann nicht anders
> als seinem Volk als Rater, Ermahner, Warner zur Seite
> stehen. [16]

The writer is thus defined as an educator in a wide sense. Indeed, the
fact that so many Swiss writers have a full-time occupation in education
is reflected in the tone of their writings [17]. Swiss literary criticism
evaluates the more positive aspects of this tradition as evidence of a
firm belief in the constructive social function of literature [18]. Martin
Kraft defines the role which the writer's work assumes in this tradition:
it is

> für den Schweizer literarischer Ausdruck seiner nächsten
> Umgebung und damit ein wichtiges Mittel zum Verständnis
> dieser Umgebung und ihrer historischen Bedingtheit. [19]

At the same time the more negative aspects of the didactic tradition
render literature and attitudes conceived in it suspect for many writers.

The situation of literature in Switzerland has been further complicated by historical events, as a result of which speakers of three
major European languages live within her present boundaries. Thus the
very medium of literature - language - gives rise to a situation of some
complexity. The bulk and strength of the literary traditions developed
beyond Switzerland cause special difficulties when their languages are
used to depict a particularly Swiss reality. This is the situation
common to Swiss writers using each of the three major European languages.
But since, for example, the differences between French in France and
French in Switzerland are relatively trivial, the problem for the French-
Swiss writer is little more than theoretical. For the German-Swiss
writer, however, the problem is significantly more acute. The fact that
the normal spoken language in German-speaking Switzerland is Mundart, a
strongly dialect-flavoured version of German, while the written language
is regarded specifically as that and called Schriftdeutsch indicates the
immediacy of the problem for him [20]. In fact the writer writes in a
language which is for him in a special sense a second language since
it is a language

> die er in Wirklichkeit weder spricht noch hört, nämlich das
> Buchdeutsche, dass er folglich seine gesamten Anschauungen
> übersetzen muss. [21]

Indeed, Peter Bichsel sees the possibility of this disjunction going
beyond the problems of the creative writer and contributing to a general
Swiss self-deception:

> In vaterländischen Dingen belügen wir uns vielleicht auch
> deshalb so oft, weil wir gewohnt sind, Vaterländisches in
> der Sprache Schillers - Schriftdeutsch nennen wir sie - zu
> formulieren und nicht in der Mundart. Eine Übersetzung der
> grossen Worte unserer Helden in unsere Mundart macht die
> Lüge offensichtlich. [22]

Literature is for the German-Swiss doubly estranged from reality, first
as literature, and secondly as being written in Schriftdeutsch.

The situation also offers two advantages, however. Firstly, Mundart
and Schriftdeutsch serve, each in its own way, to promote the development
of different perceptions [23]. The interchange resulting from these
contrasting advantages must be fruitful for the creative writer.
Secondly, Mundart establishes the political identity of German-Swiss
speakers. This constitutes the principal difference between Swiss
Mundart and similar dialects of German. Thus the existence side by side
of Mundart and Schriftdeutsch contributes not merely to the preservation
of something approaching a Swiss political identity, it also confers an
important cultural advantage by keeping German-Swiss writing in the
mainstream of European literature. Switzerland thus benefits from the
relationship to the larger German linguistic community [24]. The
preservation of a specific identity within a major European language
is also an advantage peculiar to the German-Swiss, since the centralising
tendencies of the French language have denied this to his French-speaking
compatriots. Thus Mundart can preserve the value of individuality while
Schriftdeutsch preserves the benefits of the collectivity.

During the Second World War Switzerland was increasingly subjected
to pressure from Nazi Germany, pressure which was applied through the
language which Switzerland had in common with her aggressive neighbour.
As the Nazi threat diminished, Karl Schmid, in his essay 'Die kulturelle
Lage der deutschen Schweiz 1944', assessed the danger for Switzerland
during this period of having a common Schriftsprache:

> Die Sprache, für uns immer Inbegriff der geistigen
> Verpflichtung, stand in Gefahr, zu einem von vornherein
> ausgefertigten Staatsdokument umgeprägt zu werden. [25]

To a certain extent this is indicative of the permanent situation of the
German-Swiss writer. He must continue to attempt to assert that which
is Swiss in a medium which is not peculiarly Swiss. In doing so, he
runs the risk of being absorbed into a German tradition, both by
assimilation since he is writing in Schriftdeutsch, and by financial
necessity, for the German-Swiss reading public is not large enough to
offer viable financial support, and the wider German reading public is
not certain to be interested in depictions of a Swiss reality. Moreover,
it is possible that he may have to look beyond Switzerland to find any

sort of sympathetic reaction, for Switzerland's attitude to literature
and the fact of that literature's being written in a medium perfected
elsewhere combine to create a reluctance to recognise literary and other
artistic talent until that talent has first been recognised abroad.

The case of the painter Heinrich Füssli (1741-1825) exemplifies for
Walter Muschg the fate of the Swiss artist who, though spurned in his
own country, rises to fame and fortune outside it. It was only Füssli's
triumphant career in England which established his reputation in Switzerland. Muschg sees this roundabout process persisting to the present day:

> Lesen Sie bloss nach, wie Frisch und Dürrenmatt in ihren
> Anfängen von unserer Presse behandelt wurden. Erst als sie [26]
> in Deutschland bekannt waren, hat man sie bei uns erkannt.

Dora Gerber considers this uncertainty in judgements and standards, which
requires the imprimatur of the assessments of others, to be the product
of a deep-seated insecurity in the Swiss [27]. Yet this uncertainty is
not necessarily dispelled by wider contacts. The Swiss who goes abroad
does not enjoy the prestige of an independent cultural tradition or of
political power to bolster his personal qualities. Once abroad he may
well have to contend with prejudices which belittle him and increase
his insecurity. When Thornton Wilder, so much admired by Frisch, was
told in Frisch's presence in Frankfurt in 1948 that the young Swiss wrote
plays, Wilder's reaction was deflating: ''Oh', sagt Wilder. 'Bauern-
stücke?'' (II 626). Nonetheless the urge to go into the world, despite
the attendant difficulties, must remain strong, especially when each of
the major language communities of Switzerland has access, without having
to learn a foreign language, to a large foreign country which incorporates
a major European culture. The attraction exercised by the large neighbour
is nowhere more feelingly stated than by Spittler precisely in the address
of 1914 in which he denies to that neighbour the right to exercise
anything more than attraction over the small neighbour [28]. Yet the
attraction of the stimulus which the artist expects to find outside
Switzerland is very potent. For if literary or artistic creation is by
its nature solitary, the general ethos in which it takes place can
nonetheless stimulate and enrich by its general sympathy and particular
comment. For Gottfried Keller such an ethos was not only necessary for
full artistic development, it existed in fact only beyond the frontiers
of Switzerland, it was 'nur auf den Plätzen des grossen Verkehrs zu haben' [29]. Despite Keller's subsequent return, he was as aware as Füssli
of the necessity of going forth.

Until recently, however, emigration from the country was rarely
thought to be final. There would ultimately be a return, for it was

assumed that the political spirit which the Swiss absorb is sufficiently
strong to create a sense of obligation which is seldom totally ignored.
Departure and return can be interpreted as indicating a desire to be
reconciled with the milieu in which one was raised, as a stage in the
mature assessment of one's country and its ethos, in the final analysis
as a coming to terms with oneself. Thus in 1918 the critic Eduard
Korrodi, discussing the contemporary Swiss novel, considers departure
and return, expressed in literary works, to be necessary steps towards
a full appreciation of Switzerland:

> Für den Schweizergeist der jüngeren literarischen Generation
> ...wüsste ich kein beredteres Zeugnis, als dass ihr Roman –
> als Stufe ihrer eigenen Entwicklung – auch Lehr- und Wander-
> jahre bedeutete, dass sie sogar den Konflikt erlebten, die
> Schweiz zu verlieren. Wer die Schweizererde verlor, hat sie
> dankbarer und erkennender wiedergewonnen. Der darf die
> Grenze nicht preisen, der nie im Grenzenlosen fühlte. [30]

Yet this interpretation may well imply a more painless synthesis than
Doppelbürgertum is in reality. For if the strongest binding force
exerted by a country lies in the fact of its political identity, the
departure for the larger culture beyond the borders, even in conjunction
with a subsequent return, assumes a more complex dimension. Kurt Marti
has sought to summarise this complexity by claiming that, for the Swiss
author, ''Vaterland' ist...nur als Politikum fassbar' [31]. It is implied
that for the Swiss writer there is a conflict between his debt to the
larger related culture and his political obligation to his own smaller
country. Jean Moser has discussed this general dilemma in great detail.
His is a much more sombre analysis than that of Korrodi, and arrives
finally at two alternatives which would seem to preclude all synthesis:

> La solution du conflit est dans un nouveau départ ou
> la soumission. [32]

The complexities involved in these solutions are depicted in a considerable tradition in the German-Swiss novel: they are explored in novels
by Gottfried Keller (Martin Salander 1886), Carl Spitteler (Imago 1906),
Felix Moeschlin (Wachtmeister Vögeli 1922), Albin Zollinger (Pfannenstiel
1940), Gustav Keckeis (Die fremde Zeit 1947) and Max Frisch (Stiller
1954). In these novels the return of the hero to his native country
after a period of absence provides the starting-point for the action.
In all cases the return constitutes a seeking for a role in that
community which the hero had left behind him in an attempt to come
to terms with himself.

The relationship of the Swiss writer or artist to his country is
complicated by the presence of a large cultural, but politically foreign,
element in that relationship. This entails that Swiss writing must be

examined with two different aims, firstly to establish if the
contributions in the different languages of the country have common
characteristics which might be called national, and secondly, to define
the relationship of the contribution in each particular language to the
literature of the larger culture. It is possible to approach the first
definition of literature in Switzerland exclusively in terms of language, and thus to conclude that, in this sense, there can be no national
literature [33]. It has also been argued that there exist Swiss literatures [34]. This distinction points towards the second definition. The
benefit to German-Swiss literature of the connection with Germany has
always been acknowledged. In 1841 Keller, noting Germany's advance over
Switzerland in all the arts, concluded that there was no disadvantage
to the Swiss in seeking to learn from the example of their larger
neighbour [35]. Forty years later he returned to the same idea, linking
it with a rejection of the concept of a Swiss national literature [36].
In this century, German literature is held to be the great placenta from
which German-Swiss culture draws its nourishment:

> Diese innige Verflochtenheit in die allgemeine deutsche
> Kultur ist dem literarischen Leben des schweizerischen Teils
> je und je tiefstes Bedürfnis und die notwendige Quelle seines
> Wachstums gewesen. Eine Unterbrechung oder nur eine Ein-
> schnürung des Zusammenhanges hat jedesmal mit Verarmung
> und Einengung büssen müssen. [37]

The three areas of involvement - in language, in example and in interchange - provide close ties to German life and literature. Even in
times of stress, these ties must be acknowledged. Speaking in 1948, as
a Swiss who, more than many of his compatriots, had been appalled, not
only at the horrors of the Second World War, but also at his proximity
in more than one sense to them, Frisch proclaims:

> Es gibt, darüber können wir uns nicht hinwegtäuschen,
> keine Schweiz ohne Deutschland. (II 343)

Nonetheless, within this framework of involvement and indebtedness, that
which the German-Swiss writer creates has specific and peculiar
characteristics. Alfred Zäch places German-Swiss literature within a
framework of reference which seeks to specify what its particular
contribution to German literature is. He lists these characteristics
as 'Gemeinschaftssinn', 'Hang zum Individualismus', 'eine ausgesprochene
Neigung zu pädagogischer Tendenz', 'ruhige Vernunft', 'illusionslose
Nüchternheit' and 'gesunder Sinn für die Lebenswirklichkeit' [38].

The political circumstances of the Swiss are seen to be reflected
in the characteristics of German-Swiss literature. These circumstances
have traditionally moulded the writer's thought and influenced the
nature of his work. This complex relationship between the writer and

the community has provided one of the traditional themes of Swiss
literature, and the treatment of this theme is widespread among German-
Swiss writers because it is so vital to the personal situation of each
writer [39]. The twentieth century has, however, seen an increasing
attempt, starting with the efforts of Spitteler, to widen the view of
the writer beyond merely local pre-occupations, however pressing these
might be. The Second World War was to be the catalyst for many attitudes.
It introduced deliberate policies of mass-destruction carried out by the
nation so indispensible to the existence of Switzerland. It brought
about not only the deaths of men and women, but also the death of values
by which previous generations had lived. But the transformation of social
values was more difficult in Switzerland simply because the fabric of
Swiss society had been left intact [40]. That the country had remained
inviolate generated also a feeling of guilt which led to painful self-
questioning and the re-examination of accepted ideas. Switzerland was
deprived of an obvious role in the post-war world. With characteristic
irony Friedrich Dürrenmatt diagnoses the disorientation of his country:

> Wir wurden verschont. Wir mussten unsere politische Gerissen-
> heit mit einer moralischen Einbusse bezahlen. Wir standen in
> der heldischen Welt der Kriegsgewinner plötzlich als Kriegs-
> gewinnler da, ohne Möglichkeit, uns wie die Deutschen vom
> Heldentum aufs Leiden umzustellen, wir hatten nicht einmal
> gelitten. [41]

This is a statement of the crisis of identity felt by the Swiss at
this time.

The war and its aftermath caused the pulse of impatience with traditional attitudes to quicken perceptibly, so that Frisch, on returning
from visits to the ruins of Berlin and Vienna in 1948, felt able to
write of the 'Irrelevanz unserer schweizerischen Existenz' [42]. The
urgency of post-war concerns was bound to be reflected in literature.
Writers wished to come to terms with those great problems of the age
the existence of which abroad, but not at home, seemed to point to a
stagnation of thought and experience in Switzerland. At this point
Moser's thesis that there are only two solutions for those troubled by
their relationship to Switzerland, soumission or départ, receives fresh
confirmation in respect of the Swiss writer. In 1948 Dora Gerber
maintains that the Swiss writer has two options open to him: he can
accept and affirm the best of that which is Swiss, or he can adopt a
passively or actively critical stance [43]. Yet perhaps the matter is no
longer entirely as clear-cut as both Moser and Gerber would have it, it
might be that Moser's formulation of 1934, and perhaps even Gerber's of
1948, reflect essentially pre-war attitudes, perhaps the two positions

they outline have altered somewhat.

Alfred Zäch has drawn attention to a process which is affecting all
literatures and which is bound to cause at the very least an alteration
in the premisses underlying former problems. All literature is losing
its local character, in Switzerland perhaps more so than elsewhere [44],
and in doing so, is rendering redundant the long discussion as to
whether there is a national literature in Switzerland [45]. A second
process, not peculiar to Switzerland but also significantly present
there, is a move away from traditional forms of literature to what
Marti calls 'para-literarische Äusserungsformen' [46], which tend more
and more to provide the forum where current themes are examined and
moral problems posed. Marti considers this to be a reflection of a
more politicised attitude to the problems of Switzerland and Switzerland
in the world, and this accounts for the decrease in significance of
Switzerland as a purely literary theme:

> Im Stoff-Inventar der Gegenwartsliteratur ist das 'Vater-
> land' auch als Politikum 'Schweiz' in den Hintergrund
> gerückt worden. Nicht, dass es vollends von der literarischen
> Bühne geräumt worden wäre. Es hat dort immer noch seinen
> Platz. Aber eben: im Hintergrund. [47]

In the light of these two trends the positions outlined by Moser and
Gerber require some re-definition.

Two groups of writers in post-war Switzerland point to the direction
of this re-definition. Firstly, there is the group which tackles the
traditional problems of the German-Swiss writer. There problems have
been made all the more intractable by the magnitude and apparent
insolubility of so many world problems. Marti finds that the
'traditional' literary works of this first group read like bids for
personal escape [48]. The first re-defined position is thus a form of
soumission which is constantly chafing at the bondage of Switzerland,
yet unable to dispense with it. The second group is more euphorically
radical. For its members, the claims of nationality, especially of
Swiss nationality, restrict the realisation of larger humanitarian ideals.
Not only do such writers consider Switzerland to be an 'Irrelevanz',
this second group also distinguishes itself from the first by treating
the country as such, and any claims made by the traditions of Switzerland
are simply ignored. In a programmatic statement which serves as the
introduction to a collection of short stories by younger Swiss writers,
Texte (1964), Hugo Leber finds this trend exemplified by the themes of
the stories:

> Ist es nicht auffallend, dass nur in wenigen Beispielen die
> Schweiz geographisch in Erscheinung tritt, und wo es der

Fall ist, nicht als notwendige Bezogenheit zum Thema! Was
für eine ältere Generation noch Festigkeit hatte, Ordnung,
Sinn und Tradition, bleibt für viele Autoren heute ohne Wert,
nicht mehr der Betrachtung würdig. [49]

The hall-mark of the post-war départ is that the writer dissociates
himself completely from Switzerland without leaving the country.

The traditional concern of the German-Swiss writer consists in the
attempt to establish identities: the identity of the writer in a society
which regards writing as an unimportant activity; the identity of the
writer who, while he may accept the political implications of his Swiss
nationality, nonetheless seeks to preserve and develop in literary terms
his awareness of complexity in human affairs; the identity of the writer
in German who may not wish to be assimilated into the ethos most widely
expressed in the literature of that language. This attempt at establishing
an identity is born of a heritage of tensions, tension between narrowness
of background and breadth of vision, between responsibility to the self
and to the wider world, between the urge for self-assertion and the
willingness to be assimilated. Increasingly, however, these elements
of tension are being regarded as irrelevant, and in German-speaking
Switzerland literature is now much less the expression of a coming to
terms with the experience of a particular place. Switzerland was left
intact in 1945, but the traumatic effect on traditional values and
attitudes made by the Second World War was bound to influence Swiss
writers, and one manifestation of this influence is the feeling that,
if the writer devotes himself too closely to the claims of locality, he
is not fully discharging his duty in a changed world. In this changing
situation the position of Max Frisch and his generation - Frisch was
born in 1911 - is in many ways ambiguous, and has been defined as being
an intermediary one 'entre un traditionalisme critique et le besoin de
créer de nouvelles formes'[50]. For Frisch the difficulties experienced
by his commitment to his 'Zeitgenossenschaft' and by his inevitable
involvement with Switzerland are compounded by his full and mature
concern for and with both.

2. Max Frisch as a Swiss Citizen

The influence of the Second World War on Frisch's attitude to Switzerland

In view of the continuing importance of his relationship to
Switzerland, it is surprising to find that in Frisch's earliest extant
writings there is practically no mention of his country. The first
published narratives, Jürg Reinhart (1934) and Antwort aus der Stille
(1937), do not derive their inspiration from Switzerland, but rather,
in the first case, from the author's early travels as a journalist,
and in both, from the theme of youth attempting to prove itself. Frisch
has of course recounted how in 1938 he burnt 'alles Geschriebene...
inbegriffen die Tagebücher' (II 588), so that it is not possible to
establish the nature or content of most of the early work. From the
period before 1940 there survive only two direct considerations of
things Swiss, the anecdote Mundart (1934) (I 69), and a series of three
articles written during a visit to Germany in 1935, the composite title
of which is Kleines Tagebuch einer deutschen Reise (I 84-97). In this
delineation of his views on Switzerland, the first use of the diary
form which assumes such importance in his later writings, Frisch
recognises a debt to the parent culture, albeit a debt between equals
which he feels called in question by the manifestations of Nazi power.

Writing in 1972, Friedrich Dürrenmatt draws attention to the
importance of the war years for the Switzerland of the present time [1].
Clearly, this is a statement which could equally well refer to the
effect of the war on other countries. At the same time it points to
the significance of the war even for a non-combattant country. In more
particular terms the war proved a catalyst for Frisch. Its course,
and above all, its aftermath, caused reactions in him which crystallised
his whole Weltanschauung [2], not only in terms of his relationship to
the Swiss situation, but also in terms of his attitude towards the
ideological blocs into which the world divided itself.

As Frisch's reactions to the war unfold, the nature of his evalu-
ation of Switzerland, and of its possible role in the post-war period,
becomes apparent. The outbreak and initial stages of the war, however,
gave little indication of what was to come. Thus the fact of war could
be approached without the drastic re-appraisal of values which later
became necessary. In the diary of his 'Grenzdienst', Blätter aus dem
Brotsack, Frisch hopes in 1940, as he watches the oath being taken to
the Swiss flag, that devotion to Switzerland will stop well short of

uncritical worship (I 117). This suggests the liberal outlook of a man
of almost thirty who has travelled widely, and accords in tone with the
1935 recognition of 'Doppelbürgertum' in that both are reflections of
an attitude which events have not yet seriously tested. As the war
progresses, however, Frisch becomes aware that some re-definition of
these relatively uncomplicated sentiments is necessary. He tries to
establish the appropriate attitude for his neutral country in a
situation where virtually the rest of Europe is engaged in war. In
1943 he comes to the conclusion that the position of Switzerland can
best be exemplified by a comparison between two paintings: Kreuzigung
Christi by Breughel and Exekution um Mitternacht by Goya (I 221-222).
In the latter painting, the execution dominates the canvas; in the
former, the crucifixion of Christ is only one of the events depicted.
The implication is that Switzerland can retain perspectives which an
exclusive pre-occupation with war could distort or destroy. Towards the
end of the war a second analogy appears relevant. Frisch compares the
role of Switzerland at this point in her history and in the history of
Europe to that of the chorus in Greek tragedy. He sees in the non-
involvement of the chorus in the action a parallel to Switzerland's
present position. This parallel contains pointers to a possible positive
stance for the country in post-war Europe: the chorus

> klagt, aber er klagt nicht an, er ist der Mitleidende aller,
> er verwechselt sich nie mit ihnen, nicht mit ihrer Schuld
> und ihrer Grösse, er ist ohne die Leidenschaft, welche den
> Helden macht und vernichtet...Warum hören sie ihn dennoch
> an? Weil er nichts am eigenen Leib erlitt; aus ihm spricht
> keine Rache, kein Hass, er allein hätte es leicht, Übersicht
> der menschlichen Liebe durchzuhalten und die Ehrfurcht zu
> wahren. (II 287)

Yet he is also fully aware of the ambiguity of Switzerland's own
position in setting herself up as a provider of moral succour. His
story of the young British pilot refusing to praise the civilised
aspects of his internment in Switzerland because he was shot down over
Tobruk by Swiss-made shells (IV 222) illustrates this awareness. That
its painfulness did not lessen with time is shown by the suggestion
made more than twenty years later that for the war period the Swiss
national drama ought to have been Brecht's Der gute Mensch von Sezuan
(VI 297) [3]. The irreconciliable duality represented in the figures of
Shen Te and Shui Ta seems to Frisch in recollection to be a suitable
symbol for the Switzerland of the Second World War.

If, in ascribing a role to his country, Frisch was trying, however
tentatively, to approach a definition of Switzerland, his experiences
with the defeated neighbour Germany, without whom there can be no

Switzerland, were frustrating. Reporting on his first visit to the
devastated country after the frontiers were opened, he finds in Germany
a desire that the Swiss judge the German case positively. He is being
forced into precisely the position which he sought to avoid. He expands
the nature of his difficulties in adopting a stance towards the Germans –
and in arriving at a more precise definition of his own country –, in
the well-known Drei Entwürfe eines Briefes which close the entries for
1946 in Tagebuch 1946-1949 (II 469-475). A young man who fought at
Stalingrad is irate that Frisch, a neutral Swiss, should write of death
in his play Nun singen sie wieder [4]. In the first Entwurf Frisch is
impatient with the young man's implicit claim to exclusive competence
in the field of valid human experience:

> Sie sind nicht mehr der Sieger, aber der Mann, der dabei war,
> und als solcher erhaben über alle andern, die nichts erlebt
> haben, weil sie nicht den Krieg erlebt haben. (II 472)

In his final draft Frisch stresses that those who have lived untouched
by the ravages of war need not for that reason fall silent and withdraw;
their particular experience has afforded them an advantage of
perspective [5]. By refusing to accept only the experience of war as
legitimate, Frisch stresses the importance to him of the symbolism of
the Breughel painting.

It is understandable that in the immediate post-war years so much
of Frisch's intellectual activity should be concerned with Germany,
home of the parent culture for the German-Swiss. There is first of all,
on the human level, the necessity for some kind of inventory after the
horrors. Secondly, because the trauma which was experienced as the
facts became known was so great, the attempt to avoid confronting the
trauma and so to learn from it, was equally great. Frisch discerns two
main forms of evasion of this responsibility: the first is to take
refuge in an ivory tower; the second is to minister to the suffering of
the German people in such a way as to obscure the causes of this
suffering (II 338). His fear is that, before the events of the immediate
past have been assimilated, they will be superseded by fresh ones, and
the past will be forgotten instead of helping to form positive attitudes
for the future. Frisch's third reason for concerning himself so much
with the recent history of Germany embraces the two previous reasons
and relates the whole matter specifically to himself. He shares his
humanitarian concerns with many the world over. What he does not share
with most of those others, however, but with all members of that nation
from whose midst the perpetrators of the horrors had arisen, is an entire
culture. Not merely does he have in common those aspects of culture,

such as painting and music, which know no frontier, but language itself,
the refracting medium of experience, he shares with the criminals. In
these circumstances how can he be certain that he does not possess their
proclivities? (II 629). It is in his confrontation with recent German
history within the framework of this question that Frisch arrives at a
definition of what he sees as one of Switzerland's most important and
worthwhile characteristics.

Whereas in 1935 geographical proximity and linguistic kinship
could be accepted as inevitable but fruitful, by the end of the war
the revelations of what the Germans had done inspire radically different
sentiments. For the war had produced a new and monstrous category of
man, the hallmark of whom is that he combines culture and brutality
(II 292). For Frisch the chief example is the Nazi Statthalter of
Bohemia, Heydrich, 'der Mozart spielte' (II 444). In the figures of
Heydrich and his like Frisch sees incarnated a betrayal of, and a break
with, the tenets of nineteenth century humanism in which he and his
generation were raised. The problem is not merely that of a perverse
relationship to 'Kunst'. The influences working on the individual in
the wider sphere of 'Kultur' have not apparently been sufficiently strong
to check the darker impulses of those raised within its ambit. It is
this failure which is specifically of the twentieth century. Frisch
describes this moral dereliction, when it is coupled with cultivation
of the arts, as 'ästhetische Kultur' (II 629). As he later demonstrates
with the characters in Biedermann und die Brandstifter and Andorra,
Frisch believes that this is a cast of mind which can exist only when
rigid categories of thinking obtain, when there is a failure, or a
refusal, to establish relationships between different aspects of human
experience. Since these aspects do not merge to form a whole in the
mentality which he is describing, it does not matter how unrelated and
irreconciliable they are. Indeed, their irreconciliability is the
condition of the mentality:

> Es ist eine Geistesart, die das Höchste denken kann (denn
> die irdische Schwere werfen sie einfach über Bord, damit
> der Ballon steigt) und die das Niederste nicht verhindert,
> eine Kultur, die sich strengstens über die Forderung des
> Tages erhebt, ganz und gar der Ewigkeit zu Diensten. (II 629)

The main characteristic of this mentality for Frisch is that it creates
a 'säuberliche Scheidung zwischen Kultur und Politik' (II 629).

In defining what 'Politik' appears to be for the German, Frisch at
the same time establishes what it means for the Swiss. For the Swiss,
'Politik' is a wide-ranging concept, embracing the manner in which men
live together and the nature of their social structures, upon which the

continuing existence of mankind depends. This is not the case for the
German, who regards the mundane and everyday efforts required to
maintain and improve these structures, as being unworthy of him, as
beneath the dignity of a cultured man (II 630). It is this denigration
of practical concerns, in favour of an exaggerated and dangerous obeisance
before art, which Frisch castigates. Artistic talent is sundered from
the generality of public life and put forward as a make-weight against
the shortcomings of that generality in any other sphere. A situation
which absolves the possessor of artistic talent from all moral and civic
responsibility is bluntly rejected by Frisch. Simply because it promotes
notions of complete independence from the community, talent is not the
quality most essential for the proper functioning of society. A sense
of responsibility is more important (II 445). Frisch now begins to move
towards a clearer definition of one aspect of Switzerland. He argues
that she has a different tradition from Germany, and insists on the width
of the concept of 'Kultur' in Switzerland:

> Der deutsche und vielleicht abendländische Irrtum, dass
> wir Kultur haben, wenn wir Sinfonien haben, ist hierzu-
> lande kaum möglich; der Künstler nicht als Statthalter
> der Kultur; er ist nur ein Glied unter anderen; Kultur
> ist eine Sache des ganzen Volkes; wir erkennen sie nicht
> allein auf dem Bücherschrank und am Flügel, sondern
> ebensosehr in der Art, wie man seine Untergebenen
> behandelt. (II 491-492)

Frisch becomes aware, from his consideration of a contrasting one, of
the value of the Swiss ethos. The cultural measure of the worth of a
man is his behaviour as a citizen. The matter can be stated quite
simply: 'Kunst ist kein Ersatz für politische Kultur' (V 343). The
realisation of this truth leads Frisch to make one of his most forth-
right statements of commitment to Switzerland:

> Unter Kultur verstehen wir in erster Linie die staats-
> bürgerlichen Leistungen, die gemeinschaftliche Haltung
> mehr als das künstlerische oder wissenschaftliche Meister-
> werk eines einzelnen Staatsbürgers. Auch wenn es für den
> schweizerischen Künstler eine trockene Luft ist, was ihn
> in seiner Heimat umgibt, so ist dieses Übel, wie sehr es
> uns persönlich trifft, doch nur die leidige Kehrseite
> einer Haltung, die, von den meisten Deutschen als spiessig
> verachtet, als Ganzes unsere volle Bejahung hat – eben weil
> die gegenteilige Haltung, die ästhetische Kultur, zu einer
> tödlichen Katastrophe geführt hat, führen muss. (II 631)

'Kultur' and 'Politik' are therefore not mutually exclusive concepts.

   The clear question which Frisch set himself about his relationship
to what had happened in Germany and in the name of Germany has produced
an answer which is quite unambiguous – for its moral weight is never
in doubt – but one the qualifications of which reflect the complexity
of the truth. He was provoked by an external event – the end of the

war - to map out, with the help of an analysis of a German phenomenon, part of the Swiss national identity, and hence part of his own identity. In this Frisch is following in the footsteps of two other German-Swiss writers in this century. For Albin Zollinger, the decisive event in the shaping of his political awareness was the Nazi assumption of power [6]. For Carl Spitteler it was the outbreak of the First World War which caused him to define his position towards Germany, and hence to circumscribe his own identity, in Unser Schweizer Standpunkt. By reacting to events in Germany, all three are able to move some way towards self-definition.

An understanding of the genesis of the convictions which Frisch has reached is important, since it explains the wide connotations which the concept of 'Kultur' has for him. On the one hand, 'Kultur' can be observed in a colourful and crowded Italian country bus, which, despite its festive air, represents for its occupants nothing more than the conduct of their everyday affairs (II 516) [7]. On the other hand, 'Kultur' is also the wisdom contained in a set of written precepts by which men seek to regulate their communal existence. In his lecture 'Unsere Arroganz gegenüber Amerika', Frisch suggests that many condescending European attitudes towards the United States are based on a narrow definition of 'Kultur', and this causes those adopting such attitudes to overlook the worth of the American Constitution, itself a product of 'Kultur' (III 225). It is the ethos of the community which provides the real 'Kultur' of the individual, and it is his sense of responsibility towards the community which provides for its continuing health. Only through 'die Mühseligkeit politischer Tätigkeit' (V 348) can a stable framework be established within which the individual may prosper within the community. It is without any illusion that Frisch rejects 'ästhetische Kultur', for he does so in the knowledge of the difficulty of the alternative which he is advocating: 'Politik ist eine Sisyphus-Arbeit' (V 349). It is a clear-sighted, yet firm, commitment to the politics of consensus.

False perspectives of Switzerland

The nature of Frisch's commitment has often been overlooked when he has criticised aspects of Switzerland, and when for his pains he has attracted adverse comment [1]. The continuing hostility to Frisch's criticism has not been without its effect on him. In 1960 he made his well-known refusal to consider further the problem of the writer in

Switzerland:

> Die Problematik des Schweizer Schriftstellers, des Schrift-
> stellers in der Schweiz? Persönlich habe ich mit ihr ab-
> geschlossen, sie beschäftigt mich nicht mehr, nachdem ich
> mich mit ihr jahrelang ...ausgiebig auseinandergesetzt
> habe. (IV 258)

In 1964 he confesses: 'Das Thema Schweiz bringt mich nicht auf pro-
duktive Touren' [2]. In the following year, after five years residence
in Rome, he returns to Switzerland. He confides to <u>Tagebuch 1966-1971</u>
that, although he sees much in a new light, he feels that his observations
are not sufficiently significant to yield new 'Einsichten' (VI 11),
and he resolves to maintain silence in public about Switzerland. Yet
on the next page there is an admission that the vow has already been
broken: he has just written an introduction to a book of interviews
with Italian 'Gastarbeiter' in Switzerland. That the resolution to
maintain silence on Switzerland and the breaking of this resolution
should appear in such close proximity is symptomatic of Frisch's attitude
to the matter. It is a theme to which he returns despite every
discouragement.

One aspect of Frisch's frequent travels abroad might provide the
first of two major reasons for his continuing to criticise his country
in what he believes to be a constructive spirit. For in his case travel
has so far involved a return to his point of departure, Switzerland.
This provides frequent opportunities for him to see his country from a
fresh perspective. It may be that absence has caused him to forget the
more intractable aspects of the country and its inhabitants, but return
sharpens awareness of national shortcomings (II 343). Perhaps Frisch's
most revealing view of the re-adjustments demanded by return appears in
a comment on Zollinger's novel <u>Pfannenstiel</u>. Frisch considers the
vexations which beset Zollinger's hero on his return from abroad and
concludes:

> Rückkehr eines Schweizers in seine Heimat, die, unter der
> Lupe einer wirklichen Vaterlandsliebe genommen, immer wieder
> bitter enttäuscht, zur Auseinandersetzung fordert gerade
> durch die Stille ihres eigenen Behagens. (I 207)

It is an apt summary of the response to the challenge experienced by
the returning traveller, and points to the complex nature of Frisch's
own commitment to Switzerland.

The second reason for Frisch's persistence in criticising his
country is more fundamental. It may be the consequence of his Swiss
nature to address himself to what he holds to be Swiss problems which
gives rise to conflict between his sober, even pessimistic, judgements
and his strong belief in the worth of civic responsibility in its widest

sense [3]. Frisch himself considers that the major experiences of his
life which he has undergone in Switzerland have created an indissoluble
bond [4]. He proclaims the necessity of criticism precisely because of
his emotional involvement (IV 221). He wishes strongly that this
constructive criticism, inspired by the best of motives, should be
considered as a natural and necessary part of the civic responsibility
of every member of a nation. He feels that there must be something
amiss in a situation where criticism is rejected, where the critic is
made to feel that he, and not the object of his criticism, is at fault,
regardless of his motives (V 372). For Frisch it is a matter of
legitimate concern that, despite the many foreigners who settle and
work in Switzerland, the country fails to generate in them a genuine
interest. It is a matter of even more pressing concern that this lack
of interest should extend to the Swiss themselves, for they regard their
country merely as a convenient venue for their pursuits; Switzerland is
for them 'ein Gebrauchsgegenstand, nicht mehr ein schöpferisches Unter-
nehmen' (V 392). In his definition of 'ästhetische Kultur' Frisch had
considered the lack of concern with society's shortcomings as being in
the final analysis corrosive of the entire social fabric. He had
defined 'Politik' as a concern with the well-being of the body politic,
and his own abiding concern is with the state of the Swiss body politic.
Because of the vital importance of the interrelation between the well-
being of the individual and the soundness of society as a whole, he
insists on the right to criticise that society. He has traced the
development within himself of the critical faculty allied to a sense of
commitment:

> Ich bin hier und nicht anderswo geboren, das naive Gefühl
> von Zugehörigkeit und später das Bewusstsein von Zugehörig-
> keit, ein kritisches Bewusstsein, das die Zugehörigkeit
> keineswegs aufhebt. (VI 611)

In averring that 'kritisches Bewusstsein' is an integral part of
'Zugehörigkeit' Frisch pinpoints what he feels to be the essential
nature of civic responsibility. It is on the basis of this belief that
his entire discussion of Switzerland is conducted.

The historical origins of the Swiss Confederation, or rather a
widespread interpretation of what are held to be the facts of these
origins, attracts the attention of Frisch, and from an analysis of this
interpretation he deduces some general conclusions. The central figure
in this traditional interpretation is of course Wilhelm Tell, and Frisch
finds it ironic that Tell, the Swiss hero, can equally well be seen as
a figure inimical to many cherished Swiss traditions. The fact that
Tell acted on his own, quite without reference to those about him,

renders him in Frisch's eyes, particularly unsuited to the role of
symbolic national hero [5]. The fault cannot be laid entirely at the
door of Schiller with his creation of a Tell drama, but the attractions
of yielding to self-delusion derived from a work by such a major
literary figure are probably too strong to be resisted. In an attempt
to question the unexamined assumptions of the traditional interpretation
Frisch published <u>Wilhelm Tell für die Schule</u> in 1971. In it he
demonstrates how the confrontation between Tell and the <u>Reichsvogt</u> almost
did not happen, and how, when it did, the situation was at first by no
means irretrievable. But a momentum is generated which engulfs the
participants. As he watches the crisis develop Konrad is 'erschrocken
über den Lauf der Dinge' (VI 453). Ironically, the action he takes to
defuse the crisis merely precipitates it. Events are not subject to
control: matters are now out of the hands of Konrad 'der plötzlich die
Regie verloren hatte' (VI 454). Frisch thus applies one of the central
tenets of his mature work to the legend of the origins of the
Confederation: an interpretation of events which is based on the
assumption that they could only have taken place in the way they did
must be false since it excludes the range of possibility for a different
development. Such an interpretation is at odds with the nature of
reality:

> Jeder Verlauf, der dadurch, dass er stattfindet, andere
> Verläufe ausschliesst, unterstellt sich selbst einen Sinn,[6]
> der ihm nicht zukommt. (V 581)

The Tell myth assumes that the events which it contains were predestined
to happen in the manner in which they did happen, and this imposes a
single immutable interpretation on these events. This in turn inhibits
the capacity to view the historical past creatively, and so to link it
meaningfully to the present: 'Der Mythos (löst) keine Probleme' (V 376).
If it is one of the functions of the past to influence the present
positively, a stultified view of the past must affect the present dis-
advantageously.

Frisch regards the inability to look at the past from anything but
a single viewpoint to be one manifestation of a cast of mind which he
finds widely prevalent amongst his countrymen. At the close of 1940
he comments on the reaction of the Swiss to the news of the disasters
taking place in the outside world, and sees in this reaction a general
trait of the Swiss character which he finds reprehensible. This is the
inability to come to terms with the flux and continuum of reality,
which is constantly demanding of the individual a revision of his views.
Instead, reality is looked upon by the Swiss as something fixed. This

immobility of outlook tends to atrophy the natural and necessary ability
to react and adapt to changing circumstances:

> Es ist der schweizerische Aberglaube an den Bestand.
> Man wird, indem die schöpferischen Auseinandersetzungen
> übersprungen oder verpasst werden, die neuen Bestände sehen,
> die aus dem Ereignis hervorgehen, und man wird sie, sobald
> sie zum scheinbaren Stehen kommen, jedesmal wieder für
> einen Bestand halten. Bedenklich ist es, weil man diesen
> Ruhestand des Geistes, diese gigantische Fremde vor allem
> Lebendigen, das nun einmal seinem Wesen nach ungemütlich
> und ungeheuerlich ist, gelegentlich schon mit Gesinnung
> verwechselt. [7]

This is Frisch's first full statement on the phenomenon of 'Bestand',
inertia, lack of willingness to move forward, which he considers to
characterise much of Swiss life.

The concept of 'Bestand' does not merely come from a subjective
impression which Frisch has formed, but is the result of empirical
observation from his experiences as an architect. His interest in
city planning confronted him with many specific and immediate problems,
and this led to the development of his political awareness:

> Ich habe den Weg gewählt, dass ich die politische Engagiert-
> heit nicht nur oder nicht in erster Linie in die Literatur
> hineingenommen habe, sondern dass ich das als Staatsbürger
> aktiv, mit und ohne Partei, gemacht habe, so dass ich dann
> nicht der Verpflichtung erlag, in jedem Buch seine politi-
> sche Relevanz, seine politische Engagiertheit nachzuweisen.
> So habe ich mich dann erst mit der Welt im grossen und
> ganzen beschäftigt und mit der Örtlichkeit Schweiz. [8]

For Frisch the architect, with his direct experience of the 'Sisyphus-
Arbeit' of practical politics, the concept of 'Bestand' is very real.
In a lecture given to Zürich architects on his return from America in
1953, Frisch complains that the Swiss suffer from 'Heimweh nach dem
Vorgestern' (III 236). The resulting lack of initiative, the impotence
of the imagination, are not merely debilitating, they are fatal. Five
years earlier, on the other hand, contemplating the vast task of re-
building which was being undertaken in the ruins of Warsaw, Frisch had
noted that the air was 'voll Zukunft' (II 610). It was the desire to
catch something of this spirit, to realise 'die Möglichkeit einer lebendigen Schweiz' (III 242), which brought about his collaboration with
his architect colleagues Burckhardt and Kutter in a plan to make the
'Landesausstellung' of 1964 a vehicle for all that was vital in Swiss
life. In a pamphlet published in 1955, Achtung: Die Schweiz, the three
authors attack the prevailing lack of drive, the feeble yielding in the
face of what people imagine to be the insuperable force of circumstance.
They propose the construction of a new town which would incorporate
their ideas. In 1964, reflecting that, despite all the discussion

generated by the pamphlet, nothing of the plan was realised, Frisch
states quite simply what had been the authors' aim: 'Wir wollten eine
heutige Schweiz' [9]. The failure to implement any of the 1955 proposals
is for Frisch symptomatic of the Swiss reluctance to embark on any
venture requiring breadth of vision. It is a reluctance which is brought
about by the failure to approach the present other than in terms of a
fixed interpretation of the past.

A second area in which Frisch detects the same unwillingness to
adapt to reality is the vexed question of 'Überfremdung', the designation
given to the problems created by the many foreign workers in Switzerland.
The failure to cope with these problems is but another manifestation of
the inability to come to terms with the facts of a new situation. The
image which the Swiss have of their country is static, not developing.
Into this situation the foreign workers come, and Frisch characterises
the resulting confrontation from the point of view of the mentality which
he is criticising:

> Hier das Gesunde und Ein-für-alle-Mal-Richtige und Einhei-
> mische und Weiss-Gott-Bewährte, kurzum das Schweizerische,
> und da kommen nun mitten in unseren Wohlstand unversehens
> Fremdlinge in Scharen. (V 377)

Once more Frisch insists on approaching a problem in a constructive
manner. In the phenomenon of 'Überfremdung' he sees a possibility for
Switzerland to assert herself positively by seizing the opportunity
'die Position der Schweiz aktuell zu bestimmen' (V 398).

In 1947, on his return from visiting Germany, Frisch had noted
another characteristic of the Swiss which militates against a relaxed
accommodation with reality, namely, a lack of self-confidence (II 491).
Self-confidence and 'Bestand' are inimical: self-confidence requires a
momentum alien to 'Bestand', which is a dead weight of fixed interpretations which relate to an image of what has been. In a comment
which touches directly on the problems of his major fictional heroes,
Frisch indicates that a subconscious awareness of the irrelevance of
these interpretations for the future is also part of 'Bestand': 'Fast
hat man den Eindruck, dass Zukunft überhaupt als Bedrohung empfunden
wird.' (V 381) Frisch finds this attitude self-defeating, since the
future will come in any case. However much the Swiss might wish it,
life is not fixed at one point in time. 'Bestand' for this reason
causes the past, the present and the future to stand in a distorted
relationship to one another. Rhetorically Frisch asks: 'Was will die
Schweiz von der Zukunft: ihre Vergangenheit?' (V 381). In Wilhelm
Tell für die Schule he answers his own question: in Switzerland,

Mile End Library
Queen Mary, University of London
Easter Vacation 1st - 25th April 2010

Extended Easter Vacation Loans
Ordinary Loans borrowed from
Friday 5th March
will be due back on Friday 30th April

One Week Loans borrowed
from Friday 26th March
will be due back on Wed 28th April

Borrowed items 12/05/2010 15:25
XXXXXX5294

Item Title	Due Date
The Fire Raisers : a morality	24/05/2010
* Hugo von Hofmannsthal : t	09/06/2010
* Max Frisch : his work and i	19/05/2010
* Horvath : a study	19/05/2010

* Indicates items borrowed today
Thank you
Don't forget to renew your loans
If you are going away for the vacation

refuge in images of the past is preferred to innovation (VI 439).
Public life in Switzerland is vitiated by a lack of self-confidence
which makes the past look more attractive than the future.

The chief underlying feature of the Swiss 'Aberglaube an den Bestand'
is thus fear which derives from an inability to accept the uncertain
nature of life. Indeed, Frisch sees this fear as the dominant trait
in his fellow-countrymen:

> Ich möchte die Angst vor der Zukunft geradezu als das
> Grundgefühl des Schweizer Zeitgenossen bezeichnen. (IV 258)

The symptoms of this 'Angst' are 'Minderwertigkeitsgefühl und Dünkel'
(IV 223) [10]. The high esteem in which the Swiss hold money, allied
with the stable prosperity of the country since 1945, are not sufficient
to extinguish or even to muffle the unease caused by the contrary pull
of these two emotions in the psyche of present-day Switzerland. Instead,
'Angst' and 'Bestand' are compounded in their effect by external
circumstances of material prosperity, by 'Konjunktur'. Frisch notes
the Swiss reluctance, despite monetary wealth, to invest in new ideas,
and concludes that prosperity stands in inverse proportion to the
willingness to take risks. As a result Switzerland produces nothing
which is original (IV 223). He goes so far as to call the Swiss 'ein
saturiertes Volk' (II 342). In Achtung: Die Schweiz he had asserted
that prosperity was taking the place of moral values, and had asked how
long this could continue: 'Vertrauen wir auf die Ewigkeit der Konjunktur?' (III 295). For Frisch the situation is fraught with the gravest
dangers. In 1957 he exhorts young teachers to approach the tasks of
their profession in a spirit which will dispel the pernicious influence
of 'Konjunktur' (IV 212). He wishes youth to be offered the possibility
of developing resistance to what he regards as a shortcoming in the Swiss
character, for he considers that reverence for material prosperity masks
an unfulfilled inner need. In 1974, in his most sombre assessment of
Switzerland from the point of view of its young people, Frisch considers
that obeisance to 'Konjunktur' has morally eviscerated the country to
the point where the younger generation, unlike his own, does not feel
obliged, either by circumstances or by what the country has to offer,
to concern itself very deeply with Switzerland (VI 516). In this very
real sense 'Aberglaube an den Bestand' and 'Konjunktur' are together
denying the future.

The Swiss create a false image of their standing and reputation.
They harbour the illusion that this image is a fitting representation
of their identity. But the nation as a whole shies away from an attempt
to acquire real respect through a meaningful confrontation with the

present (V 396). In this respect the close relationship between
Frisch's lectures, speeches and articles on the one hand and his
narrative and drama on the other is demonstrated, for the assumption
of a role forms a major theme in his plays and novels. In his 1957
address on the Swiss national day he relates 'Angst' to the assumption
of a role:

> Ich habe gesagt, die Schweiz habe Angst. Ich meine das
> ganz einfach: Jeder, der eine Rolle spielt, die nicht
> ganz mit der Wirklichkeit übereinstimmt, muss ja Angst
> haben, und darum erträgt er sehr wenig Kritik. (IV 221)

The role is also a manifestation of a defective relationship to the
continuum of time [11], and since it does not accord with reality, it is
not possible to talk of Switzerland's mission in Europe in the sense
that the country by its composition offers an example to others of
peaceful co-existence and mutual respect among language groups. Frisch
talks bluntly of 'das Märchen von der Mission der Schweiz' [12], and is
of the opinion that the desire to find a mission in this sense arises
in general from 'Angst' and in particular from an attempt to compensate
for political insignificance and territorial smallness. A defective
relationship to reality - the unwillingness to accept that life cannot
be defined in terms of 'Bestand' - leads to an assumption of a role -
that Switzerland could serve as a model - which creates a further divorce
from reality. The awareness of this divorce manifests itself in an
increase in the 'Angst' which lies originally at the root of the defective
relationship to reality. Although 'Angst' may be a general phenomenon
in the contemporary world, it is nonetheless valid to maintain that
Frisch's pre-occupation with this theme reflects his feeling that there
is a particular degree of enthralment to it in Switzerland. His untiring
attempts to throw light on the manifestations of 'Angst' are motivated
by the conviction that a clear definition of difficulties is the first
step towards combatting them. In this lies for him the importance of
his discussion of the negative traits of his countrymen.

The nature of Frisch's commitment to Switzerland

Frisch has shown himself to be anxious that something of a radical
and visionary nature be undertaken in Switzerland. In his 1953 lecture
to Zürich architects he quotes Zwingli's phrase 'Lass uns um Gottes
willen etwas Tapferes tun'. He emphasises the obligations towards the
present placed on everyone, and defines tradition in the light of this
obligation as

> sich an die Aufgaben seiner Zeit wagen mit dem gleichen Mut,
> wie die Vorfahren ihn hatten gegenüber ihrer Zeit. (III 237)

For this there must be available a clear concept appropriate to the
times. It is the duty of every citizen to contribute to the formulation
of this concept:

> Die Schweiz als Inhalt in unserer Zeit ist neu zu konzipieren.
> Das ist nicht die Aufgabe der Behörde, sondern unsere
> Aufgabe. [1]

Addressing architects once more, but again with wider connotations,
Frisch, in his introduction to the pamphlet <u>Wir selber bauen unsere
Stadt</u> (1953), proclaims the necessity for such a theoretical plan:
'Man ist nicht realistisch, indem man keine Idee hat' [2]. There have
been times in the past when the country behaved in accordance with
clearly defined aims. Frisch the architect points to an example in the
federal capital of a creative plan which was successfully realised: the
covered walkways of Bern contain something of the Swiss idea [3]. Frisch
also refers to the lively awareness of things Swiss discernible in the
events of 1848 when Switzerland possessed 'eine geschichtliche Gegenwart' (III 236). He evokes the 'Landesausstellung' of 1939 in similar
vein (I 133) [4]. Thus there have been achievements which have been
attained by the force of a vision, and, as a result, these achievements
have incorporated and exemplified much that was specifically Swiss. In
this manner the country was able to fulfil itself: 'Die Grösse unseres
Landes: die Grösse seines Geistes' (VI 571). But it appears that Frisch
considers that the impetus which he saw in the years 1848 and 1939 has
spent itself. During the war and at its close he saw his country
fulfilling a function with regard to her neighbours. In 1964 Frisch
describes the opportunity which existed immediately after 1945 for
Switzerland to put her neutrality to good use, to become 'ein geistiges
Genf' [5]. It was a vision of a positive function for neutrality which
was never realised.

The belief in the supreme importance of the obligation to approach
the contemporary world with the creative zest manifested by previous
generations is the motivation of Frisch's unceasing attempts to define
and to come to terms with his immediate world, his Swiss environment,
and with the wider framework of the European and world situation. For
Frisch the attempt to fulfil this obligation is the only justification
for the committal to paper of views and ideas offered to the public.
In the note 'An den Leser' which prefaces <u>Tagebuch 1946-1949</u> he makes
his attitude plain: the reader is invited

> diesen Aufzeichnungen und Skizzen eines jüngeren Zeit-
> genossen zu folgen, dessen Schreibrecht niemals in seiner
> Person, nur in seiner Zeitgenossenschaft begründet sein
> kann. (II 349)

A quarter of a century later Frisch refers to the dialogue started by
reactions to his writing, a dialogue vital to his task of giving
expression to the contemporary world: he regards these reactions 'als
Herausforderung, den eigenen Standort in der Zeitgenossenschaft zu
suchen' [6]. Implicit in Frisch's unflinching dedication to his 'Zeitgenossenschaft' is the full involvement of the writer in his particular
society. For, as a citizen, the writer cannot absolve himself of the
political and social responsibility which Frisch referred to in his
definition of 'Kultur', and a major part of that responsibility lies
in an active concern for the state of the contemporary world. Contemptuously he rejects any notion of the artist which does not contain
this responsibility as 'jene hehre Vorstellung vom Künstler...ledig
aller Zeitgenossenschaft' (II 341) [7]. Ironically it was a fellow-Swiss
who caused him to define his attitude most clearly. In his speech
accepting the 'Literaturpreis der Stadt Zürich' in 1966, Emil Staiger
decried aspects of modern literature in a way which many, including
Frisch, felt to diminish unfairly modern achievements in favour of a
return to attitudes of an imagined past which divorced literature from
everyday concerns. In an open letter, Frisch reminds Staiger of the
obligation placed upon anyone making public statements:

> Wer auf eine Bühne tritt...steht in der Zeit und hat sich [8]
> dieser Zeit bewusst zu sein. (V 461)

But to endeavour to fulfil the manifold obligations laid upon the writer
in his attempt to establish a relationship with his environment is not
an easy task. The weight of the pressures to conform is perhaps most
apparent when it is temporarily removed. Travelling in Germany in 1949,
Frisch reflects on his brief freedom from coercion to accept a national
point of view, and on the ambivalent reactions which he experiences
about his own homeland when he is abroad:

> Ein nicht unbedeutender Vorteil: dass man in einem fremden
> Land nicht meint, man müsse allem gegenüber eine heimatliche
> Übereinstimmung finden. Man erwartet nicht, was es niemals
> geben kann. Schon das gibt dem fremden Land jedesmal etwas
> Befreiendes, Erfrischendes, etwas Festliches, was uns dann
> der Heimat gegenüber oft ungerecht macht. Es sind überall
> nur wenige, denen man zugetan sein kann. Das Ungerechte:
> in der Fremde bin ich dankbar für die wenigen, in der Heimat
> entsetzt über die Menge der andern. (II 695)

As well as being a statement of general validity, this is one of
Frisch's most succint formulations of the difficulties of his relationship to Switzerland.

The qualifications with which Frisch surrounds his public statements about his commitment to his country serve to demonstrate its

basic strength. In general terms, he is aware of the extent to which a
writer is formed by his native environment. Accepting the 'Büchner-
preis' in 1958, he tells his fellow-writers: 'Wir sind abhängig von
unserer Herkunft' (IV 241). In more particular terms the progress of
his views since the end of the war in respect of Switzerland can be
traced. In 1947 he avers that he would choose to be Swiss if indeed he
had such a choice (II 492). In 1958 he states firmly: 'Ich bin
Schweizer, und begehre nichts andres zu sein' (IV 237). In the same
year he enlarges on the theme of the writer's dependence on his
environment and also makes reference to the restrictiveness of
Switzerland:

> Meine Umwelt, die nächste, ist die Schweiz. Und dafür
> bin ich dankbar. Aber die Schweiz ist nicht meine einzige 9
> Umwelt. Und dafür bin ich auch dankbar.

In 1960, the year in which he claimed that the 'Problematik' of the
writer in Switzerland no longer exercised him, he answers the question
as to why he continues to live in Switzerland and not in West Germany:
'Weil es sich hier bequem leben lässt und ich hier noch am ehesten hin-
gehöre' (IV 258). In the 1966 speech on 'Überfremdung' Frisch
formulates to his audience his commitment in an indirect manner:

> Vielleicht finden Sie, dass der Sprecher...noch nicht
> so richtig dazugehört. Selber weiss ich nur, dass ich
> nicht anderswo dazugehöre. (V 399)

On the other hand, Frisch has never minimised the personal cost of
involvement with one's native country. In 1974, after making this
general point, he goes on to relate it to his indignation at
Switzerland's attitude to contemporary events in Chile, and concludes:

> So verstehe ich mich als Schweizer ganz und gar, dieser
> meiner Heimat verbunden - einmal wieder - in Zorn und Scham.
> (VI 517)

By reacting in 'Zorn und Scham' to what he considers to be less positive
aspects of being Swiss at the present time, Frisch is accepting
individual responsibility for his country. Later in the same year,
he traces briefly the development of his relationship to Switzerland:
age and travel have diminished the intensity of his involvement, but
he acknowledges that he has been conditioned by his background and that
his outlook still reflects it:

> Insofern fühle ich mich nicht mehr so zentral schweizerisch,
> aber ich bringe meine Erfahrung mit, ich bringe die Bedingt-10
> heit mit, die man durch die Geschichte einfach hat.

Switzerland and its ethos are ineradicably a part of Frisch's deeply
personal commitment to the contemporary world. It is a commitment which
possesses validity beyond the borders of his country, and at the same time
it represents the best elements in the tradition of Swiss intellectual life.

3. Max Frisch as a Contemporary Swiss Writer

The relationship to a Swiss tradition

The interests and concerns expressed in the writing of Max Frisch
are common to those of other figures in the history of Swiss letters.
His reflections on the Swiss state, on its history and on its position
in the changing world of the twentieth century, as well as his conviction
that a critical commitment to Switzerland is a moral obligation upon
himself and his countrymen, form part of a continuing Swiss tradition.
Certainly, a similarity suggests itself between the outlook of Frisch
and that of Gottfried Keller [1]. Keller's 1848 declaration of the
necessity for commitment to the community had a general application, and
it was one from which, despite many vicissitudes, he never resiled in
relation to Switzerland:

> Wehe einem jeden, der nicht sein Schicksal an dasjenige [2]
> der öffentlichen Gemeinschaft bindet.

On the day following this diary entry, Keller had proclaimed: 'Nein,
es darf keine Privatleute mehr geben' [3]. The Nazi era, from which Frisch
draws so many lessons and which so strongly influenced his attitude to
Switzerland, was an example of what can happen to a society if Keller's
warning is ignored. There is also evidence of a temperamental similarity between Keller and Frisch. It would not be unreasonable, for
example, to apply to Frisch the words written in 1890 by C. F. Meyer in
his recollections of Keller:

> Er sorgte, lehrte, predigte, warnte, schmollte, strafte
> väterlich und sah überall zu dem, was er für recht hielt. [4]

Much of the virulence of Swiss criticism of Frisch might be diminished
if it recognised a similar concern in his attitude. It is of course
possible that, in the face of the gravity and complexity of the
problems now confronting, not only Switzerland, but the world at large,
the emotions underlying the calls for adjustment and change are
stronger, so that Frisch's tone is more intense than Keller's [5]. The
constant exhortations of both writers that there must be a high moral
framework of reference for the conduct of daily life derives from the
fact that both men spent much formative time abroad [6]. One of the most
travelled Swiss writers of his generation, Frisch has strengthened by
his journeys his conviction that a moral awareness is necessary to
counter the pull towards conformity in modern life in general, and in
Switzerland in particular. The circumstances of the lives of both
Keller and Frisch render them conscious of the necessity for an attitude
to Switzerland tempered by views garnered outside Switzerland. Yet if

the exhortations of Keller and Frisch to the Swiss are motivated by
their sense of attachment to the country in which they were born, this
sense of attachment is devoid of false sentiment: the link is accepted
as a fact of life. This has enabled them to regard Switzerland as a
microcosm of the sociological environment in general. They both draw
on their observation of human relations as they are conditioned by the
framework of this microcosm for the universal themes of their artistic
works [7]. It has been for the calibre of his artistic work, not because
he was Swiss, that Keller has been esteemed [8]. Similarly, if Frisch is
an important Swiss writer, he must be judged to be so on the quality of
his presentation of his themes, and not because of the intrinsic
importance of these themes [9].

Gottfried Keller is the chief figure in Swiss literature with whom
Frisch has affinities, but there are also connections with others. [10]
The novel Stiller, for example, is considered to link Frisch not only
to Keller, but also to Gotthelf [11]. Stiller also displays similarities
to Spitteler's novel Imago (1906). In each case the returning artist
is used as a literary device by the author to examine aspects of Swiss
society in relation to the period in which the novel is set. It is a
device which was also adopted by Albin Zollinger in Pfannenstiel (1940).
It is to Zollinger that Frisch feels most attracted among Swiss writers
this century (II 496). Frisch's admiration has not clouded his
judgement of the stature of Zollinger's work, however, and it is
appropriate to look at the case of Zollinger and at Frisch's reaction
to it, for the fate of Zollinger demonstrates the particular nature of
the pressures to which the Swiss writer is subject.

In Heimat und Fremde Hans Bänziger has given a good account of the
difficulties which Zollinger encountered. In summing up Zollinger's
position, Bänziger places him in a Swiss tradition which starts with
Bodmer and Breitinger, and indicates how Zollinger's determination to
continue this tradition differentiated him from at least two of his
contemporaries, Jakob Schaffner and Robert Walser, in the stresses of
the period in which he lived [12]. The critical spirit of this tradition
imparts a moralistic tone to Zollinger's work, and this spirit and its
literary expression form a link with Frisch. Their castigation of what
they hold to be the deficiencies of Switzerland in their work also
establishes connections with Keller's last novel Martin Salander [13].
Yet there is a clear difference in tone between the work of Frisch and
of Zollinger, and this derives from the perspective gained by Frisch
from his many contacts beyond the borders of Switzerland [14]. It is

precisely this dimension which Zollinger lacked, and Frisch claims that
it prevented his full development as a writer. Zollinger wrote his
main works under the long shadow of approaching war and during two
years of actual war. In the period from 1933 to 1941 Switzerland was
under increasing pressure from Germany and the events taking place
there, and Frisch points to one of the internal effects of this pressure
which had a direct bearing on society's view of the German-Swiss writer:
his potential Swiss audience was at this time capable only of a limited
and simplified response, and this was bound to affect him. In addition,
the increasing isolation of the country deprived him of the challenge
offered by confrontation with standards valid outside Switzerland (IV 268).
For these two reasons Zollinger was an emigré in his own country in the
sense that he could not find a foothold there; he did not have the
advantages of the real emigrés in Switzerland at that time:

> Die Emigranten hatten ein anderes Hinterland, wenn auch
> zur Zeit ein verlorenes, Berlin oder Wien oder Prag, die
> Schweiz war für sie nur eine Station, nicht ein Massstab.
> (IV 269)

There are two consequences of having an exclusively Swiss background
and audience. In the first place, the writer reduces the scope of his
artistic undertaking in order to avoid being ignored completely.
Secondly, since the urge to communicate persists even in this restricted
environment, the writer inevitably becomes parochial for he has,
outside this environment, no measure of comparison for the value of
what he can communicate. The Swiss writer, therefore, if he is confined
to a Swiss background, must reckon with a diminution of his potential.

The plight of Zollinger also illustrates, albeit in negative
fashion, the vital importance for the writer of the link between
himself and his audience. In his 1958 speech 'Öffentlichkeit als Partner', his fullest consideration of this link, Frisch identifies three
types of audience (IV 249-250). The first is hostile, but may serve
a useful purpose in impelling the writer to write with the utmost
clarity and effectiveness. The second is benevolent, but because of
this, unhelpful, since it encourages a desire to please and an over-
readiness to compromise. But the third type of audience is apathetic,
and this is for the writer not merely unsatisfactory, but positively
harmful since it provokes him to distort his manner of expression in
order to gain attention. It was the fate of Zollinger to have such a
public, which was indifferent to everything which it could not regard
as a reinforcement of the national will to survive. It was understandable, at a time when the nation was surrounded by potential
aggressors, that a dialogue should be especially difficult between the

writer and his public. Frisch sums up the frustration experienced by
Zollinger in a telling image: 'Das Gefühl, in Watte zu sprechen, war
seine bittere Enttäuschung' (I 211) [15]. Zollinger reacted to this
frustration by over-stating his case [16]. It was the double pressure of
being enclosed and being forced to raise his voice which prevented
Zollinger from expressing himself fully, and for this reason Frisch
looks upon his work as the 'Vermächtnis eines Opfers' (IV 270).

In addition to highlighting the increased difficulties of the Swiss
writer with his public at that particular time, the case of Zollinger
is a 'Schweizerspiegel' (IV 269) in a further sense. It underlines
the dependence of the Swiss writer on foreign criticism for a serious
and considered assessment of his work. The value of this assessment
is apparent only when its availability is threatened or absent. Frisch
draws attention to the unhelpfulness for the Swiss artist of the
ambivalent Swiss attitude to his work by pointing to the vital function
of the emigrés as a counter-balance in Swiss cultural life during the
period of the war (II 491). The main contribution of the emigrés was
to the productions of the Zürcher Schauspielhaus. In stressing the
importance of this contribution Frisch claims that the emigrés, with
a perspective achieved elsewhere, were able to help the Swiss towards
an awareness of themselves. But Zollinger had died before the success
of the Schauspielhaus had become established. Frisch's sympathy for
Zollinger as a man and for his plight as a writer makes Frisch aware
of the important formulative influences which his audience exerts on
the writer:

> Was aus einem Schriftsteller wird, hängt nicht nur von
> seinem eigenen Charakter und seinem Talent ab, die Umwelt
> kann ihn stimulieren oder kastrieren. (IV 250)

Zollinger was the victim of a defective relationship to his 'Umwelt',
and his tragedy is particularly Swiss: left to its own resources the
Swiss world is too enclosed to generate the forces necessary to
establish the self-awareness so vital to its well-being and that of
its artists.

The influx of emigré talent to the Zürcher Schauspielhaus meant that,
by the end of the war, the theatre had established a reputation which
was unique, since it had provided for the continuance of a tradition
impossible elsewhere in the German-speaking world. At a time, therefore,
when the new generation of Swiss dramatists, exemplified above all in
the figures of Dürrenmatt and Frisch, were coming forward with their
first ventures, there existed a firmly established theatre with a high
reputation which was prepared to stage these plays [17]. The drama which

se under these conditions was a contribution to Switzerland's attempt
come to terms with the Second World War. For Switzerland had been
red, and some sought to resolve the complex moral tensions which this
brought about by depicting these tensions on the stage. They attempted
to give substance to the apparent unreality of an intact Switzerland [18].
It was part of a search for an identity at that time in which Frisch was
one of the participants.

Another aspect of this endeavour was the necessity of establishing
contact with the outside world. The Schauspielhaus was important, but
the encirclement and subsequent emergence unscathed of Switzerland had
nonetheless produced an inward-looking mentality. Thus, if one aim of
Frisch's work at this time is to tackle the moral dilemma of being
spared, another is to attempt to establish contact. A third aim
inevitably reflects his attempt to come to terms with Germany and her
immediate past. Frisch's concern on this point finds artistic expression
chiefly in his play Nun singen sie wieder (first performed 1945).
Frisch states that the conception of the play arose 'aus einem Bedürfnis,
eine eigene Bedrängnis loszuwerden' (II 470). A younger Swiss
contemporary, Hugo Loetscher, puts the importance of the play into a
Swiss framework of reference with similar liberating connotations for
the Swiss literature of the time [19]. Even wider importance is attached
to this play and to the later Als der Krieg zu Ende war (first performed
1949), in that they were at this period among the rare attempts on the
stage in German-speaking countries to treat the problem of coming to
terms with the past. Frisch's position as a German-Swiss permitted
him to deal with a theme which no German could at that time [20]. More
than any other art form perhaps, the drama, especially in Zürich, was
at that time in a position to present in telling fashion the moral
problems of the day. It could fulfil what Frisch has always regarded
as the primary function of the theatre, to present 'die unverborgene,
sichtbare, öffentliche Konfrontation eines Werkes mit seiner Zeitgenossenschaft' [21].

It is appropriate, at the point where Frisch is beginning to
establish his reputation as a writer, to consider his view of the
intellectual, and more particularly of the writer, in Swiss society.
The attitudes of other countries to the intellectual offer a comparison
to the situation in Switzerland. In Germany, for example, the importance
accorded to the intellectual presents a contrast to his standing in
Switzerland, and Frisch notes the flattering nature of this attention
for the Swiss intellectual (II 337). When the status granted to the
intellectual by society coincides with the former's awareness of his

duty towards that society, the conditions exist for the mutual
responsibility, upon which the health of society depends, and the
intellectual can fulfil a useful social role. The intervention of
Emile Zola in the Dreyfus affair in France demonstrates this for Frisch.
It was not Zola's literary prestige which contributed to his influence
in the matter, but the importance which society placed on the sense of
civic responsibility of a notable intellect (V 348) [22]. A relationship
of respect is therefore possible between the intellectual and the body
politic. The inferior status of the intellectual in Switzerland need
not, however, inhibit him from questioning the premisses upon which
society bases its behaviour, although these attempts may be misunderstood.
Frisch is, however, much too realistic not to warn intellectuals,
especially writers, of the limits of the influence which they can exert
through their activities:

> Zu meinen, der Schriftsteller mache Politik, indem er sich
> ausspricht zur Politik, wäre eine Selbsttäuschung. (V 349)

In Switzerland an additional factor can be adduced which puts the
restricted influence of the intellectual as writer into a historical
perspective, namely the comparatively recent emergence of the writer
who seek. to support himself entirely from his writing [23]. Even today
the Swiss writer occupies a marginal situation, at least as far as
supporting himself from his literary work is concerned. Frisch points
to the contrast between the writer's position and the general prosperity
of the country (II 562).

Frisch's comments on Swiss literature and its background since
1945 give prominence to those aspects which Walter Muschg described
some years earlier: the continuing existence of a bürgerlich reading
public whose views on what Swiss literature should offer are characterised by an inability to adapt themselves to the passage of time [24]. In
1953 Frisch attacks this backward-looking mentality as being a flight
from contemporary reality to the illusory certainty offered by a
vision of a past era:

> Das Heimweh nach dem Vorgestern, das die meisten Schweizer
> zu bestimmen scheint, sehen wir allenthalben - in der
> Literatur: Morgarten und Gartenlaube sind ihre beliebtesten
> Bezirke; die meisten Erzählungen entführen uns in die
> ländliche Idylle, die als letztes Reduit der Innerlichkeit
> erscheint; die meisten Gedichte bedienen sich einer Meta-
> physik, die kaum unserer eigenen Erfahrungswelt entstammt,
> und wenn nicht mit Pferden gepflügt wird, sondern mit einem
> Traktor, liefert ihnen das Brot schon keine Poesie mehr;
> eine gewisse Wehmütigkeit, dass das 19. Jahrhundert immer
> weiter zurückliegt, scheint die hauptsächliche Aussage im
> schweizerischen Schrifttum zu sein. (III 236)

By catering for such expectations and by producing such writing, the writer is betraying his 'Zeitgenossenschaft', he is depriving literature of its link with contemporary society. Yet this need not be so. The presence of an audience whose expectations and outlook are in some way at odds with reality provides an opportunity for commenting on this disjunction through the medium of comedy. In 1958 Frisch draws attention to this positive aspect of the situation confronting the Swiss writer (IV 250). It is especially conducive to the production of drama. If the dramatist is to create an effective play, he must know 'wer im Par-kett sitzt' [25]. In Switzerland this is more likely than elsewhere. The very compactness of bürgerlich society offers in its resistance to change a challenge to the writer which, if accepted, can prove fruitful for him provided he is aware of the dangers of writing in such a situation. In 1960 Frisch exemplifies this point by reference to Dürrenmatt's Der Besuch der alten Dame and to his own Biedermann und die Brandstifter, the inspiration for both of which was drawn directly from the conditions prevailing in Switzerland (IV 259). In his sober assessment of his country Frisch is far from suggesting that the writer's existence there is not viable.

Shortly after Frisch makes his most determinedly positive statement on the possibility of literature in Switzerland, Kurt Guggenheim deplores the fact that the theme of Switzerland in contemporary Swiss literature, if it appears at all, is treated in anything but a positive fashion [26]. The form of his complaint suggests, although Guggenheim does not mention any names, that it might include Frisch since it comes perilously close to making a plea for the kind of literature which Frisch regards as 'Propaganda für die Schweiz' [27]. Guggenheim's criticism places Frisch's well-known statement of 1966 (V 372-373) about the younger generation of Swiss writers in perspective. This statement, apparently similar to Guggenheim's in that the absence of Switzerland as a literary theme in the work of this generation is discussed, is in fact of a quite different nature. In the first place, this absence is recorded as a fact, not presented as a blameworthy dereliction on the part of these writers. Secondly, Frisch feels that in neighbouring countries there exists a rapport between the writer and his environment which appears to be lacking in Switzerland. Thirdly, he continues his probing to the point where he asks if it is the fault of the country rather than of the writers that this rapport is lacking. Frisch confesses himself baffled by this question:

> Ist unser Land für seine Schriftsteller kein Gegenstand
> mehr? Und wenn es so sein sollte: Warum? Was heisst

> das in bezug auf das Land? Literatur ist eine Wünschel
> wo sie nicht in Bewegung gerät, da ist keine Quelle. Is
> das die Antwort? Ich weiss nicht. (V 373)

In Frisch's own case the link between society and himself is clear.
In so far as the world of Switzerland and the world of the Bürger,
if not exactly co-extensive, over-lap to a great degree, the difficulty
of Frisch's position vis-a-vis the Bürger world is applicable to his
entire stance towards Switzerland. Since the Bürger world (and with
it Switzerland) exists, and exists in relation to Frisch, it must be
taken seriously, and although it might aggravate to the point of
exasperation, it cannot be ignored [28]. This implies a position which
calls for a constant and strenuous effort to reconcile the demands
arising from the need to accept and also to criticise. Obviously Frisch
is concerned that younger writers have abandoned the complexity of the
position which he occupies. He is afraid that, sensing the difficulty
of influencing the backward-looking public which he had criticised in
1953, they have quite simply cut their links to this public.

The urgency of the problem posed by the writing of the younger
Swiss generation is all the more pressing for Frisch because of his
belief in the necessity of a link between literature and society. He
relates this general belief to a specifically Swiss tradition:

> Domäne der Literatur?...Heute keine Frage: die res publica.
> Das ist aus helvetischer Tradition (Jeremias Gotthelf,
> Gottfried Keller) nicht unbegreiflich. [29]

Yet there is an even more fundamental issue at stake. The real danger
lies not so much in the fact that a tradition is failing to command
respect, but that the importance of the truth which the tradition of
concern for the community contains is being disregarded. For it is
paradoxical that the first step towards personal identity lies in a
commitment to the community. Individuality can only be fulfilled by
accepting the responsibility to the community. To abjure the community
is to deprive the individual personality [30]. If this form of commitment
is important for the individual, it is vital for the writer, since he
draws on his experience of this link for his literary depiction of the
human condition (IV 239). To deny it is to forfeit the possibility
of creating valid literature. The play of interchange which the link
implies between the private and the public renders the individual
receptive to the possibilities offered by new ideas and experiences.
This openness also contains a perspective of relationship between the
local and the wider world, and this perspective is lost if one element
is allowed to bulk larger than the other. When the viewpoint centres
on the local - in this case, on Switzerland - to the exclusion of all

else, Frisch sees no difference between the assertions to which it gives
rise and the blandishments of modern advertising (VI 417). It might
be that members of the younger generation, in reacting against the lack
of perspective of such an attitude, themselves adopt a position which·
also suffers from a lack of balance, which is no less unproductive than
the attitude against which they are reacting. By dissociating themselves
from their environment in their work, they deprive themselves of the
social observation which is the basis of all literary creation. Frisch
has stressed the necessity of social experience, of being part of the
active fabric of society, for the writer. He himself admits to a
certain restriction in the scope of his social intercourse since he
gave up his architect's practice. The main source of his experience of
his environment is as a consequence his recollections of those parts of
his life when he played a recognised social role 'als Träger einer Funktion' [31]. In this he is part of a long Swiss tradition, the necessity
for which he affirms, and the apparent disappearance of which he can
only look on with regret.

The contribution to a Swiss tradition

The longest period which Frisch spent as 'Träger einer Funktion'
was twelve years as an architect. There is a similarity between his
comments on his original profession and his attitude to writing, and
this similarity shapes his view of the position of the writer in society.
In his earliest extant reference to his inclination towards becoming
an architect, he defines its attraction for him as being the practical
realisation of a plan first conceived on paper. The work with paper is
regarded as a preliminary exercise, the validity of which is then put
to the test (II 587) [1]. Frisch describes the excitement which the
bringing together of all the elements in the practical realisation of
a plan, however modest it may be, can generate in him as he is engaged
in his very first commission as an architect:

> ...der erste Entwurf, der verwirklicht werden sollte. Nicht
> immer nur blosses Papier, nur Striche, nur Worte, nur
> Bilder. Ganz wirklich, ganz greifbar waren diese
> schlanken Stämmchen. (I 113)

Frisch later describes this excitement as 'Machlust' (IV 245). It is
a powerful force. Spitteler had described the essential 'Schamgefühl'
of the Swiss writer laying himself bare to his reading public. For
Frisch this emotion, this 'Schamhaftigkeit' (IV 244), is an integral
part of the writing process for all writers, and his interest lies in
establishing what drives the writer to overcome it. The writer, Frisch
claims, is motivated by 'Machlust', and because this urge is 'naiv und

rücksichtslos, verantwortungslos' (IV 245), it is able to breach the
barriers of 'Schamhaftigkeit'. Frisch insists on the emphasis on
craftmanship which the word 'Machlust' contains. Artistic form offers
a 'Macht des Trostes' (II 381) when it is wrested from the chaos of
reality, and this artistic form can never be the result of fortuitous
and unplanned inspiration alone. Craftmanship guides and controls
inspiration. Frisch sets himself resolutely against the viewpoint which
sees art exclusively as the product of inspiration, an attitude particularly prevalent in German-speaking countries, 'wo die Literatur so
heilig genommen wird' [2]. Because literature tends there not to be
regarded as part of normal life, its genesis is ascribed to sources
beyond human control, and the idea that craftmanship might contribute
to the regulation of these forces verges on the sacrilegious. For
Frisch this is a complete misconception, and he directs his attention
to refuting it in the 1955 article Zur Chinesischen Mauer (II 220-225).
In the final analysis it is the work of art which counts, not its genesis
or the purity of its inspiration. The craftsmanship of its final form,
which it offers to those who contemplate it, is the only touchstone
for judgement. The stages in which the artist creates are revealed:
the complex inter-dependence between form and content evolves in the
manner in which they shape and determine one another in the progress
towards their final unity, in the manner in which this unity can then
communicate, and in the manner in which the artist's intention, by
being modulated by the demands of communicability, paradoxically reveals
the special nature of the artist's own insights - this involved process
of constant adjustment and re-adjustment is the artist's craftsmanship.
As in architecture, the excitement, and the difficulty, of writing
arise for Frisch from the attempt properly to combine the constituent
elements of the undertaking. As in architecture, the result is not
necessarily definitive, it is tentative, an experiment. Fittingly,
Frisch's reflections on craftsmanship in art accompany his description
of how he came to re-write his play Die Chinesische Mauer.

It is in association with his later play Biedermann und die Brandstifter that Frisch gives most plastic expression to the relationship
between the artist and his material. In the programme notes on the
occasion of the premiere in 1958 (IV 454-456), Frisch comments that a
good pewter pot can be sketched by someone who has never so much as
touched the material of which it is made. Such a sketch conveys the
idea of a pot. But the material of which the pot is made can itself
provide inspiration for the craftsman who shapes it. Frisch made a
scale-model of a stage, and learnt much from this by testing on it

what he had written, and by making the adjustments which experimentation
with the model showed to be necessary. The process of trial and error
is similar to that used by the craftsman in making ceramics. The rehearsal
of the play – the test of the validity of the playwright's idea – is
compared, in the interaction of intention and possibility, to a blacksmith working at his anvil. Frisch closes by thanking the Zürcher
Schauspielhaus for affording him the opportunity to experiment like the
craftsmen whom he has cited, and also to experiment with the craftsmen
in the theatre. These experiments have permitted him to make an
appropriate and feasible construction [3].

Clearly the architect and the playwright have at least superficial
affinities. Yet it can be seen from the similarity – amounting at times
to interchangeability – of Frisch's statements on writing and those on
architecture that Frisch conceives of both activities as part of the
same indivisible process of reaching an accommodation with reality.
The individual and his ideas meet with reality in a fashion which results
in the shaping of both reality and the individual, in the shaping of
their respective contours. Contours can be shaped by the coming
together of material and tools, reality providing the material and the
individual the tools. The potter has his hands, the maker of ceramics
his chemicals and the blacksmith his hammer and anvil. The tool of the
writer is language, and he can use it in the way in which a sculptor
uses a chisel. In a passage which stresses the need for scrupulous
care, Frisch shows how language is used to give shape to inchoate
reality:

> Wie der Bildhauer, wenn er den Meissel führt, arbeitet
> die Sprache, indem sie die Leere, das Sagbare, vortreibt
> gegen das Geheimnis, gegen das Lebendige. Immer besteht
> die Gefahr, dass man das Geheimnis zerschlägt, und ebenso
> die andere Gefahr, dass man vorzeitig aufhört, dass man es
> ein Klumpen sein lässt, dass man das Geheimnis nicht stellt,
> nicht fasst, nicht befreit von allem, was immer noch sagbar
> wäre. (II 379)

The linguistic situation in which Frisch finds himself as a German-
Swiss is especially suited to foster this attitude of extreme care in
giving verbal shape to the elusive nature of reality.

Many of the peculiarities of this situation are suggested by the
sketch Mundart (1934) (I 69). To the unnamed young German-Swiss who
is the principal figure of this anecdote, it seems that 'Schweizerdeutsch'
is useful only for such mundane undertakings as ordering wine. Once it
leaves the sphere of everyday concerns and attempts to express more
grandiose concepts, 'Schweizerdeutsch' becomes ridiculous, and thus
exposes the pretensions of the speaker. A tradition of Mundart

literature, which might have helped Mundart to acquire a more
philosophical dimension, does not exist, because there have not been
sufficient writers so deficient in commercial sense as to write in the
medium. The young man concludes by suggesting what Mundart and Hochdeutsch represent for the German-Swiss as far as literary expression is
concerned. The relationship to Mundart is likened to the clay on the
potter's wheel resisting attempts to shape it, defying the potter to
give it pleasing form. The relationship to Hochdeutsch as a literary
medium, on the other hand, resembles that of the potter's customer to
the finished products: instead of having to cope with the intractability
of the material as the potter does, the customer merely has to seek out
the vessel most appropriate to his purpose. The writers who have shaped
the consciousness of the German-Swiss offer him such 'fertige(n) Töpfe'
(I 69). Two considerations emerge for the German-Swiss writer, and for
Frisch in particular, from this anecdote and its conclusions.

Firstly, the German-Swiss writer must be influenced, and not necessarily to his advantage, by the fact that the medium of his expression,
Hochdeutsch or Schriftdeutsch, is the language of a foreign country to
which he must look for possible literary success. It is true that
Frisch, after briefly analysing the sociological composition of German-
speaking Switzerland, is of the opinion that the ratio of the reading
public to the total population is not a bad one. Comparison of the
figures for Switzerland with those for Germany puts the Swiss in a
relatively favourable light, and for this reason Frisch warns against
any bitterness on the part of the German-Swiss writer towards his
countrymen, on that score at least (II 562-563). But this does not
of course run counter to Friedrich Dürrenmatt's assertion that the
Swiss writer, if he wishes to survive as a full-time writer, must
engage in the export business; he may live and work in Switzerland,
but the economic market for his work is elsewhere [4]. The truth of
what Dürrenmatt maintains is shown in the success of Frisch himself.
The effect of this dependence on the foreign market is that the
reputation of a writer is achieved in Switzerland often by virtue of a
reputation which he has already established elsewhere. Despite many
literary prizes in Switzerland, the country does not really do very
much for her writers since most of these prizes are 'eine nachträgliche
Bestätigung schon bestehenden Ruhms' [5]. Literary reputations are
delivered ready-made from abroad, as it were. For Frisch one of the
characteristics of the general lack of self-confidence of his countrymen
is 'der bedenkenlose Kniefall vor allem Fremden' (II 491). It is
ironic that his own reputation amongst them owes at least something

48.

to this.

Secondly, there is the complex relationship of the writer to
Mundart and to Hochdeutsch. In a list of 'Dankbarkeiten' - aspects of
his life for which he is grateful - Frisch cites 'die Spannung zwischen
Mundart und Schriftsprache' (VI 235) [6]. Yet elsewhere he would seem
to suggest that the tendency towards a norm which his use of Hochdeutsch
implies, might encourage neglect of Mundart. In answer to a question
as to the possible influence on himself of a public beyond that of
German-speaking Switzerland, he admits that he has always had a German
reader in mind when writing [7]. The feeling that writing for a German
public can be a form of estrangement for a German-Swiss writer is
heightened on learning that German publishers' readers are at pains to
eradicate from Frisch's language those elements which are particularly
Swiss. They impress upon him that his form of Hochdeutsch is not
sufficiently pure [8]. But the situation is perhaps not quite as one-
sided as this suggests. Perhaps Frisch's use of the word 'Spannung'
is a good pointer to the true state of affairs. If one pole of this
tension is provided by what Frisch calls the 'Begrifflichkeit' [9] of
Hochdeutsch, the other pole is provided by the more direct relationship
to immediate reality of Mundart, the closeness of which is demonstrated
by the fact that Mundart is 'eine unbewusste Sprache' [10]. But one of
the functions of literature is to create awareness of that which is
unthinking. Part of this process of becoming aware must lie for the
writer in the very act of using language in a creative way. To the
insights afforded by this there is added for the German-Swiss writer
additional dimension: that offered by the interplay of two such closely
related yet distinct means of expression as Hochdeutsch and Mundart.
Walter Schenker concludes from his discussions with him that Frisch's
relationship to the two modes of expression gives rise in him to a form
of 'Sprachscheu' which Schenker defines as deriving from an attempt to
amalgamate what Frisch requires from the qualities of both Mundart and
Hochdeutsch:

> Sprachscheu in dem Sinn, dass sich Max Frisch weder auf die
> Sprachebene des Gewöhnlichen noch auf die des Gehobenen
> ganz festlegen will. [11]

This suggests that the qualifications in Frisch's writing, both in his
plays and novels on the one hand and in his essays and speeches on the
other, flow directly from the tension which the two modes of expression
generate for him as a German-Swiss writer.

In general terms, however, it is true to say that, if Frisch admits
that he has a German reader in mind when he writes, he is reacting as

other German-Swiss writers do to their linguistic situation and
adapting his written language towards a German norm. There is in any
case, a reluctance on the part of the Swiss to read Mundart. This
derives partly from the fact that they are used to reading Hochdeutsch,
partly from a certain contemptuous rivalry amongst the dialects [12].
Frisch himself has drawn attention to the fact that it is an accepted
convention, both inside and outside Switzerland, that, within the
framework of a novel, Swiss characters in Swiss settings express themselves in Hochdeutsch [13]. Within this general convention for the novel,
the occasional Swiss element which is found in Frisch's Hochdeutsch
need not obtrude, but can serve to reinforce the strength of the depicted
reality [14]. If, on the other hand, Swiss linguistic elements occur in
the course of a play, they encourage the spectator to relate the play
to Switzerland. To the extent that it is not natural for the German-
Swiss to speak Hochdeutsch, however, its use on the stage must
necessarily create something of a gulf between the spectator and the
play. Yet the very plasticity of Mundart does not lend itself, quite
apart from considerations of diversity, to rhetoric [15]. This
incompatibility raises technical problems which are reflected in
Frisch's reactions to difficulties posed by work on the abortive plans
for the film Zürich-Transit. Here Frisch achieves two solutions to
the problem of comprehensibility: firstly, he proposes a sound-track
with a narrative voice-off relating the action in Hochdeutsch over the
muted Mundart conversation of the figures on the screen; secondly, he
proposes that Ehrismann, the main character, should conduct two
conversations important to the action respectively with a German and
a French-speaking Swiss - conversations which are necessarily conducted
in Hochdeutsch [16]. These two solutions arise from the problem of
making the situation generally comprehensible against a very definite
Zürich setting. In the theatre the problem can only be solved by not
setting the play in Switzerland in the first place. The plays cannot
have a 'real' setting in the sense that the action does not take place
in a specific locality. The note to Nun singen sie wieder therefore
has a general application:

> Der Ort, wo diese Szenen spielen, geht immer aus dem
> gesprochenen Wort hervor. (II 137)

Thus Frisch exploits a situation which is forced upon him with two aims
in mind: firstly, he presents within it an aspect of human behaviour
which he holds to have universal validity [17]; and secondly, he destroys
the illusion that the action of the play is taking place anywhere
other than on the stage [18]. The tension between Mundart and Hochdeutsch,

which Frisch experiences in common with other German-Swiss writers,
obliges him to adopt certain conventions and technical devices in the
theatre as well as in the novel. The structure, as well as the content,
of his work is influenced by his linguistic situation.

The case of Frisch throws light on the complexities of literary
creation for the German-Swiss. Frisch himself points to a link between
his relationship to Hochdeutsch and his distrustful attitude to
linguistic expression in general: Hochdeutsch is for him 'die ver-
fremdende Sprache' [19]. The dimension which this relationship to his
medium of expression imparts to the writer, the freedom which it
bestows on him to express his view of reality from two similar and
proximate but separate perspectives which fuse in the arrangements of
the written works, the ability to probe and test - these advantages can
be elevated into an artistic principle. In a well-known passage in
Tagebuch 1946-1949, Frisch discusses Brecht's 'Verfremdungseffekt' in
the theatre. He notes that its object is to present the action on the
stage in such a way that the spectator views this action, not 'als
Hingerissener' but 'als Erkennender' (II 600), and speculates on the
effect of the application of these principles to narrative writing.
He comes to the conclusion that, if it were possible to do this, the
false reality which is attributed to literature by readers, especially
in German-speaking countries, would be destroyed. This statement is
rightly seen by Schenker to derive from Frisch's own linguistic
situation:

> Das Programm Brechts formuliert nur etwas nach, was Frisch
> schon vorher elementar erfahren hat, elementar nämlich
> von der deutschschweizerischen Sprachsituation her. [20]

The relationship between Mundart and Hochdeutsch inherent in Frisch's
works, has also forged his views on the usefulness and the limitations
of language in general. These are views which in turn colour his
assessment of the role of literature in human affairs.

In Tagebuch 1946-1949 Frisch acknowledges a link between the
Romantic and the modern eras (II 448). The predeliction for the
outline sketch, long evident in modern painting, is now appearing in
writing too. The particular qualities of this fragmentary form were
well-known to the Romantics. This 'Skizze' is the artistic form most
appropriate to the present because of its tentative and probing nature.
For the architect Frisch, the term 'Skizze' has an additional relevance
in that it signifies the preliminary stage in the accommodation to
reality of an architectural project. Frisch suggests further that to
reflect the disintegration of the modern world through form is a

possible way of coming to terms with this world: the use of the
'Skizze' springs from a distrust of inappropriate and superficial
form, it is 'Ausdruck eines Weltbildes, das sich nicht mehr schliesst
oder noch nicht schliesst' (II 448). It is in its search for an
appropriate language which can give expression to a changed reality,
that Frisch sees the characteristic nature of modern literature. This
accounts for its propensity to experiment (V 328). For the process of
disintegration, analysed by Hofmannsthal at the beginning of the century
in his famous Chandosbrief, is accelerating. There is a growing
disjunction of language and reality. As words become increasingly
sundered from the reality which they purport to represent, so they
become increasingly worthless. In 1947 Frisch expresses the view that
language — and not simply the German language — has been irreparably
damaged by political and commercial propaganda. In so far as it distorts
and misrepresents, language, the medium of communication, is inferior
to the silence of dumb creatures (II 537). The dangers attending the
use of language have not, however, been brought about solely by abuse
in the modern age. These dangers are inherent in language itself. An
awareness of this is impressed perhaps more forcibly on Frisch by his
own linguistic situation. Language contains a 'fast uferlose Missdeut-
barkeit' (IV 562) and becomes a 'Gefäss des Vorurteils' (II 536).
Frisch's reaction to the two inter-related problems of inadequacy of
language and abuse of language indicates his own conviction that
language is failing to provide a forum for human intercourse [21]. For
Frisch the major artistic question of the day is the manner in which
writers can in their work sufficiently come to terms with reality to
attempt to offer a bulwark against the increasing erosion of language.

The problem of the relationship between literature and the use of
language has been for Frisch given definitive expression by Büchner.
Frisch cites Mercier's famous speech in Dantons Tod, in which Mercier
points out the connection between the vocabulary of the revolutionaries
and the destruction which surrounds them, as the classic diagnosis of
the destructive power of language, especially of politically motivated
language:

> Sie (die Literatur) bringt, sofern sie lebendig ist, die
> Sprache immer und immer wieder auf den Stand der Realität,
> auch die Literatur, die nicht programmatisch eingreift,
> vielleicht vor allem die Literatur, die nicht programmatisch
> eingreift. 'Geht einmal euren Phrasen nach bis zu dem Punkt,
> wo sie verkörpert werden' sagt Büchner im Danton: 'Blickt
> um euch, das alles habt ihr gesprochen'. Das sagt die Lite-
> ratur, sofern sie ihren Namen verdient; der Rest is
> Belletristik. (V 353) [22]

Literature thus has a clear goal: to restore the connection between language and reality. The linguistic abstractions which deaden the force and worth of reality must be attacked so that thinking relates directly to the world of experience. Frisch has given expression to his own exhortation by exploring the link between language and reality through three forms of lack of communication in three plays. In Als der Krieg zu Ende war (1949) the heroine, a German woman trying to eke out an existence in the ruins of Berlin immediately after the war, falls in love with a Russian officer. Neither of them speaks the other's language. In his comments on the real episode which inspired the play, Frisch is struck by the paradox that absence of a common language can be the basis for communication, and finds it significant that it should be a woman with her closer ties to reality who instigates the relationship (II 536-537). On the other hand, lack of language can be subjected to as much abuse as language itself. This is demonstrated in the figure of the dumb Min Ko, Der Stumme, in Die Chinesische Mauer (second version 1955). In Min Ko, ironically known as the 'Stimme des Volkes' (II 196), Frisch shows how silence can be exploited and degraded by hostile political forces. Biedermann und die Brandstifter (1958) deals with the complete dislocation of language and reality. Language fails to cope with or analyse a potentially dangerous situation, and is seen in the play totally to negate its function. For this reason silence becomes the real hero of the play, since silence forms the tabula rasa on which meaningful communication can be restored [23].

If he embarks on the problematic attempt to communicate, the writer must also accept the fact that the modern world is different from the world of his predecessors. The consciousness of reality reflected in their work is a consciousness which no longer reflects his reality. To adopt their manner, to perpetuate their modes of writing is meaningless. It subverts the possibility of communication. Frisch compares the situation of those writers who approach the present with the attitudes of the past to people living within an outmoded interpretation of the world which is collapsing silently about them like the walls of a house. They persist in writing on these walls as if they were still in place; in fact, they are writing on air (II 450). This represents a failure to come to terms with reality through language. It is with just such a failure that Frisch charges much of modern poetry written in German. Prior to a discussion of the way in which two poems of Brecht — 'Rückkehr' and 'An die Nachgeborenen' — reflect a consciousness of reality through their use of language, Frisch complains that the poetry which does not do this is failing in its

purpose, is not using language as a 'Meissel' in the way he has already
proposed. In this poetry there is 'keine sprachliche Durchdringung der
Welt, die uns umstellt' (II 538). Frisch sees the failure of this
poetry reflected in the manner of its presentation at a traditional
Dichterlesung. The stage-management of such a performance is rendered
useless by the impingement of surrounding reality in the same way as
this poetry seems futile and irrelevant to our real concerns. The
solemn manner of reading also heightens the feeling of dissociation
from actuality. A real poem does not require this elaborately unreal
presentation because it relates itself to reality directly by way of
its language. It is the function of literature to keep alive the
'Lebendigkeit des Wortes' and to maintain 'den Kurswert der Wörter'
(V 353). The real commitment of the writer lies in striving for this:

> Es ist...ein Engagement, wenn Literatur die gebräuchliche
> Sprache auf ihren Wirklichkeitsgehalt hin testet; ein
> Engagement an die Realität. 24

Since Frisch considers the state of health of language to be a constant
obligation on the writer, he rejects inappropriate, falsely traditional
modes of viewing the world through language. He does this in the full
awareness of the double nature of language, of its ability to reveal
and to dissemble.

One literary response to the reality of the modern world which
Frisch feels to be suitable has been shown to be the 'Skizze'. The
question arises as to whether it is possible that the 'Skizze' might
be incorporated into a larger framework which would enhance its
significance. The value of the 'Skizze' lies in its exploratory
nature which creates an interplay with the reader. If a book is too
overbearing, if its concerns are inward-looking, this interplay cannot
take place. Frisch notes the stimulus, on the other hand, of a book
which is outgoing, which can create an interplay between itself and the
reader (II 447). It occurs to Frisch that the manner of this interaction can be applied to literary form. Individual sections of the
book can, by the arrangement of their sequence, react against one
another by the apparent dissimilarity of their content in such a way
as to indicate a deeper-lying affinity between themselves. The diary
form lends itself particularly to the possibility of this kind of
arrangement which resembles that of a mosaic. In Tagebuch 1946-1949
Frisch formulates the theory of the matter. In the short foreword
An den Leser he draws the reader's attention to the significance which
the contiguity of the entries seeks to create:

> Der Leser täte diesem Buch einen grossen Gefallen, wenn er,
> nicht nach Laune und Zufall hin und her blätternd, die

> zusammensetzende Folge achtete; die einzelnen Steine eines
> Mosaiks, und als solches ist dieses Buch zumindest gewollt,
> können sich allein kaum verantworten. (II 349)

Thus the principle of the interaction of the components of a mosaic
contributing to the total significance of the depiction is extended to
the diary as a literary form. This form characterises Frisch's prose-
writing from Blätter aus dem Brotsack (1940) - and the reprise of the
same theme in Dienstbüchlein (1974) -, the two diaries as such, Tagebuch 1946-1949 and Tagebuch 1966-1971, and the Erzählung Montauk (1975)
to the four major novels, of which the 'Erzählmosaike' [25] of Mein Name
sei Gantenbein (1964) is the last. The latest work, the Erzählung
Der Mensch erscheint im Holozän (1979) develops the principle to its
furthest point. The narrative is offset and interspersed with extracts,
from history books and works of reference, which are not incorporated
typographically into the text, but retain the appearance of insertions
in a scrap-book [26]. The resulting mosaic requires the synthesising
consciousness of the reader and also reflects the divergence of the
world which he inhabits [27].

Critics have drawn attention to two manifestations of this mosaic
principle at work in Tagebuch 1946-1949: firstly, to the proximity of
the section entitled 'Du sollst dir kein Bildnis machen' and the story
'Der andorranische Jude' (the basis of the play Andorra); and secondly,
to the proximity of the mention of the Communist coup in Czecheslovakia
in 1948 and the story 'Burleske' (the basis for the play Biedermann und
die Brandstifter) [28]. In each case the story gives narrative and more
tangible expression to aspects of the section which it follows. A
further example in the diary of significant proximity has escaped
critical attention. There is a connection between the description of
Frisch's meeting with the American playwright Thornton Wilder, conveyed
largely by means of a story about the son of a night-watchman - 'Frankfurt, November 1948' (II 626-628) - and Frisch's subsequent reflections
on Germany and the differences between Germany and German-speaking
Switzerland, especially in their respective attitudes to art - 'Hamburg,
November 1948' (II 628-632) [29].

The story concerns the son of a night-watchman whose neighbours
think that the boy's father is a poultry thief because he is never
seen during the day. In order to retrieve the father's reputation, the
boy visits his neighbours who happen to be acting as hosts to a visiting
wise man. Far from resolving the matter, however, the boy's visit leads
to an acrimonious dispute, and the wise man and the neighbours take
peremptory leave of the boy who reproaches himself for what has happened.

The anecdote is a further example of Frisch's belief that language
can reflect reality only by indirect means since its content is a
narrative rendering of his own position as a German-Swiss writer within
a larger German tradition. Frisch gives shape and hence meaning to
the feelings aroused in him by the patronising attitudes of both Wilder
and Wilder's German hosts. From its position in <u>Tagebuch 1946-1949</u>
the story also acquires a wider significance: it provides an instance
of personal involvement to which the theoretical considerations about
art and Switzerland, which follow, can be related.

The story highlights the elements of difficulty in establishing a
cultural respectability and identity for Switzerland against an
unsympathetic environment: the inertia of unexamined assumption, the
lack of first-hand knowledge (the neighbour with whom the dispute
starts does not personally know the boy's father), the designation of
that which does not accord with the stereotype as being exceptional in
such a way as to reinforce the stereotype by maintaining it (the boy is
an exception in his milieu), and the appropriation to the generality of
the larger group of qualities denied to the generality of the smaller
group (poultry thieves are an exception amongst the neighbours). The
boy can be equated with the young playwright Max Frisch, the neighbours
with the German hosts, and the wise man with Thornton Wilder. Even the
much admired American - who, as Frisch notes, wrote <u>Our Town</u> in Zürich
(II 626) - appears to be part of the conspiracy of disparagement. The
concept of 'Bildnis' which forms such an important theme in Frisch's
work is thus seen to arise directly from his own experience as a Swiss
writer attempting self-definition. The patronising tone which can be
so provoking, the implication that the Swiss writer has not available
for him, because of his position, the full range of human experience,
and the degeneration of the argument into self-justificatory squabbling
are aspects which have already emerged in a consideration of a similar
problem in <u>Drei Entwürfe eines Briefes</u>. In that instance, Frisch,
determinedly making use of the of the opportunity presented to him,
went on to define the Swiss posture during the Second World War. In
this instance, in 'Hamburg, November 1948', the section of the diary
immediately following the account of the meeting with Wilder, Frisch
resolutely takes that humiliating experience as the starting-point for
one of his fullest examinations of the concept of 'Kultur', and of its
different interpretations in Germany and Switzerland. At the close of
this examination, he sums up his attitude in a rhetorical question, in
which 'Spiesser' can be equated with the 'Hühnerdieb' of the story:

> Die Heidenangst, ein Spiesser zu sein, und das Missverständnis, das darin schon enthalten ist, die Bemühtheit, sich in den Sphären des Ewigen anzusiedeln, um auf der Erde nicht verantwortlich zu sein, die tausend Unarten voreiliger Metaphysik – ob das für die Kultur nicht gefährlicher ist als alle Spiesser zusammen? (II 632)

Frisch's affirmation of the Swiss ethos is the more acceptable since, following as it does on a depiction of the encounter in Frankfurt, it contains an awareness of the implications of that affirmation. In a further example of the manner in which the separate parts of the mosaic offset one another in the presentation of the whole pattern, Frisch causes a characterisation of his identity as a German-Swiss writer in the larger German tradition to be followed by a statement of his commitment as a citizen to Switzerland. He shows, by literary structure, that identity and commitment, the major themes of his creative work, are closely linked and that they derive from his own experience.

A Swiss tradition and the modern world

If language and his cultural position are two factors shaping the consciousness of Frisch the writer, a third factor is the nature of the modern world in which it is a characteristic of the writer that he knows 'seine Macht und seine Machtlosigkeit' [1]. An indication of Frisch's assessment of the influence of the writer is given in a short sketch Knipsen oder Sehen? (1934) (I 70-74). In this Frisch complains that people do not use their eyes properly. The age in which they live encourages this misuse since it makes cameras readily available, and people come to rely on these instruments to reproduce reality for them. The sketch contains the earliest treatment of the theme of Reproduktion: the ability of the camera to reproduce replicas of reality interposes itself between people and reality, and this leads to the atrophy of the faculty of vision, and in turn to a decline in the ability to analyse and appreciate. For these reasons, Frisch advises people to dispense with their cameras. After doing so, he addresses himself directly to the camera-shop owner. He apologises for what he has just said by telling the shop-owner that it is unlikely that he, Frisch, will have altered anyone's views by his remarks:

> Falls Sie mir böse sind, lieber Herr Photohändler, so überschätzen Sie unsereinen erheblich: wenn sich auf Grund dieser Plauderei (Frisch's sketch) auch nur ein einziger Mensch ändern würde, sehen Sie, dann würden wir nicht mehr plaudern, sondern predigen – unendlich Wichtigeres. (I 73-74)

By drawing this distinction at the start of his writing career (Jürg Reinhart was also published in 1934), Frisch shows himself to have a

clear idea of the limited effectiveness of the writer's ability to
alter opinions. Thirteen years later he attempts to distinguish
between the fame of a writer and his influence. In Tagebuch 1946-1949
he discusses the difficulties which a group of writers are having in
trying to agree on a manifesto protesting against the polarisation of
the world into two political and economic systems (II 522-523). This
leads Frisch to reflect, in the following section 'Zur Schriftstellerei'
(II 524-525), on the influence of the writer in the modern wold. These
reflections take the form of an imaginary conversation between Frisch
and a stranger. Frisch laments the fact that writers appear to have no
influence in the modern world, and suggests that things might be better
if they had. The other man is not sure. He recalls that as a student
he once heard on the radio the voices of two men investing their fame
in the future of Hitler: those of Gerhart Hauptmann and Max Schmeling.
Fame is possibly irrelevant, certainly fragile; influence, on the other
hand, stems from a demonstration of some comprehension of the matter
in hand:

> Einfluss hat man immer nur dort, wo man etwas von der
> Sache versteht, wo man der Welt bewiesen hat, dass man
> etwas von der Sache versteht. (II 525)

It would seem that this quality, if present in the writer's work,
could have at least a potential influence.

As a first step to establishing the nature of this potential in
writing in particular and in art in general, Frisch considers art
which is devoid of it. The theatre of the absurd is, for Frisch, an
example of art which sends the spectator back to reality with a sense
of relief. It confers no dimension of insight; it establishes no new
relationships in the mind; it promotes acceptance of reality as it is
at present interpreted [2]. But in attempting to define further what is
valid in art in the sense that it can influence fruitfully, in however
limited a fashion, Frisch is compelled to examine his own motives in
creating art.

Frisch discerns three strands of motivation in his writing. The
first is the urge to establish personal identity, to sketch out,
however imperfectly, the contours of individuality. This develops into
a voyage of discovery the surprises of which can be unpleasant, and the
difficulties of which indicate the limits of what can be expressed by
language (II 361). The struggle for expression has its own rewards,
however. The approximation of what the writer wishes to express to
what he can express, his striving for form, is the second strand of
motivation in his writing. Frisch has already described this as

'Machlust'. The creation of form, be it simply of a sentence, is not
only an achievement in itself: it acts as a bulwark against the
meaningless chaos of reality. To wrest form from the inexpressible is
the same as wresting meaning from interior and exterior chaos (II 381).
In so far as form is the prerequisite for communication, the writer's
struggle with form is allied to his desire to communicate, and
constitutes the third strand in the motivation of the writer. Frisch
considers this desire to be an existential one, comparable with the
elemental urge which caused the cave-dwellers to paint on the walls of
the cave: expression goes some way towards exorcism. Frisch stresses
that these are personal motives, arising from deep-seated needs in the
individual writer (V 350) [3]. Inevitably the manner in which the
writer seeks to satisfy these needs will be coloured not only by his
personality, but also by the age in which he lives. If, in writing,
the writer seeks primarily to give an account of himself to himself, he
is also reflecting in this account the concerns of his generation [4].
The three chief strands of the motivation of the writer thus spring
from personal needs. However much these needs are coloured by the
environment, their expression does not come from a sense of social
responsibility in the writer.

Frisch does not of course wish to deny that the writer does have a
social responsibility. He merely insists that the primary motives of
the writer are personal. In his fullest exploration of the link
between personal motivation and social responsibility in the writer,
his 1958 address 'Öffentlichkeit als Partner', he asserts that
responsibility is a feeling which is secondary and acquired. One
result of his own writing has been his realisation that in the past
he misunderstood his own motives:

> Spreche ich...von mir selbst, so müsste ich sagen, dass ich
> die gesellschaftliche Verantwortung des Schriftstellers
> nicht bloss angenommen, sondern mich, rückläufig sozusagen,
> sogar zum Irrtum verstiegen habe, dass ich überhaupt aus
> solcher Verantwortung heraus schreibe. (IV 247)

Yet if it is accepted that the primary motives are personal - a need to
establish the writer's own identity -, and if it is accepted that the
writer, like all other citizens, has a responsibility to those around
him, it is necessary to establish a link between the need and the
responsibility. Frisch does this by elaborating on the nature of the
need to communicate. Part of the search for personal identity
consists in establishing the difference between the individual
personality and those around it:

> Man möchte nicht so sehr gefallen als wissen, wer man ist.
> Bin ich ausgefallen, so wie ich meine Zeit erfahre, oder
> bin ich unter Geschwistern? (IV 246)

That which the writer creates is thus partly a confession, partly an
appeal. To the extent that this appeal is inherent in every work of
art, it forms the basis for communication, since the creator of the
work of art has gone half-way, has imagined a possible partner in a
dialogue. Every work of art, because it presupposes a public, assumes
a social responsibility for the reactions it evokes. The responsibility
towards his own personality developed in the writer's search for his
own identity necessarily widens into a social responsibility [5]. Frisch
has thus been at some pains to indicate at which stage awareness of
social responsibility manifests itself in the writing process, for he
also believes that the writer must ensure that it is directed to
appropriate tasks.

   In his correspondance with Walter Höllerer, Dramaturgisches (1969),
Frisch makes a full statement of what he considers to be the relationship
between literature and politics. He underlines the right of the
individual to be active politically. He also accepts the possibility
of literature having an effect on society. What he finds debatable,
however, is the linking of political activity and literature:

> Es gibt keine Literatur, die nicht engagiert ist. Wenn
> wir heute von Engagement sprechen, meinen wir allerdings
> immer das direkt-politische Engagement: Literatur als
> Propaganda für eine Ideologie. [6]

In 1972 Frisch enlarges on the admissibility of the concept
'Engagement' in the personal political sphere, and goes somewhat
further in questioning its application to the sphere of literature:

> Ich glaube, mein Engagement als Staatsbürger, also das,
> was man tut oder leider meistens nicht tut, ist sehr viel
> weniger radikal als das schriftstellerische. Es ist
> natürlich pragmatischer, denn eine staatsbürgerliche
> Tätigkeit richtet sich nach der Realisierbarkeit aus.
> Sonst ist Politik Dichtung, und wenn Politik Dichtung ist,
> ist es schlechte Dichtung. [7]

A situation must not be permitted to arise in which the reader is
encouraged to equate a political outlook similar to his own with
literary quality. The aim of literature is above all the 'Darstellung
des Konkreten' [8], and this cannot be realised by the fervour of
political persuasion nor judged by it.

   The writer can become the object of social pressures. One danger
for him lies in success, which is liable to distort his own conception
of his role in that he tends to assume other roles irrelevant to his
main one. The danger is that the writer's material comes to be

dominated, not by the desire to express, but by the desire to fulfil
these other roles:

> Man sieht sich dann, von Auflage zu Auflage, unversehens
> in der Rolle eines schriftstellerischen Seelensorgers,
> Eheberaters und Rattenfängers, beziehungsweise Jugend-
> führers. (IV 248-249)

Such pressures must be resisted. The quality of representation must
transcend other considerations. Frisch's commitment to this principle
is accompanied by definitions of two opposed attitudes, neither totally
inimical to the principle, but both harming it in some way. One
attitude reserves art for the ivory tower, the other seeks to use it
as an instrument of political change (IV 247). Frisch makes a rigorous
distinction between the political writer and the writer who imagines
that, because of his 'Engagement', his work has a political effect:
'Nicht jeder, der schreiben kann, ist Jean-Paul Sartre'[9]. Indeed, it
is precisely the combination of artistic stature and political commitment which proves the dubiety of a claim for the political effectiveness
of art. This is exemplified by the case of Brecht, whose greatness as
a dramatist is not in question, yet whose art has had no political
repercussions. The futility of imagining that art has a social
influence in the practical political sense is strikingly illustrated
by the lack of effect which Brecht's work has had [10]. Even with his
clear awareness of this example before him, however, Frisch admits that
writing generates a momentum and an enthusiasm which he must resist if
he himself is not to lapse into the illusion that his writing is in
some way an effective programme for political reform [11]. Thus an
element of restraint is called for if the writer's contribution to
literature is to remain within its legitimate boundaries. For if
creative writing is placed beside other human activities, it must be
recognised that it is not literature which has pushed back the frontiers
of knowledge in our century. This has not, however, rendered literature
superfluous. On the other hand, the attempt to link literature and
political action as a spurious justification for literature cannot be
condoned. Literature still has its primacy in the field of exploring
the reaction of the individual to reality:

> Manche Schriftsteller halten die Literatur gerade in
> politischen Dingen für untauglich und bevorzugen die direkte
> Aktion; ich denke: zu Recht. Das geht zugunsten der Politik
> und zugunsten der Literatur. Die Domäne der Literatur?
> Was die Soziologie nicht erfasst, was die Biologie nicht
> erfasst: das Einzelwesen, das Ich, nicht mein Ich, aber ein
> Ich, die Person, die die Welt erfährt als Ich, die stirbt
> als Ich, die Person in allen ihren biologischen und gesell-
> schaftlichen Bedingtheiten; also die Darstellung der Person,
> die in der Statistik enthalten ist, aber in der Statistik

>nicht zur Sprache kommt und im Hinblick aufs Ganze
>irrelevant ist, aber leben muss mit dem Bewusstsein,
>dass sie irrelevant ist – das ist es, was wenigstens
>mich interessiert, was mir darstellenswert erscheint:
>alles was Menschen erfahren, Geschlecht, Technik,
>Politik als Realität und als Utopie, aber im Gegensatz
>zur Wissenschaft bezogen auf das Ich, das erfährt. 12

The social function of the writer is therefore to stimulate the awareness of the individual.

Commitment to the reality of the individual has been an abiding
concern with Frisch. A passage in Blätter aus dem Brotsack illustrates
the manner in which the involvement of the individual gives significance
to wider concerns involving entire nations, and how, conversely, lack
of individual involvement enables discussion of these wider questions
without any awareness of the reality involved. Once when Frisch had
just returned to Zürich after a spell of 'Grenzdienst' he was astonished
at the casual breadth of the conversation at a social gathering of those
not directly involved in the defence of Switzerland:

>Man trinkt...einen Kaffee, staunt über die sauberen Tassen
>und darüber, wie alle von den grossen Dingen reden, von
>Staaten und Schlachten und Völkern, von Erdteilen und
>Geschichte, – während für uns alle Fragen viel näher sind,
>darum auch kleiner, Fragen aber, wo man um so zuständiger,
>um so verantwortlicher ist. (I 131)

There is here a clear juxtaposition between the density of reality,
and the significance with which the individual invests it, and the
tendency of language to dissociate itself from that reality and so to
become destructive. It is the duty of the writer to combat this
tendency of language towards abstraction by his commitment to
individual reality. Frisch returns to images of war and bloody struggle
in his 1958 'Büchnerpreisrede'. To his fellow-writers he compares the
dangers of language dissociated from reality to stockpiles of weapons
which it is the duty of writers to attempt to render harmless with the
concreteness of their language (IV 236). This is also part of the
social function of the writer. But his task is made more difficult by
the nature of reality itself, by its ceaseless flux, by the fact that
it has always moved on from the position in which language last fixed
it. In a little-regarded section of Tagebuch 1946-1949, significantly
entitled 'Unterwegs', Frisch examines the dangers of the relationship
between language and reality:

>Jeder Gedanke ist in dem Augenblick, wo wir ihn zum ersten-
>mal haben, vollkommen wahr, gültig, den Bedingungen ent-
>sprechend, unter denen er entsteht; dann aber, indem wir
>nur das Ergebnis aussprechen, ohne die Summe seiner Bedin-
>gungen aussprechen zu können, hängt er plötzlich im Leeren,
>nichtssagend, und jetzt erst beginnt das Falsche, indem wir

> uns umsehen und Entsprechungen suchen...so stehen wir denn
> da und haben nichts als ein Ergebnis, erinnern uns, dass das
> Ergebnis vollkommen stimmte, beziehen es auf Erscheinungen,
> die diesen Gedanken selber nie ergeben hätten, überschreiten
> den Bereich seiner Gültigkeit, da wir die Summe seiner Be-
> dingungen nicht mehr wissen, oder mindestens verschieben wir
> ihn - und schon ist der Irrtum da, die Vergewaltigung, die
> Überzeugung. (II 544)

It is the task of the writer to attempt to prevent the formation of such
an 'Überzeugung'. At this point the writer as a guardian of the worth
of language merges with the writer as a craftsman faced with the
technical difficulties presented by his task. The writer expresses
himself in a form suited to the realisation of these complex aims: the
'Skizze'. In an image appropriate to the technological age, an image
which also retains the idea of movement, Frisch demonstrates the urgency
of the writer's undertaking: 'Es geht nicht um Vergnügungsreisen,
sondern um Testflüge' (V 328). Frisch sees the function of literature
in society as 'die Irritation, dass es sie trotzdem gibt' [13]. The
writer must call in question the values and tenets of the society in
which he lives in order to prevent the stasis which spurious conviction
imparts. Alfred Andersch, an almost exact contemporary of Frisch,
considers that the quality of his Swiss colleague resides in the fact
'dass er zweifelnd erzählt' [14]. In the writer's commitment to the
individual a framework of doubt is essential.

Frisch's hope for the effectiveness, however limited, of the
writer, is strengthened by a feeling of spiritual community with other
writers. The uniting factor in this community is not the discredited
notion of 'Berufung', but a shared concern for the condition of the
individual in a world riven by idealogical clashes (IV 242). It
behoves the writer

> eine Sprache zu erarbeiten, die wieder etwas besagt, die
> unseren Erfahrungen in dieser Epoche standzuhalten ver-
> möchte, die unsere Skepsis nicht einfach beurlaubt, um
> sich poetisch geben zu können, und die Gläubigkeit nicht
> mit Wunschdenken verwechselt, die vor Realitäten nicht
> zu erröten braucht, die einzubeziehen wagt, was sie zu
> überwinden hofft: die Kloake und die lichtscheuen
> Räume. (V 463)

The means of realising these aims are 'Ironie' and 'Arbeit' (IV 240),
and writers are inspired by the hope that they may help to change the
perspective from which reality is viewed. Speaking more particularly
to his fellow playwrights, Frisch sees this, and not the fostering
of the illusion that it can re-create reality, as the function of the
theatre:

> Unser Spiel, verstanden als Antwort auf die Unabbildbar-
> keit der Welt, ändert diese Welt noch nicht, aber unser

Verhältnis zu ihr. (V 346-347) [15]

Literature can help to create doubt about the validity of the interpretations which the individual has forced upon him (V 353). It is
here that Frisch sees the possible effectiveness of literature, of a
political commitment in the widest sense:

> Dadurch, dass die Literatur die Dinge darstellt, wie sie
> erlebt werden, verunsichert sie die Sprache. Damit wäre
> ich bei dem, was ich das indirekt politische, bewusstseins-
> bildende Engagement der Literatur nenne. Ich selber bin
> der Meinung..., dass diese Art Engagement die viel grössere [16]
> Wirkung hat als das direkte, also das Agitprop.

But writers must also be fully aware of the daunting nature of their
task. The well-known close to the 'Büchnerpreisrede' unites the
various strands of Frisch's attitude in a restrained statement of the
writer's role in the modern world:

> Es ist eine Resignation, aber eine kombattante Resignation,
> was uns verbindet, ein individuelles Engagement an die
> Wahrhaftigkeit, der Versuch, Kunst zu machen, die nicht
> national und nicht international, sondern mehr ist, nämlich
> ein immer wieder zu leistender Bann gegen die Abstraktion,
> gegen die Ideologie und ihre tödlichen Fronten, die nicht
> bekämpft werden können mit dem Todesmut des einzelnen; sie
> können nur zersetzt werden durch die Arbeit jedes einzelnen
> an seinem Ort. (IV 242-243)

It is an undertaking, muted though the tenor of its programme may be,
which is sustained by the nearest approximation to a vision of better
things to which Frisch has ever given expression: a society which
accepts and which incorporates into itself the intellect and its
concerns:

> Ziel ist eine Gesellschaft, die den Geist nicht zum
> Aussenseiter macht, nicht zum Märtyrer und nicht zum
> Hofnarren. (II 397)

Frisch's sober view of the role of the writer and the function of
literature represents an adjustment to the second half of the twentieth
centure of a Swiss tradition of concern that each member of society is
obligated to contribute by his activity to the well-being of the
res publica. In this commitment, the individual establishes his
own identity.

II   <u>THEMES IN THE WORK OF MAX FRISCH WHICH RELATE</u>

<u>TO HIS SWISS BACKGROUND</u>

64.

Introduction

The statements of Max Frisch on his country, his definition of the situation of the German-Swiss writer, and his views on the role of the writer in the modern world lead to the conclusion that the complex distinctions and qualifications of his outlook can be subsumed under the two concepts of identity and commitment. The central position which these concepts occupy in Frisch's thinking reflects not only his relationship to a tradition of German-Swiss writing, but also circumscribes his place in contemporary German-Swiss writing. The atmosphere in which the German-Swiss author writes has evolved substantially since Frisch began his writing career. The political and monetary stability of Switzerland, and its compact and intact social structure contrasted, and still contrast, with the rapidity of social change which started in Western Europe as a consequence of the upheaval caused by the Second World War. Switzerland's gradual adaptation of its traditionally neutral role has lead to a greater involvement with the world at large, but the extent of this involvement has not kept pace with the stress and flux of change beyond its borders, and thus the country, and what it can yield to them, appears increasingly irrelevant to her younger writers. Switzerland's political and social conservatism has long been a source of concern for Frisch, and in a sense this concern characterises the generation of writers of which he is the leading figure. For, despite his impatience with many aspects of Switzerland, Frisch can accept that Switzerland has legitimately exercised an influence on his Weltanschauung, whereas the younger generation find such an acceptance much more difficult.

Frisch's complicated relationship to the peculiarities and difficulties of Switzerland provides the basis for the themes of his literary works. He suggests that it is easier to detect the formative influence of background in the writer than in others: the writer's profession entails a self-revelation which is written, and thus open to detailed scrutiny. He is of the opinion that an examination of his own writing leaves no doubt as to his origins. As proof of this connection, he relates a number of his key works to his Swiss background:

> Versammle ich die Figuren meiner Erfindung: Bin auf seiner Reise nach Peking, Stiller, der in Zürich sich selbst entkommen möchte, Homo Faber, der sich selbst versäumt, weil er nirgendwohin gehört, der heimelige Herr Biedermann usw., so erübrigt sich das Vorzeigen meines Schweizer Passes. Andorra ist nicht die Schweiz, nur das Modell einer Angst, es könnte die Schweiz sein; Angst eines Schweizers offenbar. Gantenbein spielt den Blinden; um sich mit der Umwelt zu vertragen.

> Graf Öderland, Figur einer supponierten Legende und seinem
> Namen nach eher skandinavisch, greift zur Axt, weil er die
> entleerte und erstarrte Gesellschaft, die er als Staatsan-
> walt vertritt, am eigenen Leib nicht mehr erträgt. (VI 514-515)

It is not simply that Frisch treats local difficulties in his work, but
rather that he sees the difficulties which arise in Switzerland as
aspects or manifestations of wider issues. The Swiss background is
transmuted into universal significance. Thus aspects of life which
are for Frisch thrown into prominence by the fact of being a German-
Swiss establish themselves as themes in his work. The locality of
Switzerland, which has rendered him aware of identity and commitment,
becomes symbolic in his writing [1].

A. IDENTITY

1. Identity and the Impact of Time

Time and the social framework

Frisch has asserted more than once that Schiller in his play Wilhelm Tell created a figure and contributed to a mystique which has seriously misled the Swiss [1]. In his fullest statement of the charge that the idealised figure of Tell prevents a proper assessment of national characteristics (VI 509), Frisch makes three points: firstly, that the existence of a national figure such as Tell derives from myth rather than historical fact; secondly, that Schiller, legitimately enough for his own purposes, ascribed to the figure in his play a quality more appropriate to the age and ethos in which Schiller himself lived; and thirdly, that it behoves the Swiss, if they are not to misunderstand themselves, to revise their perception of the legendary Tell from time to time. A continuing assessment of this national figure is all the more necessary since a small country has special difficulties in coming to terms with itself [2]. It is thus harmful to cling to an erroneous idea of freedom which surrounds Tell, and which derives in great part from Schiller's presentation.

It was avowedly to set something against the sterility of this fixed interpretation of Tell that Frisch wrote Wilhelm Tell für die Schule [3]. Significantly, however, this was not his only motive in writing the book. The historical material attracted him primarily as a writer. He is intrigued by the general phenomenon that a writer, by his use of the preterite tense in his narrative, can create an air of authenticity around his story which contrasts with the fact that the story is an invention. In the particular case of the legend of Wilhelm Tell, Frisch heightens this illusion of authenticity by including in his account a scholarly apparatus of footnotes. In fact these footnotes serve to highlight the speculative nature of the narrative. Its central figure is thus stripped of the solid and unquestioned role which time has caused to accrete round him. By presenting the Tell legend in the framework of an interacting contrast of styles, Frisch seeks to permit a critical approach to it. In attempting to do this, he is adhering to his belief that there is no absolute truth. Interim positions are established in the full knowledge that they are interim and therefore liable to change and alteration. Constant re-assessment involves moving forward, intellectually and experientially, within the

medium of time which is itself moving forward. If, on the other hand,
this forward flow is regarded as destructive, fixed perceptions of the
past offer an illusion of stability. The myth of Wilhelm Tell, as it
is unquestioningly accepted in Switzerland, is a major manifestation
of a debilitating relationship to time. The belief in the myth is an
attempt to preserve identity in a world in which it is becoming
increasingly difficult to establish identity. The Swiss attitude to
the legend of Tell is the local manifestation of a universal problem:
man's relationship to time in the modern world.

The broadest canvas for the treatment of this theme is offered by
the novel Stiller, for in no other work is a society - in this case
that of Switzerland - so fully depicted [4]. The chief malaise afflicting
Swiss society as it is portrayed, and from which all other ills stem,
is a distorted relationship to time. The dead weight of time, in the
sense that the past inhibits all action in the present, is shown to be
a stultifying factor in Swiss life. Awareness of this permeates the
novel at all levels, but significantly its major explicit expressions
occur in the presence of three characters with important connections to
Stiller. The first is Stiller's 'amtlicher Verteidiger' Dr. Bohnenblust, representative of the Swiss establishment and product of the
education provided by that establishment, who, ironically, has been
charged with looking after the interests of Stiller. The second is
Julika, his wife, who is unable to accept Stiller except in terms of
his past life. The third is the ambitious young architect Sturzenegger,
who, despite the progressive claims which he makes about himself, is as
much in the conservative mould as Bohnenblust.

The first description which Stiller gives of Bohnenblust is not
altogether unsympathetic: he is 'ein argloser Mensch', 'gerecht' and
'nicht dumm' (III 373-374). Yet his mind is stocked with wholly
undigested views of the Swiss past. So in thrall is he to a received
interpretation of the past that his relationship to the future is
clouded with deepest foreboding: 'Jede Verwandlung ängstigt ihn. Er
verspricht sich mehr von der Vergangenheit' (III 544). Clearly, to
the extent that he is 'Sohn aus gutem Haus' (III 373), Bohnenblust is
intended to exemplify widely-held opinions. Indeed, Stiller feels that
his opinions are sufficiently representative for him to be able to
extrapolate some general points from his defence lawyer's remarks.
The historical notion of freedom in Switzerland - so closely linked to
the Tell legend - is rejected by Stiller as a chimera: the Swiss lack
of relationship to the present day - 'Geschichtlosigkeit' (III 547) -

is a result, not only of their fixation with the past, but also of their lack of importance. Stiller, for his part, refuses to make his views public. He is aware that, however potent an influence heritage might be, it is in the last analysis the individual who is responsible for his own freedom (III 548). If Stiller does not finally succeed in his quest, he knows what it entails. Whereas Bohnenblust vicariously draws importance from what he holds to be the 'official' perception of Switzerland, Stiller does not abdicate his own moral responsibility, at this point in the narrative at least, because of what he holds to be the shortcomings of his country.

The section of the novel in which Stiller has his first outing from prison with Julika also contains a short description of Zürich. Stiller describes the pleasant bustle of cultural activity which, for the visitor, alleviates the boredom normally felt in the provinces. This activity - even that of the Swiss-born artists - is imported, since it is provided by those whose international standing has nothing to do with Zürich or Switzerland (III 431). Two points relate this consideration of Zürich to the wider concerns of the novel. Firstly, it immediately follows the important section containing the story of Rip van Winkle (III 423-428), the man who was unable to find a role for himself either in the time-structure of the mountains or of his native village. Frisch here employs the mosaic principle in order that Rip van Winkle's personal 'Geschichtlosigkeit' may illuminate that of the city of Zürich and of Switzerland, for in Rip's case lack of relationship to time brings about loss of identity. Secondly, it is in the course of this first outing that the diametrically opposed attitudes of Stiller and his wife become apparent. She cannot see him except in terms of his past life. He, on the other hand, has suppressed all memory of a common past life with her - which is not recounted until the 'Zweites Heft' - and wishes to be accepted as he is at present, without reference to his past. It becomes clear that compromise will not be possible (III 434). The dead hand of the past will triumph. In terms of their relationship she cannot accept the present and he cannot incorporate the past. Their disorientation in time harmonises with the setting of Zürich.

The third explicit criticism in relation to the Swiss concept of time is in a monologue by Stiller in the presence of the young architect Sturzenegger. The Swiss, Stiller maintains, are not content merely to preserve the best of the old in their buildings, which in itself would be praiseworthy. They continue to build in the present and for the future 'im Massstab einer vergangenen, und zwar endgültig vergangenen Zeit' (III 595). Stiller asks why the Swiss do not rebel against such ossification of thought, which is a perversion of a true tradition - 'Mumifikation...als Heimatschutz' (III 595). As the monologue progresses, it becomes clear from Sturzenegger's interjections that, despite his veneer of liberalism, he is quite content to function within the existing system, and Stiller falls back on his own reflections. He broods on Sturzenegger's exoneration of Switzerland from Stiller's charges that the country is not a democracy, for he finds that the stasis of the general attitude of the Swiss is entirely at odds with any concept of democracy. Sturzenegger, and also Bohnenblust, the first by his lack of probity, the second by his lack of awareness, combine to sustain the inertia against which Stiller reacts in attempting to define himself, an undertaking doomed by Stiller's failures of communication with them. Yet Sturzenegger and Bohnenblust are representative figures of the society which has imprisoned Stiller in the hope that he will accept a 'Bildnis' of himself based on the past [5]. Stiller perceives that it is a society which, because of its distorted relationship to time, is as fettered in its actions as he is in his physical movement (III 548). Stiller's individual fate is at this point the dramatised representation of the fate of a society.

Just as the external aspect of Swiss architecture, its 'Mumifikation', permitted conclusions to be drawn about those who design and build it, so external aspects of their environment influence Frisch's characters and are indicative of their state of mind. In Die Schwierigen, Ammann, the colonel and pillar of Swiss society, prevents 'die beschlossene Verschandelung eines alten Zunfthauses' (I 482), which was to have become a municipal employment office, by raising sufficient money to have it restored. Symbolically, the younger generation, in the figure of his daughter Hortense, has a serious accident in the gutted building while restoration work is in progress. On her return from hospital Hortense, the representative of the future, finds in her father's house 'alles beim alten, vertraut wie ein Museum' (I 493). The immediate environment, because of its lack of relevance to the needs of the individuals at present in it, exercises an inhibiting effect on them and distorts their concept of time. Before Yvonne, spurred to emulation by the example of Hauswirt in his commitment to herself and to the child which he has not fathered, finally achieves self-acceptance, she tries to avoid her responsibilities to herself. Her house is described as being 'dornröschenhaft' (I 417), as is her

holiday cottage in Tessin (I 464). Like the princess in the fairy-
tale and like Rip van Winkle, Yvonne wishes to render herself unconscious
to the passing of time. Stiller tries to escape the passage of time by
fleeing to America. On his return, one of the visitors to Stiller/White
in prison describes to him 'den dornröschenhaften Zustand von Stillers
verlassenem Atelier' (III 679). Similarly, the imitation 'ferme
vaudoise' to which Stiller and Julika retreat on his release from prison,
described by Stiller first as 'das Haus unseres Lebens' (III 733) and
then as 'das Haus meines Lebens' (III 735), is the external manifestation
of the rootlessness of his life. Structures can reflect the faulty
relationship to time of those who inhabit them.

To the extent that the environment is created, and tolerated, by
society, the parallel between the individual and the buildings which he
inhabits and has about him is symbolic of the relationship between the
individual and society in general. Society conditions the individual,
and the individual, in his behaviour, reflects society. An awareness
of time figures prominently in this relationship. In the final version
of Graf Öderland (1961) Frisch depicts the social order as wholly
responsible for making the flow of time meaningless for the individual.
The tendency of modern society to reduce the individual to anonymity
elicits two opposing responses: submission, and hence negation of the
personality, or revolt and, as the development of the play shows,
bondage to a different set of forces. The Staatsanwalt, as he signs
the papers for the yacht which he imagines will take him away from it,
berates society which he calls 'Öderland': the monotony and standardisation of modern life devalues time, so that the individual's response
to it becomes negative (III 55). Time, on the precise measurement of
which so much modern technology depends, is being excised as a
qualitative entity from the life of modern man.

The individual experience of time

A reaction to the ephemeral nature of life is recorded in Blätter
aus dem Brotsack (1940). This reaction is positive, displaying an
uncomplicated acceptance, and is evoked by the contemplation of an
autumn landscape (I 126). Ephemerality receives a sharper focus five
years later in Bin, where the passing of time is related to the narrator's
own life. He is prompted to set out on the symbolic journey to Peking
with Bin by the realisation, which suddenly erupts into the unreflecting
pattern of his daily round, that half his life is over (I 604). Since
similar realisations about time in relation to the individual provoke

a diminishing response in subsequent Frisch heroes, it is worth under-
lining that 'Bin', the 'companion' on the journey, represents that
element of potential for action in all men which time and the
intractibility of reality erode ^{6}. In Bin there is a clear awareness
of the abrasive effect of daily life on this element of the personality
which can see beyond mundane concerns (I 624), but despite the time
claimed by everyday demands, they are accepted as part of the necessary
fabric of life.

This acceptance later becomes unsettled in the male characters of
Frisch by querelous fretting at the futility of these repetitive tasks.
In most of the women, on the other hand, acceptance continues. In
Die Schwierigen, Reinhart and Hortense meet years after their affair is
over. Hortense, now married with children, tells of her daily life,
which is conditioned by the seasons of the year and by the growth of
her children. She concludes her account by asserting that the fulfilment
of these duties is in itself a sufficient justification for her carrying
them out - further reflection is, for her, unnecessary (I 586-587).
In Stiller, Sibylle, during her stay in the United States, is impressed
by the efficiency with which the Americans arrange the details of their
everyday lives, details which are, as she realises 'das Drum und Dran,
das neun Zehntel unseres Lebens ausmacht' (III 659). Since they accept
that so much of life is taken up with trivial activities, the women in
Frisch's works are able to realise their identity much more fully than
the men. The men look upon themselves as being accountable for the use
which they have made of their time. For the women identity tends to
reside in activity. For the men identity tends to be a state of mind
which they could confer on themselves only after they are satisfied
that their activities are significant. As a result, the multitude of
necessary trivial tasks in everyday life hinders the achievement of this
state. Even the relatively well-balanced narrator in Bin is not entirely
free from the feeling that his identity must be justified in terms of
what he has done (I 652) ^{7}. The problem of accounting for oneself is
rendered easy for many, who, by subsuming large sections of their lives
under some generalised activity - '40 Jahre bei der Bundesbahn' (VI 703)
- justify themselves to themselves and to others. The early Bin
constitutes an attempt to establish identity, however imprecisely,
within the time left to the individual and outside the framework of
these generalised activities. Yet the narrator in Bin is fully aware,
in the last words of his account, of the lack of any conclusive
developments arising from such an enterprise: he refers to 'Peking,
das ich nie erreichen werde' (I 658). He accepts that this does not

invalidate the journey. Characters in later novels, above all in
Gantenbein, do not.

The second aspect of time which concerns Frisch relates to the use
made of a human lifespan. The situations in which he depicts the matter
all demonstrate that it is essential to maintain a fine balance between,
on the one hand, the sheer necessity for some activity, however undemand-
ing, with which to occupy oneself for at least part of this time, and on
the other, the flight into activity, however pointless, as a means of
escaping confrontation with the more reflective aspects of life. In
the Nachwort to Stiller, Rolf, visiting Stiller in his inauthentic
'ferme vaudoise', quickly realises that even Stiller regards his
activity as a potter as meaningless. Rolf asks himself how it is
possible to face life without some activity or role, the external
demands of which can distract from the more fundamental questions:

> Was macht der Mensch mit der Zeit seines Lebens?...Wie hält
> dieser Stiller es aus, so ohne gesellschaftliche oder
> berufliche Wichtigkeiten gleichsam schutzlos, vor dieser
> Frage zu sitzen? (III 741)

Not to be shielded from the full force of this question is to run the
risk of the decline which gradually befalls Stiller. Reinhart the
failed painter in Die Schwierigen - in many ways the forerunner of the
more complex and more fully realised Stiller - is aware of the danger.
At the lowest ebb of his life, as he drifts indecisively, he finds the
passage of his days wearisome in the extreme 'denn sie waren ja ohne
Halt an einer Arbeit' (I 576). The inner moral support derived from
work and implicit in Reinhart's feeling, is also mentioned in Tagebuch
1946-1949, where Frisch goes a considerable way towards defining his
own attitude to the demands of a job or profession. As he prepares to
leave Siena, the last stage of an autumn holiday in 1947, to return to
his desk, he concludes that the very confines which work imposes on the
pattern of existence heighten the appreciation of life (II 517).
Almost thirty years later he emphasises in Montauk the psychological
necessity to himself of work (VI 725). To seek to be absorbed in work
is not so much a quest for a narcotic as a realisation that the great
questions of life can possibly only be answered through consideration
of the details which work demands.

Work, however lowly, also confers a form of identity. Reinhart, as
he begins to escape from the moral despair into which he has fallen,
takes a room and agrees, in part-payment of the rent, to perform menial
household tasks. He is aware, in his still deeply troubled state, of
the status, minimal though it is, which this work confers on him: 'Es

reihte ihn ein' (I 578). He has become 'Träger einer Funktion' in
society once more. It is this role, this justification of his time
and existence, which involves the core of a man. Other social
relationships are secondary, even irrelevant. Gantenbein, jealous of
Svoboda because of the latter's previous involvement with Lila, tries
nonetheless to be fair in his assessment of him: a man cannot be
judged purely in terms of his relations with the opposite sex since a
man's work occupies such a key role in his life (V 256). A strong
note of male sexual identity is also conferred by work. Sibylle
watches Stiller at work as he prepares material for an exhibition of
sculpture: 'Nie ist ein Mann so schön, fand sie, wie bei einer hand-
werklichen Arbeit' (III 629). In the same tenor, but altogether more
problematic because of his defective relationship to the opposite sex,
is Faber's defiant statement: 'Ich lebte, wie jeder wirkliche Mann,
in meiner Arbeit' (IV 90). Work is an aspect of life which can be
controlled and directed, relations between the sexes cannot. As well
as being a form of identity, work provides, not only for Faber, a
refuge from emotional entaglements [8]. Yet it is also because of the
ecstasy attending successful creative work, which can confer a vibrant
sense of identity, that work acquires such an important, almost spiritual
value. Reinhart describes this ecstasy: it is generated by excitement
and pleasure at the work in hand, but its fullness is such that the
individual is also receptive to contact with others during it as at no
other time (I 433) [9]. Self-realisation - the full, meaningful
exploitation of one's time - cannot take place without a positive
relationship to work. Since work takes place in a social context, that
context can help to provide part of the framework for personal identity.
Fulfilled identity in turn enriches the social context.

The social context can also impede self-realisation, however.
Frisch depicts the meaningless activity of modern office life and the
effects which it produces. At one point in Die Schwierigen Reinhart
works in an office. He observes one man who marks the passing days on
a calendar, and hears him one day declare with pleasure that there is
only one week left until pay-day. Reinhart is prompted to consider the
thousands of people who have a similar attitude to time (I 494) [10].
Loss of personal dimensions results from this kind of work which distorts
the relationship to time. This process is most fully examined in Graf
Öderland in the figure of the bank clerk who has murdered the janitor
in the bank where he works [11]. During a conversation in his cell with
his defence lawyer, he indicates the similarity of his cell to his

place of work, and it is part of Frisch's purpose that the clerk should
remain unaware of the full irony of this similarity (III 19). The clerk
characterises the fashion in which the present has ceased to have meaning
for him: the present can be borne only by contemplating the prospect of
a future at work. The clerk's ambivalent attitude to the week-end makes
this disorientation clear (III 43). The disjunction between the smooth
functioning of the bank and the mental unrest of those who work there,
manifested in the clerk, has a parallel with the individual's relationship to modern society [12]. Inevitably in a society where the impersonal
nature of work makes abundantly clear to each worker that he or she is
replaceable, the awareness of identity, because of the lack of relationship to time, must slacken to the point of extinction. The clerk
reflects on the fact that the janitor has only acquired identity as a
distinct human being through having been murdered, unaware that he too,
the prepetrator of this apparently motiveless act before which all stand
baffled, has similarly conferred identity on himself. Violence is the
only recourse open to the individual who seeks to escape the impoverishment which modern society imposes. Frisch sees this impoverishment as
deriving directly from a disturbed relationship to time: the present
is debased by the activities which occupy it. The individual, if he does
not revolt against this debasement, loses his identity in a perpetual
longing for a more fulfilling future. The Staatsanwalt, who has the
task of prosecuting the clerk, speculates on what would happen if this
longing were ever to be removed so that it could no longer sustain the
individual in the face of the present - the individual's attitude to the
present, and so to society, would undergo a revolution with far-reaching
consequences (III 10-11). Thus the manner in which the individual is
constrained to envisage the flow of time has a profound effect on his
awareness of himself and conditions the extent to which he can realise
himself in time.

The third aspect of time which concerns Frisch is that individual
experience of time is also conditioned by the manner in which time is
defined. A notable feature of Frisch's attempts to define time is the
frequency with which he compares time to the phenomenon of light. The
narrator in Bin ponders on the extent to which the present, the past
and time itself are baffling concepts for the individual. His
relationship to those who are dead, for example, is akin to his
perception of light from stars which are extinct (I 637) [13]. The
narrator is here considering the concept of time from a perspective
which is unusual for him. He is looking upon it as an experiential

unity instead of as an experiential sequence. But Frisch indicates a
paradox: it is impossible to bring together the experience of time
and its definition. Again he draws on the analogy of light to
demonstrate this: time viewed as a 'Nacheinander' is

> ein Hilfsmittel unserer Vorstellung, eine Abwicklung, die
> uns nacheinander zeigt, was eigentlich ein Ineinander ist,
> ein Zugleich, das wir allerdings als solches nicht wahr-
> nehmen können, so wenig wie die Farben des Lichtes, wenn
> sein Strahl nicht gebrochen und zerlegt ist. (II 361)

To define is to separate into component parts, and in this sense the
nature of the sum of these parts is lost. The unconscious restores
unity to this process:

> Unser Bewusstsein als das brechende Prisma, das unser
> Leben in ein Nacheinander zerlegt, und der Traum als die
> andere Linse, die es wieder in sein Urganzes sammelt;
> der Traum und die Dichtung, die ihm in diesem Sinne
> nachzukommen sucht. (II 361-362)

There is thus a constant dichotomy between the intellectual perception
of time and the emotional experience of time.

In accordance with the idea that the experience of time is 'ein
Zugleich', Frisch sets himself against what he considers to be two
misconceptions about the nature of the present. In the first place,
he rejects the view that experience is fully achieved in the present.
To do so, he draws once more on the analogy of light. A photograph is
the chemical reaction of light on a sensitive filter, and he sees in
this process a parallel to the nature of experience. Viewing a
beautiful landscape in Italy, Frisch registers in himself a certain
disappointment at his sensations (II 451-452). He is not, however,
having the full experience of the view; that will come later. His
present experience is like the exposure of a film which memory will
later develop and make complete. He is thus led to reflect on the
peculiar nature of the present, and concludes that it is a transition
between the past and the future, which are the real areas of experience.
To this extent the present is curiously neutral, which does not however
imply that it is without significance, since experience is dependent on
the quality of the material gathered in the present. The second misconception is that the present forms the point at which the fullest
perception on a given matter has been reached. Frisch calls this
assumption 'die Anmassung aller Gegenwart' (II 360) as he tells a
writer that it is the writer's early works which he likes best. When
the writer is clearly displeased, Frisch feels that the writer is doing
himself an injustice by thinking that his later works are necessarily
better.

76.

The idea that perception is cumulative runs parallel to the idea
that time is sequential. An early sketch, Kleine Erinnerung (1934),
illustrates the point anecdotally. The story of Rip van Winkle has
been much in the narrator's mind as he has been visiting places where
his youth was spent. While his memory of these places has remained
static, they have almost all altered in reality. In particular he
recalls a harmless, but at the time important, episode involving a
school-fellow, who was fascinated by the theatre, and an actress. By
chance he meets this school-fellow after many years, and asks if his
interest in the theatre has continued:

> (Er) blickte mich mitleidig überlegen an, wie wenn man
> einen Grossvater zum Kinderspiel einlädt, und lächelte
> nur...Dann komme ich mir immer, wie gesagt, so zurück-
> geblieben vor wie Rip van Winkle. (I 79)

In this sketch the 'Nacheinander', which is essentially the definition
of time, has conditioned the experience of the former school-fellow.
The 'Zugleich', the reality of time, is, on the other hand, related to
the sphere of the unconscious which does not normally come to the fore,
and which obtrudes embarassingly like the gaffe of a child. With years
and the consequent assumption of dignity, the 'Nacheinander' tends to
take the upper hand, which is what Jürg Reinhart means when he claims
that growing up is 'ein Verarmen' (I 275).

Time and Rip van Winkle

The story of Rip van Winkle features prominently in Frisch's
depiction of the relationship between identity and time. If its first
use in 1934 is an attempt to contrast attitudes to time, subsequent
uses of it and references to it depict failure to adjust to the complex
nature of time [14]. The story offers a vehicule for the ideas which pre-
occupy Frisch about the individual's relationship to time: the speed
of time, which inexplicably causes long periods to elapse without an
awareness of their passage; as a consequence of this, an unsettled
attitude to activity in the present; and thirdly, in this baffling
situation, the impossibility of establishing identity.

The first account of the story as such is given in the Hörspiel
Rip van Winkle (1953), a forerunner, as regards plot and themes, of
the novel Stiller. In the Hörspiel the Staatsanwalt closes his account
of the story of Rip van Winkle by strongly emphasising the ultimate
disorientation of the central figure (III 820-821). The situation of
the hero of the Hörspiel, who is significantly known as Der Fremdling,
is thus closely parallel to that of the hero of Stiller, which contains

the fullest treatment of the story.

While still, as in the anecdote of 1934, referred to as 'ein amerikanisches Märchen', the story as narrated by Stiller has originally been
read by him in a 'Buch von Sven Hedin' (III 422). The mention of Hedin
(1865-1952), a Swedish explorer and author of voluminous writings on his
travels, provides a clear indication of the function of Stiller's
version within the framework of the novel: it is an exploratory trip
in search of his identity, an attempt to bring together his past and
his present into a meaningful whole, 'ein Versuch zur Klärung seines
neuen Ichs' [15]. It is instructive to compare the differences between
Frisch's version as related by Stiller with Hedin's version of Washington
Irving's original tale in order to understand where the weight of
Frisch's interest in the story lies [16]. Whereas Hedin characterises
his hero as 'ein gutmütiger Schelm', Frisch's Rip van Winkle is 'ein
innerlicher Mensch' (III 423); Hedin's Rip is 'ein Erzfaulenzer', and
although Frisch's Rip is 'ein geborener Faulenzer', he feels that he
ought to have 'einen männlichen Beruf', and in general, at the age of
fifty, 'er hatte mehr von sich erwartet' (III 423). Rip's wife in
Hedin's tale is shrewish to the point where she herself comes close to
creating a legend in that respect, while with Frisch the wife's
behaviour is toned down and is presented as largely justified because
of Rip's irresponsible behaviour. Hedin gives his version a very clear
political background, provided by the American War of Independance,
whereas Frisch, apart from situating the story on the banks of the
Hudson River, presents a version which is much more generalised and
mythical. Hedin's Rip is required to serve drinks to the strange
company in which he finds himself in the mountains, and on taking a
draught himself falls asleep. Frisch's Rip, on the other hand, is
obliged constantly to set up the skittles for the never-ending game,
exhausting work which is described as a 'Fron' (III 426), and from
which the only rescue would be to wake up [17]. The hero in Hedin's tale
appears to lose his identity completely in that, on his return, he
finds that his son now carries the designation Rip van Winkle, but his
own declaration of identity is eventually accepted and he acquires a new
dimension as a result of the story he has to tell of his adventures in
the mountains. In Frisch's story, on the other hand, Rip feels obliged
to tell his daughter on his return that her father is dead, and as he
continues to fail to make contact in this strange world, he is forced
to ask himself if his return has been pointless, for he is 'ein Fremdling
in fremder Welt' (III 428). Frisch's Rip is thus a more complex
character than the original. Before the accidental encounter with the

party in the mountains, there was already a firm taint of failure about him. Moreover, he was dissatisfied with the circumstances of his life without having formed any resolution to dissipate this dissatisfaction. His return, far from offering him a fresh start, disorientates him completely, since it denies him the possibility of re-integration. For, contrary to the case of Hedin's hero, his story is not accepted: 'Umsonst erzählte er die wunderliche Geschichte mit den Kegeln' (III 427). He has become 'geschichtlos'.

The story of Rip van Winkle, as here narrated, has clear parallels with the life of Stiller: Stiller's growing dissatisfaction and frustration up until his flight at the end of 1945; his failure to put down roots in the United States, his discovery that he has merely exacerbated and given a different setting to his perennial problems; and his despair on his return, when all - with the significant exceptions, among the major figures, of Rolf, and among the minor, of Knobel the warder, neither of whom knew him prior to his flight - relate him to what they have previously known of Stiller. Furthermore, they disregard, or fail to comprehend, his attempts to communicate to them the nature of his problem by means of stories such as that of Rip van Winkle. In these stories he is confronting his past and his present in an attempt to establish a new identity which he feels will free him from the leaden weight of the failures accruing to the Stiller whom everyone thinks they know. The famous opening to the novel, 'Ich bin nicht Stiller!', is his cry of anger against that fixed image, and his stories, none more so than that of Rip van Winkle, represent his efforts to demonstrate the truth of his assertion that he has changed. These stories are also a plea for help from Stiller. He believes he has made a perception about his identity, and he wishes others to become as aware as they can of this perception in order that they might alter their view of him accordingly [18]. Given a sympathetic hearing, Stiller feels he might be able to re-integrate himself, not only with his Swiss environment, but also with his past. Stiller gives an unmistakable indication of the symbolic nature of these stories. At the close of his story about the Carlsbad Caves, he is asked by Knobel if he is the hero Jim White, whom Stiller has depicted in such grim struggles with himself. Stiller replies:

> 'Nein', lache ich, 'das gerade nicht! Aber was ich selber erlebt habe, sehen Sie, das war genau das gleiche - genau'. (III 521)

It is a clear statement of intent, the irony of which lies in the fact that it is made to Knobel. For Knobel, the only person who initially

accepts Stiller as Mr. White, has done so because his mind has been so
conditioned by his reading of 'Illustrierten' that he can only react
to a one-dimensional view of reality, and has thus given literal
credence to the more sensational aspects of the stories. Other
dimensions which they may contain are not accessible to him.

Publicly, Stiller wishes to have nothing more to do with that part
of him which is fixed, as it were, namely his past, whereas those about
him persist in seeing him only in these terms. His final defeat and
failure stem from the fact that the attempts which he makes in private
with those about him to achieve a synthesis between his past and his
present - his stories - are received with incomprehension or dismissed
as the phantasies to which he was prone in the past. At the conclusion
of the Rip van Winkle story, the baffled Dr. Bohnenblust asks: 'Was
hat das wieder mit unserer Sache zu tun?' (III 428). In the course of
the first interview in prison with Julika, as Stiller tries to impress
upon her the fact that he has changed, she refers three times to his
'Hirngespinste' (III 408-409). Directly after this interview, Stiller
makes one of his most important statements about the incommunicable
nature of identity (III 412). He has fled from himself because he
felt that the pressures about him were causing him to destroy his true
personality. He now realises that flight itself was a betrayal, and
that the only solution is to take the knowledge of his dereliction upon
himself even if it cannot be communicated. This is the final parallel
between Rip van Winkle and Stiller, in that the conclusion of the
narration of Rip's story points forward to the close of the novel.
Rip tells his daughter that her father is dead because he does not
want to step back into the role which the villagers have in readiness
for him. He subsequently fails to find an identity in the community
which he left twenty years before. In a sense Rip is more perspicacious
than Stiller since he accepts the impossibility of the venture which
Stiller embarks upon: the creation of a new identity in a community
which once knew him. Rip is aware that aspects of identity cannot be
communicated. In his reflections after the first interview with Julika,
Stiller shows himself to be intellectually aware of this also. He
senses that the break in continuity in his relations with the community,
far from offering him an opportunity to start afresh in the community's
perception of him, has rendered any hope of such change quite impossible [19].
Emotionally, however, he feels the need to communicate. But his stories,
in which he attempts to reveal himself, are doomed to failure, because
his listeners rely for their perceptions of him on their memories of
seven years before, or are incapable of perceiving more than the surface

meaning of these stories. 'Der Traum' and 'die Dichtung' are the means
by which the individual tries to grasp the 'Urganzes' of life.
Presumably in a society in which Dr. Bohnenblust, at the very start
of the novel, can exhort Stiller to write 'nichts als die schlichte
Wahrheit' (III 362) in the confident expectation of this being possible,
stories such as that of Rip van Winkle can carry no symbolic meaning.
It is not only Knobel who has simplified reactions.

In the most recent treatment of the theme of Rip van Winkle in
<u>Tagebuch 1966-1971</u> (VI 398-400), Frisch reverses the traditional story
in so far as Rip undergoes a transformation while the world remains
unchanged. Instead of being unaware of the passage of time, and hence
being unable to adjust to change in his surroundings, Rip experiences
a vision - its nature is, significantly, never disclosed - the intensity
of which is such that he assumes that a considerable period of time must
have elapsed. Furthermore, when Rip returns in the early morning, it is
he who finds the villagers asleep: 'Sie schlafen nur, die Zeitgenossen'.
This formulation stresses the contemporaneity of the villagers with Rip,
as opposed to the villagers of Stiller's Rip, and in doing so it underlines all the more the extent to which this Rip nonetheless feels
estranged from those around him as a result of his vision. For, in
common with the other Rip, his story is not accepted, either by his wife
or in the village itself. The nature of the vision, which is a real
part of his experience, and hence of his identity, cannot be communicated.
It is only the observable activities of his daily round which are held
to constitute his life. His profession also hints at the fact that full
communication between the individual and those about him is never
possible. He is a cooper, and, in that he makes receptacles, resembles
the later Stiller, who is a potter. In so far as identity lies partly
in what the individual feels to be the erroneous perception of others,
the figures of Stiller the potter and Rip the cooper, by their products
which can be filled with whatever the purchaser chooses, hint also at
the random nature of that aspect of identity [20].

Rip van Winkle is a symbol of the difficulty of relating the 'Nacheinander' of time, in which social life is lived, to the impact of
experience which transcends this 'Nacheinander'. It is impossible to
communicate the nature of this experience, and as a result the
individual in Frisch's work tends to remain 'muré dans une subjectivité
impuissante' [21]. He cannot establish a viable relationship with his
own experience, which is the prerequisite for establishing a viable
relationship with society. Because of this double estrangement, he is

not shielded from or buoyed up against his own annihilation in time.
Rip van Winkle, with his permanently dislocated relationship to time,
is a fitting parallel to the major Frisch heroes, who successively
evince an increasing fear at the passing of time.

Avoidance of time

The strongest expression of this fear at the passing of time is
contained in the novel <u>Mein Name sei Gantenbein</u>. Frisch himself has
stressed that the novel opens with a death (V 331), and it closes
with an unidentified body in a coffin being swept down the River Limmat
in Zürich, a clear pointer to the fate of individuality in time. The
story begins with the narrator in an empty flat, which has still traces
of those who occupied it, and the story closes in the same deserted
flat. For the narrator, the opening scene in the flat is reminiscent
of the ruins of Pompei, fixed for ever at a specific point in the flow
of time: 'Alles noch vorhanden, bloss die Zeit ist weg' (V 20). The
final description of the flat, in which the remnants of decaying food
in the kitchen and the general atmosphere of neglect are emphasised,
thrice contains the narrator's interjected 'Ich kenne das' (V 313-314)
in reference to his surroundings. Thus the framework of the novel
contains those elements which dominate its course: the arrest of time,
a feeling of futility at what appear to be life's repetitions, and death.

Frisch has rejected the contention that time, as developed in the
novel, is stationary, and in doing so, has placed great emphasis on time
as a ceaseless and transitory process (V 331). The suggestion is always
present in the novel that an awareness of the fleeting nature of life
exercises a debilitating influence, that, as this awareness grows, a
form of mental paralysis in the face of life increases. One way of
avoiding this awareness, a method perhaps not consciously formulated,
is to allow habit, especially the habit of another's company, to dull
reactions to time. This form of avoiding identity in time is exemplified
by the couple who have lived together long enough to imagine that they
each know sufficient about their partner's past and present to live
hermetically sealed from further reflection (V 136-137). Only when
this vacuum is ruptured, when, for example, the couple change house,
does time itself resume movement for them, as it were, and with the
movement of time comes pessimistic, if not morbid speculation on that
movement in relation to the lives of the couple. Habit can insulate
against the consciousness of time. The protection thus afforded is of
the thinnest, however, because the re-establishment of the awareness

of time renders its effects more obvious and its significance in
relation to the individual more devastating.

Habit implies a frequency of repetition and the acceptance of that
repetition. A second and more conscious form of reaction against the
passage of time cannot accept such repetition, especially in the
relations between the sexes, and takes refuge in the pretence that it
is possible to maintain one dimension of time only. The man and the
woman who meet in a bar at the beginning of Gantenbein and who spend
the night together, are of one mind in this matter. They wish for an
eternal present, devoid of past - 'Geschichte' - and of future - 'Wiederholung' (V 73). They are aware of the impossibility of clinging to
the present, but they resemble other Frisch characters in that they
suppress this knowledge. With satisfaction the man reflects that they
have not known one another for twenty-four hours yet, so that the verbal
paraphernalia which attaches to the passing of time cannot weigh down
their relationship. But as he ponders further, he becomes oppressed
with the weight of the approaching future, 'die Zukunft, die mit seinem
Erinnern schon begann' (V 74) [22]. Memory is already tainting the
future, so that further meetings between the couple will assume a pre-
determined and repetitious character. The young painter Reinhart, in
the course of his inconclusive relationship with Hortense, expresses
similar doubts about the nature of the future with her, and in doing so
condemns their association to a lingering end. He wishes for a
relationship 'ohne Vergangenes, ohne Zukunft, ohne Angst, ohne Zuver-
sicht' (I 513). The restricted pattern of their meetings reflects
Reinhart's fears. The affair between Stiller and Sibylle also expresses
its inner disharmony in its repetitive outward conduct (III 625).
Frisch conveys the blind, unreasoning nature of Stiller's fear of
repetition by causing the expression of this fear to stand isolated
from the rest of the text towards the close of the 'Erstes Heft' of
the novel:

> Meine Angst: Die Wiederholung - ! (III 420) [23]

The latest in the line of Frisch heroes who blight the future by
imagining that they know it from the past is Kürmann in Biografie.
The Registrator describes this central fault to him:

> Sie verhalten sich nicht zur Gegenwart, sondern zu einer
> Erinnerung. Das ist es. Sie meinen die Zukunft schon zu
> kennen durch Ihre Erfahrung. Drum wird es jedesmal die-
> selbe Geschichte. (V 492)

The repetitions of life are not mechanically interchangeable since the
continuum of time renders everything unique. The fear of repetition

is a simplified response to life, and implies a lack of trust in the
shaping forces of life as opposed to its destructive forces. To the
extent that time is regarded as permanently inimical, it cannot be
harnessed to the establishment of identity.

A third approach to the perplexing problem of time is quite simply
to try to deny its existence. Aware that his affair with the woman
whom he met in the bar the previous afternoon is likely to lead to the
kind of emotional involvement which he detests, the man in Gantenbein
sets out the next morning for a museum, which, for him, stands outside
the framework of time: 'Jenseits der Zeit wollte er sein' (V 72). The
museum offers him a refuge where he no longer requires to realise himself
in relation to his contemporary environment. For his everyday world is
one which, by virtue of its technology, appears to create a superfluity
of time. In Die Chinesische Mauer Don Juan reproaches Columbus for
having discovered the world, since his discoveries have been transformed
by air-travel into useless time (II 184). Just as the man sought refuge
from time in the museum, so Gantenbein seeks similar refuge in the most
modern symbol of the meaninglessness of time, the airport. The figures
in Gantenbein are 'geschichtlos' because they remain immobile before a
plethora of possibilities, such as are suggested by the destination-
board in the airport departure lounge. Since the possibilities are
interchangeable, they are meaningless, and thus time itself becomes
meaningless, becomes a vacuum which must be filled with distraction.
As Gantenbein paces the floor of the airport lounge awaiting the arrival
of Lila, he muses idly on the nature of time, and his casual reflections
gradually cease as his mindless pacing comes to resemble, in the rhythm
of the passage, the ticking of a clock. He has begun to pace because
he was bored with the repetitive nature of his thoughts. By linking
satiety with these thoughts to the visual image of the jerking clock-
hands, Frisch succeeds in suggesting that they have been circling like
the clock-hands, and that they, like time itself, must be evaded;
Gantenbein is 'froh um das Muster auf dem Boden, das die Zeit gliedert'
(V 310). The future is an eternal meaningless present in which Gantenbein envies Patsch the dog who has no consciousness of time, who is
'ein Hund ohne Zeit' (V 310).

If the present and the future are negated, the past has no meaning
either. It is not only Walter Faber who is obliged to look back on
the 'Ruinen seiner Vergangenheit' [24]. Reinhart's suicide and Stiller's
gradual decline in Glion are indicative of their failure to come to
terms with their past lives. Gantenbein, sitting at the opening and

at the close of the novel in the empty flat which is a symbol of a broken
marriage, and also a symbol of his inability to accept the failure of
his past, is in the same mould. He abdicates knowledge of what has
happened - 'weiss nicht, was geschehen ist' (V 314) - in such a fashion
as to indicate clearly that he is afraid to admit to his contribution to
that past. His guilt suppresses the truth. This is characteristic of
all Frisch heroes in respect of their past. But if Reinhart and Stiller
both feel that time is passing without them achieving anything, in
Faber, Gantenbein and Kürmann this feeling is all the stronger because
they are aware that they have less time left to them. Ironically, their
denial of time reinforces its power to destroy their lives.

A fourth manifestation of the disequilibrium in time is reflected
in deficiencies in the attitudes of Frisch's characters towards the
opposite sex. These are expressed in the terminology of incest,
traditionally the indication of the gravest disharmony between the
sexes. This disharmony stems from the dislocated sense of time since
the relations in question are almost always characterised as being
between the generations and rarely between siblings. The first relationship so described - that of an older woman with a younger man - provides
the formulation for the much graver maladjustments in later works. In
Jürg Reinhart, Jürg describes his affair with the older Dutch baroness
as 'verkehrt und unpassend' (I 260). This designation is applicable
to failed sexual relationships in both Die Schwierigen and Stiller. In
the former novel, Yvonne, shortly after her marriage to a contemporary,
Hinkelmann, realises that her role in their relationship is that 'einer
fehlenden Mutter' (I 401). Hinkelmann the archeologist can establish
a viable relationship with the dead past, but not with the living
present. Yvonne, increasingly aware of this, on discovering that she
is pregnant, resolves to leave her husband. Twice she explains herself
to the thunderstruck Hinkelmann: 'Man bekommt kein Kind von seinem
Sohn' (I 402, 405). In similar fashion, as their unsatisfactory
relationship breaks up, Sibylle comports herself 'nicht ohne Mütter-
lichkeit' (III 645) towards Stiller. The destructive nature of these
two relationships is symbolised by abortion (I 410, III 635). It is
as if time revenges itself on those with dislocated relationships to
it by denying them the possibility of continuing in time through
offspring.

Homo Faber represents the culmination of the theme of incest,
because the novel does not merely use its terminology, but incorporates
the act itself. Walter Faber is the clearest example of the way in

which a misunderstanding of the nature of time distorts sexual relationships. His first sexual experience was with a much older woman (IV 99),
his current mistress is young enough to be his daughter, and in general
his attitude to the sexual act, the basis of all life, comes near to
horrified revulsion (IV 93). Against this psychological background,
he makes the acquaintance of his daughter Sabeth, and begins thus his
long self-deception as he suppresses the accumulating evidence that she
is his daughter, a fact assumed by the outside world (IV 86). Sabeth
herself, partly as a result of her youth, has a somewhat ambivalent
attitude to the opposite sex. On the one hand, with immature confidence
in her own experience, she rejects her contemporaries. Yet on the
other hand she is not entirely at ease with Faber, who has the over-
protective attitude of the much older man, and Sabeth's comment on this
ironically points to the real situation between them: 'Du tust wie ein
Papa!' (IV 115). The two descriptions which Faber gives of Sabeth's
physical appearance are devoid of sensuousness or femininity. In both
cases, it is her youthful grace which moves him. The first, on board
ship, describes her with the dispassionate eye of a man for whom the
body is a functional instrument: 'Ich fand sie schön, aber nicht auf-
reizend' (IV 87). The second description, in Italy, has the impersonal
att ri butes of antique beauty. Sabeth is 'schlank und senkrecht, dabei
sprachlos wie eine Statue' (IV 115). The tone of these descriptions
permits two conclusions. Firstly, Faber the engineer who goes in such
fear of all manifestations of life, is responding, however faintly, to
grace in human form, as the shift in emphasis from the functional to
the statuesque in the two descriptions demonstrates. Secondly, it can
be concluded that the emotional composure of both descriptions gives
an indication of the strength of the sexual relations between Faber
and Sabeth. The relationship with his daughter reflects not only
Faber's warped, but also his diminished responses. Faber, the apostle
of technology, has, in trying to insulate himself against all human
reflexes, so dulled himself that his reactions fail to relate to
manifestations of time. His tragedy is that when he does begin to
respond, the young woman should be his own daughter. So accustomed is
he to suppressing instinctive knowledge that he can only react to her
sexually [25], yet the suppressed knowledge of the truth, together with
his general attitude to sex, inhibit his sexual response. The major
irony the novel is that the re-assertion of her instinctive reactions
in Sabeth causes her death. Bitten by an adder as she lies on the beach,
she cries out, and as Faber comes to her from the sea, she looks with
slowly dawning realisation at the ageing naked man, retreats before him,

falls and sustains the undiscovered fracture of her skull (IV 157-158).

Faber has rejected the fact that time imposes a shape on the
individual human life. Birth, growth, maturity, decline and death are
concepts which he has rigorously excluded from his thoughts because
they derive from the natural world which, unlike that of technology,
is not fully explicable. Influenced by his training and profession,
Faber has transferred his simplistic outlook to the complexities of
life, and has wreaked havoc. He relates that Hanna, his contemporary
in years and the only woman with whom he has experienced sexual fulfilment (IV 100), tells him how he has misused the all-important dimension
of time: he has deprived life of its mysterious and inexplicable
possibilities, and life has revenged itself in the destruction of his
daughter:

> Du behandelst das Leben nicht als Gestalt, sondern als
> blosse Addition, daher kein Verhältnis zur Zeit, weil
> kein Verhältnis zum Tod. Leben sei Gestalt in der Zeit.
> (IV 170) [26]

'Gestalt in der Zeit' is a concept which has never established itself
in the mind of Faber, who wishes life to be as much subject to control
as a machine. For Faber the technologist, the high priest of modern
life, the realities of life are as one-dimensional as they are for
Knobel the warder [27]. Faber's failure to live with time has caused him
to imagine, at the age of fifty, that life is as repeatable as a
mechanical movement, and the monstrous relationship with his daughter
has resulted. That Faber imposes repetition by violence in the belief
that life can be repeated is an indication in the difference of his
outlook from that of Kilian in Bin. In his important conversation with
the young girl Maja, Kilian denies the existence of repetition in life.
For Kilian they are two criteria by which the individual measures the
shape which time is giving him. There is first of all comparison: 'Die
Jugend wird immer jünger. Das ist das eine' (I 652). The second
criterion is the growing awareness that it is necessary to accept that
certain forms of involvement with others are inappropriate. Maja takes
her leave of Kilian, and writes a note expressing her regret. As Kilian
and Bin study the note, Bin asks:

> 'Sie hat dich geliebt, - weisst du das?'
> Kilian wusste es durchaus.
> (Das war das andere). (I 652-653)

The two elements which Kilian singles out as contributing most to a
sense of the passing of time, an awareness of the movement of life and
an acceptance of personal renunciation in this movement, are both alien
to the mechanistic conception of life held by the technologist Faber.

It is only negatively, through the magnitude of his appalling experience
of his betrayal of life, that Faber can perceive the rightness of an
attitude such as Kilian's. Hanna verbalises his own perception when
she reminds him brutally of his disregard of time: 'Wir können uns
nicht mit unseren Kindern nochmals verheiraten' (IV 139). Experience
cannot be repeated. Faber's attempt to avoid establishing his identity
in time has destroyed him.

Variations on the end of time

The failure of the major Frisch characters to come to terms with
the passage of time is attended by decline and death: Reinhart commits
suicide, Stiller is condemned to lead a meaningless existence, Faber
has terminal cancer, Gantenbein closes with death, and Kürmann has only
a few years to live. The figures in Gantenbein contain the
characteristics which are present to a greater or lesser degree in
the Frisch hero in all the main works: an obsession with passing
time, with sickness and with death. There is no longer the self-
confidence, manifest in some of the earliest writing of Frisch, which
derived from an acceptance of the limitations of life. Death could
then be seen as a disciplining agent, in much the same way as work
could increase the awareness of life by imposing a meaningful pattern.
The story of Kilian in Bin bears witness to a commitment to the
succession of generations and the cycle of birth and death which is
without parallel in the later works. Kilian, challenged by a
traditional figure of death to come with him or to send someone in
his stead, unwittingly designates his father just at the point where
his own son is born. The dying father affirms the organic cycle
(I 656). The constants of life are never again envisaged with such
acceptance in Frisch's imaginative work.

The reality of death, which is directly experienced in Bin, can be
masked by technology in a way which deprives death of the meaning
bestowed on it by the natural cycle. In the sketch 'Der Harlekin' in
Tagebuch 1946-1949, the emissary of the devil depicts the unreality
of modern death. If Gottlieb Knoll, the hero, agrees to the death of
a mandarin in distant China, he will receive untold riches. As Gottlieb
cavils at the thought of killing, the emissary outlines for him the
advantages of technology in the matter, the chief of which is that
Gottlieb does not have to meet his victim face to face (II 658-659).
Technology is not subject to organic laws, in which death forms the
last stage, and it therefore stands independent of an organic framework

of time. Technology has been harnessed to bring about human destruction
on a massive scale, and the ease with which this destruction can be
effected is rupturing the consciousness of life and death which the
organic laws impart. Der Heutige in Die Chinesische Mauer, alive to
the potentially destructive capacity of the atomic bomb which technology
has created, envisages a world from which the organic laws, and hence
human dimensions - above all that of time - have been banished (II 207) [28].
Yet this is merely a logical extension of the world of Walter Faber, in
which technology is regarded as a victory over time. Surrounded as he
is by apparently incontrovertible evidence of the supremacy of technology
over organic matter, the individual is diverted from a proper acceptance
of his own finiteness. Faber, in his brief vision in Cuba of the
immense possibilities of life, denounces the Americans, whose civilisation
has the most highly developed technology in the world, for their
'pornografisches Verhältnis zum Tod' (IV 177), the obscene pretence
that death is not part of life. It is against this general background
that the individual contemplates his own death.

However much he has looked away from the subject, the individual is
aware within himself that the longer he exists, the more imminent his
death, which will fix his identity for all time, becomes. From having
been a theoretical matter, the question of death assumes the highest
personal relevance. Frisch, as he approaches his mid-sixties, examines
his mental attitude to his own death (VI 750-751). He distinguishes
between 'Angst vor dem Alter' and 'das Todesbewusstsein'; the former,
which is so strongly present in his later years is 'melancholisch',
while the latter is a more subtle all-pervading awareness which is
present 'auch in der Freude'; he is much in contact with younger people,
but he can make no more commitments; he is as heedful of the renunciatory
aspect of ageing as was Kilian more than thirty years before; he knows
'dass es sich verbietet, eine jüngere Frau an diese meine Zukunftslosigkeit binden zu wollen' (VI 751). Yet whereas Frisch might accept death
and the end of identity in relation to himself, his 'Zukunftslosigkeit',
he cannot resist the opportunity to experiment, not with the possibility
of cheating physical death, but with the possibility of casting off
identity by means of a death which is presumed by others. It is a more
refined form of the evasion of identity than that practised by Stiller,
who merely sought to run away, and it is an evasion which is made
possible by the technological age. The experiment is carried out in
the story told to Camilla Huber in Gantenbein (V 248 ff.), later
expanded into the film-script Zürich-Transit (1966), about the man who
attended his own funeral. The modern world makes it possible for a man

to witness the social conventions surrounding his own presumed death,
and this offers him the possibility of a retreat from his social
identity. After the funeral, he calls for the last time at his empty
apartment and, apart from the inexplicable fact that his keys are
later found in the letter-box, there are 'keine Spuren von ihm' (V 255).
In the film-script the matter is expanded, but the essence of the story
remains the same. Ehrismann, the counterpart of the unnamed man in the
novel, sloughs his social identity. As he strolls about his home town
of Zürich after the funeral, he reflects on the extent to which time
has been placed at his disposal by the absence of an identity: 'Ich
hatte Zeit wie noch nie' (V 429) [29]. As he buys a one-way air-ticket
to Nairobi, he is surprised at the ease with which he can leave Zürich.
He cannot bring himself to take the flight, however, and returns once
more to the empty flat. The film-script, like the original story,
closes with Ehrismann walking away from the building in which the flat
is situated. The modern world has permitted a fresh start, in the
sense that the previous identity is no longer available. Yet,
significantly, both the story and the film-script end there, for the
fresh start is valueless, it represents life in a vacuum and is a form
of 'Zukunftslosigkeit' which is more anguishing than that of physical
death. As physical death inevitably approaches, the experiment in
casting off identity reinforces the instinctive knowledge that it is
not only not possible to start again, but more importantly, that it
would be profitless if it were possible.

Speculation about the emotional impact of living one's life, or at
least part of it, over again, has never been absent from Frisch's work.
In Prague in 1947, Frisch recalls that thirteen years have passed since
he was last in the city, and he asks himself how he would react if he
had to live these thirteen years over again without the least
alteration (II 486). This note of enquiry, as regards volition and
ability to go through life again, is later altogether banished. To
re-live life would be to experience 'Wiederholung' on an unbearable
scale. The narrator in Gantenbein, speculating on the possibility of
re-living Enderlin's life, or part of it, finds the prospect appalling.
It would not be possible to temper apprehension about the future with
hope, there would instead be the devastating prospect of certain
knowledge (V 123). Kürmann, offered the possibility of shaping his
life as he wishes on the stage, reacts in similar fashion and is
horrified at the thought of having to repeat the experience of his
relationship with Antoinette again, when its development is known in

advance (V 541). It is as if the intellect were trying desperately to
reconcile itself with the nature of time. The man who attended his own
funeral created a living death for himself since, stripped of identity,
he nonetheless continues to exist in the medium of time. For the
narrator in Gantenbein and for Kürmann such a living death would lie
in a repetition of a part of life, however small. They are trying to
coerce themselves into accepting that there is but one life by depicting
to themselves a repetition in terms which would be unbearable. It
represents an attempt to come to terms with the inevitable.

The inevitable relates not only to the future, but also to the past.
The individual's behaviour has been registered by himself and by others,
and this has fixed his identity in the past. Time cannot record the
possibilities for behaviour which actual behaviour has excluded. Increasingly, the Frisch hero feels that in this respect time is one-
dimensional. He regrets that he cannot set the record straight, and
leave the world an account of the possibilities which faced him. The
Staatsanwalt in Rip van Winkle suggests that, in order truly to know a
person, one must be aware of the courses of action upon which he did
not embark, because they form the personality of the individual as much
as the actual behaviour does. He berates the Verteidiger for imagining
that the whole truth about the personality of Der Fremdling lies in his
external behaviour (III 813). Gantenbein goes further, finding
dissatisfaction with his past because it does not reveal this dimension
of possibility. He complains that the immobility of his actual past,
by which those about him identify him, bores him and that speculation
on what might have been - 'unvergessbare Zukunft' (V 59) - is all that
renders life bearable. The Frisch hero attempts to counterbalance his
lack of significant activity in the past by drawing attention to what
might have been. The reluctance to accept that identity involves
irreversible and irrevocable choice in time stems from an immaturity
which envisages life as being capable of complete control. Paradoxically,
the quest for totality ends in self-betrayal. Since half-measures are
not acceptable in the matter of identity, no measures at all are undertaken, and identity remains a welter of unrealised possibilities. The
Frisch hero can commit himself neither to what is nor to what has been,
and so the observable external life - the one possibility which has
been realised - becomes, as the years pass, more and more embarrassing
since it provides such a poor reflection of what is held to have been
the potential. The weight of guilt towards this unrealised potential
leads to suicide (Reinhart), physical escape (Stiller) and to mental

escape in Gantenbein, who has not the decisiveness for either of these
acts. Life is only bearable 'als Hirngespinst' (V 59) because the
past cannot be altered. To this cast of mind the unchangeable nature
of the past is as frightening and debilitating as the inevitability of
the future.

It is not that there is a lack of awareness of the immutables of
life. There is, however, especially in the major figures, an increasing
disjunction between intellectual perception and emotional acceptance
of the limits and confines of the personality. It is clear that the
variety of mental exercises which are undertaken constitute an attempt
to bridge this gap: constant confrontation with the incontrovertible
might induce acceptance. Gantenbein, for example, as he sets out to
cast new roles for himself, is aware that these roles will all shape
themselves to the nature of his basic personality. He compares this
to the unchanging shape of his body in respect of buying clothes - his
body will always have the same effect on the clothes (V 20-21). Kürmann
is offered the possibility of changing his life on the stage, the undertaking which Reinhart, Stiller and Gantenbein embark upon in reality.
Yet the opportunity to alter the past, not in reality, but on the stage,
as a 'Spiel', demonstrates that even within this dimension alteration
is impossible. The licence permitted by the stage cannot dispense with
the irreducible core which forms the personality and which cannot be
changed (V 503). Kürmann, in a fashion similar to that experienced
by Stiller, also finds that there is a further element in his life
which he cannot change: those about him. He cannot erase his
disastrous marriage with Kattrin, his first wife, for to do so would
entail revoking the child of their union. He cannot now decide to
remain in San Francisco at the outbreak of the Second World War, since
that would mean that the Jewish refugees whom his chance intervention
had allowed to slip into Switzerland, would now be lost. Despairingly,
as he sees the interaction of his own past with that of others, Kürmann
recognises the impossibility of alteration to his life in the rhetorical
question: 'Wie soll ich anders wählen?' (V 514). The immutability of
the individual merges with the immutability of the past to forge the
identity of the individual whether he will or not. The only possible
stance to the past and to the actions of the individual therein is to
rationalise and make sense of past identity by assuming that events
were meant to happen in the manner in which they did. In this way
identity arises from an act of belief (V 565). The mortal condition
of man obliges him to posit meaning, a point made in Blätter aus dem
Brotsack. As he reads Homer, Frisch reflects on the immortality of

the gods. They do not seek for a meaning to life, only mortals do
that. The short space of time which mortals are allotted would not be
capable of being borne if they did not (I 146). Faced with the fact
that so much of life is subject to change which is not within the
control of the individual, the individual sustains himself by believing
in retrospect that these events were inevitable. Only in this way can
harmony be restored between intellect and emotion in respect of the past.

Frisch illustrates acceptance of the irreversible nature of life in
an anecdote in Tagebuch 1946-1949 (II 493 ff.). A young man and a
young woman fall in love and plan to marry. He feels that he cannot
accept this responsibility, however, and breaks off the relationship.
Years later they meet by chance, and discover that they are both married
with children. The young woman, like the majority of Frisch's female
figures, is firmly rooted in life. She expresses her pleasure at
meeting again, but as she thinks of the past she refuses to ponder on
what might have been. To do so is to beat futilely against the
unassailability of what did in fact take place. That it did not take
place belongs to the realm of acceptance, not to the realm of speculation.
Since the past is both his and irreversible, it is pointless for the
individual not to accept it, since he has had a determining influence,
however minimal, on it. For the characters in the early Santa Cruz, the
play constitutes the 'Aufdeckung ihres unveränderlichen Seins' [30] to the
extent that they ascribe a place to 'Sehnsucht' in their lives in the
full knowledge that the wishes it generates in relation to the past will
never be realised, and in relation to the future only rarely. They move
towards accepting themselves as they are since they know, in the well-
known statement of Tagebuch 1946-1949, that time can develop them, but
never transform them (II 361). The conditions of life cannot be
removed without removing life itself, a fundamental truth which the
later Frisch characters find increasingly impossible to accept. The
naked man at the opening of Gantenbein, desperately seeking a new role
for himself, still wears his spectacles and his watch (V 16), symbols
of the ability to perceive and of the framework of time, two constants
of the personality which no individual can eradicate. Increasingly
aware that he cannot change his life even on the stage, Kürmann learns
from the Registrator that the only freedom of choice which he has is in
the behaviour he will adopt to the fact of his own mortality (V 573).
The inability of the major Frisch figures to accept themselves in a
framework of time, to cease to fret about what is a condition of life,
saps their spiritual strength. They may perceive the nature of time
intellectually, but they cannot bring themselves to accept it

emotionally. They are destroyed by their disorientation in time.

There can be traced, principally in the prose works of Frisch, an
increasing unease at the relationship between the individual and the
medium of time in which his identity evolves. As the relative
certainties of the earliest works are left behind, the Frisch hero
becomes more and more pre-occupied with warding off what he sees as
the depradations of time upon his personality. In the course of this
progression, the idea that the personality can fulfil itself in time
is gradually replaced by the feeling that the progress of time
annihilates the personality. The relationship to time, from being
one of acceptance, changes to one in which the identity of the
individual cannot be realised.

The change of the relationship to time can be measured against the
affirmatory note struck in the diary of 1940. Caught up in the boring
routine of frontier soldiering, the narrator in Blätter aus dem Brotsack
envies a colleague who has managed to obtain leave. He reassures himself, however, with the thought that leave, especially at this time of
national emergency, does not after all constitute a dispensation from
the responsibility of living: 'Es gibt doch keinen Urlaub von der Zeit!'
(I 116). This affirmation yields in Die Schwierigen to a Romantic
melancholy which is inspired by the thought that the individual is
powerless to alter or influence the flow of time in any way (I 516-517).
The propensity to be mesmerised by the phenomenon of time, already
beginning to be apparent in Die Schwierigen, is fully depicted in Stiller.
Stiller, realising that the geographical change from Switzerland to the
United States has not altered his personality, and has in fact increased
his difficulties, attempts the final rejection of his identity by
suicide. The attempt is not successful, and as he lies under sedation
in hospital he experiences a frightening feeling that he is totally
unrelated to any normal point of orientation in time. He suffers no
physical pain, but the sensation of being suspended in time is unbearable
and derives principally from the fact that the awareness of time, in
which action is possible, is no longer a functioning part of his
consciousness. He has as a consequence an overwhelming feeling of
impotence (III 725-726). Stiller's condition at this point offers a
symbol of his lack of relationship to time, of his disorientation which
prevents him from establishing his identity.

Homo Faber suggests that it is not possible to attain personal
identity in time within modern civilisation, or at any rate, within the

framework of everyday concerns which civilisation normally imposes on
the individual. Faber visits Herbert, the young German engineer - whom
he first met on the plane as Herbert was setting out to look for his
brother Joachim - in the jungle village where they, together, had found
Joachim's body. Herbert has now severed all ties with the civilised
world. Faber and he sit in his hut during a rainstorm 'wie in einer
Arche Noah' (IV 166) because there is no light. Herbert has withdrawn
totally from society. The primeval forest, the antithesis of modern
technological society, either destroys - Joachim committed suicide -
or demands subservience to its own rhythms: 'Herbert wie ein Indio'
(IV 168). For Herbert at least, identity involves the rejection of
civilisation. Faber's own single direct experience of the potential
of life occurs outside the framework of his normal existence. He ends
his four-day stay on the island of Cuba with the firm declaration:
'Ich preise das Leben!' (IV 181). But this declaration must be seen
in a wider context. It is true that there is a contrast between Faber's
normal dissection of time and his unified experience of time in the
Cuba episode [31]. But the importance of this experience must be
qualified by its marginal nature. Indeed, it is doubly marginal.
Firstly, Faber is a tourist, and it is not certain that he will be able
to transfer his Cuban experience to his daily life. Secondly, it is an
experience of time which ignores all political framework. The repressive
dictatorship of Battista's Cuba - the time is 1957 - is utterly
irrelevant to the central personal experience. Similarly, the
conclusion of the novel in a sense takes place outside a social
context. Faber cannot imagine a future with Hanna (IV 192) - quite
apart from the fact that she no longer has a flat in Athens (IV 199) -,
he has already resigned from his job before reaching Athens (IV 197),
and he is sufficiently aware of the advanced state of his illness to
sense that the operation will in all probability achieve nothing
(IV 198). If, in this situation, Faber manages to establish a relationship to time, to sustain the vision of life which he experienced on Cuba,
then this relationship - like the Cuba experience - is established on
the margins of society and on the margins of life itself.

In Gantenbein the lack of contact with experience, and hence with
time, is much more obvious. Significantly, the opening and closing
deaths take place in Zürich, which was described as 'geschichtslos'
(III 431). It is the second episode of death, the one with a nameless
body in a coffin on the River Limmat, which fascinates Gantenbein.
The man, 'der nicht einmal einen Namen hinterlassen wollte' (V 314),
has contrived to leave without an identity. All that is known 'von

diesem Zeitgenossen' (V 314) is that he must have lived since his body
provides proof of that. Patsch the dog was briefly envied because it
was 'ein Hund ohne Zeit'. With the unidentified man Gantenbein's
reaction is altogether more forceful. He, after all, once shared the
same consciousness of time with Gantenbein, and with this handicap
almost achieves a feat which commands Gantenbein's unstinted admiration:
had it not been for the fact that a chance current stranded the coffin
against a weir, he would have managed to float away without having
committed his body to an identity. He would have succeeded: 'Abzuschwimmen ohne Geschichte' (V 319). In fact, Gantenbein's admiration has two
causes. Firstly, the man has avoided involvement with the bureaucracy
without which the technological society could not function - even
Gantenbein, for his imaginary role as a blind man, required to obtain
'die gelbe Armbinde' (V 42). Secondly, after his multifarious and
exhausting attempts to avoid commitment to a fixed identity, Gantenbein
cannot hide his delight that someone else should almost have achieved
his own most desired goal. Stiller's relationship to time is
characterised by pain at his inability to make contact with experience.
Gantenbein, on the other hand, has almost totally withdrawn from any
concept of responsibility towards himself in time. The conjectural
element in the title Mein Name sei Gantenbein is thus not so much
indicative of a search for a new identity as a device to posit endless
possibilities and so to escape identity. For Gantenbein the unidentified
man in the coffin is a symbol of success in this endeavour.

The medium of time is increasingly felt to be an irksome condition
of life. The fabric of modern life, dominated by technology which
exists and functions beyond organic time, interacts with the personality
of the individual to create a vacuum in the present. In this vacuum
the protagonists struggle in an alienated atmosphere to establish an
equilibrium in time. It is a struggle which declines into purposeless
day-dreaming, and of which Rip van Winkle symbolises the failure.

96.

2. Identity and the Forces of the Environment

'Sehnsucht' and the environment

Two early statements by Frisch deal with the two main areas of
difficulty which the individual experiences in his relationship to the
environment. In the first statement, in Freunde und Fremde (1932)
(I 27-31), Frisch attempts to reconcile the continuing process of life
to the immobility of the environment. To demonstrate the difficulties
of such a reconciliation, Frisch places himself in a mountainous
landscape. As he contemplates the heights above him, he registers his
fear: to scale the immediate peak will provide merely temporary respite
from the 'Sehnsucht' which is driving him forward. That particular
achievement will serve only to give rise to a longing for fresh achievements which will drive him to other environments. 'Sehnsucht', one of
Frisch's recurring motifs, is, in one of its first extant uses,
presented as disturbingly unquenchable. Yet, since 'Sehnsucht' is still
at this point linked to the immediate environment, albeit to the
challenging and changing environment of a mountain range, life and the
environment are not considered to be irreconcilable within the
consciousness of the individual.

If this first statement on the relationship between the individual
and the environment gives some indication of the extent of the former's
dependence on the latter, the second, in Ein Mensch geht weg (1932) [1],
shows the way in which the individual must seek to be independent of the
immediate environment because the environment cannot reflect the
multiplicity of the strands which connect the individual to the elusive
process of life. This would be to demand too much of the environment,
and at the same time would be a betrayal of the human capacity to
transcend the environment. Frisch considers that such a betrayal would
be manifest in the failure to keep alive the memory of a loved one who
is no longer present in the immediate environment. This would be a
dereliction of duty towards the principle of human interdependence
which causes us to live on in one another long after separation. Thus
the individual must also extend himself beyond his environment to
encompass dimensions which it cannot contain.

This is a process of which the conscious mind is not always aware.
Manifestations of the unconscious mind, such as dreams, make the individual cognisant of realms beyond the environment in which he lives.
As the Second World War draws to its close, Frisch seeks to cast light
on why the Swiss writer, who has been spared the horrors of war, is

justified in continuing to write. It is in the Swiss writer's faculty, through the mechanism of the dream, to add dimensions to the experience which he has culled from his immediate environment, that part of his justification lies (II 289). His dreams, associating him with the sufferings of others elsewhere, are evidence of the human interdependence which transcends the environment. Dreams approach a totality of vision which the conscious mind is either unaware of, or at pains to limit [2]. Just as the environment does not constitute the whole of life for the individual, although it can do much to sustain life, so the bare biographical facts of the individual life can yield only a partial picture of the individual (V 327). Throughout his work, Frisch has juxtaposed the factual observable life of the individual, which is capable of being expressed, with the inner life, known only to the individual and, if capable of being expressed at all, then only indirectly. The gradual emergence of these two aspects of life as wholly irreconciliable opposites charts the course of Frisch's career as a novelist and dramatist. It is for this reason that the early works, notably Santa Cruz [3] and Bin, occupy an important place in the oeuvre, for it is in them that a reconciliation takes place between what are later seen as opposing poles. In these early works the individual is shown arranging matters in such a fashion that he balances the claims of his immediate environment and those of his inner life [4]. The initial frustration that the visions of the inner life cannot be realised, which expresses itself as dissatisfaction at the constrictions of the environment, gives way to an awareness of the dangers which arise from lack of control over the longings and wishes of the inner life, and to a realisation that a synthesis must be achieved. In view of the fact that later Frisch heroes devote themselves to untrammelled speculation about developments and experiences possible in their lives, if they were not in the situations in which they find themselves, it is appropriate to emphasise the existence of this awareness in the earlier characters.

The tendency of the inner dimensions of the personality to denigrate life in the everyday environment is expressed in the first published work of fiction, Jürg Reinhart. Jürg, in a fashion similar to later theoretical statements made by Frisch, refuses to accept that failure to come to terms with the environment can be compensated for by alleged intensity of the inner life (I 304). Balz Leuthold in Antwort aus der Stille, on the other hand, has in a small measure that which is so to plague later Frisch heroes: the fear that the unrealised possibilities within him could have greater significance than those

possibilities which have actually been developed [5]. This is a fear
which is always accompanied by a belief in the transforming power of
the grand gesture. The penchant for dramatic action has its inherent
dangers more spectacularly highlighted when it is transferred to the
political sphere. The power of 'Sehnsucht' in yearning for a different
political framework to life is explored in the play Nun singen sie
wieder. Eduard, one of the young airmen fighting against Germany claims
that the beauty of music is the only thing which cannot be destroyed by
bombs. For him music exemplifies a 'Sehnsucht', an 'Illusion', which
lies beyond the confines of the environment (II 94). Yet, as he
develops the concept of 'Illusion' in human affairs into the political
sphere, he demonstrates, possibly unwittingly, its amoral nature. The
power of 'Illusion' can be harnessed indifferently to creation or to
destruction. The destruction of all that the environment contains is
not regarded as too high a price to pay for the attempt to realise
visions, the product of 'Sehnsucht'.

If the power of 'Sehnsucht' in the political sphere is amoral, its
undue hold on the emotional life of the individual is harmful, even
destructive. To the extent that 'Sehnsucht' derives its power from the
individual's desire to be something other than he is, the individual
can combat this power by a ruthless commitment to his own limitations.
Such a commitment can call for harsh decisions. Significantly, it is
a woman, Yvonne, who exemplifies this method of combatting 'Sehnsucht'
in the early work. Her break with her husband Hinkelmann in Die
Schwierigen is motivated by her determination to come to terms with
her situation. She has realised that it is futile for her and Hinkelmann
to attempt to construct a life together. She advises him that he can
do nothing because 'Niemand kann aus seiner Haut heraus' (I 406).
More important, she has the strength to act on her insight. It is the
same kind of strength in Hauswirt which later causes Yvonne to admire
Hauswirt's commitment to herself and her child (I 596-597). Yet not
everyone has the innate strength of character possessed by Yvonne and
Hauswirt. For the narrator in Bin, it is the weight and fullness of
lived life which combats 'Sehnsucht', so that he questions whether he
has any right to 'Sehnsucht'. To Bin he enumerates the details of his
good fortune which he and his wife enjoy in terms of the abundance of
nature and in terms of child-bearing (I 630-631). In so far as this
accommodation with the force of 'Sehnsucht' demonstrates that a
bürgerlich environment is not necessarily totally inimical to personal
fulfilment, the balance achieved by the narrator in Bin - and by Yvonne
in Die Schwierigen - is not very different, as will be shown, from that

achieved by the Rittmeister and Elvira in Santa Cruz. Frisch himself
attests to a continuity of aim in the works of his early and middle
periods. In his introduction, published in the Neue Zürcher Zeitung
in 1954, to a passage from his new novel Stiller, he draws attention
to the connection between these works:

> Die Linie, die in früheren Arbeiten wie Santa Cruz, Nun
> singen sie wieder und Graf Öderland, dann auch in der
> kleinen Erzählung Bin oder Die Reise nach Peking begonnen
> worden ist, wird weitergeführt; Simultaneität von gewesenen
> Leben und ersehnten Leben, Dialektik zwischen Tat und Traum,
> die zusammen erst die Realität eines Menschen ergeben, be-
> stimmen die Komposition dieses Romans. 6

In Santa Cruz and also in Bin, which was written at the same period 7,
Frisch presents the attainment of a balance between longing and reality
in the lives of his protagonists, whereas in later works longing and
reality are increasingly seen to diverge. After Bin and Santa Cruz, the
Frisch hero never again comes so close to establishing an identity in
which a relationship to the environment is a concommitant part of that
identity.

Possible locations for the establishment of identity

The two aspects of life which take on physical shape in Santa Cruz
had already been defined by the hero in Jürg Reinhart. Out sailing,
Jürg reflects on his own character, and comes to the conclusion that
there are two streams of mental activity within him: the one concerned
with the finite reality of his life, and the other with the infinite
possibilities beyond that reality, possibilities as infinite as the
vastness of the sea (I 243). The play Santa Cruz is essentially a
depiction of the power which this second strand of mental activity has
over the individual, and the course and close of the action indicate
the manner in which this power can be contained and made fruitful,
rather than be allowed to grow in destructive fashion. In a programme
note to a later play, Frisch outlines the considerations which led him
to write Santa Cruz (II 217). He wishes to indicate the strength of
unfulfilled longing in the character of the Rittmeister by incorporating
this longing in the separate figure on the stage of Pelegrin. He finds
that this visible representation is in keeping with the reality of the
manner in which longing consciously or unconsciously influences daily
decisions. The Rittmeister testifies to the power of unfulfilled
longing over himself and his actions by acknowledging the separate
identity which this power has assumed:

> Ich möchte ihn noch einmal kennenlernen, ihn, der mein
> anderes Leben führt. (II 21)

He dismisses his wife's objection that this is all a figment of his imagination. The force of this power can only be represented by imagining a separate figure which for its existence is usurping the Rittmeister's own vitality. The vision of this figure undermines the defences which the Rittmeister assembles against it. Even a very conscious enumeration of the benefits and advantages of his present situation cannot act as a counterweight against his urge to reach out for that which is symbolised by Pelegrin. The worth of reality is unsettled by this yearning (II 22). The Rittmeister's formulation of his difficulties is sober and restrained, and indicates the confrontation within himself of a desire to commit himself to the here and now, and his increasingly painful awareness that his environment, and the circumstances arising from it, could have been different. In wishing to erase the consciousness of other possible courses which his life could have taken, the Rittmeister has so restricted himself mentally and emotionally to his present framework of existence that he has unwittingly given that consciousness a strong and increasing hold over himself.

A further aspect of the polarisation which has taken place in the Rittmeister's mental and emotional life between reality and longing is provided in the 'Vorspiel' to the play, where the revered Pelegrin appears as a shabby tramp. This demonstrates that the passage of time has also played a part in the creation of the dichotomy in the Rittmeister. For the Rittmeister's longing, and its immoderate growth, centre in an episode in his life seventeen years earlier (II 60). His phantasy about the decision which he might have made at that point in his life, as opposed to the one which he actually did make, relates to the young man who he then was. The possibility of another decision is timeless in the sense that it has not developed [8]. Time is related to what the Rittmeister feels to be the suffocating restrictions of the castle, timelessness to the decision which he could have taken in Santa Cruz [9]. Lack of relationship to time is one of the factors which nourishes the force of longing.

The attractions of the way of thought symbolised by Pelegrin lie in the contrast which he offers to the claims made on the individual by reality. Pelegrin is a powerful figure because he is a negation of reality, a figure for whom the endlessness of possibility is at odds with the limitations of action. He has achieved nothing, can achieve nothing. His own words indicate that he is incapable of finding satisfaction in reality. In a speech to Elvira he contrasts the 'knowledge' of the imagination with the reality of the external world:

> Elvira, ich kenne eine Muschel, die es nicht gibt, eine
> Muschel, die man nur denken kann, so schön ist sie, und
> wenn man an den Küsten aller Meere streifte und wenn man
> Tausende und Hunderttausende von Muscheln eröffnete, sie
> alle zusammen, nie sind sie so schön wie die Muschel, die
> man sich denken kann. (II 34)

His repetition of these words to Elvira's daughter Viola, (II 71),
symbolises, immediately prior to his being obliterated by the synthesis
which Elvira and the Rittmeister bring about between the two levels of
their lives, that longing is part of the human condition. This longing,
as depicted in Santa Cruz, can acquire an immeasurable dimension which
precludes contact with reality. The servant, reporting to the Rittmeister the arrival of Pelegrin in the village tavern, tells of
Pelegrin's fantastic tales (II 19). Pelegrin himself, the siren
voice, tempts Elvira with the limitless possibilities which he can
offer her. He speaks of 'Die uferlosen Nächte da draussen, unsere
Nächte' (II 50). He describes to her in glowing terms the dawn of the
fresh start for which later Frisch heroes so crave (II 36). The
Rittmeister, dictating his letter of farewell to Elvira at the point
where he feels that he must break with his present life, pauses in his
dictation to reflect on the imagined advantages of the life upon which
he is about to embark: 'Noch einmal die Weite alles Möglichen' (II 43).
Sudden drama, impulsive reaction and complete lack of restraint
characterise the world of imagination which Pelegrin represents.

Parallel with the depiction of Pelegrin's world appear manifestations
of the finiteness of reality which that world does not recognise. As
an indication of its lack of identity in the real world, Pelegrin's ship
is obliged to sail bearing an 'übermaltes Wappen' (II 54). Pedro the
poet, symbol of reason and insight, appears in chains, and his
pronouncements and warnings are ridiculed and rejected by the crew of
Pelegrin's ship (II 31 ff.). Only the Rittmeister pays heed to
Pedro's words about the futility of denying actual existence by
reflecting on the different courses which life might have taken (II 54).
Significantly, as he foretells the imminent demise of Pelegrin just
before the resolution achieved in the fifth act, Pedro appears 'nicht
mehr gefesselt' (II 60). For Pelegrin is to die in the morning with
the coming of light [10], when Elvira and the Rittmeister unite the two
levels of their lives and thus restore the full dimension of reality
to their relationship. Their confrontation with Pelegrin after seventeen
years has provided 'die Ausgangsbasis für eine Selbstwahl der Partner' [11].
Thus they rob Pelegrin of his independent existence. Yet even at the
close of his life, Pelegrin cannot abandon the simplistic attitudes

102.

which he nurtures in others. For him life, as symbolised in himself
and the <u>Rittmeister</u>, is a matter of irreconciliable alternatives:

>Der eine hat das Meer, der andere das Schloss; der
>eine hat Hawai – der andere das Kind. (II 72)

With Pelegrin dead on stage, Elvira comments on the harmfulness of
such attitudes and on the necessity of availing oneself of the capacity
for synthesis contained in the human psyche. At the close of the play
she reads the letter which the <u>Rittmeister</u> was to have left for her, in
which he set out his motives for quitting the castle. She admits that
she has experienced similar longings, which she had suppressed, but
which she now knows she must incorporate: 'Wir müssen die Sehnsucht
nicht töten' (II 74). The threat to themselves, and to their marriage,
posed by their secret longing lying dormant, has been made dramatically
real by the re-appearance of Pelegrin. Their reactions to this appearance prepare the way for their commitment to the environment in which
the constrictions of the castle can be seen as necessary and fruitful.
In committing themselves to their environment they have paradoxically
risen above its limitations.

Hawai, where the <u>Rittmeister</u> longed to be, is the first of four
place-names – Hawai, Peking, Santorin, Peru – which occur in Frisch's
work. None of the characters, in whose lives these place-names play an
important role, ever reach them as they imagined them to be, and this
inaccessibility symbolises the impossibility of the yearnings of these
characters. The chronological sequence of these place-names in the work
indicates in the characters in question an increasing dissociation from
their immediate environments. The achievement of Elvira and the <u>Ritt-
meister</u> lies in committing themselves to their environment and thus
releasing themselves from a mental state in which, in the confines of
their castle, they were essentially as rootless as Pelegrin. This is
an achievement not always possible for other characters in respect of
their imagined goals. It is true that in <u>Santa Cruz</u> the dilemna and its
resolution are presented in artistically less sophisticated terms than
in the later works. At the same time, a proper recognition of the intent
of the play enables it to be seen, within the context of Frisch's work
as a whole, in a clearer perspective. Frisch himself looks upon the
synthesis portrayed in the play as a form of commitment which every
individual must undertake in order to establish and fulfil his identity.
It is a measure of the positive intent which Frisch ascribes to this
synthesis that the concept of 'Wiederholung', which is so to terrify
later characters, is here envisaged by him in a formative role:

>Denn erst da, wo sich ein Damals und ein Heute in unserem

> Erleben begegnen, erst da, wo die Wiederholung uns dazu
> verhilft, gewinnen wir die Erkenntnis, dass wir offenbar
> ein Schicksal haben, ein Kreuz, das man auf sich nehmen muss,
> eine Cruz oder Crux, um spanischer zu reden. (II 76-77)

Elvira and the <u>Rittmeister</u> have subsumed the paradoxes of reality and
longing within the continuing process of life. By establishing a harmony
within themselves they have established a viable relationship with their
environment, and have thus accorded it its rightful place, which neither
exaggerates nor underestimates its importance in their lives.

The course of the 'Erzählung' <u>Bin oder die Reise nach Peking</u>
represents, as in the case of <u>Santa Cruz</u>, a 'Bewusstseinsentwicklung' [12].
If, in <u>Santa Cruz</u>, this development takes the form of restoring substance
to an environment devalued by longing, in <u>Bin</u>, during the symbolic
journey, balance eventually ensues from the confrontation between
reality and expectation. The boundlessness of the latter is restrained
and contained by the finiteness of the former. Experience tempers
longing, and the process by which this is done is depicted in the
narrative. The narrator is accompanied by Bin, the incorporation of
his possibilities [13]. Bin is not always present in the narrator's
consciousness, but the reality of Bin to the narrator is never in doubt.
Although so closely allied to the narrator, Bin is unobtrusive and
always permits the narrator to draw his own conclusions from the
experiences which occur on the journey. The most significant of these
conclusions occurs when the narrator believes himself to be within
striking distance of his goal, the city of Peking, which he knows to
lie on the seashore. At the point where the sequence of events which
prompts the conclusions in question starts, he is the guest of an
important Chinese with whom he goes riding each morning. His description
of these outings, in its contrast between the actuality of the real drab
and misty scenery and the vision of the imagined scenery which the
narrator has within him, shows that the narrator still cherishes some
notion of the realisability of his dreams:

> Ich hoffte stets, dass...das Meer, das wirkliche, läge vor
> uns, das grenzenlose, das die schwebende Kugel unserer Erde
> umspült. (I 641)

One morning his host announces that the prince is coming, and since
they are so close to Peking, the narrator can only assume that this
must mean the prince of Peking. Yet, when the meeting takes place, the
expected 'otherness' of the prince does not manifest itself, because
the whole encounter is so redolent of the narrator's own reality. His
host demonstrates to the prince how his (the host's) house was built
in accordance with the designs of the narrator; the prince's conversation

relates to the narrator's own background, and displays close knowledge
of it. The culmination of the narrator's insight is reached when the
prince embarks on a story, the unseemly tenor of which causes the
narrator to withdraw and to observe the proceedings from outside in
mounting disillusion (I 648-649). The expectation that Peking, and
all that has to do with it, would be as immaculate as the city of the
narrator's vision, has been disappointed. All human experience is
alloyed, only in the imagination can there be no blemishes. From this
point onwards, the actuality of the narrator's own life becomes
increasingly the subject of the narrative, and the balance between
reality and dream is achieved at the close in the realisation that he
will never reach Peking. In this sense the journey undertaken in Bin
'führt wieder nach Hause' [14]. The symbolic going forth was intended to
cast off the shackles of an impoverished environment. The confrontation
with his expectations has instead brought the narrator back to himself
in that environment, just as the confrontation with Pelegrin did in the
case of the Rittmeister and his wife. In both cases, the power of
longing is demonstrated, in Santa Cruz in respect of an unrealisable
past, and in Bin in respect of an unrealised future. 'Hawai' and 'Peking'
are arbitrary designations [15] of mental and emotional states to which
the individual must pay proper heed. This implies the synthesis which
figures in the paradoxical outcome of both works: in Santa Cruz, by
remaining, Elvira and the Rittmeister go forth; in Bin, by going forth,
the narrator remains.

In Graf Öderland the vision of the ideal life which the unfettered
imagination invents is once more, as in Santa Cruz, represented by a
ship roaming the high seas at will. In the third scene of the play,
entitled 'Der Staatsanwalt greift zu seiner Axt', which is intended to
convey his rupture with bürgerlich life, the Staatsanwalt describes
this ship, of which he was captain, to Inge, who is to be his female
companion on the journey to Santorin:

> Mein Schiff hatte drei Maste, der Bug hatte einen Schnabel,
> den ich heute noch zeichnen könnte, wie ein Adler. Wir
> fuhren nach allen Küsten der Welt. Kreuz und quer. Ohne
> Ziel und Zeit. (III 27)

Yet the promise contained in the name of the ship, 'Esperanza' (III 32),
has never materialised. The vibrant abundance of the imagination has
given way to the reality of an ornamental ship in the Staatsanwalt's
study. He feels that the ornamental ship represents the extent to which
his public life has diminished him as a man. It is because he has been
so exemplary in the discharge of his public duties that he has felt the

need to disappear. Mario, the clairvoyant engaged to help in the
search for him, describes how the Staatsanwalt's life appeared to
society as 'Arbeit und Pflichterfüllung' (III 31). The play calls in
question the social approval implicit in Mario's words. In the section
of Tagebuch 1946-1949 immediately preceding the sketch 'Der Graf von
Öderland', the first draft of the play, Frisch draws attention to the
dangers of elevating all work, however trivial, to the level of a moral
imperative (II 406). Even the clairvoyant is so imbued with the social
value of 'Arbeit als Tugend' (II 406) that he cannot see beyond the
facade of the Staatsanwalt's public life. When the Staatsanwalt admits
his inner reality to his wife, it becomes clear that it is his awareness
of this inner state which has created the bond between himself and the
bank clerk who has committed the motiveless murder [16]. It is ironic
that the bond should be symbolised by the axe which they both wield.

The axe is an indication of the extent to which the nature of
society in Graf Öderland prevents the individual from reconciling
reality and imagination. An accommodation was reached with this
experiential problem in Santa Cruz because the social dimension there
was sufficiently nebulous not to interfere with the progress towards
such an accommodation. If the lyrical note of the earlier play is
absent from the harsh atmosphere of Graf Öderland, this is attributable
to the more clearly defined social background of the later play. The
Staatsanwalt describes to Inge the way in which the fulfilment of his
duties in society fell short of fulfilling him as a man:

> Ich konnte tun, was immer meine Pflicht war, und ich wurde
> es dennoch nie los, das Gefühl, dass ich meine Pflicht
> versäume mit jedem Atemzug, nie. (III 26)

The importance of his social position, so much in contrast to that of
the bank clerk whom he has to prosecute, cannot act as a counterweight
to his dissatisfaction. But the Staatsanwalt is not larger than society
in the sense that what he seeks goes beyond the capacity of society to
provide. By linking his dissatisfaction and protest with that of the
inarticulate clerk, Frisch shows that it is the social structures in
which they live which have failed both men. In the nature of their
protest Frisch perceives that both men point to a deficiency in their
society: its inability to cater for a human dimension beyond that of
time-serving. Frisch comments on his aim in depicting society as he
does in Graf Öderland:

> Es wird von dieser Gesellschaft gesagt, dass sich
> Vitalität darin nur kriminell äussern kann - wir müssen
> also eine Gesellschaft suchen oder immer wieder herstellen, [17]
> in der Vitalität soziabel wird, das ist das Fernziel.

The energy of this 'Vitalität' is irresistible, and if it is not
harnessed, its eruption can only have negative consequences. In despair
because the ship of his dreams has become 'ein Nippzeug' (III 32), the
Staatsanwalt breaks violently with the constrictions of his bürgerlich
life. The nature of his subsequent bondage in the living nightmare of
Santorin is presaged in his visit to the charcoal-burners in the wood.
The contradictions of his own position are highlighted by a member of
this group proclaiming freedom while in thrall to alcohol (III 40).
The 'reality' of the Staatsanwalt's Santorin is anything but that of a
dream come true. Santorin, the symbol of the place where everything
was better because free from all constraint, ironically becomes the
scene of the most oppressive social and political anarchy.

It is significant that the first description in the play of the
island of Santorin comes not from the Staatsanwalt, but from the clairvoyant who is trying to find him. The clairvoyant's information is
specific as to geographical situation and political conditions:

> Zwischen Griechenland und Kreta. Zur Zeit, wie es heisst,
> in den Händen der Rebellen. (III 36)

The specificity of the clairvoyant's description is wholly lacking in
that given by the Staatsanwalt later in the play. He has seen the
island only on photographs, and since he has no direct experience of
the place, the warmth of his description imbues it with a worth which,
by implication, is absent from his present surroundings (III 54).
For the Staatsanwalt, Santorin, the 'locus amoenus seiner Sehnsucht' [18],
is attractive because it offers a contrary vision to his everyday life.
It is this aspect which tempts the Gendarm, another person paid by
society to uphold its fabric and values. The fleeing, and as yet undiscovered Staatsanwalt invites him to crew on the yacht which he is
about to buy for the voyage to Santorin. Once more the fascination of
limitless possibilities takes hold as the Gendarm muses on the offer:

> Wenn man so denkt, was man anfangen könnte mit diesem Leben,
> um die ganze Welt könnte man segeln, und was man hier in
> Wirklichkeit tut. (III 51)

The monotony induced by the social environment encourages such escapist
visions. The political situation in Santorin is referred to a second
time by Dr. Hahn, ostensibly the seller of the yacht which the Staatsanwalt wishes to buy. He too claims to have heard that the island is
occupied by rebels, whom he defines as 'Feinde des Gesetzes, Feinde der
Ordnung' (III 54). In defending the theory of the rebels' revolt,
before he has experienced the reality of the situation which they have
created, the Staatsanwalt voices Frisch's contention that a society in
which vitality can only manifest itself in a criminal fashion is a

society which requires reform. To Hahn the <u>Staatsanwalt</u> suggests that
it is possible that the concepts of law and order have been applied so
constrictively in society that they encourage rebellion. In doing
this, he identifies himself, at this point, with these rebels (III 54).
Yet Santorin proves to be the opposite of what he expected. Inge, his
companion, complains that they are, in the place so praised and longed
for, obliged to live

> in einer Kloake, und sobald einer die Tür aufmacht, stinkt
> es nach Abwasser...Und das nennt sich Santorin! (III 63)

Physical unpleasantness is accompanied by mental anguish, which is
ironically of the kind which the <u>Staatsanwalt</u> experienced in <u>bürgerlich</u>
society, and from which he imagined he would free himself in Santorin.
For he is obliged by the rebels to preside over this anarchy. The
vicious circle which his action of revolt has described is made plain
to him:

> Wer, um frei zu sein, die Macht stürzt, übernimmt das
> Gegenteil der Freiheit, die Macht. (III 89)

He cannot free himself from the nightmare into which he has plunged.
The play closes with his plea that he might wake in order to be
released from the responsibility of what he has done.

Santorin, as a place where wishes are realised and where dreams
come true, is similar to Hawai and Peking in that it is never reached
as it was imagined. Dreams, as both the <u>Rittmeister</u> and Elvira become
aware, can never fully be realised because the imagination can always
outstrip the possibilities of reality. But the couple can come to
terms with this fact relatively easily because of the almost complete
absence of a definable social situation. For the narrator in <u>Bin</u> the
problem is more acute, in so far as he is obliged to come to terms with
himself against a specifically Swiss background. But, despite the fact
that this background is firmly indicated, it still does no more than
provide the barest framework for the realisation of the private dilemna.
Not until <u>Graf Öderland</u> is society held responsible for not merely failing
to help, but actually preventing, the individual from realising himself.
It is not simply that the <u>Staatsanwalt</u> discovers to his horror that
Santorin is the opposite of what he has expected. What is worse is that
society has forced him to seek Santorin through violence. In the section
of <u>Tagebuch 1946-1949</u> preceding 'Der Graf von Öderland', Frisch
emphasises the way in which the unnatural attitudes of modern society
will attract retribution:

> Das einzig Natürliche an diesem babylonischen Unterfangen,
> das wir Zivilisation nennen: dass es sich immer wieder
> rächt. (II 406)

The action of the _Staatsanwalt_, a member of the social establishment,
in parallel with that of the bank clerk, a lesser cog in the soulless
social machinery, is a manifestation of this retribution. In this way
the play strikes a warning note [19]. But it also underlines the inter-
dependence of the state of society as a whole and the emotional health
of the individual. The individual must make his reconciliation between
the claims of reality and imagination in a social structure. These
goals of the imagination which are never reached - Hawai, Peking,
Santorin - all serve to emphasise, in differing fashion, the indissoluble relationship between individual and society.

Hawai, Peking and Santorin, originally symbols of ideal environments where the heroes could more fully realise their identities than
in their actual surroundings, all contribute in some measure to the
heroes' later true perception of reality. This is not the case with
Peru in _Gantenbein_. Peru is doubly a phantasy, since it occurs within
the framework of that which is already a product of the imagination,
the 'Geschichten' invented by the narrator of the novel under the rubric
'Ich stelle mir vor'. Peru is completely dissociated from the narrator's
circumstances and experience. Observing himself acting out his role of
the man who has met a woman in a bar, the narrator is aware of this:

> Peru, sagt er, sei das Land seiner Hoffnung!...Man
> plaudert also von Peru, das ich nicht kenne. (V 62)

In her flat he deflects the woman from her intention of showing him
'die Strassenkarte von Peru' (V 74), since this would oblige him to
relate Peru to an actual location. It amuses him that she should take
the matter of Peru seriously, yet at the same time the physical reality
of love-making is devalued by the presence of Peru in his consciousness:
'Peru! Das wurde der Name, den er in der Umarmung als einzigen aus-
sprach' (V 75). It is not clear whether he is associating the act of
love with her with the kind of experience he would expect to find in
Peru, or whether he still longs for Peru over and above this act of
love. Peru obtrudes, however, into the fullness of the experience.
Only at one point does the same imagined character, as he lies ill
with terminal cancer, see Peru in its true perspective as a designation
for an awareness of something other than the here and now (V 152).
The mocking overtones with which Peru is generally mentioned in the
novel, however, indicate that it is regarded as something unreal.
Longing appears to have ceased to be something which can be
incorporated positively and actively into life.

There is thus a progression in the relationship between the
characters and the places where they imagine their identities can best

flourish. In <u>Santa Cruz</u> the <u>Rittmeister</u> and his wife achieve an equilibrium between the past and the present, expressed in Pelegrin's words
of defiance, which the <u>Rittmeister</u>, at the close of the play, makes his
own as an indication of acceptance:

> Ich verwünsche nichts, was ich erlebt habe, und nichts, was
> ich erlebt habe, wünsche ich noch einmal zurück. (II 74)

Hawai thus ceases to be external, and is incorporated fully into the
consciousness of the <u>Rittmeister</u>. In <u>Bin</u>, where the social background
is more clearly defined, the action closes with the young architect
returning home from military training. As he makes contact with his
wife and child once more, and as he moves about his flat, he feels
constrained by the restrictions of his surroundings. But there is an
implicit awareness that this is the reality of life, and that Peking,
far from being an attainable goal, is the designation for the process
of life which also contains the longing, the realisation of which
Peking once symbolised for him. At the close of the 'Erzählung', the
narrator takes his recently born child on his knee and relates the
child, and himself, to this process of life (I 658). In <u>Graf Öderland</u>,
because he is almost totally defined by his social function, the
<u>Staatsanwalt</u> feels compelled to re-assert his individuality by
attempting to reach by violence his goal of complete freedom, Santorin.
But instead, he releases the contents of a Pandora's box, and the
freedom which he had imagined and longed for becomes disillusioning
anarchy. He laments the destruction of <u>bürgerlich</u> order. Ruins did
not figure in his vision of freedom (III 85). The balance achieved
in <u>Santa Cruz</u> and <u>Bin</u> is no longer possible. An impasse has been
reached: the constraints of society are so suffocating as to demand
action. But that action, instead of bringing hoped-for release, ends
in the nightmare of Santorin. If <u>Graf Öderland</u> demonstrates the
insolubility of the problem of identity in the environment under
certain circumstances, Peru in <u>Gantenbein</u>, by virtue of the fact that
it is never taken seriously, indicates resignation in the face of what
appears to be the intractability of the problem. Peru is neither a
goal nor a process. Because it is so dissociated from reality, it is
a way of defining a malignant perception of personal insufficiency in
the present. For all the self-mockery with which Peru is treated, the
fact that what it symbolises has not been incorporated into the
consciousness presents a constant danger to the value of the here and
now. It is a danger which is made explicit in the case of the couple
who are symbols of habit. They long, like the <u>Rittmeister</u>, for a
different environment in which the pattern of habit might be broken.

But, unlike the case of the Rittmeister, this longing does not lead to
action, but corrodes the present to the point where the very vessels of
experience, their bodies, are held to be the main obstacle to the
realisation of their longing (V 136). At such a point, where the real
is perceived as countering and nullifying the imaginary, all hope of a
balance between the two has been abandoned. The four place-names,
Hawai, Peking, Santorin and Peru, mark a progression from an initial
inability to come to terms with the environment to an outright rejection
of the possibility of such an accommodation.

Avoidance of the problems of identity in the environment

There are three strands to the problem of identity in the environment: the capacity of 'Sehnsucht' to resist the lessons of experience,
the structure of individual character and, compounding these two, the
nature of contemporary society. In Santa Cruz, within an imprecisely
defined framework, a balance has been reached, possibly because the
third strand of the problem has been ignored. In Bin, the narrator,
on his journey to Peking explains how important it is not to suppress
awareness of this unrealised or unrealisable aspect of the personality,
for to do so creates an imbalance:

> Zu lange haben wir den Traum aus uns verstossen; er lebt
> ohne uns, wir ohne ihn. So sind wir niemals ganz. (I 636)

This dimension of the personality, if it is ignored, creates an ever-
increasing disruption in the flow of life. In a striking image, the
narrator compares this impediment to the amount of snow accumulating
in front of a moving snow-plough (I 640). Unless care is exercised,
there must come a point where the amount of snow prevents forward
movement. The general problem of balancing experience between longing
and reality in such a fashion that the one may complement the other,
is also bound up with the peculiarities of the individual temperament.
The characters whom Frisch portrays at grips with this problem have a
tendency to look too far beyond the limits of the possible. Too
imaginative and self-conscious an awareness of one's limitations causes
events in the environment to be interpreted exclusively in terms of
these limitations. Typical of the attitude of mind of so many Frisch
characters in this respect are Yvonne in Die Schwierigen and Don Juan.
The former, 'deren Urteil so gerne zum Masslosen neigte' (I 418),
searches beyond the horizons of everyday life for her own identity.
The latter pays the price exacted by the absolute demands of his
intellect by boredom at the finite nature of his actual experience.
He suffers from

die Langeweile eines Geistes, der nach dem Unbedingten
dürstet und glaubt erfahren zu haben, dass er es nie
zu finden vermag. (III 173-174)

The fact that they both have situations thrust upon them which involve
the creation of life and which they come to accept, however gracelessly
at first, is an indication that life possesses an inherent stabilising
factor. The third element of difficulty in establishing identity in
the environment is provided by the nature of the contemporary world,
which, by means of the mass media and the general ethos of the consumer
society, creates artificial needs and longings. These longings are not
satisfied by the acquisition of material possessions, nor by the
massive provision of escapist entertainment [20]. It would appear that
Frisch is suggesting, by the behaviour of many of his characters, that
the nature of the modern world is such as to make the problem of
identity scarcely admit of a solution.

A good example of the general nature of the difficulties experienced
in his immediate environment by the Frisch hero is provided by the
episode in Die Schwierigen in which Reinhart takes Hortense sailing on
the Zürichsee (I 484-487) [21]. He has spoken to her so enthusiastically
of sailing that Hortense believes in his skill as a sailor. But it is
clear, as soon as they set out in a hired boat, that Reinhart has very
little idea of what he is about for they collide with the first marking-
buoy. In the midst of these difficulties, Reinhart recalls his other
experience of sailing. This was 'am Meer, damals' (I 485), and the
impression is created from the scenic details that this took place in
Greece, where Reinhart first met Yvonne. But, significantly, the scene
is never specifically identified, and the generalised description could
refer to any coast in the area of the Mediterranean. In Reinhart's
recollection the atmosphere was one devoid of limitations and restrictions. He makes an unfavourable contrast between his recollection and
his present situation: 'Hier merkt man jeden Blödsinn, den du begehst'
(I 486). The whole episode redounds to the discredit of his immediate
environment. Memory has convinced him of his viability as a sailor, and
his poor performance on the Zürichsee does not cause him to revise that
memory. Instead, the present environment is seen as inimical to his
efforts.

The environment and what takes place there is subject only to the
most limited control and direction by the individual. This is a fact
which Frisch characters find increasingly difficult to accept, and
increasingly the environment is regarded, not merely as indifferent,
but as hostile. For Reinhart the petty restrictions of the Zürichsee

ran counter to his memory of himself as a sailor. For the narrator in
Gantenbein, the involvements of social intercourse can be avoided only
by flight from them. He observes Enderlin waiting on a plane in order
to avoid involvement with the woman whom he met in the bar. He has
sympathy with Enderlin: 'Ich verstehe seine Flucht vor der Zukunft'
(V 127). In the section which follows, entitled 'Hütet euch vor Namen!'
(V 127-129), he goes on to describe the manner in which a man and a
woman, when they first come together, talk of people they know in
general terms, without specifically mentioning names. To the extent
that these people are unidentified they have no reality, and so can
offer no resistance to the narrative whims of the couple. Inevitably,
however, names are mentioned. The indeterminate personalities of 'ein
Kollege von mir; eine Tante von mir; ein junges Mädchen' (V 127)
gradually take on a reality. Some are known to the other person, or
the other person knows someone who knows them. The intricate web of
relationships which composes society is built up. The narrator
experiences this process as both limiting and menacing: 'Die Einkrei-
sung ist nicht zu vermeiden' (V 127-128). The only solution is flight:
'Man müsste fliehen. Wohin?' (V 128). But there exists in all the
possible destinations which he mentions for such a flight a person
known directly or indirectly. There appears to be no environment which
has a social tabula rasa which the individual could people to his liking.
To the three difficulties involved in coming to terms with the environment there is therefore added a fourth: the social environment is
experienced by the Frisch character as being by its very nature
constricting. The constituent elements of society impinge so strongly
on his personality that he cannot sustain his attempts to establish
his identity against what he sees as a concerted attempt to define him.
All relationships are therefore sources of dissatisfaction. It is not
so much that society makes relationships difficult which appears to
trouble him, as the necessity of having to create relationships in the
first place. It is because the environment contains a multitude of
human relationships that the Frisch character finds his position in it
unsatisfactory, even untenable, and thus seeks forms of escape. It is
not only physical flight which holds out the promise of relief from
this oppressiveness, however, although this is the most obvious.
Change of social identity, and emotional and mental retreat from
aspects of the environment are two other possibilities envisaged.
All prove futile.

In two of the works already considered, physical flight, or its
prospect, represents an attempt to escape what are held to be the

suffocating constrictions of everyday life. In <u>Santa Cruz</u>, the
<u>Rittmeister</u> packs his bags and writes a farewell letter to his wife,
as he prepares to leave the confines of his snowbound castle. In the
end he does not leave, because he comes to the realisation that what
he is leaving to seek is actually within him. Similarly, the narrator
in <u>Bin</u>, appalled to discover one evening as he sits at his customary
café table that half of his life is over, sets out on what he thinks
is a journey with a specific destination, only to discover that the
journey is life itself and that there is no destination, only the
journey. Thirdly, in <u>Die grosse Wut des Philipp Hotz</u>, Hotz wishes to
leave the conjugal residence to join the Foreign Legion (IV 441). At
the close of the play, he returns home to be re-united with his wife,
claiming that he was not accepted as he was 'zu kurzsichtig' (IV 453).
By implication he was also originally too short-sighted to see the
possibilities within the limitations of his home situation. For all
their differences, these three works, in their treatment of the initial
naive belief in the efficacy of geographical change as a counter to the
apparent constraints placed upon the individual by the environment,
demonstrate that the environment does not play the decisive role
originally imagined.

A second method of attempting to avoid the reality of the environment is to alter the outward social identity of the personality.
Reinhart in <u>Die Schwierigen</u>, after his inconclusive involvement with
Hortense, disappears. In an effort to throw off the bad heritage which
he believes to be dogging him, he re-appears as Anton the gardener.
Some considerable time later, he is recognised by Hortense. Reinhart
tells her that he has sought a new life as Anton because he wished to
cast off the failures of his old life. As she listens to him
masochistically creating a philosophical structure which his failures
justify, Hortense becomes depressed by his theories which for her
constitute an avoidance of life (I 592). If Reinhart seeks to be
unobtrusive with his attempted change of social identity, Stiller is
more dramatic, not so much in his assumption of a new identity, as in
his denial of his old, in his attempt to avoid the complexities of his
own past involvement with the Swiss environment. Yet to do this he is
obliged to run counter to the recollections and relationships of all
those who constituted that involvement, and thus his undertaking is
doomed to failure from the outset. Instinctively, he is aware of this
and conveys this awareness in one of his 'Geschichten'. He attends a
Negro church service in the United States, and with sadness observes

114.

the women's cosmetic attempts to appear whiter than they are:

> Ich...sah nur eine eigene Not einmal von aussen, sah die
> Absurdität unserer Sehnsucht, anders sein zu wollen, als
> man ist! (III 542)

The most radical attempt to cast off social identity is depicted in the
case of Ehrismann in Zürich-Transit. He seizes the opportunity to
allow his identity to be formally buried. Freed thus of all ties which
the environment had formerly placed on him, he imagines that he can
create a new identity. Instead, he finds that these very ties were
his identity. The belief in a new identity proves to be as naive as
the belief in a new environment, for the ties of the old identity,
although they may be modified, can never be totally denied in the
manner which the belief in a new identity presupposes. Reinhart
commits suicide, Stiller leads a pointless and lonely existence in
Glion, and Ehrismann simply disappears. The fates of the three men
point to the dangers of attempting to sever these ties.

A third method of attempting to avoid responsibility in the environment consists in devising a stratagem which enables the individual to
escape into a partial interpretation of the world. In this imagined
world, the pressures of the real world, which the individual feels to
be inhibiting the establishment of his identity, are no longer present.
Yet this imagined world is fragile, constantly threatened by the real
world and ultimately destroyed by it. The first example of such a
world is created by Agnes, the heroine of Als der Krieg zu Ende war.
Hemmed in by the squalor of her life in a cellar in the ruins of Berlin
during the Russian occupation of 1945, and further burdened by the
knowledge that her husband has been a member of the 'Waffen SS', she
seeks refuge from the reality of her environment in her relationship
with a Russian officer who has requisitioned the premises above the
cellar. Since she does not understand Russian, and he does not speak
German, it is clear that the relationship, apart from its physical
aspect, exists largely in her own mind. It consists of her interpretation of what she understands to be happening [22]. Agnes creates a
false identity which is destroyed when her husband appears and his true
identity is revealed to the Russian. If Agnes seeks a world of
imagined emotions, it is precisely the entanglements of emotion which
Don Juan wishes to relinquish for the certainties of the intellectual
exercise of geometry: 'Mir graust vor dem Sumpf unserer Stimmungen'
(III 131). In this admission to his friend Roderigo, he equates himself
with the bawd Celestina, for whom emotions merely represent disruption
to the smooth and business-like functioning of her brothel. In geometry

Don Juan seeks release from the involvements and the loose ends of life [23]. His final acceptance of life is not of his own choosing. Life itself, in the pregnancy of Miranda, coerces him, and his acceptance of responsibility towards the new life constitutes 'seine erste Bewegung zur Reife' (III 171). It is also life which compels Walter Faber to re-examine his attitude, not by bringing him to an awareness of the continuity of life as in the case of Don Juan, but by mercilessly providing him with incontrovertible evidence of his own approaching and inevitable end. Faber, meaninglessly journeying the earth so that his environment at any given moment has scarcely any concrete reality for him, clings to the explicability of technology when faced with the apparent absurdity of his own existence. Since, in his life, there is no fixed environment at which he can cavil and from which he can flee, he seeks to establish himself in technology, only to be dislodged from this refuge by the forces of life which he has wilfully ignored, and against which his partial interpretation of life does not protect him. In the apparent solidity of his bürgerlich environment, Gottlieb Biedermann has also imagined that he is protected, above all by his social position, but scarcely less by his reputation for 'Gutmütigkeit'. This latter quality enables him to gloss over aspects of his environment which are unpleasant, or which do not accord with his interpretation of that environment. But 'Gutmütigkeit' does not protect him against the determined onslaught mounted on his security by the two intruders. In a final ironic insult he is asked to provide the matches for the explosion which will destroy him.

The imagined role of the narrator of Gantenbein as a blind man is in a sense the last resort of the personality which has attempted all other devices to avoid contact with the environment. The vision of a distant and ideal environment has proved to be a chimera, the attempted assumption of a new social identity leads not to a re-definition of the personality, but to an increased alienation from society, and attempts to escape the environment by taking refuge in carefully constructed interpretations of it have been doomed to one kind of failure or another. Thus the only remaining solution is to continue in the environment, but to assume a role which frees the individual from the normal responsibilities attached to being in an environment. Gantenbein, with his dark glasses, is still able to see his environment, but is absolved from having to adapt his behaviour to the conclusions to which his sight leads him, since society accepts that he is blind. Gantenbein is the abnegation of all responsibility towards the self in

116.

the environment. He has gone as far as it is possible to go in depriving
himself of a social function without actual incarceration or confinement
to permanent care [24]. His aspirations shrink so that he is flattered
by guests admiring his ability to carry out simple tasks such as pouring
wine. Ultimately, his lack of social definition becomes emotionally
untenable. Yet when he imagines the scenes which would ensue if he told
his wife Lila the truth, they are so painful to contemplate that he is
obliged to resign himself permanently to the role which he has chosen.
Once more, the attempt to avoid the consequences of being in an environment creates a prison of the individual's own making which causes more
anguish than the original problem.

Change of environment and the consequences for identity: Stiller

It is rare for the Frisch hero to seek out an actual geographical
location in an attempt more fully to realise himself there. The
essentially passive nature of most of the heroes confines their dissatisfaction to the realm of the imagination, and an actual break with
the given environment in a decisive attempt to dispel this dissatisfaction
is not contemplated. Even Walter Faber's important experience on the
island of Cuba, which illuminates briefly and fitfully for him the real
possibilities of life, is not the result of any determination on his
part to come to terms with himself and the course of his life. Faber,
for whom external reality has resolved itself into a monotonous and
indistinguishable succession of airports and aeroplane flights, arrives
in Cuba through an accident of airline schedules. After his second
visit to Palenque in South America, he wishes, as he returns to Europe,
to avoid at all costs going via New York, which has become for him a
symbol of his lack of contact with life [25]. He is therefore obliged
to fly KLM, the airline which provides a routing avoiding New York
(IV 172). In Cuba he is jolted briefly by his impression of the
environment out of his numbed and unresponsive toleration of what goes
on around him into a more positive and meaningful participation in life,
but it is chance, and not design, which leads him to the island.
Frisch argues that change can be regenerative in that it breaks with
the detrimental effects of habit and routine [26]. Because it is in this
sense positive, he does not wish to call a change of environment,
motivated by the clear intention to break with habit, an escape, since
this would be a negative designation. He goes on to cite the example
of the Indian tribes of South America, for whom it was a religious duty
to move periodically to a new settlement, after ritually destroying

everything in the old. Frisch cannot regard this as flight. But for
Faber the process of decay has gone too far to be arrested. The experience which he undergoes by chance in Cuba can have no permanent effect.
It is only in the novel Stiller that Frisch sets out seriously to
explore the regenerative possibilities of wittingly transferring, even
for a brief period, to a new environment. The United States, Mexico,
and the Italian city of Genoa provide the locations against which
different attempts to solve the problems of identity are examined.

Stiller, beset in Switzerland by what he holds to be constant
reminders of his failures in life, stows away aboard an Italian ship
bound for the United States (III 683). He leaves his home city of
Zürich for the much wider and less clearly defined spaces of the New
World. This slackening of definition in the new environment is
reflected in Stiller's selective and impressionistic cameos of his
life there which do not permit an exact chronology of the years spent
in America to be established [27]. America forms the background to the
story of his symbolic struggle with himself in the Carlsbad caves in
New Mexico (III 507-521), to his period of residence in Oakland
(III 413-415, 536-544), where he makes an attempt at suicide (III
725-727), and to the time which he spends in New York (III 526-532).
Thus, although Stiller is not a novel about America, America appears
as 'a significant element in a psychological emotional crisis' [28].
America assumes an even wider role in the novel, however, since, as a
counterpoint to Stiller's unresolved struggles with himself, Sibylle,
at the height of the crisis in her marriage to Rolf, leaves with her
son Hannes for the United States. Furthermore, it is in New York that
Rolf visits her to resolve this crisis by suggesting a new commitment
to one another. The United States, by linking three of the main
characters, thus offers a location in which contrasting responses to
the demands of identity can be set and compared.

The symbol of the fact that Stiller has merely transferred his
existential dissatisfaction to the United States, and not disposed of
it en route, is provided by the cat Little Grey. Stiller takes a small
house in Oakland for which, instead of rent, the absent owner requires
his cat to be fed. His lack of money has obliged Stiller to accept the
arrangement, despite his aversion to cats. Almost immediately, however,
he has difficulty in coping with the animal and its feeding habits, and
as he recollects this period of his life later in 'Untersuchungshaft'
in Switzerland, he concludes that the cat was 'der erste Vorbote'
(III 413) that all was not going to go well in America. His failure

with the cat expresses itself in physical maltreatment of the animal,
and Stiller admits: 'Ich wurde mit diesem Tier nicht fertig' (III 414).
Florence, the mulatto girl who is his neighbour, is aware of 'meine
inneren Kämpfe mit dieser schwarzen Katze' (III 537). Stiller is very
much attracted to Florence, although he is deeply conscious that she
would never reciprocate this attraction. Because of her concern for the
cat, however, he is unable to prevent his pleasant memories of Florence
from being impaired by his unpleasant recollections of Little Grey
(III 544). Little Grey also acquires a wider significance. In the
'Siebentes Heft' of the novel, shortly before the juridical confrontation
in his former studio, Stiller reviews what are for him the defeats of
his life in the hope that he can come to a conclusion. One of these
defeats is the episode with Little Grey. Another is his marriage to
Julika. He ends the review by rehearsing to himself what he feels he
ought to say to his wife at the confrontation. The main point which
he wishes to make echoes the language which he used of his relationship
to Little Grey: Julika and he have been unable to surmount their
difficulties with one another: 'Wir sind nicht fertig geworden mit-
einander' (III 689). There is not merely a linguistic similarity in
Stiller's description of his failures with Julika and Little Grey.
The two images of failure come together. Stiller relates how, as he
lay in the City-Hospital of Oakland after his suicide attempt, he was
plagued by recurring dreams of which he now recalls very little. But
he has a clear recollection of the dream which brought the cat and his
wife together (III 726) [29]. The dream, in which the more recent
failure with the cat combines with the long-standing failure with Julika,
symbolises also the failure of the spell in the United States. Stiller,
in so far as he assimilates the elements of his new environment to
reinforce his own image of himself as a failure, has not drawn any
regenerative strength from his change of location.

Whereas the United States becomes for Stiller merely a different
backdrop against which to act out the problems which he had imagined
he was leaving behind, the same cannot be said of Sibylle in New York.
She has also left Europe as a result of an acute emotional crisis, but
unlike Stiller, who merely continues in the States his drifting and
indeterminate style of life, crossing the Atlantic presents Sibylle
with an entirely new set of circumstances. In order to support Hannes
and herself she is obliged to work. She is thrown back on her own
capabilities, and hence will stand or fall by her own efforts (III 655).
Since she does not demand anything of her environment, it cannot dis-
appoint her in the way it disappoints Stiller. Stiller waits to see

if the new environment will rid him of his problems, and he has thus a
passive relationship to that environment. Hence Stiller can convey,
apart from a few descriptions of scenery, very little of the reality of
that environment. Sibylle, on the other hand, is able to register the
tone and atmosphere of the foreign society in a way impossible for
Stiller. She notes the absence of any real contact between people,
and records that the American attitude to emotions is much like their
attitude towards cars (III 658-660). Sibylle has thus a relationship
to her environment but at the same time is independent of it. Because
she is not wholly dependent on external circumstances, she is in time
prepared for a reconciliation with her husband Rolf. She can resume
that relationship without the dead weight of the past condemning it to
further failure, as is the case with the resumed relationship between
Stiller and Julika. Sibylle's spell in the United States demonstrates
the regenerative power which a change of environment may have.

If it is not possible to establish with accuracy from his account
a timetable of Stiller's activities in the United States, the relationship in which Stiller stands to Mexico is even more problematical.
Mexico, as far distant as the United States, yet much more exotic than
her northern neighbour, figures in the novel as a theme contrapuntal
to that of Switzerland, but it is at no point made entirely clear whether
Stiller is always describing his own first-hand experience of the country
or whether he is sometimes drawing on a notion of what Mexico might be
like. The latter view is lent weight by the very obvious manner in
which Mexico is contrasted with Switzerland, the burgeoning and un-
restrained natural growth of the one highlighting the careful and pain-
staking husbandry of the other, a contrast drawn by Stiller in his cell
in Zürich (III 380 ff.). Mexico, in the story of the corrupt
machinations of a government minister, becomes once again the antithesis of Switzerland and the very self-conscious rectitude of Dr.
Bohnenblust, Stiller's defence lawyer (III 391). A third time, Mexico
becomes the scene of dramatic action and decisive reaction in the story
of how Stiller coped with the consequences of a volcanic eruption when
he was working on a tobacco plantation there, and provides a stark
contrast to Stiller's introspective and impotent inaction in his cell
in Switzerland (III 398-400). Clearly, there is an element of phantasy
and self-dramatisation in these accounts, which are in this respect
reminiscent of Stiller's other 'Hirngespinste'. Yet there is also an
element of lived experience in his portrayal of Mexico, which strengthens
the supposition that he has learnt about the country 'nicht durch
Graham Greene' (III 535), but from his own observation. Furthermore,

Mexico can also provide meaningful pointers to Stiller's own situation. In this connection, the last mention of Mexico in the novel is of particular significance. Stiller, at the behest of the authorities, who are hoping in this way finally to establish his identity, has just paid a visit to the dentist. Afterwards he registers his annoyance that he has allowed himself to be addressed by the dentist's receptionist as 'Herr Stiller', without correcting her. Yet if he were to correct everyone who addressed him thus, he would face an impossible task, 'eine Sisyphos-Arbeit' (III 666). Without transition he thinks involuntarily – 'Ich weiss nicht unter welchem Zwang' (III 666) – of All Souls Day in Mexico, for which he has the authority of his own observation: 'wie ich ihn auf Janitzio sah' (III 666). For Stiller the abiding impression left on him by the vigil of those remembering the souls of the dead is that of the participants' acceptance of the cycle of life: 'Eine Hingabe an das unerlässliche Stirb und Werde' (III 668). Mexico provides a contrast between this massive acceptance of that which cannot be changed and his own fretful and self-destructive assaults on what Stiller imagines might be changed: his own nature [30]. Mexico is presented as an actual geographical location in which a viable mode of living with the constants of life has been evolved. Yet this mode is accessible to Stiller only as an ideal and not as something realisable.

The flight of Rolf to the Italian port of Genoa at the height of his marital crisis, on the other hand, causes Rolf to realise very clearly that the resolution of this crisis is entirely in his own hands. The flight and its attendant circumstances have similarities and parallels with Stiller's flight to the United States. Stiller stows away 'als blinder Passagier' (III 683) on board ship in Genoa, and it is in Genoa that Rolf, fully aware of his 'Ziellosigkeit' (III 551), finally comes to a halt on the journey which he had begun 'blindlings' (III 551). Stiller vanishes without trace from Zürich, and Rolf leaves 'ohne ein Wort gesagt zu haben' (III 560), departing from the same city 'froh wie ein Flüchtling' (III 551) and in the hope that this dramatic action will by itself resolve his dilemna. But his consuming jealousy that his wife has been having an affair does not desert him in his new surroundings. On the contrary, he discovers that this emotion, temporarily forgotten during the excitement of the train journey to Genoa, returns with sufficient force to transcend the reality of the Italian environment (III 556). For Stiller the link to his past and his unresolved problems was provided in America by the cat Little Grey.

In Genoa this link is provided for Rolf by the packet of 'fleischfarbener Kleiderstoff' which he is tricked into purchasing, and which
constitutes 'sein einziges Gepäck' (III 557) when he checks in at a
hotel. On his arrival in Genoa Rolf had never in his life felt 'so
wehrlos' (III 552). If, on the one hand this feeling is inspired by
self-pity, on the other it is also a true reflection of Rolf's defencelessness against life. The parcel of cloth and Stiller's cat represent
the wearisome consequences, which are in both cases emphasised by the
change of environment, of failure to come to terms with the individual's
problems. Yet the essential difference between the journeys of Rolf
and Stiller may be symbolised by the fact that the city which is the
starting point for Stiller is the point where Rolf's flight from himself
ends. Rolf puts a much smaller distance between himself and the seat
of crisis, but in a sense travels very much farther than Stiller, in
that he is finally able to come to terms with himself and his situation.
Rolf is much less passive than Stiller because he is prepared ultimately
to learn from his experience. Thus the ludicrous nature of the entire
Genoa episode eventually has a value. He describes the entire undertaking as 'die lächerlichste Strapaze seines Lebens, nicht die nutz-
loseste' (III 559). What he finds most taxing about it is the painful
self-knowledge with which it confronts him. In contrast to Stiller's
passivity symbolised by his suicide attempt in the United States, Rolf's
reaction to the Genoa episode contains an angry awareness of the part
which he himself must play in eliminating the problem (III 564-565).
The return to Zürich enables him to begin the long and painful process
of coming to grips with the situation [31]. But the memory of the
situation into which his rejection of self-knowledge had propelled
him prior to his journey is a painful one, as he confides to Stiller
seven years later (III 570). The confidence which flows from having
confronted his problem in a new perspective of self-knowledge enables
him many months later to present Sibylle with clear alternatives about
their future (III 661), and he does this in America, the scene of
Stiller's second failure. The stability of the union, re-established
between Rolf and Sibylle in 1947, is indicated in 1952, the year of
Stiller's arrest, by the birth of a child to Sibylle [32], reported in
the mosaic of the novel immediately after the account of Rolf's Genoa
escapade.

The lesson with which Rolf returns to Zürich enables him eventually
to tackle his problem. This is not the case with Stiller who, like the
Doktor in Andorra (IV 490), returns as a failure for whom home is the
last refuge, and who will there continue as a failure. There is no

clear and coherent account of the motives for Stiller's return to
Switzerland. Nonetheless there can be no suggestion that he has
returned home to find the emotional sustenance of a locality where he
felt at one with himself, nor is there evidence of a conscious desire
on his part to come to terms with an environment which has influenced
him in a formative fashion, but which requires sober re-appraisal
before he can live at ease in it again. The opening scene of the novel
characterises Stiller's relationship to his country. It is in
accordance with his expectations of Switzerland that the uniformed
customs officer asks him not to re-board the train in order that he may
answer questions about his identity. Stiller's lack of inner balance
when confronted with such a request causes him to make the ineffectual
gesture of knocking off the official's cap. For Stiller, Switzerland
represents unwarranted interference and irksome restriction, and his
enforced stay in his cell confirms his expectations on his return home.
Stiller is not like Der Pope in Nun singen sie wieder who, as the tides
of war sweep over his village, explains his refusal to leave: 'Mein Ort
ist hier' (II 115). Stiller is not capable of such a voluntary
commitment. It is ironically during his period of incarceration that
Stiller comes closest to putting down roots into himself. After his
abortive stay in America, Stiller knows that the idea of a different
life is illusory. He no longer has, like his predecessor Reinhart in
Die Schwierigen, a vision of 'die eigentliche Heimatlichkeit der Ferne'
(I 448). His prison notebooks provide evidence of a gradual and painful
coming to terms with himself. The two very searching self-analyses, one
at the end of the 'Fünftes Heft' (III 600-601), and the other in the
course of the 'Siebentes Heft' (III 681-688), offer strong hope that
he is at last laying a foundation for self-acceptance. Yet his behaviour
at the juridical confrontation and his subsequent release dash these
hopes. His friend Rolf visits him and Julika in a place of transit, a
hotel in Territet. Here Rolf notes the 'beziehungsloses Hotelzimmer'
(III 731), in which 'nichts gehörte zu ihnen' (III 732). Even their
more permanent residence, the 'ferme vaudoise', to which Stiller
welcomes Rolf wearing one of Rolf's old suits (III 738), is a monstrous-
ly tasteless conglomeration of the shabby detritus of the age of
imitations, a counterfeit 'Schwyzerhüsli' (III 740). By designating
it as 'das Haus meines Lebens' (III 735) Stiller himself proclaims his
rootlessness. During his second visit there Rolf records of Stiller:
'Er nahm es an, Schweizer zu sein' (III 757). This can only be construed
as unwittingly ironic on the part of Rolf, for, given the tawdriness of
the surroundings, such a commitment can only be an implied criticism of

Switzerland in the modern world, and at the same time be an indication
of the spiritual bankruptcy of Stiller.

Stiller, dissatisfied with the environment in which he has grown
up, sets out for the New World, in the hope of realising himself there
in the wide spaces traditionally so full of promise. But the manner
of his departure runs counter to any positive interpretation of his
action. His disappearance is characterised by furtiveness and not by
the resolve to assert himself in a fresh set of circumstances. The
irony of his seven-year absence lies in the fact that he returns to
the status quo ante, for he does not possess the inner substance to
return to Switzerland having accumulated abroad the emotional and moral
capital which his mercenary Swiss forefathers did in terms of money.
Stiller is a failed mercenary, whose inability actively to re-integrate
himself with his country once more is evidence of his introspective
pre-occupation with his own problems [33]. The move to another environment is thus doomed to failure. In so far as Stiller imagines that he
can establish his identity in another environment, in so far as he, in
the confines of his Swiss prison cell, conjures up a vision of fulfilment in Mexico, he is creating a disjunction between reality and
imagination. That such an attitude is impoverished and negative, not
merely in terms of individual lives, but in terms of the much wider
political framework of society, Frisch has already shown in Nun singen
sie wieder. Those aspects of bürgerlich culture which divorce themselves
from reality permit the advent of a destructive and brutal political
reality. The Oberlehrer, who has taught the young Fascist officer
Herbert, is representative of such a divorce, and this is his political
and moral guilt. Thus the paradox arises that the intellectual, in
creating another world for himself in his imagination, permits reality
to assume forms from which flight into the refuge of his imagined world
becomes increasingly necessary.

An important feature of this imagined world is the creation of an
ideal environment, different in every way from the actual environment,
but chiefly in that the individual is freed from the constraints which
so irk and deny him in the latter. The figures of Pelegrin, the narrator
in Bin, the Staatsanwalt in Graf Öderland, and Stiller all have in common
their move towards another life in another environment [34]. The
circumstances of their quest, however, oblige all of them to recognise
that the search for an imagined environment, the 'other life', does not
offer a solution to the problem of identity. They have confused this

'other' life with 'real' life [35]. But of the four figures, only the
narrator in <u>Bin</u> accepts this truth. For most of Frisch's characters,
and certainly for all the later ones, this acceptance proves too
demanding of them, and they seek escape in the boundless realms of
posibility and speculation.

Yet if the environment, in that it cannot transform individual
lives, occupies a much less important role than Frisch's characters
expect, it might be hoped that the environment could offer some measure
of support, however small, to the individual in his search for himself.
The environment of the modern world, as depicted by Frisch, offers no
such support. It is Reinhart in <u>Die Schwierigen</u> who gives fullest
expression to this lack of fruitful relationship between the individual
and the environment (I 578-579). Reinhart has abandoned his attempts
to be a painter, and has taken lodgings in a working-class area. Here
he realises for the first time the full extent of the emptiness in
society. Society is dominated by a senseless pre-occupation with the
trappings of status. The activity which nonetheless takes place in this
atmosphere devoid of encouragement and support, Reinhart likens, in a
telling image, to the dissipation of energy of a bee trapped between
two panes of glass. Frisch himself attributes complicity in Reinhart's
downfall and suicide to this impoverishment of the environment. Reinhart
is wrong to accept his failure exclusively 'als <u>sein</u> Ungenügen und nicht
als das Ungenügen der Gesellschaft' [36]. Devoid of resonance for
individual needs, the environment in the modern world tends to stifle
growth, rather than to promote it. In this situation, the earthquake
becomes the symbol of the repression of natural forces. <u>Der Fremdling</u>
in <u>Rip van Winkle</u> describes his exultation at having witnessed this
natural manifestation: the eruption restores a lost perspective to
life (III 819). The <u>Staatsanwalt</u>'s rejection of his former life in
<u>Graf Öderland</u>, the bank clerk's murder of the janitor, and Stiller's
flight to America are all forms of failure not wholly caused by the
characters' inadequacies in coming to terms with themselves in the
environment. The modern world itself offers a poor framework for
human existence.

The outward orderliness of Switzerland is a particularly suitable
setting for showing the extent to which the modern world fails the
individual in his quest for himself. The realities of life are obscured
by attention to this superficial orderliness. The indifference of such
an environment to the deeper needs of the individual is bound to turn
the individual in upon himself. The environment does not offer an

opportunity for fulfilment in society. The individual seeks solace in
his imagination since his surroundings cannot cater for 'das letzte
menschliche Heimweh, verstanden zu werden' (I 595). Stiller, self-
critical and with an inferiority complex which his continuing failures
in terms of bürgerlich success can only increase, seeks a fresh and
less constricted environment, only to discover that the nature of his
personal problems does not change with the environment, and he returns
home as much a failure as he had left. Despite all his perceptive
insights into his own situation, he is unable to act, and is thus
responsible for this failure. Yet all that the environment can offer
him are the meretricious trappings of modern life. The fact that he
identifies the counterfeit 'Schwyzerhüsli' as the 'Haus meines Lebens'
is an indictment, not only of Stiller, but also of his environment.
Stiller, the most rounded and successfully realised of the Frisch
characters who seek their identity in the environment, also has the
most specifically depicted environment for his quest. His failure is
symbolic. The modern environment, as represented by the Swiss background to the novel Stiller, is, with its reproducable monotony, ceasing
to offer support to the attainment of identity.

The relationship between the main characters in Frisch's work and
the environment in which they find themselves is complex. It is a
relationship which always reflects the difficulties experienced by the
individual in coming to terms with himself. In some of the early works
a reconciliation with the estranged environment is part of the
accommodation which the individual reaches with these difficulties.
This reconciliation springs in large measure from the realisation that
the environment, far from playing a decisive role which could transform
existential dissatisfaction into fulfilment, does little more than
provide a framework for living. In the middle and later works, however,
dissatisfaction with the immediate environment indicates a failure to
attribute the difficulties and frustrations experienced by the
personality to anything other than the restrictions of that environment.
Ironically, the environment of the modern world is in these works shown
to be in many respects inimical to the individual. The belief, bordering
on the delusion, that the role of the environment is paramount in life,
accumulates real and imagined evidence about the pernicious effect on
the individual of the immediate environment, and this in turn creates
impossible expectations about the changes which transfer to an imagined
environment might cause. The relationship with the environment thus
becomes the symbol in the later works of a lack of balance in the

126.

personality, and it is in this sense that the defective relationship
with the environment indicates a failure to establish identity in
the modern world.

3.   Identity and its Limitations

Identity, in the eyes of the Frisch hero, is subject to ceaseless
external assault, and the nature of this hero's mind is such that he
finds it difficult, if not impossible, to envisage any form of accommodation with the forces against which he sees himself pitted. On the
one hand, the relentless passage of time denies him the possibility of
establishing a foothold, however temporary, from which he might review
the situation more calmly in the hope of thus devising a permanent
strategy. As a consequence, he resorts to devices which, far from
creating the illusion that time and its problems do not exist, ironically
render him even more painfully aware of the omnipotence of time. On the
other hand, his attempts to avoid confrontation by flight to other
environments, real or imagined, are futile, because these other environments produce, in their different ways, the same conditions of battle
from which he seeks to flee. The environment is as hostile as the
element of time.

The Frisch hero is thus aware of the problems which beset him.
Indeed, because of what he interprets as undeserved checks and reverses
in his attempts to solve these problems, he is exaggeratedly aware of
their difficulty. This exaggerated awareness is itself an obstacle,
for it provides a picture of difficulty so clear and total that it can
be countered only by an equally clear and total picture of solution.
Since such a solution is, in the nature of things, an impossibility, it
is replaced by an illusory solution, the salient feature of which is
its totality. When Don Juan's friend Don Roderigo expresses surprise
that Don Juan, in the midst of his personal and dynastic involvements,
should long to plunge into the study of geometry, Don Juan explains
that its fascination for him lies in its unassailable exactness, the
quality most lacking in human affairs (III 131-132). Don Juan
consciously rejects the concept of balance which adjustment to the
possibilities of life presupposes in favour of the concepts of constancy
and immutability which geometry offers him. But the quality of
immutability, so much admired by Don Juan, must be at odds with the
flexible response which life demands. By taking refuge in a science
created by man but not subject to the organic laws governing man,
Don Juan, like Walter Faber, ironically renders himself more vulnerable
to the unpredictable functioning of these laws: he becomes, contrary
to his intentions, a father. While he is exhorting Roderigo, however,
he is as yet unaware of the treacherous nature of his intellectual

refuge. Instead, he sees it as a bulwark against the magnitude of the
dangers which he must confront if he tries to establish his identity in
the flux of reality, for he knows that such attempts are not conducive
to the untroubled living of life (III 133). He is aware of, and seeks
to avoid, the eternally difficult relationship between the unreflective
and the reflective sides of life. In this Don Juan is representative
of the Frisch hero. The propensity of the Frisch hero to reflection
has led him to an awareness of complexity and difficulty in life, but
he lacks the moral energy to persevere with attempts to establish himself within that framework of complexity and difficulty. Partial
solutions involving balance are rejected in favour of total solutions
involving absolutes, such as geometry and technology. Yet, by ascribing
totality to these latter aspects of human activity, he renders these
solutions themselves debilitatingly partial. In denying the nature of
the world, the Frisch hero denies himself.

Identity and language

One major difficulty in the establishment of identity is the
problem of language. The search for identity reveals that language,
far from being a means of communication capable of conveying nuance
and subtlety, is instead a medium which, by virtue of its own laws,
imposes form and structure on the speaker and writer which at times
appear only marginally less intractable than the reality which language
purports to express. Language presents four main areas of difficulty.

1. The first problem stems from the awareness of the individual that
the expression of his essential individuality transcends the limits of
language. In the deepest sense, the individual is incapable of
expressing himself. Stiller, instructed at the beginning of his spell
of 'Untersuchungshaft' by Dr. Bohnenblust to write down 'nichts als die
schlichte Wahrheit', later raises the question of language with his
defence lawyer, and argues that language does not possess the capacity
for totally expressing reality (III 417-418). Stiller, obliged by
physical restriction to concentrate seriously for the first time on
the nature of human existence, can at this point perceive only the
crippling inadequacy of language. He continues to commit the past and
present events of his life to paper in the 'Hefte', however, and to
intersperse these records and reports with reflections on his identity
and on how this identity relates to the observable exterior of his life.
The juxtaposition of a verbalisation of the events of his life with his
reflections on this verbalisation renders gradually less diffuse the

personality of Stiller. While the authorities, during Stiller's
'Untersuchungshaft', examine the case against Stiller, the writer of
the 'Hefte', ironically aided by the man officially in charge of the
case against him, examines the case for the writer. This results in
the gradual coming together in the consciousness of the writer of the
personalities of James Larkin White and Anatol Ludwig Stiller. This
process has not gained sufficient momentum, however, to withstand the
dissipating effects of the physical freedom accorded to the writer at
the close of the official investigation. But the important point is
that this move towards integration is achieved through language.
Language does not, and cannot, reproduce the reality of Stiller, which
is inexpressible, but language can define the area around that which
is inexpressible and so impart a contour to the inexpressible. This is
the position which Stiller feels that he has attained in the 'Siebentes
Heft', the last one written by him. He has asked about the possibility
of these pages being read, and comes to the conclusion that it does not
matter whether anyone, even himself, reads them again, for they have
achieved their end:

> Schreiben ist nicht Kommunikation mit Lesern, auch nicht
> Kommunikation mit sich selbst, sondern Kommunikation mit
> dem Unaussprechlichen. Je genauer man sich auszusprechen
> vermöchte, um so reiner erschiene das Unaussprechliche, das
> heisst die Wirklichkeit, die den Schreiber bedrängt und
> bewegt. (III 677)

Thus the paradox arises that language, despite its shortcomings, helps
towards the establishment of identity:

> Wer schweigt, ist nicht stumm. Wer schweigt hat nicht
> einmal eine Ahnung, wer er nicht ist. (III 677)

But Stiller's personal decline into apathy results from the fact that
his insight never generates a mode of behaviour consistent with its
own truth.

2 The second difficulty with regard to language arises from the fact
that language misleads the speaker or writer into thinking that what
he says or writes is capable only of the interpretation which he is
imparting to his words. Since this is not the case, his expression
tends to become divorced from his intentions and to pursue its own life.
The fact that language is never final in the sense that it conveys
exactly the meaning desired, but instead merely offers a basis for a
variety of interpretations, first strikes Frisch at the rehearsals of
his plays. Here he discovers that his written text is capable of
interpretation by the actors in ways quite unsuspected by him (IV 562).
For Stiller, this aspect of language represents a barrier to his
attempt at communication. Language lends itself to such a variety of

interpretations that Stiller despairs at its duplicity. Because he
feels himself no longer to be the former Stiller, he has travelled the
world on his counterfeit American passport. But it does not represent
his true reality either, and as a measure of his attempt to find himself
he has admitted the counterfeit to his defence lawyer. It emerges in
the 'Drittes Heft', however, that the defence lawyer has not believed
him, since Bohnenblust now triumphantly proclaims that he has discovered
that the passport is false (III 525). He has interpreted Stiller's
confession in his own fashion. Thus language is by its nature ambiguous.
The extent to which language is an attempt to represent reality or to
misrepresent reality, the extent to which a statement is, or is not,
truthful, is a matter to be decided not by the speaker or writer, but
by his listener or reader.

Instead of acting as an intermediary between reality and interpretation of reality, language itself becomes a surrogate reality. The
spoken word acquires a status which usurps the actuality which it seeks
to represent. Sibylle, bitterly hurt that Stiller had gone to Paris
without her and that her marriage to Rolf seems to be beyond repair,
has tried to revenge herself on life by sleeping with two different
men on consecutive nights. On Stiller's return, she is on the verge
of confessing to him when she is interrupted by the landlady of the inn
where they are sitting. This prompts Sibylle to reflect on the way in
which her words would have lent importance to her essentially unimportant
behaviour (III 651). In this sense there is a final, irrevocable
aspect to language. Once launched into the realms of human intercourse,
its power to motivate behaviour cannot be undone. This is the sombre
realisation made by the narrator of <u>Gantenbein</u>, as he imagines what
would ensue if he were to tell Lila that he is not really blind. The
desolate irretrievability of the situation which he has created by
announcing that he is blind and by adapting his behaviour in the light
of that announcement is symbolised by the words 'Gesagt ist gesagt'
(V 166). The fact that language not only acquires an existence of its
own, but an existence which can be inimical to those who use language
is symbolised for Stiller in his experience in the Carlsbad caves in
New Mexico. The caves, and Stiller's struggles with a man who has the
same name as himself, depict the difficulties which he has encountered,
and is still encountering, in his attempt to come to terms with himself.
The grotesque and petrified shapes of the stalactites and stalacmites
are, as he tries to describe them, reminiscent of the distortions lying
in the unconscious: 'Alles ist hier versammelt wie in einem unter-
irdischen Arsenal der Metaphern (III 514-515) [1]. The distortions are

created by language, and the unconscious thus becomes a storehouse of images which can also destroy when they emerge as written and spoken language. Language, as it offers itself for interpretation when the individual seeks to communicate with others, does not remain neutral, but appears to participate in this interpretative process in malevolent fashion.

The nature of life is such as to cause proximity to and contact with other human beings. This contact gives rise to the third problem connected with the use of language in establishing identity in society. For this contact stimulates the inborn wish to communicate through language. The more intimate and close the contact, the more forceful is this desire, although paradoxically it is precisely in such close relationships that what the individual most wishes to express is least capable of expression. Thus for Frisch a depiction of the difficulties caused by language in relationships between men and women indicates the general difficulty especially well. A passage in his first novel Jürg Reinhart contains the données of this particular problem. On the ship which is taking him away temporarily from various emotional involvements, Jürg considers the extent to which experience can be distorted by the compulsion, inspired by the presence of others, to formulate it into words. For this reason he tends to avoid company 'weil das Sprechen so viel durchschneidet, was zwischen zwei Seelen lebt' (I 353-354), and he concludes that human sympathy is best conveyed by lack of language: 'Freund sein kann man nur, indem man zusammen schweigt' (I 354). The manner in which Jürg presents the problem and the nature of his solution are to hold good for the next forty years in Frisch's work. Jürg's depiction of the matter alters in subsequent works only to the extent that it becomes darker, more complex, and less amenable to the solution which he envisages.

If language in one sense represents the means to break out from the loneliness of individuation, the relationship with a member of the opposite sex might represent a similar kind of undertaking. The most socially permanent form of this relationship, marriage, could be viewed as a form of insurance against this loneliness. A passage in Die Schwierigen warns explicitly against such an assumption (I 551). Marriage presents itself as being feasible under the strict condition that the impossible is not expected of it. It cannot be used as a method of breaching the impenetrable. The belief in the efficacy of language in establishing links is here especially illusory and dangerous since it is in marriage that the temptation is greatest to believe that

132.

language is in this sense creative. That it can be destructive in such
a situation is demonstrated by the resumed relationship between Stiller
and Julika. Stiller, released from 'Untersuchungshaft', appears to
have abandoned any idea which he might have had of modifying his
behaviour in the light of the insights which he acquired during the
composition of the 'Hefte'. Re-united with Julika, he has resumed his
self-justifying speeches. His awareness of the limits of language
appears to have vanished. Rolf, on his first visit to the 'ferme
vaudoise', observes the obvious loneliness of Julika:

> Ich glaube, nie einen einsameren Menschen gesehen zu
> haben als diese Frau. Zwischen ihrer Not und der Welt
> schien eine Wand zu sein, undurchdringlich, nicht Haltung
> allein, eher etwas wie eine Gewissheit, nicht gehört zu
> werden, eine alte und hoffnungslose, nie wieder zu
> tilgende, ebenso vorwurfsfreie wie unheilbare Erfahrung,
> dass der Partner doch nur sich selbst hört. (III 747)

Paradoxically, the more Stiller sees the gap between them widening,
the more he contributes to its widening by his attempts to bridge it
through language.

The situation between Stiller and Julika, as described by Rolf in
the Nachwort to Stiller, prefigures the many instances in Gantenbein
of the way in which language increases the area of incomprehension
between couples. One example does duty for the others. The narrator
imagines himself and Lila as Philemon and Baucis, the exemplary married
couple of legend. In a tense confrontation between them, which has
been caused by his jealousy, he seeks to restore harmony by confessing
to a peccadillo which he has committed (V 193). But his attempt to
retrieve the situation only worsens it, for language is more deceptive
than silence:

> Geständnisse sind maskenhafter als Schweigen, man kann alles
> sagen, und das Geheimnis schlüpft doch nur hinter unsere
> Worte zurück, Schamlosigkeit ist noch nicht die Wahrheit,
> ganz abgesehen davon, dass man nie alles sagt. (V 193)

A relationship between the individual personality and language becomes
possible if it is accepted that language cannot express that personality.
The stability of the relationship between the couple, on the other hand,
depends on acting on the awareness that language must not be permitted
to depart from the narrow possibilities of communication between the
partners. The narrator adopts the guise of a blind man so that he will
have imposed on him a role which will protect him from making the kind
of involuntary comment on the behaviour of Lila which can only lead to
misunderstanding. He does this consciously in order to prevent his
love for her from being eroded (V 81). He is obliged, in order to act
in consonance with his role, to select from the variety of subjects on

which he might comment in relation to his wife. This selection is
inspired by a desire not to restrict the feeling of freedom of action
which she derives from her assumption that he is blind. The narrator
calls this selecting principle 'Takt', and concludes: 'Vielleicht ist
die Ehe überhaupt nur eine Frage des Takts' (V 105). For Gantenbein,
the role as a blind man is his way of ensuring, as he hopes, that he
respects the individuality of Lila, that he continues to permit her to
act from the complexity and contradictoriness of motives which acquire
coherence only through the continuity of the personality involved. The
variously motivated actions of the individual are not open to explanation
in language. Aware of the inexpressible nature of his own individuality,
Gantenbein assumes his blind role as a device to live with the same
phenomenon in Lila. It might be a dangerous device, in that it is
open to discovery, but he considers that this is a necessary risk for
the sake of their relationship:

> Erst das Geheimnis, das ein Mann und ein Weib voneinander
> hüten, macht sie zum Paar. (V 104)

Protecting the 'Geheimnis' of his role gives Gantenbein, initially at
any rate, a feeling of happiness which he has never known with a
woman (V 104). In another imaginary situation, Ehrismann, the hero
of Zürich-Transit, pictures a reunion with his wife after it has been
established that he was not in fact killed in a car accident. They
resolve to introduce an element of 'Takt' into their future relationship,
and Ehrismann proposes a toast to this resolve:

> Achte das Geheimnis deines Nächsten, auf dass du lange
> lebest mit ihm! (V 432)

It would seem that all human intercourse is dependent for its harmonious
functioning on the severely restricted use of language.

The bringing into alignment of the reality of experience with the
artificiality of language is the fourth problem posed by language. It
is possible to establish a modus vivendi with language on condition
that language is recognised as an artefact. Frisch himself knows, from
his complex relationship to dialect and standard German, of the manner
in which the interplay between the two makes him aware, when he is
writing, of this aspect of language (VI 511). In an important section
of Tagebuch 1946-1949 Frisch relates how he once visited one of the
famous Swiss watch factories (II 703). It was for him a most
distressing experience, but he has been unable since to communicate its
nature [2]. In order to be able to communicate something of his
experience, Frisch must construct in language a communicable
approximation to that experience. Paradoxically, the essence of the

experience is not communicated by attempting to verbalise the material
of the actual experience, but by finding in the artefact of language
linguistic material capable of communicating that essence:

> Jedes Erlebnis bleibt im Grunde unsäglich, solange wir
> hoffen, es ausdrücken zu können mit dem wirklichen Beispiel,
> das uns betroffen hat. Ausdrücken kann mich nur das
> Beispiel, das mir so ferne ist wie dem Zuhörer: nämlich
> das erfundene. (II 703) [3]

Stiller's stories represent his attempt to overcome this problem, but
his listeners, responding for the most part to a register which contains
a superficial relationship between language and reality, do not always
appreciate the resonance of these attempts. Thus, reviewing his
situation at the close of the 'Erstes Heft', Stiller feels that he can
find no form of communication which will convey to others what his
experience of himself is (III 435-436). In the figure of Stiller
Frisch examines the endless problems caused by the urgent need to
communicate, which is in permanent conflict with the limits of
communication. In being obliged to write the seven 'Hefte', Stiller
embarks on a 'saisie du réel par la voie des mots' [4], but he fails
ultimately to establish the necessary compromises in his use of language.

If Stiller is so involved with his problems that he cannot stand
back sufficiently form this involvement to permit dispassionate judgement, Gantenbein wishes to stand so far back that he does not become
involved at all. This constitutes another form of the impossible. For
him, language becomes an end in itself without any relation to reality.
But others act with serious intent on Gantenbein's words, however
frivolously he may have spoken. Thus the figure of Gantenbein is an
extreme formulation of the existential dilemna facing all men in regard
to language. It is also the dilemna of Frisch the author, who wishes
to portray the shortcomings of language in the medium which he wishes
to criticise [5]. The author, writing, is thus re-enacting his own
existential problem in so far as he is exploring the extent to which
he can communicate. His method of doing this is to depict through
narrative situations the difficulty of establishing a relationship to
language.

The search for identity

It is necessary to establish a working hypothesis of identity in
order to function in society. But language and identity are inextricably
entwined. The inherent danger in language is that it arrests any
additions or modifications to such a hypothesis, so that what is
intended as temporary becomes permanent. Frisch maintains that most

people are unaware of the extent to which their identity is a creation
of language. He gives this assertion forceful exemplification by
claiming that language can create identity in such a way as to reproduce
seven different identities from the same set of circumstances [6]. Since
the persons concerned do not regard their interpretations of themselves
as being one possibility amongst others, they adapt the entire reality
of their lives to one interpretation. Frisch goes on to elaborate on
the manner in which a man who has made an image of himself as a 'Pechvogel' is in fact taken over by this image. Not only does he adapt
reality to suit it, he comes to the point where the image becomes a
psychological requirement for him to the extent that, if it were taken
from him, he would require to establish an entirely new relationship to
himself. The example of the 'Pechvogel' acquires narrative form in the
course of the novel Gantenbein (V 51-52). The subject of the story in
the novel is shown as prepared to go to any lengths to preserve his
idea of himself. Preceding the story of the 'Pechvogel' is the anecdote
of Otto the milkman (V 50-51). Otto, widower, teetotaller and exemplary
citizen, one evening, 'aus Gründen, die ihm selbst verschlossen blieben'
(V 50), hurls all the pot-plants from the balcony of his flat, as a
result of which he is removed to an institution. The narrator of the
anecdote offers his own interpretation of it:

> Sein Ich hatte sich verbraucht, das kann's geben, und ein
> anderes fiel ihm nicht ein. (V 51)

Thus Otto and the 'Pechvogel' represent two consequences of the working
hypothesis about the nature of the self going awry: with Otto, the
hypothesis and reality have become so divorced that the link between
the two finally snaps, and with the 'Pechvogel', the link is tenuously
preserved by his intervention in reality.

The inventions about themselves which Otto and the 'Pechvogel'
create are shown to be defective, not because they are inventions –
which they must necessarily be, since they are conditioned by language –
but because neither man is aware of his invention. One of the most
difficult attainments for the individual is to realise that his
invention stands outside himself and is not his actual reality. Shortly
before he relates the anecdotes of Otto and the 'Pechvogel', the
narrator comments on the reason why a 'Geschichte' is accepted as an
invention, whereas the creation of an identity is not:

> Man kann sich selbst nicht sehen, das ist's, Geschichten
> gibt es nur von aussen. (V 49)

If it were possible to lessen personal involvement in the invention of
identity, the individual might be able to live more at ease with his

own behaviour. This thought occurs to the narrator when he goes to
visit the 'Bäckermeister', whose 'Geschichte' the narrator has heard
from his friend Burri (V 111-113). The 'Bäckermeister' has shot his
journeyman, whom he has discovered to be his wife's lover. After the
incident, the 'Bäckermeister' comports himself 'wie jemand, der von
aussen dazu kommt' (V 113) by taking the injured man to hospital and
by then handing himself over to the police. The narrator, intrigued,
goes to the man's shop and sees him there, temporarily released,
'ahnungslos wie ein Gendarm, der solche Taten immer nur von aussen
sieht' (V 113). Yet ultimately the 'Bäckermeister', for all his outward composure, is as unaware as Otto or the 'Pechvogel' of the real
nature of his actions. If the individual could consciously view himself
'von aussen', he would in a sense be adopting the viewpoint of language
itself, and by adopting this viewpoint he would free himself from the
deceptive illusion that the inventions of language are reality. One of
the main aims of the novel is to indicate the disparity between
expression and reality through its own fictions, and in doing this, to
demonstrate the fiction of identity.

The invention of an identity through language involves a process of
selection from the reality of the individual. One of the criteria
governing this selection is the extent to which the available material
lends itself to being shaped, and not distorted, by language. Stiller
is aware of this difficulty. In the 'Siebentes Heft', immediately prior
to the court's sentencing him to be Anatol Ludwig Stiller, he gives an
account of his attempt in Oakland to commit suicide. He closes the
account with the admission that he has never before tried to communicate
to anyone the experiences which he underwent during that period of his
life (III 726), for in shaping the experiences for communication through
language he might impart a meaning to them which they did not have for
him. Thus at this point Stiller appears to accept the disparity between
his inner reality and his outward identity. His ensuing personal
tragedy arises from the fact that he cannot sustain this knowledge, he
cannot withstand the temptation to overburden language and so destroys
any possibility of creating an identity. In addition, Stiller has not
sufficient faith in the strength of his own invention about himself not
to be pre-occupied with the inventions which others have of him. Like
many other Frisch characters, he is haunted by the shape, the 'Bildnis',
which others make of him in their minds. Don Juan is obsessed with the
fact that he shares the fate of other famous men in that there is a
disparity between that part of his personality observable to others and
his inner reality (III 148). One interpretation of Andorra is to view

the entire play as a depiction of this obsession. Since the Frisch
character always feels that the inventions of others in regard to himself are unfavourable, the hostile environment which Andri experiences
in Andorra could be construed as a coming together of all such unfavourable inventions. It is an externalisation of the belief held by
Andri, and by other Frisch characters, that those about them not merely
misunderstand them, but wilfully misunderstand them. Thus Andri is
obliged to pin all his hopes for his own positive identity on his
relationship with Barblin: 'Ich liebe einen einzigen Menschen, und das
ist genug' (IV 499), he says in front of the door behind which Barblin
is being defiled by the Soldat. When he discovers what has taken place,
Andri no longer has an identity, because he has made his identity
conditional on what he believed Barblin to be. In this deprived state,
he says to the Pater: 'Immer muss ich denken, ob's wahr ist, was die
andern von mir sagen' (IV 505). In a sense, it is Andri who permits
the inventions of others to become his reality.

It is of course true that a variety of contact with others is vital
for the stability of the individual identity. At the simplest level,
such contact, however superficial, offers respite from the loneliness
of the self. Having sought the 'Urwaldstille' to be alone, the fisher-
man whom Stiller sees in the distance in the country not far from New
York, is nonetheless ironically drawn to make contact (III 531). A
second function of contact with others is the establishment of self-
esteem. In Biografie, the Registrator points to the dossier which
contains the external facts about Kürmann's life and comments on its
contents: 'Ein Leben, das sich sehen lassen darf' (V 502). If the
individual is aware that his behaviour meets in some way the expectations
of society, this can instil confidence into his social intercourse.
But the main function of contact with others is to enable the individual
to establish his inventions, a process described by Kleist in his essay
'Über die allmähliche Verfertigung der Gedanken beim Reden' [7]. It is
precisely the reciprocity of the process described by Kleist, the
gesture of offering in order to receive and so to enhance, which is
lacking in the relations which the major figures in Frisch's works have
with those about them [8]. They appear to lack the confidence to make
the initial offer. At times it almost seems as if the individual has
abdicated his responsibility in this matter. The introduction to Rip
van Winkle, the precursor of the novel Stiller, announces a hero who
has so abdicated:

> Das ist die Skizze von einem Menschen, der nie gelebt hat:
> weil er von sich selbst forderte, so zu sein, wie die
> andern es von ihm forderten. (III 783)

Even more alarmingly, a passage in <u>Montauk</u> suggests that the individual
might have no means of establishing an identity except through the
inventions of others. The narrator imagines that a meeting and
discussion between those who have been involved with the individual,
or who could in the future be involved with him, would render the
individual powerless to oppose anything against their findings (VI 714-
715) [9]. Contact with others must be taken seriously at all levels, but
the function exclusively to establish the contours of his identity which
the Frisch character by implication accords to others, can never set
such contacts in a true perspective.

The Frisch character finds it difficult to accept that there should
be a balance, a meeting-point in human communication, in the sense
described by Kleist. A prevailing view interprets the malfunctioning
of human relations in Frisch's works exclusively as a result of the
manner in which individuals impose 'Bildnisse' on one another. But it
is possible to interpret the breakdown of human relationships depicted
by Frisch as a consequence of the refusal of the Frisch character to
accept that the assessment of others can contribute in any way except
negatively to the creation of his identity [10]. The obsession of the
Frisch character with the damage others do to him by their assessments
reaches its culmination in the episode with the tape-recorder in
<u>Gantenbein</u> (V 266-271). The narrator contrives in his imagination to
have a tape-recorder register the conversations of his guests when he
is no longer present in the room. He is so pre-occupied with himself
that he finds something abnormal about people who would not seize the
opportunity to talk about him once he is out of earshot. He cannot
believe that others are not concealing their thoughts about him when
he is present, and this is his reason for installing his tape-recorder.
Very soon, however, he begins to appreciate the impossibility of his
undertaking. As he plays back the tapes and does not hear himself
being discussed in the recorded conversations, he concludes that the
speakers are waiting for the tape to run out before they begin to
discuss him. As he erases the tape, he realises not only the futility
of what he is doing, but also that he can only envisage his relations
with others in negative terms:

> Ich lösche die Spule, die mich nur eines gelehrt hat:
> Ich lechze nach Verrat. Ich möchte wissen, dass ich bin.
>
> (V 270)

His essential fear of reality manifests itself in his desire to know
all reality, at least all reality which he thinks pertains to himself.
Because he is fearful of reality, he can only assume that its judgement

of him will be negative. Yet neither the tape-recorder, nor even the film-camera [11], can capture the evanescence of reality. The narrator is obliged to realise that not even modern technology can be harnessed to his absolutist demands on reality. In a postscript to the episode, he considers that his strong feelings of jealousy are an example of his constant readiness to seek betrayal of himself in others. From his description of the reason for his jealousy, there emerges once more his uncompromising attitude, the totality of the claims of which must jeopardise the possibility of a viable relationship between a man and a woman:

> Eifersucht als wirklicher Schmerz darüber, dass ein
> Wesen, das uns ausfüllt, zugleich aussen ist. (V 270)

Jealousy highlights the relationship between the absolutist demands of the narrator and his ceaseless experiments with possibilities. To accept one of the imagined possibilities as a working hypothesis for behaviour, in the clear-sighted knowledge that it is merely a hypothesis, would imply that a compromise has been reached. The episode with the tape-recorder makes the narrator aware of the Sisyphian nature of his task if he continues to deal in possibilities without a framework of purpose. At its conclusion, the narrator, shaken, decides to create such a framework. He resolves: 'Mein Name sei Gantenbein! (Aber endgültig)' (V 271). It seems that a compromise has at last been reached.

The decision to adopt an identity involves a compromise between what the individual wishes to communicate of himself and what he is able to communicate. To this extent identity represents a move towards living in harmony with himself in a social context. Ideally, the invention of an identity provides an interpretation which is both acceptable to the individual and to others. Part of the difficulty for the Frisch hero in finding a public role for himself is his feeling that the one to which he gravitates most naturally, that of the intellectual, is one which in the modern world must lead inevitably to the eclipse of self-esteem. Der Heutige in Die Chinesische Mauer is in this sense representative of all Frisch heroes when, at the end of the 'Vorspiel', which introduces what he promises will be a 'Farce' (II 145), he points to his own ineffectual part:

> Ich spiele darin die Rolle eines Intellektuellen. [12]

Der Heutige expresses the feeling of impotence in his social role which so overwhelms the Frisch hero. As the farce of history, represented by a cast of well-known historical figures, is enacted around him in a way which reminds him that mankind fails to learn from it, Der Heutige recalls the traditional inability of the intellectual to influence

events. In modern times this awareness of inability is reinforced by
the knowledge that mankind has invented annihilating weapons of
destruction [13]. For Frisch the fact that he casts the majority of his
heroes in the role of the intellectual creates a useful artistic device.
Through the spectrum of the concerns of his heroes he is able to examine
the nature of the modern world. The fate of Der Heutige, who is misunderstood by the people, terrorised by the forces of repression, and
then ridiculed, and rendered socially harmless by these same forces
who appoint him court-jester, bleakly depicts the impotence of the
modern intellectual. The re-working of the play Die Chinesische Mauer,
from its first version in 1946, through its second version in 1955,
its unpublished version of 1965 to its Paris version of 1972, spans the
most important years of Frisch's creative life and testifies to his
abiding concern with the subject of the play. Over the same period,
this concern finds varied, more detailed and artistically more fully
realised expression in the figures of his plays and novels who have an
affinity with Der Heutige and with his concern at his lack of social
function [14]. Faced with the opposing forces and the entrenched
ideologies of the modern world, all these figures incorporate to a
greater or lesser degree what Frisch described to his fellow-writers
in his 1958 'Büchnerpreisrede' as

> die geistige Not des einzelnen angesichts solcher Fronten,
> das Gefühl unserer Ohnmacht. (IV 242)

Narrative lends itself to a fuller depiction of such a problematic
state more than drama, and it is in the figures of Frisch's major
novels that the debilitating interaction between awareness of social
helplessness and the inability to express private reality finds its
fullest expression in their search for an acceptable identity. It is
especially in the figures of Stiller and Gantenbein that this interaction is examined most closely. Significantly, it is Stiller, the
most exhaustive compendium of the problems of the modern intellectual [15],
who fails to establish a compromise between himself and society. His
failure to establish an appropriate identity leaves a vacuum within
him, which finds its external correlative in the futile creations of
modern mass-production.

The retreat from identity: Stiller

The manner in which Stiller rejects a compromise between society
and himself which could represent his identity is of considerable
interest and importance. It occurs in the first paragraph of the
'Erstes Heft' of the novel, immediately after Stiller's well-known

denial of himself 'Ich bin nicht Stiller!' (III 361-362). He relates
how, since his committal to prison, he has not ceased to deny that he
is Stiller. He has demanded whisky to sustain himself in continuing to
make this denial, for he is liable otherwise to yield to the influence
of others in the matter of his identity, and so to assume a role not
suited to him. Two points emerge from this opening statement. Firstly,
it is clear that Stiller fears the compromise which it would be
necessary for him to make in order to admit to an identity acceptable
to others. He can conceive of such an identity having use only for
others. Secondly, he is subconsciously aware of the fact that identity
can only be established in collaboration with others. He knows that he
requires the influence of alcohol, the creator <u>par excellence</u> of self-
delusions, to imagine that an identity can be created in any other way.
The demand for whisky thus represents a retreat from an attempt to come
to terms with himself. Stiller's initial statement is also true of his
final situation as depicted by Rolf in the <u>Nachwort</u>. The same elements
are all still present there as at the beginning of the novel: hyper-
sensitivity to contact with others as manifested in the mutually
destructive relationship with Julika and the verbose self-justifications
made to Rolf; self-delusion manifested in his increasing drinking; and
the mesmerised inaction manifested in his toleration of the situation
in Glion. If Stiller has progressed by the time he arrives in Glion,
it is not in the sense that he has moved towards a solution of his
problems, but in the sense that he has, through the accretion of insight
unrelated to activity, rendered his immobility unbearable. The opening
paragraph of the novel is therefore programmatic.

The fervour of Stiller's initial defiance subsides, however, albeit
to yield to a mixture of petulance and self-abasement as he denies all
validity to his past. In seeking to eradicate his previous life he
disrupts the dialectic between the irrevocable past and self-acceptance
in which identity can be established. Yet after denying his past, he
goes on to imagine that the role offered him by others must also be a
form of denial. Hence not all of his stories are attempts to communicate.
Some seek to confuse so that others cannot contribute to his identity.
He wishes to be left alone with what he hopes to be the totality of the
void within him. To accept a compromise involving others would be to
flee this void:

> Wozu mein Geflunker? Nur damit sie mir meine Leere lassen,
> meine Nichtigkeit, meine Wirklichkeit, denn es gibt keine
> Flucht und was sie mir anbieten, ist Flucht, nicht Frei-
> heit, Flucht in eine Rolle. (III 401)

Yet Stiller is himself no stranger to flight or to the imposition of roles on others. His involvement in the Spanish Civil War had been motivated as much by a desire to flee from himself as by political ideals (III 489), and his later disappearance to the United States is motivated wholly by a desire to escape himself. He returns from Spain with the self-attributed role of 'Versager', the 'Auslegung' of his experiences there is 'von Wiederholung abgenutzt' (III 491). Years later, when Sibylle visits his studio for the first time, he forces her, as he re-enacts for her his failure in the war, to adopt the role in which he has cast her in his 'Ich-Theater' [16] (III 617). Stiller cannot, at least at that point, sufficiently detach himself from his own emotions to imagine the feelings of others, yet he is constantly outraged by what he holds to be the unfeeling treatment which he receives from others.

In the 'Fünftes Heft' of the novel Stiller begins to define the extent to which the establishment of identity necessitates distancing himself intellectually, if not emotionally, from the problems which beset him. Basing himself on his awareness that he cannot escape from himself, he wonders how it will be possible for him to bridge the gap between his knowledge of himself and what others imagine they know of him. Aware that his initial defiance in rejecting the assumptions which others made about his identity did not succeed in altering these assumptions, he now envisages a situation in which he would accept this mistaken identity created by others, but would not at the same time confuse his own reality with it:

> Man müsste imstande sein, ohne Trotz durch ihre Verwechslung hindurchzugehen, eine Rolle spielend, ohne dass ich mich selber je damit verwechsle, dazu aber müsste ich einen festen Punkt haben. (III 590)

Even if he lacks 'einen festen Punkt', the moral stamina to maintain a 'Rolle', and this lack is to be his stumbling-block, it is nonetheless true to say that he is at this stage evolving a viable attitude. The self-abasement which followed on the beginnings of self-assessment is giving way to the first stages of self-acceptance. In addition, he is beginning to accept the fact that his social identity must be a compromise between the impression others have of him and what he feels himself to be. Significantly, this statement follows the account in the 'Viertes Heft' of Rolf's journey to Genoa and the episode there with the 'fleischfarbener Stoff', the episode which was instrumental in helping Rolf to come to terms with himself. It is understandable that Stiller should preface his record of Rolf's story by admitting that it 'will mir nicht aus dem Kopf' (III 551), for the parallels to his own story are only too obvious to him. More significantly, the statement precedes Stiller's most dispassionate account so far of how he imagines others see him (III 600-601). His next statement on the matter of identity, in the 'Siebentes Heft', goes even further. He accepts that the concept of 'Rolle', previously rejected as an unwarranted imposition by others, does have a positive value for him. More, he sees that it is possible for him to choose the nature of this 'Rolle', and so he can acquire a shaping influence on the admittedly imperfect nature of his social identity. All these insights have been the product of his confrontation with himself by means of the written word:

> Kann man schreiben, ohne eine Rolle zu spielen? Man will
> sich selbst ein Fremder sein. Nicht in der Rolle, wohl
> aber in der unbewussten Entscheidung, welche Art von
> Rolle ich mir zuschreibe, liegt meine Wirklichkeit. (III 677)

In his awareness that he can mediate between himself and the outside world lies the possibility of moral freedom for Stiller. Rolf, who has become his friend, senses that Stiller is beginning to detach himself from his crippling self-pre-occupation, is beginning to accept the permanent inadequacy of his 'Rolle', and to look beyond himself in order to see himself (III 700). Reinhart, the hero of Die Schwierigen, whose problems are similar to those of Stiller, expresses the same truth which Stiller is beginning to see:

> Jede menschliche Grösse und Reife fängt damit an, dass
> man fähig wird, über sich selbst hinauszudenken, über sich
> selber hinwegzugehen. (I 590-591)

But Reinhart expresses his insight shortly before he commits suicide. It appears that, in Stiller's case, given the manner in which the novel ends, his detachment from himself is conditional on lack of physical freedom. Self-detachment and physical freedom are burdens which together prove too onerous for Stiller.

During the final period of his incarceration, however, Stiller can contain in meaningful tension the paradoxes inherent in identity. He is aware, for example, of the ambiguous, not to say dangerous role played by language in the establishment of identity. He sums up the paradox that language, the medium of communication, also creates awareness of the incommunicable, namely personal reality: 'Wir haben die Sprache, um stumm zu werden' (III 677). It is therefore apparently possible to accept at face value the statement with which Rolf opens the 'Nachwort': that Stiller's 'Verstummen' constitutes 'ein wesentlicher, vielleicht sogar der entscheidende Schritt zu seiner inneren Befreiung' (III 730). Yet the subsequent behaviour of Stiller, his

144.

desperately fanciful letters, characterised by Rolf as a form of 'Fla-
schenpost' (III 735), his telephone calls in the middle of the night
(III 737-738), and his loquaciousness when Rolf visits him, are too
reminiscent of the Stiller portrayed at the start of his own 'Hefte'
for Rolf's statement to be taken at face value [17]. Rolf wishes to see
that Stiller, for whom he appears to have developed a genuine regard,
is making progress. But Stiller is not. Figuratively speaking, the
walls of his prison were able to support Stiller as he gained insight
into himself and into the human condition. This insight is essentially
into the loneliness of individuation which can never be communicated to
another person. It is supremely difficult, however, to maintain silence,
to resist the illusion that it is possible to communicate fully. Perhaps
Stiller sees the situation clearly enough, but does not begin to
comprehend the difficulty of living in it permanently. Gantenbein is
aware of the difficulty of remaining silent, as his envy of the relief
provided by the Catholic ritual of confession makes clear (V 99). The
tension of the paradoxes which Stiller perceived slackens and he
collapses morally, because this tension is not sustained by action.
Frisch shows the moment for action which Stiller lets slip in the
juridical 'Lokaltermin' immediately prior to his release. The awareness
that he could break out of his moral imprisonment comes upon him, and
for an instant he yields to its power: 'Eine Weile lang...lasse ich
mich führen' (III 715). But he resists moving in the direction
indicated, and instead of incorporating his past, 'wie aus einem
albernen Traum erwacht' (III 715), he presently sets about destroying
it in the shape of his figures and bronzes (III 721 f.). The vacuum
which he leaves within himself by not acting is filled with the trash
of modern civilisation symbolised by his 'Schwyzerhüsli'. He has fallen
short of the ultimate responsibility of the individual to himself,
which is not merely to perceive a possible identity, but to act it out.
Whatever the drawbacks of society, the failure lies at Stiller's own
door. He pays the highest price, the loss of his identity, for
shirking the difficulties of translating insight into action.

Identity as performance: Gantenbein

In his imagined interview, 'Ich schreibe für Leser', which appeared
concurrently with the publication of Gantenbein, Frisch indicates how
the novel concerns itself with the establishment of identity (V 329).
It is essential for every human being to be able to construct an
identity which he feels he can accept. In so far as identity is also

a selection from other possibilities, it is a restriction of the reality
of the individual for the purposes of social intercourse. It therefore
represents a role in society. The depiction of the process of selection
and presentation interests Frisch as a writer, as he had already
explained in 1961:

> Jedes Ich, das erzählt, ist eine Rolle. Das ist es, was ich
> darstellen möchte. [18]

The novel Gantenbein is an attempt to depict the state of consciousness
of the individual who adopts temporarily the role of Gantenbein as a
blind man. The role, since it is an external projection of that state
of consciousness, becomes the medium for contact with the outside world.
By showing the consciousness experiencing the advantages and disadvantages
of the role which it has selected, Frisch is able to portray the constant
assessment of, and reflection on, his contact with others which the
individual ceaselessly makes. Frisch is thus attempting to show that
identity is a process, and not an immutable condition. Identity is also
a positive matter, requiring the individual to step forth into the world
in the awareness of the partial nature of his role. Since Gantenbein
consciously embarks on his role as a blind man, he is, in this respect
alone, a more positive figure than Stiller, the weakness of whose attitude
is indicated by the fact that his identity is finally determined by his
environment. But the irony of Gantenbein lies in the fact that the
narrator observes his role-playing gradually degenerating from a
diverting process into an imprisoning state.

It is important to note the premisses and expectations behind the
decision of the narrator of the novel to adopt the role of Gantenbein,
the blind man. He will embark consciously on his life as a role, but
will heighten the idea of performance implied in the role by dissembling.
His assumed blindness is, therefore, on the one hand a device to remind
him of his role, and it is also something which he can consciously with-
hold from others. He hopes that the role will impart to him a freedom
of action vis-a-vis others, since he will be able to observe the
behaviour of others unknown to them (V 21). Thus the narrator envisages
'ein Leben als Spiel' (V 21), his life as a performance. Howard S. Babb,
in his comments on Jane Austen's Pride and Prejudice, indicates the
range of meaning which the concept of 'performance' can acquire when
it is applied to the relationshps which the individual creates with
those around him:

> Performance - whose meaning...ranges from a show, an
> exhibition, to a total act, a deed integrated with one's
> entire nature...The word refers to behavior itself: a
> person can be known only by the qualities of his perform-
> ance, whichever kind it might be, and in either sort of

performance one mediates between society and oneself.[19]
Initially, of course, it is in the sense of 'show', 'exhibition', that
the narrator plays his role as Gantenbein. In the optician's in Zürich
where he is about to buy the dark glasses for his role, he resolves to
speak only in Hochdeutsch, which always gives him the feeling that he
is acting (V 25). The image of theatrical performance, evoked in the
German-Swiss context by the fact that Hochdeutsch is the language of
the theatre there, is continued after Gantenbein's visit to the Amtsarzt
to obtain a blind person's yellow armband. The interview has been
extremely taxing for Gantenbein, and after its successful conclusion he
describes himself as being 'entspannt wie ein Schauspieler hinter der
Kulisse' (V 47). Once the initial excitement of successfully acting
a part before others has subsided, however, the realities of the
situation which he has created begin to emerge. For Gantenbein, the
major advantage in the creation of his role has been the preservation
of his relationship with the actress Lila. Gradually he becomes aware,
however, that his role does not confer any new freedom on him, as he
had at the outset imagined it would. The real theatre functions only
at specific times, a role on the other hand is continuous with life.
The narrator, in the role of Svoboda, listens to Lila tell him of her
unfaithfulness to him, and muses ruefully: 'Leider fällt kein Vorhang'
(V 227). And as the scene between himself and Lila continues, his
unhappiness takes the form of a question: 'Warum, ja, warum fällt
jetzt kein Vorhang?' (V 231). The repetition of the question (V 232)
constitutes the third mention of the curtain which will not fall. It
is not Lila who has betrayed him, but the idea of a role as such. The
narrator discovers that, regardless of the detachment with which a
role is played, a role is enacted in reality.

The first public performance as Gantenbein, the blind man, can
however be regarded as successful within the framework of the narrator's
original expectations. Gantenbein, involved with Camilla Huber in a
minor street accident, is invited home by her, where he quickly perceives
that she is not a manicurist as she claims, but is instead a call-girl
(V 38). Perception has led on his side to an awareness of the real
situation, and in the course of his subsequent visits to her, during
which he continues to accept that she is a manicurist, she becomes
aware that he is not blind. She proposes a pact which would preserve
their respective roles (V 263). In the case of Camilla at least, one
of the hopes which had prompted him to adopt his role, namely that his
apparent blindness would encourage situations where silence about the
other's behaviour would accord the other freedom of behaviour, appears

to have been fulfilled. But the relationship with Camilla only emphasises his misunderstanding of the connection between detachment and involvement. He believes that, because he has acquired a measure of detachment towards himself in that he is aware of the role which he is playing, he is in a certain sense no longer involved in society, for he imagines that others will know that his role as a blind man is only one possible role for him. Yet for others it is preceisely this role which for them is his reality. This is symbolised in the trial which follows the murder of Camilla, and at which Gantenbein is cited as a witness. In order to preserve his role as a blind man, Gantenbein cannot tell the court that he saw the accused far from the scene of the crime at the time when it was being committed (V 278). Gantenbein cannot choose to be both blind and sighted: 'Jede Rolle hat ihre Schuld' (V 279). The function of the Gantenbein-Camilla relationship in the novel is to demonstrate that individuals can accord one another a certain freedom by accepting one another's roles, but that this freedom is by no means complete.

The situation in the relationship between Gantenbein and Lila is more complex. In the case of Camilla, the disparity between what she claims to be and what she actually is does not trouble Gantenbein, since he is not emotionally involved with her. With Lila his attitude is based on an assumption about her - that she is unfaithful to him - under which the disparate, even contradictory, facts of her observable behaviour can be subsumed. But he believes that his love for her is strong enough for him to accept the role which he has accorded to her. He feels that this belief is important to the relationship, especially when she returns from engagements in other theatres to which he has been unable to accompany her (V 84). He can imagine that Lila is leaving him the same latitude for the same reason: that she loves him and so accepts his role. After a visit together to Lila's dressmaker, where Gantenbein has been acting as Lila's eyes by obliging her, in his questions about the dresses which she is trying on, to describe them in relation to herself, Gantenbein asks himself if she has been discreetly accepting his assumed role (V 95) in the knowledge that he is not blind. He exercises his own discretion in the myriad household tasks which people living together require to do. In her absence he does most of this work, but not in such a fashion that she will notice. When she does not notice, and hence continues in her belief that house-work is not a major chore, he remarks: 'Alltag ist nur durch Wunder erträglich' (V 108). He finds no difficulty in remaining silent on such matters of detail.

Yet the development of the novel shows that his ability to maintain silence about his own role is under increasing strain. It is not that he is not fully aware of the virtues of silence as the story of Alil and Ali (V 161-163), which he tells to Camilla, demonstrates: Ali, an Arab shepherd boy, marries a blind girl Alil; her sight is restored, and she sees that Ali is not as handsome as the other shepherds, but she continues to love him 'denn er hatte ihr alle Farben dieser Welt geschenkt durch seine Liebe' (V 162). He in his turn goes blind, is obsessed with jealousy when she has to leave the tent, and makes love to another girl who mysteriously visits him. With his sight unexpectedly restored, he discovers that his visitor has been Alil. For Gantenbein, the story is true (V 163) because it highlights the virtues of silence in a relationship between a man and a woman, Alil's silence on discovering her husband's appearance, and her later silence in offering herself to him when he is blind. In the first instance, Alil maintains silence about his identity, in the second about her own. After recounting the story to Camilla, Gantenbein imagines what would happen if he were to tell Lila that he is not really blind, if he were to break silence about his role. The imagined consequences of his action are so appalling that he resolves: 'Ich bleibe Gantenbein' (V 199). As in the case of his more public appearance in the court of law during the trial of Camilla's alleged murderer, he finds that his role involves him with reality. Yet the irony of his role as the blind Gantenbein lies, vis-a-vis Lila at any rate, in the fact that it has brought about exactly the situation which the assumption of the role had sought to avoid. The role has destroyed the flexibility of his response to life, because it is based on a pre-conceived notion of Lila's behaviour. The belief on which the role was based is that she is deceiving him, hence, on his discovery that she is not, his role collapses (V 311). He completes the collapse by admitting to her that he has never been blind (V 312), and the next scene shows the narrator sitting in the deserted flat as at the beginning of the novel (V 313-314). The novel closes with the story of the body in the River Limmat which almost managed to drift away 'ohne Geschichte' (V 319). When he embarked on the role, Gantenbein's hybris misled him into thinking that he would by this role accord a large measure of freedom to his fellows. But in the event the role proves so inflexible that it does not prevent sentence being passed on an innocent man, it diminishes Lila in that his conduct towards her is based on the assumption that she is deceiving him, and he has betrayed himself by entering in such a cavalier spirit into the utterly serious business of playing a role.

The nature of Gantenbein's response to others is based on deception, not on genuine 'Takt' which incorporates knowledge. The relationship with Camilla is overtly based on a 'Vertrag' (V 263), whereby the contracting parties each makes his contribution towards the preservation of the freedom of action of the other. Perception is not denied, but its verbalisation is controlled in the interests of co-existence. But in reality the contract provides for a protection of deception. Camilla pays for her deception, in the marginal social position which she occupies, by losing her life to the socially uncontrollable forces which she is exploiting. Gantenbein pays for his deception by the loss of his relationship with Lila, and since his social role is negligible, he lacks an impulse genuinely to come to terms with himself, and in this limbo his desire is 'Abzuschwimmen ohne Geschichte'. The parallel between his relationship with Lila and that with Camilla is that he believes the former, like the latter, to be based on deception. When he discovers that Lila is not deceiving him, he cannot maintain silence about this perception, and so betrays his own deception. Gantenbein, anxious to protect himself against others who might perceive his deception, has no protection against his own insight, and he unmasks himself to discover that he has no resources behind the mask. The role of Gantenbein has proved inflexible because it was suitable only for pre-determined situations [20]. Its inflexibility is demonstrated by the ease with which it collapses when it is faced with the problem of incorporating into itself the truth provided by perception. His role has been merely a 'show', and 'exhibition' without substance. The essentially frivolous attitude of Gantenbein is evidenced by the glee-ful manner in which he sets about his deceptions. But like the teacher in Andorra he comes to learn that 'die Lüge ist ein Egel' (IV 497). The fiction whose intent is to deceive assumes a much more independent life than the fiction which has no such intention.

The opposite end of the scale in Babb's definition of performance is a 'total act, a deed integrated with the entire nature'. An instance of this kind of performance in Gantenbein is provided by the story of the ambassador, (V 118-120), a 'Gegenfall' (V 118) to that of Enderlin, and also to that of the minor characters such as Otto, the 'Pechvogel' and the 'Bäckermeister'. The story occurs at the point in the novel where the narrator, in his role as Enderlin, is being tormented by indecision following the offer of a chair at Harvard University. The chief reason for his indecision is that he cannot believe in himself in the role of professor. He has believed that it is possible to create an identity by the quality of his achievements. At the height of the

crisis, he perceives that achievements are a method of seeking approval
for himself from those about him. Yet, like Stiller, he cannot tolerate
any disparity between his identity and what he believes his reality to
be. In this contradictory position, he is immobilised and cannot
assume an identity (V 118).

The ambassador, representative of a major power, collapses whilst
on holiday. It is not a physical ailment which has struck him down,
but 'eine Einsicht' (V 119). He has discovered that he is not the
person the world appears to think he is. He feels that this situation
calls for his resignation, and he even prepares a letter to that effect.
Instead of sending it, however, he takes upon himself the greater burden
of not resigning, of continuing to fulfil his official functions in the
full awareness of his perception:

> Er wählt das Grössere: die Rolle. Seine Selbsterkenntnis
> bleibt sein Geheimnis. Er erfüllt sein Amt. (V 119)

He will not disabuse others of their belief that he is who they think
he is. In contrast to Gantenbein, who deceived himself as well as
others by thinking that suppression of perception created belief, the
ambassador incorporates perception into his identity. He discovers that
this distance between himself and his public identity releases energies
which enable him, not merely to perform his duties, but to perform them
better than hitherto. His awareness of his performance increases its
effectiveness [21]. This benefits not only himself, but others also, as
indicated by the fact the he intervenes successfully to save a city
from being destroyed by bombardment. Acceptance of the fact that the
'Rolle' is at best an inadequate reflection of the individual makes
available for more positive ends the energies consumed in failing to
achieve the impossible task of co-ordinating completely individuality
and identity, or in lamenting this failure. The core of the story of
the ambassador lies in his awareness of the burden of silence which
self-knowledge is obliged to bear. The desire to explain to others
the innermost reaches of the personality not only overtaxes the limits
of language, the desire itself springs from vanity. It is motivated by
the futile intention that others should become apprised of the
individual's awareness of himself. In reality, it is an exercise
which, even in the most intimate of relationships, is doomed to fritter
away individuality in meaningless proliferations of language. Yet
language can, if its possibilities are respected, help in the task of
coming to terms with the personality. For language calls the insights
gained in this task self-knowledge. That this knowledge is for the
self, and for no other, is the central guiding insight of the ambassador:

> Er weiss: jede Selbsterkenntnis, die nicht schweigen kann,
> macht kleiner und kleiner. Er weiss: wer nicht schweigen
> kann, will erkannt sein in der Grösse seiner Selbsterkennt-
> nis, die keine ist, wenn sie nicht schweigen kann, und man
> wird empfindlich, man fühlt sich verraten, indem man von
> Menschen erkannt sein will, man wird lächerlich, ehrgeizig
> im umgekehrten Grad seiner Selbsterkenntnis. Das ist
> wichtig: auch nicht unter vier Augen. (V 119)

The discipline of silence enables the individual to come to terms with
external identity. The loneliness of individuation is paradoxically
heightened by the attempt to verbalise, since the finest nuances of
external identity become matters for the most precise definition, and
the individual, embroiled thus in futile linguistic exercises, is
totally in thrall to the idea of his 'Rolle'. The story of the
ambassador indicates the extent to which the individual can play his
'Rolle' and yet be morally free of it [22].

In Stiller, Rolf the Staatsanwalt had commented to Stiller on the
fact that many achieve insight into themselves, but few, by transforming this insight into behaviour, demonstrate their acceptance of
this insight (III 669). The story of the ambassador offers an example
of the manner in which self-acceptance is achieved. Stiller fails to
adapt his behaviour and brings about his decline, and in this he
contrasts with the ambassador, whose self-acceptance accords him the
dignity and strength which Stiller fails to achieve [23]. The death of
the ambassador enhances the dignity with which he has behaved during
his lifetime. The incommunicable nature of his individuality, his
secret, departs with him. The wreaths and speeches at his funeral
emphasise this, for they cover 'seine Selbsterkenntnis für immer'
(V 120). Those present cannot deny that there is a trace of greatness
about him, for he has had the courage to accept his identity without
seeking the approval of others. His commitment to his impenetrable
mystery inspires their respect (V 120). It is a commitment to the
individuality of which the 'Rolle' forms a part. The narrator in
Gantenbein could not accept that his 'Rolle' was only a part of him,
hence his fretful search for the perfect role. The ambassador canalises
his energies, his conscious decision to accept himself 'führt nicht in
auswechselbare Geschichten, sondern zur Geschichte' [24]. The insight of
the ambassador leads, with difficulty, to decision and action, the
concomitants of commitment. Commitment also implies self-acceptance,
and the prerequisite of self-acceptance is silence. Stiller had
conjectured to Dr. Bohnenblust that this might be the case: 'Vielleicht
ist das Leben, das wirkliche, einfach stumm' (III 418). That this is
in fact so is the experience of the ambassador. It falls to him, the

representative of a country, to demonstrate that identity can only be
representative of the full reality of the individual.

The inability to establish a fruitful interaction between perception
and behaviour characterises the main figures in the works of Frisch.
Their desperate search for an identity bears witness to this lack of
interaction. All their attempts to establish an identity posit it as
a state. It is not regarded as a process in which every individual
must involve himself through action, if he wishes to respect and nurture
his individuality. Action and perception are separate, almost unrelated,
modes for the Frisch heroes. In this way they are representative of
modern man as depicted in Die Chinesische Mauer. The failure to
translate awareness about past behaviour into terms of political
action is seen there as being suicidal in the face of the threat posed
by modern weapons. But the close of the play promises that the farce
will begin all over again, because no action has been taken. In Biedermann und die Brandstifter, the Chorführer, at the end of the long and
fruitless confrontation between Biedermann and the chorus – which acts
at this point as his conscience – points to the fear of change brought
about by action as being the main cause of Biedermann's moral immobility:

> Der die Verwandlungen scheut
> Mehr als das Unheil,
> Was kann er tun
> Wider das Unheil? (IV 360)

The Frisch hero is resistant to change in the sense that he will not
moderate his behaviour in the light of his perceptions. But change is
in the nature of life. Frisch presents his characters with situations
which underline the necessity for change in their attitude to themselves [25]. But the major figures, while they may be roused to examine
these new situations, and in the greatest detail, cannot bring themselves to draw conclusions for action from their examinations. Their
newly awakened awareness renders them conscious of their own inadequacy
both in the face of their own expectations and the expectations which
they attribute to those around them. The former induce a sense of
failure and the latter a sense of constriction, and thus identity
becomes for them something quite unattainable.

Stiller and Gantenbein, the two main vehicles for the examination
of identity, both begin their odessies with a false conception of
'Rolle'. For Stiller, 'Rolle' is initially negative, but in prison he
gradually comes to an appreciation of its efficacy as a device for med-
iating between the individual and society. Outside prison and alone,
he cannot muster the strength necessary to behave in accordance with

his insight. In his last long conversation with Rolf, as Julika lies
dying in hospital, he refers hopelessly to the strength of his
perception of his situation: ''Wenn es mit Wissen getan wäre!''
(III 767). But he fails to impose change on himself. For Gantenbein,
on the other hand, 'Rolle' is an unserious activity. The role of the
blind man is socially minimal, and existentially irresponsible. Such
a narrowly-based conception does not stand up to the rigours of reality.
When the 'Rolle' collapses, Gantenbein can only recount with envy the
story of the corpse in the River Limmat which was almost swept away
without being identified. If Stiller depicts a lack of connection
between thought and action, Gantenbein demonstrates the futility of
unconsidered action. The cheerful remark at the beginning of the novel,
'Ich probiere Geschichten an wie Kleider!' (V 22), foreshadows the
absence of purposive behaviour which is to characterise the close of
the novel. Obliteration of the personality, not its affirmation, is
what Gantenbein appears to desire [26]. Identity no longer involves the
fashioning of a response to a challenge, a response which will direct
the energies of the individual and so help to shape him. In Gantenbein
identity disintegrates into possibilities of response which disperse
the individual into amorphousness. The personality surrenders its
individual nature.

The discursiveness of the novel is best suited to the characters
whom Frisch depicts. For these characters are essentially portrayals
of indecision, a mental state which the exigencies of the stage render
difficult to realise. This indecision springs from an over-sensitivity
at the way in which a decision excludes the possibility of other
decisions. The Frisch character consistently fails to come to terms
with this fact. He is overwhelmingly and harmfully aware of the
possibility of which he is depriving himself by taking a decision. He
is convinced that people who take decisions are so deprived. This
exaggerated reverence for potential makes relationships with others
fraught with every conceivable difficulty. The mentality is present
and explicit in the first novel hero, Jürg Reinhart, and points to the
fates of the later heroes Stiller and Gantenbein, who are basically
variations of the same character [27]. The Frisch character remains
constant in his intense suspicion of all limitation. Limitation is
never regarded as fruitful, as a necessary device to direct growth and
canalise energy, but always as an unjustified encroachment on the
limitless extent of potential. Paradoxically, however, this is not a
manifestation of the intensity of his concern for the individual, but

is indicative of a deeply frivolous outlook: he cannot accept
commitment and its implications as facts of life.

The picture of indecision and inaction presented by the heroes is,
however, countered by a feature not sufficiently commented on by
critics. In the four major novels of Frisch a contrastive figure or
episode, through its relationship to the structure of the narrative,
provides an example of the behaviour which the hero is seeking to
avoid, and so puts the hero into a moral perspective. In Die Schwierigen Hauswirt accepts Yvonne and her child by Reinhart [28]. In Stiller,
the figure of Rolf provides a contrast to Stiller, above all in Rolf's
assimilation of the Genoa episode, on the basis of which he is able to
come to terms with himself and later to re-establish his relationship
with Sibylle [29]. In Homo Faber, the Cuba episode, for all the
qualifications with which it is surrounded, displays an attitude
which is more attune to the realities of life than that habitually
adopted by Faber. And in Gantenbein, the story of the ambassador
contrasts with the indecision and inaction of the narrator's role-
playing, since the ambassador commits himself to the compromise with
which life presents him. The figure of the ambassador incorporates the
paradox that personal identity acquires meaning for the individual only
if it is regarded as a performance, but a performance demanding the
full deployment of the individual's resources as a human being. In
his 1964 speech 'Der Autor und das Theater', Frisch defines the theatre
as an aesthetic response to the resistance of reality to expression:

> Wie immer das Theater sich gibt, ist es Kunst: Spiel als
> Antwort auf die Unabbildbarkeit der Welt. (V 345)

The ambassador's behaviour demonstrates that he has applied this
definition to the concept of identity, of 'Rolle', and in doing so has
not restricted himself but has released the full possibilities of the
personality. The ambassador and the position of the artist are similar
in that both are aware of the necessity of a commitment to performance [30].
Only by this conscious assumption of identity can the individual overcome the fear of change in time, create a link between perception and
action, and so offer resistance to the corrosive forces of the modern
world. In this sense, identity is the prerequisite to commitment.

B. COMMITMENT

1. Fear of Commitment and its Consequences

Rejection of responsibility

Continuity of theme in the works of Max Frisch, manifested in his
lifelong interest in the story of Rip van Winkle, is apparent also in
his treatment of fear of commitment. This recurs in a variety of guises
in all the works. It is characterised by an inability to accept the
limitations of the individual personality and circumstances. There
exists in the figures who suffer from it an ineradicable conviction
that commitment is synonymous with self-deprivation. Because this
inability usually remains hidden from those who have it, its
manifestations are almost always defined and commented on by others.
Thus Frau von Reisner, in Jürg Reinhart Eine sommerliche Schicksalsfahrt,
deplores the manner in which the young men of her acquaintance concern
themselves so noisily with the trivia of existence at the expense of
central issues. She wishes that some of them at least had sufficient
moral fibre to confront themselves as they really are (I 278-279).
The situation of these comments in the structure of the novel relates
them also to the hero Jürg and to his reaction to the range of experience
with which the situations of the novel present him. The inconclusiveness
of the character of Jürg derives in part from his youth, and his
ineffectualness in coping with his problems is caused by his uncertainty
about the viability of alternative courses of action as he sets out on
the 'Schicksalsfahrt' of his life. But if uncertainties about commitment
relate, in the case of Jürg, to the future, thirty-three years later a
situation is presented in which they relate to the past of a different
hero. Once more it is a spectator, this time somewhat more privileged,
since he has possession of the dossier containing the facts of the hero's
life, who comments, albeit more indirectly, on the lack of commitment
on the part of the hero to the life set forth in the dossier. The
Registrator in Biografie expresses the hero Kürmann's belief that he
could have conducted his life, not merely differently, but by
implication, in a manner more appropriate to his conception of himself
(V 560) [1]. The course of the play demonstrates to Kürmann the
impossibility of changing the past. All that he can hope to change
is his relationship to the past. His freedom is restricted to accepting that that past represents him. His dissatisfaction with his past,
and his wish to change it show Kürmann's affinity to other Frisch heroes.

Although the Frisch hero may be aware of the impossibility of realising what he desires, his every action, by being directed to surmounting the impossibility, in fact reinforces it.

The narrator in Bin, one of the few successful travellers of the many created by Frisch, is aware of the paradoxical relationship to possible goals which exists in his own mind, as he sets out towards Peking:

> So hinauszuwandern in eine Nacht, um keine Grenzen
> bekümmert! Wir werden schon keine, die in uns liegt,
> je überspringen. (I 604)

His awareness, and above all his acceptance, of this ambiguous relationship contribute in no small measure to the success of his journey to Peking, for within this framework of ambiguity he can cope with the unpredictability of reality. In this he is not typical of the major heroes who follow him. Their inflexibility might best be characterised by reference to a minor character in Homo Faber who does not actually appear, Hanna's second husband, the Communist Piper. Hanna reports that his devotion to the ideology which he has espoused transcends all that could reasonably be expected. His blinkered attitude has divorced him from reality: 'Was er verloren habe: ein spontanes Verhältnis zur Realität' (IV 144). The manner in which he subsumes all to his vision is identical with the way in which the Frisch heroes seek to render the impossible realisable. If these figures are tragic, it is in the ceaseless harnessing of energy to the dissipation of their substance as human beings, since a fraction of the same energy directed within a limited framework of commitment could impart richness and meaning to their lives. The major figures are explorations of the mentality which draws back from commitment, and of the consequences which follow upon this withdrawal.

A striking feature of the withdrawal from commitment is envy of animals for being beyond the pressures of responsibility. The narrator of Bin, momentarily depressed in the course of his journey to Peking, strolls along the banks of the lake and reflects on the lack of existential difficulties which the swans swimming there have (I 630). Hortense in Die Schwierigen, intoxicated by the apparent timelessness of high summer on the country estate of her godmother, looks back on the complications of her relationships in her daily life in the city, and longs for the uncaring existence of an animal (I 527). The absence of the complex functioning of the human mind is a major source of envy. Ironically noting that it is precisely this mind which can create within itself the agonising emptiness of boredom, Frisch sees an

extreme contrast to its functioning in the supine attitude of the
salamanders at the zoo, for whom bodily function determines all
(II 647-648). Enderlin, consumed by boredom at the airport, is
rendered all the more frustrated at his condition by seeing a 'Hund
ohne Zeit', and concludes: 'Ein Hund hat's gut' (V 310) [2]. In
Montauk dogs are praised for their inability to gossip (VI 661).
That these comments on the ease of animal existence are not merely
random images of oppositeness, but form a strand in the theme of lack
of commitment in the work of Frisch is indicated by a question in
Tagebuch 1966-1971, the last in the first of the ten questionnaires
which Frisch addresses to the reader:

> Möchten Sie lieber gestorben sein oder noch eine Zeit
> leben als ein gesundes Tier? Und als welches? (VI 9)

Animal existence is not only clearly linked with the negation of human
life, the absence of ratiocination which is the main object of envy is
here enhanced by the exclusion of the only other possible element of
difficulty about animal life which the writer can imagine, physical
pain. A healthy animal represents the irreducible limits of existence
in that individual responsibility can be extirpated no further.

    Yet for two major Frisch heroes, Stiller and Faber, that which
links them to this envied animal existence, their own physical functioning, is a source of unpleasantness, if not of downright disgust. This
constitutes a little noted link between the two figures. In the 'Zweites
Heft' of Stiller, it is recorded that for several years Stiller daily
swam over the Zürichsee and back, 'oft noch im Oktober' (III 459). He
was prompted to do this, not simply for exercise but also to rid himself
of his own perspiration, the presence of which rendered him incapable
of normal social intercourse. Ironically, his flight from this society
with which he is unable to cope is attended by the same physical
manifestations which so embarrassed him there. As he crouches in the
intolerable heat of the hold of the ship on which he is stowing away
to America, perspiration is a reminder of failure for him. It is so
hot that

> der Schweiss aus allen Poren rann, ich begriff sehr wohl,
> dass die schöne Julika sich ekeln würde vor diesem Schweiss.
> (III 683)

Walter Faber is even more extreme than Stiller in his attitude to
bodily functions. When he is delayed for five days in the humid jungle
settlement of Palenque as he and Herbert journey towards Joachim's
plantation, his one activity is to shower constantly (IV 38). Another
physical manifestation which causes Faber constant concern is his beard

(IV 10). After the crash-landing in the desert, where he has no
opportunity to shave, he elaborates on this dislike:

> Ich habe dann das Gefühl, ich werde etwas wie eine
> Pflanze, wenn ich nicht rasiert bin. (IV 27)

Retribution for this particular aspect of his unnatural obsession with
the natural is visited on him in New York, when he delays leaving his
flat in order to repair an electric razor, and is thus there to take
the telephone-call from the shipping company which causes him to sail
on the liner on which Sabeth is travelling. After the tragic encounter
with his daughter, as he lies dying in the Athens hospital, Faber still
regrets that the framework of human life, flesh and its manifestations,
is not perfectible: 'Fleisch ist kein Material, sondern ein Fluch'
(IV 171).

The fascinated dislike with which Stiller, and more strongly, Faber,
regard the functioning of the human body derives from the same outlook
which envies animals the ease of their existence. Thought and reflection
have ceased to be anchored in the reality which constitutes the individual
and his environment and has drifted into the realm of speculation on the
impossible. His relationship to his physical nature and his envy of
unthinking animals form a part of this imaginary world. Envy of animals
is not the fleeting emotion which might occur at a moment of particular
difficulty in life. In Tagebuch 1946-1949 Frisch comments on the
difficulty of the human condition (II 488). The ability to choose
characterises this condition and distinguishes it from that of the
animals. The burden imposed is accepted as a necessary prerequisite
of this difference. The easier life of the seagull is cited as a
measure of the burden, not as an object of envy. This affirmation of
the strenuousness of life represents a commitment to the individual
which none of the heroes in the major fictional works is in a position
to make. Envy of animals is the hallmark of this failure, and is an
indication of the existential irresponsibility of the Frisch heroes.
The choice before these heroes has been defined by Schiller, when he
warns against a similar kind of envy, envy of an imagined tranquillity
in human affairs which the sight of the tranquillity of inanimate nature
inspires. Visions of ease are not compatible with human life, and after
advising the reader how to maintain the difficult balance between freedom
and necessary constriction, Schiller concludes:

> Jene Natur, die du dem Vernunftlosen beneidest, ist keiner
> Achtung, keiner Sehnsucht wert. Sie liegt hinter dir, sie
> muss ewig hinter dir liegen. Verlassen von der Leiter, die
> dich trug, bleibt dir jetzt keine andere Wahl mehr, als mit
> freiem Bewusstsein und Willen das Gesetz zu ergreifen oder

rettungslos in eine bodenlose Tiefe zu fallen. [3]

The quagmire evoked by Schiller is one in which all the major Frisch heroes founder. They are incapable of committing themselves to the moral necessity which is the only alternative.

The consequences of failing to reject what Schiller calls 'eine bodenlose Tiefe' are for the Frisch hero paradoxical, frustrating and eventually crippling. They are paradoxical in that he fails to establish a dimension of perspective in his life for the very reason that he is exclusively pre-occupied with himself [4]. This lack of perspective entails that he does not possess 'einen festen Punkt' (III 590), as Stiller, the most perceptive of the heroes, realises. Thus his ability to judge himself in relation to the environment becomes dislocated, and he turns to standards outside himself. But these external instances are not yardsticks in the sense that he uses them as models for emulation. Their function is different.

Hinkelmann, Yvonne's first husband in Die Schwierigen, and a pre-liminary sketch for the more fully realised figure of Reinhart, has his ordered world shattered by Yvonne's decision to leave him. Vainly, he hopes for a reconciliation; repeatedly he calls with flowers at the hospital where Yvonne has had their child aborted. He cannot cope with a situation where he has no outside support, he is devoid of inner resources upon which to draw in his emotional crisis:

> (Er) dachte..., wie das Kind an seine Mutter, stets an Yvonne, deren Achtung oder Verachtung ja sein letzter Massstab blieb in all dieser Wirrnis. (I 412)

Hinkelmann's reaction, indicating that at the age of thirty-five he still requires an emotional umbilical cord, highlights also the key problem of the immaturity displayed by so many Frisch characters: they are unable to evolve an attitude within themselves or create an interior set of values which will withstand the unpredictability of the situations with which life presents them. They seek safety from life, even obliteration of life. Thus, Don Juan wishes to withdraw to the controllable world of figures and calculations. Stiller also abrogates his responsibility. In his case, it is Julika, not he, who must carry the responsibility for the success or failure of their marriage. Stiller, locked within his own concerns, is quite unaware, even at the highest point of his self-awareness - in the 'Siebentes Heft' immediately prior to the juridical confrontation with her - of the magnitude of the imposition which he is thus making on his wife. He formulates very clearly the gravity of her responsibility in the matter: 'Letztlich wird alles von Julika abhängen, nur von Julika'

160.

(III 707). At the confrontation itself he does not shrink from remind-
ing Julika of her duty. He asks her whether she loves him or not:

> Nur darauf kommt es jetzt an. Nur auf dich, Julika,
> einzig und allein auf dich! (III 713) [5]

But it is not merely his marriage which Stiller banishes from the
purlieu of his accountability. It is life itself, as Rolf's reaction
to Stiller's attitude after the former's first disquieting visit to
Glion makes clear:

> Darum ging es ja doch, um Verwirklichen oder Versagen, um
> Atmen oder Ersticken, in diesem Sinn um Leben oder Tod,
> richtiger: um Leben oder Versiechen. (III 752)

The checks and reverses which form part of life are for Stiller and the
other major heroes manifestations of the injustice of life to them.
This sense of injustice is further heightened and their passivity receives
further vindication, when external agents such as Yvonne or Julika, whom
they have designated as their rescuers, fail them.

The frustrating aspect of the failure of the Frisch character to
make a moral commitment to himself resides in the fact that, since he
can only define himself in relation to the injustice which others mete
out to him, he can never be independent of others. Yet he can never
have genuine contact with others, for he possesses too little impulse
to move towards others to establish contact. But paradoxically, since
he is so supinely dependent on others, the Frisch character can never,
despite his self-absorption, possess the strength to be alone. At the
moment of the greatest crisis of his life, Hinkelmann realises the
cardinal virtue of the ability to be alone:

> Eine Ahnung davon, dass er die Einsamkeit lernen müsste,
> einen Grad von Einsamkeit, den er sich vorzustellen bisher
> noch niemals Anlass hatte; dass er das lernen müsste, bevor
> man zu irgendeiner Gemeinschaft taugte, eine Ahnung davon
> hatte er schon. (I 412)

The ability to be alone pre-supposes resources which sustain that aloneness, resources on which, in society, others can draw, and which they
can in their turn replenish. Stiller, in his most detailed review of
the stations of his life (III 681-688), centres his account in his
permanent inability to sustain aloneness. Continually he was plagued
by 'Hoffnung auf eine grossartige Begegnung an der nächsten oder über-
nächsten Strassenecke' (III 682). He pinpoints the period when he
first became a sculptor as the one spell in his life when his creative
drive enabled him to be alone, but this did not last long:

> Schon war der Ehrgeiz da, die Freude in Hinsicht auf
> Anerkennung, die Sorge in Hinsicht auf Geringschätzung.
> (III 682)

The account closes with further revelations of his maltreatment in

Oakland of the cat Little Grey. As a result of his brutality, the cat
no longer came about the house in the way which had annoyed him so much.
But he had nonetheless still not freed himself from the animal, for he
constantly expected its return (III 686). Stiller's failure to be
alone is also a failure to relate himself to what lies beyond him. Of
all the Frisch characters, he demonstrates most clearly that the self-
centred personality creates around himself an unbreachable wall of
loneliness which prevents replenishment of the vital forces by human
intercourse [6].

The failure to make the moral decision to accept and affirm the
limitations of the individual is ultimately fatally crippling since the
individual cannot free himself from 'die Totalität immanenter Wert-
urteile' [7] which holds him in thrall. If the individual insists that
those about him relate themselves to him, he can relate himself to
nothing, since he cannot accept the right of others to an existence
independent of him. An early minor character in Antwort aus der Stille
exemplifies the point. Barbara, the fiancée of the hero Balz, admits
to the selfish and self-centred role which she has played in demanding
that Balz should virtually be an extension of herself [8]. Unlike
Barbara, later minor characters do not resolve the matter, but continue
in the harmful delusion that the world has no importance other than for
themselves. Philipp Hotz, in a speech to the audience, humorously
asserts that he forms the most important topic of conversation for his
wife and mistress (IV 438). The manner of delivery does not altogether
disguise the underlying seriousness of the statement, but reveals the
frame of mind which later causes Gantenbein to imagine the experiment
with his tape-recorder. A third minor character gives a wider framework
of reference to the inability of the individual not to see everything
about him in terms of himself. Can, the teacher, in Andorra, has rejected
Andri's request to marry Barblin. The Mutter, Can's wife, although at
this stage ignorant of the real reason for the refusal, nonetheless
finds its manner and Can's further comments entirely in accord with her
knowledge of his character:

> Du schweigst in dich hinein, weil du eifersüchtig bist,
> Can, auf die Jungen und auf das Leben überhaupt und dass
> es jetzt weitergeht ohne dich. (IV 495)

The resentment in Can that the world does not relate to himself as
fully as he would wish is a manifestation of the larger inability to
establish a stable and balanced relationship to life.

Egocentricity is also the dominating trait in the major characters.
Julika, for example, is obsessed with herself, and this constitutes for

her the principal attraction of the ballet: her sexual excitement, as she stands on the stage, the focus of all eyes in the theatre (III 451), and her delight that her photograph should appear on the 'Titelseite einer schweizerischen Illustrierten' (III 477) with its dissemination throughout the world, leave no doubt on that score. There is thus a pernicious link between Julika and Stiller which they can never break. Yet Stiller's narcissism is more destructive and consuming than that of his wife, as Rolf tries to point out to Stiller, ironically as Julika is undergoing the fatal operation. Stiller has been expressing fears that Julika will die, and that this will be his punishment for his conduct towards her. Rolf tries to point out his error:

> Wer stirbt schon einem anderen zuliebe oder zuleide! Du
> überschätzt deine Wichtigkeit, ich meine: deine Wichtig-
> keit für sie. Sie braucht dich nicht, wie du gebraucht sein
> möchtest. (III 765)

Although the focus of attention in the course of the novel is very much more on Stiller than on Julika, the interest of their relationship lies in the fact that it is the only major relationship in Frisch's work where both partners are, so to speak, similarly deprived. Usually, the woman is the better balanced partner, being more firmly rooted in life. Stiller has had a relationship with such a woman, Sibylle, which ended by her aborting their child. This indicates that the more balanced characters have a better instinct for survival and are preapred to take the necessary action to maintain that balance. The egocentric characters have no such developed instinct and so cannot take such action. Hence Stiller and Julika are re-united by the circumstances of the novel, the one to die, the other to sink into decline. They lack a dimension in which they can communicate with each other, or which would enable them to separate for good. Julika is the exception among the female characters in that she has the same problems as the male characters Stiller and Don Juan. Die Dame points out the latter's central failing to him: 'Du hast immer bloss dich selbst geliebt und nie dich selbst gefunden' (III 145). Narcissism, an impotent and deadly fascination, characterises the marriage of Julika and Stiller, and their relationship exemplifies all that is fatal in any lack of self-affirmation. Yet their prison and their demise, actual and symbolic, are of their own making, for they, like Gantenbein, cannot discern a link between liberty and volition. The characters of Frisch cannot grasp that commitment is a liberating act.

The spiritual rootlessness of the Frisch characters has its external correlative in the provisional and sketchy nature of their

living arrangements. Reinhart has 'eigentlich kein Zuhause' (I 448),
and Sibylle notes that the studio of Stiller, Reinhart's more fully
developed successor, possesses 'den Zauber des Provisorischen' (III 603).
But the enthusiasm of her initial reaction is qualified as she gradually
draws conclusions from the state of the studio and its contents about
the personality of the man who occupies it. She decides that his
selection of books is 'eher jünglingshaft' (III 610), and her general
impression is that the place offers an accurate reflection of Stiller's
immaturity (III 611). Stiller commits the seven 'Hefte' to paper in
prison, surroundings which are not of his choosing, although from the
outset he is fully aware of the nature of his own contribution to his
being in prison: prison is merely the external manifestation of a much
deeper bondage (III 373). Faber, the modern counterpart to Pelegrin
the wanderer, quarters the globe ceaselessly. His constant journeying
is a different form of imprisonment from that of Stiller. That he
cannot break out of this particular prison is symbolised by the fact
that, when he telephones his pied-a-terre in New York, his one fragile
link to the possibility of a life not circumscribed by movement, he is
told three times that no-one of his name lives there (IV 163-164).
The narrator of Gantenbein begins and ends his imaginings in the desolate
emptiness of the flat in which his marriage came to an end. The evidence
of life that once took place there emphasises his desolation of spirit,
and the menace contained in the covered furniture underlines the
impossibility of escape:

> Alle Polstermöbel sind mit weissen Tüchern bedeckt.
> Komisch anzusehen: als spielten sie Feme. (V 19)

The ironic counterpoint to his enclosure is: 'Die Welt ist voller
Ziele' (V 82). It is not therefore that the Frisch character has the
disregarding attitude to his immediate surroundings of one who lives
an intense inner life. Instead, these surroundings make their own
particular contribution to the oppressive sense that he is surrounded
at every turn by malevolent forces which are inimical to him, and which
prevent him putting down roots.

Attempts to dissemble the hollowness at the centre of the
personality are always exposed by these malevolent forces. The
macabre close to Die Schwierigen illustrates this. Reinhart, in his
role as Anton the servant, takes his own life. To the general horror,
as his body is being lifted into the coffin, his wig, of which the
others were ignorant, falls off (I 599). Reinhart's attempt to be
someone else was a failure symbolised by suicide. It is ironic that
in death his real self should be revealed. In the case of Stiller,

the attempt to dissemble gradually ceases to seek to convince. The
impression is created that he pettishly and irresponsibly feels that
if the world wishes to have him as Stiller, then it should provide for
him as Stiller. This is borne out by his lack of serious attempt to
find some financial basis for his life with Julika on his release. His
pretence is fully revealed during Rolf's first visit in October 1954 to
the 'ferme vaudoise', at the time of which Stiller is forty-two years
of age [9]. Yet Rolf describes his appearance, in one of Rolf's old
suits, as that of a gauche adolescent (III 738). The naked man at the
beginning of Gantenbein is an even more extreme form of an attempt to
dissemble inner emptiness. He runs naked through the streets of Zürich
because 'er habe einen Schrei ausstossen wollen' (V 18). He is finally
brought to a halt on the stage of the opera-house and covered with a
cloak, 'himmelblau mit goldenen Quasten, ein Königsmantel' (V 17).
Ironically, his protest, the nature of which never becomes clear, is
muffled by the trappings of illusion, its motor force, since he had
imagined that his action of running through the streets would acquire
significance. Even more ironically his nakedness relates him to Gottlieb Biedermann, representative of all those most scandalised by a
naked man in the streets. For Biedermann's possessions also represent
a form of estrangement [10]. The trappings of bürgerlich life are the
cloak with which he tries to cover himself, and they are as illusory
as the power implied by the 'Königsmantel'. For the latter leads to
the asylum and the former are destroyed. Biedermann is, in his dis-
semblance, as essentially rootless as the other Frisch characters.
Accumulating material possessions is as much a manifestation of inner
fear as wearing a wig, donning borrowed garb or running naked through
the streets. These activities are all symbols of a lack of commitment,
and they all represent futile evasions of the individual's responsibility
to himself.

'Angst'

One of the main emotional consequences which flow from the evasion
of the individual's responsibility to himself is fear, which indicates
his subconscious awareness of insecurity. The major characters are not
only aware of their 'Angst', they are also aware that they are seeking
or adopting devices which will lessen or extirpate this 'Angst'. For
Reinhart, 'Angst' is at first the hallmark of the insincere and insecure
bürgerlich society in which he lives. As a painter in this society he
imagines that others consider that his social role consists in hiding

this 'Angst' by his work (I 453). Later he finds that the 'Angst' which he sees about him has almost acquired the structure of a philosophy (I 534-535). Ultimately he is destroyed not by what he sees about him, but by his own unresolved 'Angst'. Stiller the sculptor, on the other hand, gives shape to his 'Angst' in the 'Hefte' [11], but retreats from the implications of this shape. There is a striking similarity between the situations of Biedermann and Faber. Biedermann, unable to prevent the initial intrusion into his home, is terrified by what is happening there, and as a consequence he pretends that the real meaning of what he is seeing is not registering in his brain. This gives rise to the lament of the chorus: 'Blinder als blind ist der Ängstliche' (IV 347). Faber also refuses to act on the implications of what he can see before him, and as a result defiles and destroys his own daughter. As he dines in the restaurant car of the train taking him to Zürich for the last time, he wishes to destroy his eyes, those organs which he feels have betrayed him (IV 192). One of the motivations of Gantenbein's role as a blind man is also that the consequences of sight should be avoided. He seeks with his dark glasses to make others 'frei von der Angst, dass man ihre Lügen sehe' (V 44). If it is inevitable that a writer of fiction in the demythologised twentieth century should reflect in his compositions aspects of the widespread lack of transcendental values, of which the 'Angst' of the individual is one manifestation [12], the figures created by Frisch are symbolic of the age.

If the manifestations of 'Angst' in the psyche of the individual lend themselves more to depiction in the novels, the social consequences of 'Angst' figure more prominently in the plays. The protagonists there, drawn in much more schematic form than those of the novels, appear as examples of the society in which they exist. The public behaviour of these figures thus displays not merely the 'Angst' of the individual, but also of society at large. In Graf Öderland, the Staatsanwalt, fascinated by the apparently motiveless murder committed by the bank clerk, disappears from society under the influence of this fascination. The clairvoyant, summoned by the family to help in the search for him, considers that the rows of filing-cabinets in the study where the Staatsanwalt first conceived the idea of flight, mask the 'Angst' which is the keynote of 'Zivilisation' (III 37). The Staatsanwalt takes forceful action in an attempt to rid himself of pervasive fear. Herr Biedermann in the 1953 Hörspiel Herr Biedermann und die Brandstifter points forward to the passivity of future characters in so far as he internalises his 'Angst' and thereby increases it. He is

also the first in the line of those who react to reality by denying
the evidence of their own eyes. In a sense he cannot afford to react
to the reality around him for that would be to admit to a guilty
conscience for not having reacted to previous events. He is thus
caught in an inextricable position (IV 312). If the faculties of
perception are not put to proper use, they will atrophy, so that they
can no longer convey adequate information for the individual to make an
assessment and take a decision. Thus Biedermann, in the play of 1958,
lives in permanent and irrational fear of reality (IV 347). The social
consequences of Biedermann's personal failure are demonstrated by the
fact that the fire-raisers select his house because it is nearest to
the gasometer, and by setting fire to it they can thus cause most damage.
The intruders represent another feature which gives rise to 'Angst' in
modern society - violence. Schmitz makes much of his former profession
of wrestler to Biedermann (IV 330). The fact that Biedermann is ripe
for coercion must not osbscure the fact that he is coerced. The
depiction of the violence of society reaches its culmination in
Andorra. Society, far from sustaining the individual, destroys him.
Yet, however much society is responsible for inducing 'Angst' in the
individual, the Frisch character cannot attribute his problems entirely
to the shortcomings of society, nor can he hope for personal improvement
from a reform of society [13]. It is in the individual psyche that
liberation must take place, and this is a conviction which Frisch,
despite his polemics against the ills of society both in his works and
his journalism, never loses.

No single relationship in the work of Frisch exemplifies more fully
than that between Stiller and Julika that the ills of society in the
final analysis play only a contributary, not a central, role in the
difficulties of the individual. Neither Stiller nor Julika are able
as individuals to commit themselves to what they are, their relationship
exacerbates the difficulties which this lack of commitment causes, and
leads finally to her death and his spiritual decline. Their relative
failure in the public sphere - he as a sculptor and she as a dancer -
are the result of their personal inadequacies and not of a social
situation capable of improvement. Their inadequacies are characterised
by 'Angst', which in both cases has its roots in deep-seated fears of
sexual inadequacy. Stiller's longing for the impossible is to a large
extent responsible for his involvement with Julika, since, like Faber
and Biedermann, he does not adapt his behaviour to what is plain to all -
other men instinctively sense Julika's frigidity (III 437). Yet his

perseverance with the relationship, even if he lacks the perceptions
which previous experience might have afforded, is in defiance of his
own instinctive awareness of the limitations of the situation. Indeed,
Stiller makes a perverse virtue of respecting these limiations despite
his real inclinations, as Julika is for her part aware (III 439).
They are attracted to one another by an awareness of their inadequacies:
'Sie brauchten einander von ihrer Angst her' (III 440). Yet there is
a difference in their attitudes in that Julika has no false expectations
beyond what she perceives to be the limitations of their relationship,
which she sees as being viable if the sexual element remains excluded
(III 439). Stiller, on the other hand, has expectations beyond these
limitations and is permanently wounded by the undisclosed word used by
Julika to express her repugnance 'in ihrer ersten gemeinsamen Nacht'
(III 458). Since he relates everything to no wider framework than
himself, he can only construe what she says exclusively as evidence of
his failure as a man

> so dass er Worte, die Julika möglicherweise jedem Mann
> hätte sagen können, ganz und gar auf sich bezog. (III 458)

If Julika enters marriage with Stiller in the expectation that their
sexual relations would play a minimal role, they become for Stiller a
'Bewährungsprobe' (III 496): his achievement of sexual ecstasy for
them both would be a final and triumphant assertion of his manhood and
a victory over the actual possibilities in the relationship. But in
his last interview with Julika in Davos before he disappears to the
United States, Stiller admits to the impossibility of the task which
he undertook in respect of their relationship (III 496-497).
Paradoxically, his failure in that self-imposed task bound him even
more closely to her, as 'Angst' encouraged the vain hope that he
might nonetheless succeed. Even here, at this moment of apparent
truth, he is not able to look upon Julika's tuberculosis as anything
but punishment for his failure in the impossible. Because he can
never be entirely truthful about himself and his relationship with
his wife, he can never come to terms with their relationship in a
manner which would allow him either to accommodate himself to it or
free himself from it. As a result, his release from prison offers
no possibility of a fresh start in his re-union with her. In their
desolate hotel room, even for the indulgent observer Rolf, they are
like 'zwei Gefesselte' (III 733). Stiller's final words to Julika
in Davos before he disappears therefore assume, in the light of
subsequent events, the bravado of a man still dependent on external
acclaim:

> Nämlich ich weiss jetzt, dass nicht du es bist, was mich
> bis heute gehindert hat, wirklich zu leben. (III 501)

The truth of these words is at odds with his ability to act upon them.

The resolute pursuit of truth is put forward by Reinhart in Die
Schwierigen as the only means by which the debilitating emotion of
'Angst' can be countered. To his long-suffering mother, he claims that
no price is too high to pay to be rid of the paralysing effect of
'Angst' because 'aus der Angst kommt nichts heraus, überhaupt nichts!'
(I 531). Significantly, the passage occurs during a discussion of his
father's alcoholism, for the largely unfocussed 'Angst' which besets
the Frisch character is also a form of addiction. This is the conclusion
which must follow from the many instances where detailed and precise
knowledge of the problem of 'Angst' fails to resolve it. The victim
remains in thrall. This is true even at an apparently advanced stage
of self-liberation. Self-acceptance can itself prove fettering if the
individual is constantly at pains to demonstrate that he has accepted
himself as he is. Rolf explains to Stiller that this is also a manifestation of 'Angst' (III 670). Stiller is able to record, in a somewhat
self-congratulatory tone, an instance where his behaviour appears not
to be determined by a force other than his own volition, namely, the
expectations of others. This concerns precisely the matter of drinking.
Stiller has been released on bail for the afternoon, and as he sits with
Julika in a café, she asks him not to drink so much. Stiller eventually
decides against ordering more whisky 'denn Trotz ist das Gegenteil von
wirklicher Unabhängigkeit' (III 435). It might be that Stiller's
motivation in not drinking is simply to convince Julika that he is not
the same person as the one who disappeared seven years previously. But
the incident, although trivial, suggests that he might move towards
liberating the larger areas in which his behaviour is not free. In the
novel, direct comment of a more reliable nature about the way in which
individual behaviour can be reduced to a reaction to the behaviour of
others comes from independent witnesses. The consumptive young priest
whom Julika encounters during her stay in Davos draws her attention to
the way in which her behaviour, not merely towards her husband, is not
genuinely free (III 483). Julika obliges him to explain further, and
he describes her lack of freedom in another way, by drawing her attention
to her refusal to commit herself to her own life:

> Sie wollen nicht erwachsen werden, nicht verantwortlich
> werden für Ihr eigenes Leben. (III 483)

Another witness, Rolf, places Stiller's lack of freedom into an ontological framework in which Stiller's pride at his independence of Julika

in the matter of a glass of whisky becomes insignificant. For Rolf,
Stiller's attempt at self-acceptance has been doomed to failure
because they have never been conducted in relation to a wider sphere
of reference, in relation to 'so etwas wie Gott' (III 775) [14]. Such
a sphere of reference would provide the perspective which Stiller lacks
in which to come to terms with his real stature, in contrast to his
grandiose dreams of himself. Until he relates himself to such a sphere
of reference, his insistence on his insignificance is simply a form of
masochistic castigation that he is not what his dreams would have him
be (III 775-776). This insistence is a form of pride. Just as he
refuses to accept the limitations of his relationship with his wife, so
he cannot accept his own limitations. Stiller has a vision of what he
could be like without these limitations. The vision and the damage which
it causes by its contrast to reality Frisch calls 'Selbstüberforderung'
(III 668). It is the gravest manifestation of the individual's failure
to commit himself to his own personality.

'Selbstüberforderung'

'Selbstüberforderung' designates the attempts made by the individual
to define himself outside the framework of the possible. In so far as
the individual fails to perceive that true freedom resides only in a
full commitment to the possible, to the limitations of the individual
character, 'Selbstüberforderung' is the main manifestation of his lack
of freedom. For under 'Selbstüberforderung' are subsumed all the
personality traits which contribute to the moral subjection of Frisch's
characters [15]. The presence of these traits which lead to 'Selbstüberforderung' blights the individual's contact with those around him and
paralyses his ability to organise his behaviour purposively.

The beginnings of the concept of 'Selbstüberforderung', later to
find its fullest realisation in Stiller, can be traced back to Frisch's
earliest extant creative works. It first manifests itself in a generalised dissatisfaction with the manner in which the possibilities of
youth seem in later life to have become restricted to an unproductive
daily round. Antwort aus der Stille treats of a young man who breaks
temporarily with all that his daily life represents in order to make a
dramatic gesture towards the achievement which he feels to be within
him. In a Mundart broadcast in 1937 on the novel [16], Frisch comments
on the hero's motivation. He sees the dissatisfaction which prompted
the hero to action as widespread: the individual is aware of the
special nature of his life, yet cannot reconcile this with the mundane

round of chores and minor events which constitute its passing. To some
extent, this dissatisfaction, which also causes the narrator in Bin to
set out for Peking, is socially conditioned. The individual lives in
society, the values of which he absorbs, and the yardsticks of which he
uses to measure himself. Indeed, the Frisch character is most likely
to be conditioned by society to the extent that he reacts against its
expectations. The outstanding example of this particular form of social
conditioning is provided by the character-sketch of himself by Stiller
at the end of the 'Fünftes Heft' (III 600-601) of how he believes
others see him. Ironically, this is a most precise portrait of Stiller,
yet at the point where self-acceptance and hence commitment are
mentioned, Stiller stands back and rejects self-acceptance because
others expect it of him. Before his departure to the United States,
Stiller knew a young homosexual, Alex, who commits suicide during
Stiller's absence. Later Stiller is visited in prison by the parents.
Professor Haefeli, the father, comments on the necessity for the
individual to live with his weaknesses, and goes on to question,
apparently with the agreement of Stiller, the psychological stability
of those who require constant social approval (III 588-589). Yet in
the major public gesture of his own life, his participation in the
Spanish Civil War, Stiller suffers what he considers to be a loss of
public esteem from which he cannot recover, from which he does not
permit himself to recover. Masochistically he recounts at social
gatherings his failure to shoot at a group of Nationalist soldiers,
who then tied him up and left him to be rescued ignominiously by his
own side [17]. Sibylle, to her embarrassment, is not spared, on her
first visit to his studio, a re-enactment of his defects in this
incident. Her balance and her firm grasp of the priorities of life
enable her to define his situation to him (III 616). But Stiller is
unable to draw conclusions, as Sibylle does, from the disparity between
his actual performance and his expectation of his performance. It is
not clear to what extent Stiller has internalised in his own inflated
expectations of himself his interpretation of society's expectations
of him. But it is reasonable to assume that, however much the contours
of the idealised personality of the individual in thrall to 'Selbstüberforderung' are fashioned by personal phantasy, the social ethos
provides clichés which nourish that phantasy.

The most immediate anticipation of the formulation of 'Selbstüberforderung' in Stiller occurs in the Hörspiel Rip van Winkle. The
Staatsanwalt, in conversation with the Verteidiger of the significantly

named Fremdling, the hero, emphasises one symbolic aspect of the story
of Rip van Winkle: the profitless drudgery of setting up the skittles
for the game of ninepins in the mountains is likened to the manner in
which the individual's exaggerated expectations of himself cause him
ceaseless frustration (III 827). In Stiller it is also the Staatsanwalt, Rolf, who describes 'Selbstüberforderung' and its deleterious
consequences, and in doing so, provides a contrastive figure against
which the main figure of Stiller may be set. Rolf begins his definition
by emphasising the destructive nature of 'Selbstüberforderung'.
Basically, the malaise results from a discrepancy between the emotions
and the intellect: modern man is subject to emotions of which he is
intellectually ashamed. Drawing on and learning from his own experience
in a manner foreign to Stiller, Rolf sees his awareness of the general
problem as having been awakened by the incident with the flesh-coloured
cloth in Genoa. The situation of which the Genoa episode was an
expression must be confronted. The two most widespread tactics of
evasion are futile: the smothering of the life of the emotions, and
the pretence that the emotions are not emotions. Both forms of 'Selbst-
belügung' (III 668) lead inexorably to 'Selbstentfremdung' (III 668).
The classic symptom of the denial of this aspect of the psyche is the
ironic belittling of emotions. This dissociation of intellect and
emotion provides the psychological background to 'Selbstüberforderung',
the central aspect of which is a discrepancy between expectation and
performance. The emotional hall-mark of 'Selbstüberforderung' is the
permanent frustration of a bad conscience that the discrepancy is not
being bridged (III 669). The siren voice of vanity, 'die kokette
Stimme eines Pseudo-Ich' (III 669), tempts the individual away from
the path towards his true self. Stiller's disregard of this most
explicit warning leads directly to the paltry mendacity of the 'ferme
vaudoise'.

At this point, Rolf's monologue is interrupted by a short report
on a discussion between Rolf and Stiller on the famous assertion by
Manto in the second part of Goethe's Faust: 'Den lieb ich, der Unmög-
liches begehrt'. It is important to emphasise the nature of this
conversation as it is reported, for it relates directly to the role of
the contrasting figures and episodes in the four major novels. The two
men agree on the danger inherent in Manto's statement. It is dangerous
because it contains an invitation to disregard the bounds of the
possible:

> Dieser Vers...ist eine Einladung zur Neurose, hat mit
> einem wirklichen Streben (er redet ja auch nicht von

> Streben, sondern von Begehren) nichts zu tun, das die
> Demut vor unseren begrenzten Möglichkeiten voraussetzt.
>
> (III 669)

There is thus no question of equating 'Selbstüberforderung' or Stiller
himself, its fullest exemplification, with undertakings which are not
misconceived and utterly harmful [18]. In addition, the agreement between
the two men on this point further highlights the contrast between them,
since it underlines Stiller's failure to act. Rolf's interpretation
of Manto's statement is at one with his experience and behaviour,
Stiller's is not. The function of the break in the monologue is to
emphasise Stiller's essentially negative relationship to its content.

Rolf, as he resumes his monologue, draws attention to Stiller's
representative status in that for many perception by no means always
leads to action (III 669) [19]. In a statement which points forward to
the story of the ambassador in Gantenbein, Rolf is of the opinion that
such perception should remain silent, and emphasises that, of itself,
perception only constitutes a beginning. It is also erroneous to assume
that the translation of perception into action, the final stage which
Rolf calls 'Selbstannahme' (III 670), will come with the passing of the
years. Unless the individual acts, his increasing age will merely
induce a false sense of resignation at the injustice of the world in not
recognising and rewarding him. That is no escape from spiritual bondage.
True self-acceptance can only take place within a wider ontological
framework which can provide a valid moral perspective. 'Selbstannahme',
the antithesis of 'Selbstüberforderung', is a man's greatest venture
and requires the deployment of his entire resources: 'Es braucht die
höchste Lebenskraft, um sich selbst anzunehmen' (III 670). It is a
commitment to what is possible which harnesses energies and leads to
achievement. Any retreat from such a commitment must result in the
dissipation of substance.

The course of the novel, in so far as he is unable to realise his
personality, in so far as he remains in thrall to 'Selbstüberforderung',
charts the dissipation of Stiller's substance. The 'Nachwort'
demonstrates this clearly. The self-questioning and the ceaseless self-
analysis conducted in prison have not been a prelude to action in freedom, indeed, they appear to have reduced Stiller to impotence, for the
problems which seemed soluble in the safety of prison assume in the
'Nachwort' the guise of invincible spectres in Stiller's eyes. It might
even be that the 'Nachwort' demonstrates that his time in prison was a
period of regression, since all the manifestations of 'Selbstüberforderung' are present in reinforced strength after his release. Once more,

the relationship with Julika is for Stiller the measure of all his ills.
His belief that matters would have been different in different circumstances appears ineradicable. Forlornly, Rolf attempts to disabuse him
of the illusion that a relationship with another woman, with Sibylle
for example, would have altered him (III 764). Stiller prefers to
ignore the fact that Sibylle was prepared to commit herself to him
until she perceived his moral tergiversation (III 635). The destructive
irrationality of Stiller's attitude is underlined by his continuing belief
in miraculous transformation. Prior to his first visit to them in their
hotel in Territet before they rent the 'ferme vaudoise', Rolf had noted
that Stiller and Julika appeared to be living 'von der Hoffnung auf
weitere Wunder' (III 731). Now, as Julika lies dying, Rolf tries to
impress upon Stiller the folly of expecting too much from his assertion
that he loves his wife:

> Du erwartest von deiner Liebe wirklich so etwas wie ein
> Wunder, mein Lieber, und das ist es vermutlich, was nicht
> geht. (III 769)

As always, it is Stiller himself who gives the clearest and most precise
formulation to the matter. He compares his return to Julika with the
return to the gaming-tables of a gambler, who, having lost heavily,
still cannot accept that he has lost, and continues to gamble because
gambling has set up its own momentum in the individual and he has not
the moral energy left to stop. For a similar reason, Stiller is unable
to cut himself free from his wife and forget her (III 768). The
strength and destructive power of 'Selbstüberforderung', as exemplified
in the fate of Stiller, are indicated in the language and imagery of
addiction. 'Selbstüberforderung' evolves a behaviour pattern which
prevents the hapless victim from reaching out, mentally or spiritually
from the confines of the personality. He is thus unable to break out
of the self-generating vicious circle which surrounds him [20]. There is
one thing which the individual in the grip of 'Selbstüberforderung' and
the individual committed to himself have in common: a vantage point
from which they can observe their behaviour. But whereas the latter,
as in the case of the ambassador in <u>Gantenbein</u>, observes his actions,
which are fuelled by the energies which he has released by his commitment, with an intense sense of surprise at the extent of the potential
being realised, the former, as in the case of Stiller, observes his
actions, the predictable pattern of which he knows only too well, with
an appalled fascination: 'Ich hatte immer wieder einmal so einen eiser-
nen Willen mit verkehrter Steuerung' (III 683). Part of the horror of
the 'bodenlose Tiefe' to which Schiller saw the individual consigning
himself by not committing himself to his nature is that futility is not

shapeless, but has a pattern which is agonisingly repeated.

The related characters Reinhart, Don Juan, Faber and Stiller all
share to a greater or lesser degree the hybris which is one of the
driving forces of 'Selbstüberforderung'. They all imagine that they
can alter an aspect of reality. Reinhart imagines that he can change
himself by changing his social designation, by becoming Anton the
gardener, and pays for this illusion with his life. Don Juan believes
that it is possible to live in a social limbo, independent of others.
Life revenges itself on him by making him a father. Faber, placing
his faith in the non-organic world of technology, imagines that he is
beyond the dictates of organic laws, and kills his only creation,
Sabeth. Stiller, unable to come to terms with himself, imagines that
he can change the nature of his relationship with Julika, without the
necessary first step of active self-adjustment. Indeed, his pride
goes so far as to cause him to imagine that he can change Julika herself.
Rolf pleads with him to abandon this delusion, born of hybris and doomed
to failure (III 772). With something approaching despair, Rolf
realises that the man who has become his friend has made no progress
towards an acceptance of himself and his situation, that he is still
in bondage to 'Selbstüberforderung' in that he imagines that he can
miraculously redeem Julika and himself from the hell which they have
created for themselves. In urging Stiller to come to his senses, to
see the reality of his situation, Rolf attributes to Stiller the wilful
blindness which is such a notable feature of all the major Frisch
heroes (III 764). Rolf perceives that Stiller has denied his experience
and that his odyssey has in this sense been circular and self-consuming.
Stiller inhabits a world in which grand gestures are merely the stuff
of day-dreams. These day-dreams are Stiller's compensation for the fact
that the world is at it is. In his insistence that, if his day-dreams
are not realisable, they at least ought to be, there is a ridiculous
element to Stiller [21]. If he is in the final analysis a tragic figure,
his tragedy results from impotence and not from action. It is a
tragedy in which moral dimensions are implied by their absence rather
than indicated by their presence.

In the figure of Stiller the entire gamut of existential problems
faced by the modern intellectual has been delineated. In so far as
Stiller has many traits in common with the other major Frisch heroes,
he can be said to be representative of them. Yet a distinction must
be made between Stiller as such a representative and the figure of
Biedermann. For although Biedermann shares many of the shortcomings

of Stiller, such as moral evasion and wilful blindness, the 'Nachspiel'
to Biedermann und die Brandstifter demonstrates that he possesses one
attribute in which Stiller is wholly lacking: the capacity to survive.
His imperviousness to every argument constitutes his very protection [22].
He survives having learnt nothing. Adelheid Weise has established
distinctions between the Bürger whom he represents, and the intellectual
whom Stiller represents [23]. In her definition of the Bürger, the
attention which the Bürger pays to his material existence not only
precludes his paying attention to the moral sphere, he has no knowledge
of such a sphere. If the Bürger is too pre-occupied with actuality to
see the possibilities of life, the intellectual cannot come to terms
with actuality because he is too pre-occupied with its possibilities,
and his attitude is thus one of flight. This is nothing less than the
'Selbstüberforderung' demonstrated by Stiller. For 'Selbstüberforderung'
is a description of the condition of the intellectual caught between a
reality which he finds unacceptable, and on which he therefore turns his
back, and an ontology to which he does not relate his activities
because he cannot submit. It is not a tenable position, and the aura
of desolation which surrounds the major Frisch characters testifies to
their awareness that they have failed to achieve a viable philosophy.
Only Biedermann who, in a special sense, is not of their number, survives, complacent and uncaring, the holocaust to which he has contributed.
For the others, suicide, malignant disease and diminution of the pulse
of life are the tolls exacted for their failure.

Destruction and the personality

The awareness of the Frisch characters that they are not destined
to flourish and multiply is manifested in the pattern of destruction
which surrounds them. This is not destruction for the sake of renewal,
the replacement of that which no longer enhances life. Destruction in
the works of Frisch is wholly negative. Just as the spiritual rootlessness of the Frisch character is indicated by the provisional nature of
his living arrangements, destruction is the external symbol of his
inner barrenness. At a superficial level destruction occurs in the
breaking of minor domestic objects. In Rip van Winkle, Stiller, Gantenbein and Biografie such objects, often drinking glasses, are thrown
against walls. The incidence of these breakages is sufficient for them
to form part of the theme of destruction, and their frequency, not only
over Frisch's work as a whole, but within the framework of the individual
works, can legitimately be construed as an indication of permanent

emotional tension. It is a minor symptom of the existential frustration
which besets all the major Frisch characters.

That they suffer from the curse of a blighted heritage is an idea
present in several Frisch characters. This is apparent from the bizarre
circumstances, always attended by destruction or attempts at destruction,
in which these figures confront their fathers. The brooding, resentful
relationship between Reinhart and his father in Die Schwierigen, the
most fully-documented of these father-son relationships, reaches the
most acute point of its animosity when Reinhart attempts to shoot his
father (I 583-584). Circumstances contrive to underline Reinhart's
impotence against the heredity which he believes to be tainted: his gun
is empty since he has already used his ammunition to shoot at birds, and
so his father is not harmed. Afterwards Reinhart reflects that it would
have been a pointless action to kill his father, since it would have
been an avoidance of the necessity to confront himself (I 584). Yet
so convinced is Reinhart that his heredity has harmed him that he feels
that it is in any case pointless to confront himself, and his subsequent
suicide is the outcome of this conviction. In Bin the destructive
relationship to the father occurs within the framework of the cycle of
birth and death (I 656). Since the time of Kilian's father's death
coincides with the birth of Kilian's child, it appears that Kilian, in
order to become a father, must consent to the death of his father. Any
such continuity of life is absent from the parallel confrontation in
Stiller between Stiller and his dead father in the Bowery district of
New York (III 526-528). Stiller admits to the Staatsanwalt that the
man is in fact his step-father. Since the step-father actually appears
at the juridical confrontation in Stiller's studio (III 720) long after
Stiller's period in the United States, the imagined incident in the
Bowery symbolises his dislike of his spiritual heritage and his
destructive feelings towards it. The culmination of the theme of tainted
heritage occurs in the figure of Faber, himself a father. Not only does
he bring about his own collapse, he destroys also that part of him which
could have lived on beyond him, his daughter Sabeth. His awareness of
his guilt forms the content of his last observation before the operation
which will confirm the fatal disease within him: he laments that Sabeth
was destined to meet her 'Vater..., der alles zerstört' (IV 203). The
measure of Faber's barrenness of spirit is the destruction of his
offspring.

The best-known example of destruction by fire in Frisch's work
occurs in Biedermann und die Brandstifter. The opening stage-direction,

according to which Biedermann lights a cigar (IV 327), points to the
way in which Biedermann himself lights the conflagration which is to
engulf him. Yet Biedermann survives the holocaust with untroubled
complacency. For other Frisch characters, destruction by fire is a
consequence of the moral pollution which they have caused. Reinhart
returns with Hortense to the inn where he began his ill-starred
association with Yvonne to find that it has burned down (I 514). The
sanatorium in Davos, where Julika spent many months, and which was the
scene of Stiller's unsuccessful attempt to put an end to their harmful
relationship, has burned down by the time Stiller returns from America
(III 420). As the narrator in Gantenbein at the beginning of the novel
contemplates the empty flat, symbol of the failure of his marriage and
of his failure as a person, he considers setting fire to the ruins of
his past. But he has no matches, and contents himself with imagining
the scene (V 20). But even this imaginary scene is attended by
impotent farce: the objects and materials fail to catch fire properly.
Everything would require to be soaked in petrol. In the atmosphere of
ineffectualness which the narrator creates for himself, even the
purifying element of fire requires to be stimulated. It is a typical
and ironic contrast between intent and inept execution.

The theme of destruction culminates in the destruction of personal
achievement or creation. Convinced of his inner bankruptcy, Reinhart
consigns his pictures to the flames (I 496), despite the fact that
their creation imparted to him the most vibrant sensation of being
alive which he had ever experienced (I 433). He never again attempts
to create. Stiller, in the course of the juridical confrontation in
his studio, destroys the figures which he had modelled, and in doing
so experiences briefly something akin to the emotional and mental poise
with which he had created them. But this sensation is fleeting, and
yields to a feeling of desolation unparalleled in his life, 'der erbärm-
lichste Augenblick meines Lebens' (III 722). Stiller's destruction of
the figures is not an act of liberation. Like Reinhart, he never again
creates [24], and his final decline dates from this moment of destruction.
Faber's destruction is the most heinous. Not only does he destroy
another human being, that human being was created by him. His
instruction, as he lies in hospital, that all his papers should be
destroyed in the event of his death (IV 199), seems like an act of
pedantic tidiness beside his monstrous crime, yet it is understandable
that he should wish to erase all traces of himself. The narrator in
Gantenbein, in his role as Svoboda, wishes to destroy the scene of his

life with Lila, and with his Swiss army rifle begins methodically to
shoot up the apartment where they lived. Since Svoboda is an architect,
this is also an indication of his destructive relationship to what he
creates. Even this action does not entirely eradicate the element of
phantasy present in the Frisch character, however. Peru was the illusory
land where everything was better, and Svoboda's bullets fail to destroy
it: 'Dann ein beschämender Fehlschuss auf den tönernen Inka-Hund aus
Peru' (V 261). In a sense the destruction of that with which Kürmann
has identified himself in Biografie is the cruellest in that he is not
the agent of the destruction. Kürmann, in the course of his research,
discovered a reflex vital to the state of the behavioural sciences at
the time (V 516). But subsequent research has invalidated Kürmann's
discovery (V 560). The entire spectrum of professions occupied by the
modern intellectual is seen to be unproductive, since for Reinhart the
painter, Stiller the sculptor, Faber the engineer, Svoboda the architect
and Kürmann the scientist the products of their creativity are doomed
to destruction. Significantly, it is for the most part they themselves
who carry out this destruction.

The obsessive quest for an illusory freedom in which all potential
will be realised ends in destruction, the symbol of failure and
spiritual bondage. The vicious circle created by bidding for this
illusory freedom is typified by the fate of Graf Öderland: in apparently
breaking out, he merely draws tighter about him the chains which he has
created for himself in his imagination. Öderland is spritually self-
destructive, not a political martyr [25]. In Kürmann, the latest major
hero, the illusion of untramelled freedom is present as strongly as in
Öderland. The essential irresponsibility of the Frisch character in
this yearning to shed the necessary ties of life is linked to the theme
of destruction. The urge to destroy is unleashed by the awareness that
the imagined freedom is an illusion. The Frisch character cannot
accommodate the knowledge of the confines of life. This inability is
typified by Walter Faber, whose desire to destroy his eyesight after
the death of Sabeth is a desire to eliminate the knowledge of his
complicity in her death. Knowledge destroys the illusions of the Frisch
character, but he cannot accept the advent of knowledge as a necessary
process in living life. He does not possess sufficient inner resources
to cope with knowledge. Hence his reaction is to destroy. It is a
reaction which may be different in degree, but certainly not in kind,
from that of throwing a glass against a wall.

The fates of the major Frisch heroes indicate, however, that even

if they resist incorporating knowledge into the motivation of their
behaviour, they are nonetheless undermined psychologically by the
awareness of that knowledge. To the extent that they do not act upon
their knowledge their decline is self-induced. In the figures of
Stiller and Faber knowledge penetrates despite their resistance, but
does not lead to action. The disjunction between knowledge and action
in the Frisch character is the source of his debility. Commenting on
Brecht's Furcht und Elend des dritten Reiches, Frisch expresses the
opinion that, if humanity were capable of recalling with clarity the
stark reality of the past, then humanity would either commit suicide
or arrange matters so that there was no possibility of the mistakes of
the past recurring (II 328). The dilemna of the Frisch character is
that, despite the clarity of his memory and his knowledge, he does not
have the moral vigour necessary to effect a change in his attitude, and
if he attempts suicide he is not always successful.

The reluctance to leave the realm of the imagination is shown by
the behaviour of two later Frisch characters: by the narrator's role-
playing in Gantenbein, and by Kürmann's attempt in Biografie to substitute an imaginary life for his actual life. The same reluctance is
present in the very first hero Jürg. He is fully aware of the plenitude
of the life of the imagination. At his age and in his circumstances,
he has difficulty in conceiving a form of happiness which does not
involve a relationship with a woman. Yet he has sufficient experience
of the discrepancy between imagination and reality to prefer to keep
solely within his mind any happiness beyond such a relationship:

> Wenn auch die Frau nicht das Glück bedeutet: ich weiss
> nicht, wo man das Glück dann suchen soll. Und ich bin so
> feige, dass ich dieses Unbekannte nicht einzulösen wage!
> Weil es vielleicht so viel mehr ist, solange man es nicht
> kennt. (I 295)

It is precisely this fear of renouncing possibilities, however remote
or impossible their realisation might be, which is at the heart of fear
of commitment. Possibilities are always of the imagination, and the
imagination is always under the complete control of the individual.
Since the reality of the present, of the here-and-now, is for the
Frisch hero deficient because it is not capable of being controlled,
renunciation of possibility is regarded as an unwarranted deprivation.
The more the individual takes refuge in his imagination, the more he
requires to do so. The confrontation with reality becomes increasingly
painful, the individual becomes more and more dissociated from the idea
that he must adapt to reality if he is to realise himself. This
dissociation manifests itself in external destruction, itself an

indication of the deeper self-destruction which is taking place.

Encapsulated within himself, the Frisch character leads a life of perpetual torment which cannot be resolved because he cannot commit himself to meaningful action, which is the expression of inner resolve. The mocking comment of the Verfasser to Herr Biedermann in Herr Bieder-mann und die Brandstifter on the latter's failure to take action against the intruders in his home indicates the psychological situation of the Frisch characters:

> Es muss eine schwere Zeit für Sie gewesen sein, Herr
> Biedermann, all diese inneren Kämpfe, die immer wieder
> damit endeten, dass Sie nichts unternehmen konnten. (IV 301)

Stiller, generalising from his own predicament, considers that encapsulation is a feature of the modern age. Seeking to explain to Knobel the warder the nature of his 'Morde', his designation for the breakdown of his personal relations with a variety of people, he mentions the emotional release which actual murders would have afforded. In the fact that action has taken place lies the attraction of actual murder, because action, even destructive action such as murder, is a form of relief from the strain of living (III 476). Past ages such as the Renaissance period are admired by Stiller for having characterised themselves by such action; today, on the other hand, all is internal-ised. Stiller's vision of liberating action is of a piece with his belief that he could realise himself in the vastness of the United States. Reality disproves both illusions: the United States does not solve his problems, and the act of destroying his figures, which he supposed would liberate him from his past, in fact creates a void which he is not destined to fill. All Stiller's actions are attended by inflated expectations, and his corrosive petulance when these expectations are not fulfilled increases his unwillingness to come to terms with the true nature of life. Pelegrin, the early incorporation of inadequacy, is dubbed a 'Feigling vor dem wirklichen Leben' (II 66). It is a designation which could apply to all the major Frisch characters in their failure to reach an accommodation with what is outside them and so to commit themselves to the shape of their identity against that wider reality.

Fear of commitment in the major figures in Frisch's work derives from their inadequate relationship to reality. They do not adapt their outlook as a result of contact with, and observation of, reality. Instead, they constantly demand that reality should conform to their pre-conceptions of it, and prefer to disregard the evidence of their

perception when it does not so conform, but continues to offer contrary
evidence. But the Frisch character still clings to these pre-conceptions, setting his face resolutely against the notion that he might
learn from reality. In this respect the disbelief of the narrator in
Gantenbein in the evidence of his own eyes is typical:

> Ich kann nicht glauben, dass das, was ich sehe, schon der
> Lauf der Welt ist. (V 314)

With these words the narrator introduces his closing phantasy about the
body which almost succeeds in floating away in the river Limmat without
being identified. The story represents the attempt of the individual
to avoid the final commitment to himself, to his own death, the act
which completes his identity. It is in the failure to submit to
immutable facts of life, such as the inevitability of death, that the
Frisch character is gradually worn down by reality. For his outrage at
the manner in which reality develops in relation to himself is permanent.
The teacher in Andorra reflects this attitude:

> Ich weiss nicht, die Welt hat einen Hang, immer grad die
> mieseste Wendung zu nehmen. (IV 492)

The sense of outrage stems from the fact that the failure of reality
to measure up to the extravagant dimensions expected of it is always
interpreted as a personal insult. The obsessive pre-occupation with
himself prevents the individual from realising that reality treats
others in a similar fashion.

The failure to appreciate that he has this bond with others
increases the isolation of the Frisch character, and puts a further
obstacle in the way of his breaking out and establishing contact with
others, and so ultimately with himself. In this sense the Frisch
character never has the feeling that he forms part of a community.
Imagining that he is excluded from society confers a certain status
which reinforces his ego. The truthfulness of a dream reveals to
Stiller the posturing nature of this special status. In the dream he
re-lives his first outing with Julika after she comes to visit him in
Zürich during his spell in prison. Through the windows of the café
where they sat, he watches himself as he makes a public display of the
fact that he imagines himself to be an outcast (III 415). The similarity of Julika's character to that of Stiller is indicated by the fact
that, in the dream, she is similarly marked. Gantenbein sets himself
apart from society by his yellow arm-band, a form of disguise which
exploits the goodwill of others. The belief that he is in a category
apart absolves the Frisch character of the necessity of having to
come to terms with the world of reality as others do, and consoles him

for his failure in that world.

The Frisch character is not unaware of the loss of dimension which
his life has incurred, but does not necessarily attribute this to a
lack of commitment. In content, and in the manner in which it is made,
Kürmann's admission to Antoinette is typical of the obfuscations with
which the Frisch character surrounds the most obvious of truths. This
admission is not conveyed directly to Antoinette, but is read out to
her by the Registrator from a note which Kürmann has left. Further,
Kürmann also implicates Antoinette in the failure of their relationship,
although she, like Sibylle, is a character with a firm commitment to
reality, as her decision to leave Kürmann shows. Kürmann's message to
her is a lament over the paucity of their relationship:

> 'Wir haben einander verkleinert. Warum haben wir immer
> verkleinert. Ich dich, du mich. Wieso hat sich uns alles,
> was möglich wäre, so verkleinert. Wir kennen einander nur
> verkleinert'. (IV 575) [26]

Yet, if the Frisch character is aware of the loss of dimension to his
life, it is also true to say that he remains sufficiently undisturbed
by this loss to bestir himself to action. There is an element in him
which prevents him from approaching life with the seriousness which it
deserves. This element is a fundamental lassitude of spirit which allows
him to tolerate what he knows from direct experience to be the
deficiencies of his life by belittling the entire framework of human
life in a manner which verges on the frivolous. A passage from Homo
Faber, (IV 92-93) demonstrates, as possibly as no other in the entire
work of Frisch, the range of these negative characteristics: the concern
to seek distraction from the business of living, the fretting at aimless
and boring activity, and the existential isolation trivialised by the
passivity of the reaction to it. Faber, in his apartment in New York,
describes his loneliness which not even attempts at communication –
writing letters – have been able to alleviate; he plays the radio which
emphasises his solitude [27]; he listens to his own footsteps in the empty
apartment; he comments on his distaste for the gin which he nonetheless
continues to drink; all this constitutes his weariness at the pettiness
of life: 'Alles ist nicht tragisch, nur mühsam' (IV 93). This is the
most precise and concentrated description of the desolate passivity
which afflicts the Frisch characters. They fail to commit themselves
to what they are because they fear restriction, and paradoxically create
a world wholly lacking in dimension. As a result, the indeterminate
nature of their lives gradually immobilises them in spiritual lethargy.
Their world, as Faber recognises, is not one which can accommodate the
amplitude of tragedy.

2.   Commitment, <u>Reproduktion</u> and Technology

The main characters in Frisch's work have been seen to be
irresolute. Each one is fearful of the consequences of taking
decisions in those areas of life over which he, in common with other
individuals, has control. Since he fails to take the decisions which
would give direction and purpose to his life, he retreats more and
more into an attitude of dissatisfied passivity. His intelligence
registers the minutiae of this dissatisfaction, his emotions clamour
for release from it, and in this frustrating situation he comes
gradually to believe that all the external circumstances of his life
are conspiring to prevent him realising himself as a human being.
There is some justification for this belief. The world which he
inhabits is, as depicted by Frisch, characterised by the domination of
technology. The influence of technology in the modern world is such
that it has not only created the conditions necessary for physical
survival in the developed countries, but it also determines the nature
of human experience. This determining influence is exercised
principally through <u>Reproduktion</u>, the process whereby technology enables
verbal stimuli and visual images to be endlessly reproduced and disseminated. This artificial process interposes itself between the individual
and his experience of reality. Indeed, this process becomes his reality,
so that his experience bears the marks of uniformity and repetition,
the two chief characteristics of <u>Reproduktion</u>. Thus the nature of the
modern world militates against all forms of individuality. For this
aspect of the condition of modern man the main Frisch characters become
a symbol. Their pusillanimity proves fatal in face of the ceaseless
barrage of the impersonal forces which they encounter daily. The
vitality of a moral dimension, by its absence in these characters, is
shown to be necessary for psychological survival in a world which
thwarts the development of such a dimension. In the various defeats
of his characters, Frisch portrays the difficulties with which individual
commitment must contend in the second half of the twentieth century.

The two main figures through which Frisch examines these
difficulties are those of Stiller the artist and Faber the technologist.
Traditionally the artist communicates his perceptions of life through
his chosen medium. But in a world where perception is becoming less
and less dependent on the insights of the individual, since the perceived
world is becoming increasingly subject to standardisation, this
traditional function of the artist is being eroded. Ironically, it is

the artist who displays the rapidly diminishing possibilities for
individual commitment. Stiller's retreat into silence — Rolf sees him
'nicht als Sonderfall' (III 669) — is thus symbolic. If the changing
nature of the individual's reality is undermining the traditional function
of the artist, it might be expected that the technologist, the custodian
of this new reality, would supplant the figure of the artist as an
interpreter to his fellows. Ironically, this is not the case. Stiller
the artist fails because he cannot penetrate as an individual to an
experience of reality which he could imbue with universal validity, and
in the world of Reproduktion he becomes immured in his own self-centred
concerns. But for Faber, the technologist, making the machine the centre
of the world is equally limiting because, despite the omnipresence of
the machine, there is no universal significance to be extracted from it
which would link the individual to a wider metaphysical framework.
Faber is also representative. He is not only the figure of the
technologist, in him as a human being are reflected the effects of the
kind of world which he himself is helping to create [1]. It is important
to emphasise a further link between the figures of Stiller and Faber.
In the portrayal of both men there is depicted a point of struggle with
the nature of the modern world. In the one case, the struggle is waged
and lost between a not insignificant artistic talent, capable of insight
and perception, and the impersonal forces of the mass media and mass-
production, the world of Reproduktion. In the other case, the struggle
is waged and lost between, on the one hand, a mentality which has become
so imbued with a regard for the machine that all reality is viewed from
a mechanistic standpoint, and, on the other, the forces of life itself,
which finally demonstrate their superiority over the machine. Frisch's
depiction of the intensity and relevance of these two struggles represents his major artistic achievement. It might be that the dynamism of
the struggles imparts a momentum to the two novels which accords them
special status in the corpus of Frisch's works, for in the later Gantenbein the point of struggle has been passed. There, the narrator's
games of the imagination are merely games, and this in itself offers a
comment on the individual's freedom in the modern world. Stiller and
Faber suffer because they are aware of their failure as humans. Awareness of failure implies a positive standard of measurement. Such a
standard is contained in moral commitment to the realisation of
individuality, the only defence against the impersonality of the
modern world. By their protracted and losing struggles, Stiller and
Faber show where the path of salvation lies.

The world of Reproduktion
_____

The manner in which the mass media succeed in imposing an image of
reality on the consciousness of the individual before he has the opportunity directly to experience that reality is a theme which recurs
in the work of Frisch. He discusses the dissociation of experience
and reality in the modern world in Tagebuch 1946-1949 (II 512-513).
The room in Florence which Savonarola once occupied contains a picture
of his execution by fire. The picture reveals a directness of
experience which characterises that age as opposed to the modern age:
Savonarola's judges are directly involved in the decision which they
have taken to the extent that they are witnessing the execution. For
them too, the execution retains its full impact. The modern age, on
the other hand, lives, not with reality, but with images of reality.
Frisch contrasts the direct experience of past ages with the situation
which has been brought about by techniques of mass communication which
results in the individual having 'eine Anschauung, ohne geschaut zu
haben' (II 512). Experience of reality is anticipated by the media of
communication and dissemination. The narrator in Bin sees the Wall of
China 'die anzusehen war, wie man sie von Bildern eben kennt' (I 605).
Despite the fact that the Staatsanwalt in Graf Öderland is obliged to
say of Santorin, the location where his ideal vision of life will be
realised: 'Ich kenne es nur von Bildern' (III 54), he is nonetheless
able to give an exact description of how it must look. In Stiller,
the man with whom Stiller has travelled from Paris in the train is
able to suggest to officials a possible clue to the identity of the
man with the false passport, because, as Stiller records, 'dieser Herr
mich mit einem Bild in seiner Illustrierten verwechselte' (III 365).
The irony is here enhanced by the fact that Stiller is later officially
designated as the person the 'Illustrierte' says he is. Stiller's only
confidant during his first few days in prison, Knobel the warder, knows
about the jungles of South America 'aus Kulturfilmen' (III 377), and
so provides a sympathetic audience for Stiller's more lurid tales. For
the narrator in Gantenbein, in his role as Enderlin the traveller,
Jerusalem has no surprises for him since it is as he had imagined it
from the images he has seen of it (V 154). Because reality is for the
individual pre-determined to the extent that he knows the appearance of
everything which he is likely to see from images, he has no direct
contact with reality.

Since the individual is becoming unaccustomed to direct experience
of reality, he comes to accept, and even to require, what appears to be

the mediation between himself and reality offered by Reproduktion.
Walter Benjamin, in his essay 'Das Kunstwerk im Zeitalter seiner technischen Reproduzierbarkeit', discusses this phenomenon and the extent
to which the individual's perception of reality acquires the characteristics of technical mediation: printed pictures and film transmit an
image of reality which is both superficial and endlessly repeatable,
and which contrast with the uniqueness of the image of reality contained
in a painting [2]. Whereas the painting can act as a mediator between the
individual and reality, Reproduktion has moved to a position where it
is arbiter of what reality is. The products of Reproduktion thus
provide the measure against which the validity of experience can be
gauged. Stiller's experience of a market-place in Mexico is confirmed
in its reality for him through its close approximation to the image
which he has of a Mexican market-place from films which he has seen
(III 381). Later, as he drives out of New York, he notes that the
countryside 'gleitet vorüber wie ein Farbfilm mit Wald und See und
Schilf' (III 530). In the story of Isidor, the hero, strolling in
Marseilles, notes that the Mediterranean 'leuchtete wie auf einem Plakat'
(III 393-394), while for Faber the air-hostess calming the passengers,
as the plane from New York to Mexico City is about to crash-land, is
'lächelnd wie Reklame' (IV 18). The modern mind, replete with images,
automatically relates reality to them, not only in the brief and
fragmented sights of everyday life, but also in its more permanent
attitudes. A passage from Als der Krieg zu Ende war illustrates in
ironic fashion how the eternal human capacity for prejudice is exploited
by Reproduktion. Horst, Agnes's husband, asks her for a description of
the Russian officer. Her answer mocks the stereotyped images which
people his mind in general, and concludes of the officer in particular:
'Denk an die Illustrierte! Genau so sieht er aus' (II 262). With the
development of her relationship to the Russian officer, Agnes is
beginning to appreciate the poverty and harmfulness of stereotypes.
But the experience vouchsafed to the individual will not always be of
sufficient intensity to enable him to cast aside these images. Knobel,
in his fourteen years as a prison officer, has encountered only mild-
mannered, even colourless, men in the cells for which he is responsible:
'Wenn er Verbrecher hören will, muss er ins Kino laufen (so sagt er) wie
jeder andere' (III 377). Reality is acceptable to the extent that it
coincides with a received image of itself. To the extent that it does
not, it must be subjected to a corrective confrontation with the image.

In the world of Reproduktion the greatly increased mobility of the

individual paradoxically reduces, rather than enhances, his capacity
fully to experience reality. The traveller has such clear images,
received from countless sources, of the places and sights which he
has not yet visited, that when he does actually see them, he cannot
recognise them for what they are because the substance of the images
of these sights and places prevents the reception of reality in his
mind. Enderlin, as he locks his car in Jerusalem, realises only then
that he has driven past the Mount of Olives (V 154). Enderlin cannot
establish any relationship between himself and what he sees, and his
concluding comments on Jerusalem record the mental and emotional vacuum
in which his visit to the seat of Christendom has taken place: '(Ich)
weiss nur, was ich bei meiner Ankunft schon gewusst habe' (V 156).
Enderlin is the archetypal tourist, uncommunicating and incapable of
receiving communication. Encapsulated in his experiential aloneness,
the modern tourist not only departs unchanged from the places which he
has visited, he also arrives in these places with all the reminders of
the reality from which he thought he was escaping. Hans Magnus Enzensberger, in his essay 'Eine Theorie des Tourismus', shows how this lack
of real change is symbolised by the presence of other tourists around
the traveller [3]. Of the fact that modern travel, advertised as a
release from the reality of daily life, offers no escape from oneself
there is no more forceful exemplification than the three occasions
when circumstances oblige Walter Faber to look closely at himself in a
mirror. In the washroom at Houston, Texas, in the restaurant in Paris,
and in the hospital in Athens (IV 11, 98, 170-171) Faber sees three
reflections of himself which record his progressive physical decline.
At these three strategic points in his journey towards death, Faber,
the traveller who has seen everything and experienced nothing, is
forced painfully and exceptionally to endure sight as an experience
directly related to himself.

In an attempt to restore experiential content to the act of seeing,
Gantenbein imagines himself as a tourist guide in Greece (V 199-201).
In his feigned blindness he would ask tourists to describe what they
are seeing, instead of describing to them what they are seeing, namely
things and places which they have in any case already seen in picutres.
Only in this way will tourists learn to make use of their eyes. He
also imagines an advertisement for his services which might restore some
meaning to the empty clichés of travel brochures: 'Reisen Sie mit
einem Blinden!...Ich öffne Ihnen die Augen!' (V 201). Just as Gantenbein's advertisement would seek to revitalise the language of the

travel agent, so he would try to bring back a lost dimension to travel
itself, because he would put to the tourists 'Fragen, die mit der
Kamera nicht zu beantworten sind' (V 200). For the mobility of the
tourist is not employed to enrich experience, but is used to confirm
that the reality which he sees conforms to the image of it which the
world of Reproduktion has given him. The tourist's ceaseless
photographing confirms the image and not the reality [4]. The brief
sojourns which his mobility enables the tourist to make in a variety
of widely separated places provide no more experience for him than that
offered by Reproduktion through images of the same places. And since
his own photographs of these places act as a substitute for his experience of them, Reproduktion comes to have more substance for him than
reality itself. In this sense modern travel is a denial of the reality
and uniqueness of the individual, as Faber's three experiences of seeing
himself so disruptively remind him.

In the world of Reproduktion human experience requires to be authenticated by the products of Reproduktion. The corollary to this is that
experience which cannot be so authenticated must be subject to doubts
about its validity. Yet, ironically, since Reproduktion can only record
'Augenschein' (V 156), its inability to register anything other than
surface appearance renders it uniquely unfitted to authenticate more
profound experience. Stiller realises this as he tries in vain to
convince his defence-lawyer of the real meaning, as opposed to the
surface appearance, of his stay in the United States (III 412). The
ability of the individual to be a valid repository for his own experience
is increasingly being called in question. The figure of Stiller is
important in this respect. For Stiller is obliged to struggle on two
fronts. Not only is he at grips with the vagaries of his own nature,
he must also combat the forces of Reproduktion which have a fixed and
superficial image of him, as symbolised by the photograph in the
'Illustrierte'. Reproduktion cannot adapt itself to the changes in his
inner reality, but its power in the world is such that its image of him
will prevail. The symbol for this is provided by Stiller's first outing
in Zürich with Julika, when she persuades him to assume the pose of a
photograph taken years before (III 431-432). The static image of
Reproduktion takes precedence of Stiller's claims over his own
experience.

In the figure of Walter Faber the intrusion of the world of Reproduktion upon the individual's relation to his own experience is shown
as having progressed a stage further. For Faber, constantly filming,

has abrogated his right to experience the world, and himself, to the
camera, which becomes the repository of his reactions. More precisely,
since the camera is the repository merely of what it records, the
process of filming bypasses a relationship to what is being filmed, which
as a consequence never impinges on the consciousness of the photographer.
Faber's reaction to the environment is as mechanical as the functioning
of the camera. Indeed, his reaction, when he is not actually filming,
can be conditioned by the fact that he has already filmed a similar
scene, and thus there is no obligation upon him to react to the present
one (IV 15). Face to face with reality, he can only remain passive,
awaiting a stimulus from outside. Gradually the camera becomes the
symbol, not of Faber's desire to record his environment, but of his
profound indifference to it. As the ship on which he will meet Sabeth
sails out of New York harbour, the object of his filming moves from Ivy
his mistress waving from the pier, to the Manhattan skyline to the sea-
gulls accompanying the ship (IV 68) - they all acquire the same
importance since they are all pictures on a film. The indifference of
the camera erodes any scale of values in its operator, and this gives
rise to the indifference and lassitude which make Faber unable to
distinguish what is real and what is not. It is only the unreproducible
uniqueness of death which can cause him to break through to direct
experience. Three times he has experienced a vision of his own impend-
ing death in his mirror reflection, and it is only after Sabeth's
death, when he interrupts his return journey to Athens in Cuba, that
he realises the futility of his filming (IV 182). Yet Faber, once
having abandoned the responsibility of perception to his camera, is
not spared the final punishment for this dereliction. With his newly-
found knowledge that the film is merely a facsimile of reality, he is
obliged to watch in Düsseldorf as a film of the dead Sabeth is run
through in error (IV 185-192). In perceiving that the film cannot be
responded to as reality, he also perceives that he has never responded,
and will now never be able to respond, to the reality of his daughter.

The chief feature of the machine-controlled age of Reproduktion is
its assault on the realities of human experience and its devaluation
of empirical perception as a means of establishing those realities.
The faculties of perception are assailed by so much that is a facsimile
of life that the individual ceases to have defences against the
inauthenticity of experience which these facsimiles contain. Their
ubiquity and their deceptive similarity to the surface of reality
combine to hinder recognition of the fact that they are artefacts. In
past ages artefacts could not only be recognised as such, but could

also be accepted as having an interpretative function since the
individual possessed a direct relationship to reality which was not
impinged upon by these artefacts. The genre of the novel is itself
an example of the way in which an artefact, literature, has come to
lose its substance in the world of Reproduktion. The interpretative
artefacts of the past have been to a large extent replaced by the
products of Reproduktion, which refer to no reality beyond themselves [5].
The disposable successors to the artefacts of former times evoke an
ambiguous response in the individual. On the one hand, their very
availability imparts to them an aura of authority – omnipresence
suggests omniscience. The attitude to the contents of the newspaper,
one of the most widely disseminated products of Reproduktion, bears
witness to this assumed authority. The policeman in Graf Öderland
cites the authority of the newspaper for the veracity of his information:
'Steht im Abendblatt' (III 47). On the other hand, it is the same
policeman who shortly afterwards displays a different attitude to the
omniscience of the products of Reproduktion. As the Staatsanwalt urges
him to consider flight, attended by violence, from his everyday
existence, the policeman admits to having had thoughts of this order,
although they have not been suggested to him by the newspaper (III 50).
The policeman is thus aware that the newspaper cannot offer referential
authority for all aspects of human life. Yet at the same time, those
aspects which do not have this authority acquire a dubious status in
the eyes of the individual who is accustomed to legitimise himself
experientially by reference to the products of Reproduktion. Since
these products can only reflect the surface of reality, the individual
distrusts all that is not of this surface. To his cost as a sentient
being, he adapts his experiences to the capabilities of Reproduktion,
the inauthenticity of which promotes inauthenticity of experience.

The way in which experience becomes inauthentic can be seen in a
comparison of the differing responses of the narrators in Bin and Homo
Faber to the phenomenon of the newspaper. In the former, the narrator
is fully conscious of the fact that the newspaper constitutes an
invitation to vicarious experience: its perusal deflects the individual
from direct experience. The nature of this deflection, as described by
the narrator, is further highlighted by the irrelevance of the newspaper for the young girl, in whose company he is (I 651). Here, human
contact and reflection impart a framework of perspective to the newspaper, for which, ironically, the narrator even finds a minor practical
use as a fan. Walter Faber, on the other hand, has no such contact and
indulges in no such reflection. For him the newspaper has become

exclusively a diversion from the all-pervading tedium of life, the sole
worth of which is the novelty of its contents. Thus the newspaper
which the air-hostess distributes at the start of the flight from New
York is of no interest to him because he has read its main sensational
story in an earlier edition (IV 7). The newspaper, provided it contains
novelty, passes the time, and apparently does nothing more. It certainly
conveys nothing significant, for the scraps of unconnected information
which it imparts cannot cohere in any meaningful fashion in the mind of
the individual. Yet on the basis of what is acquired from newspapers
knowledge is posited. Hence the sarcasm of Stiller on his arrest as he
enters Switzerland is understandable: 'Jeder Zeitungsleser scheint hier
zu wissen, wer Stiller gewesen ist' (III 369). The inauthentic
experience offered by the newspaper and illustrated magazine leads to
an inauthentic perception of the individual.

The inhabitant of the world of Reproduktion is, in Frisch's opinion,
deluded into thinking that the products of the mass media are necessary
for his orientation in the conduct of his daily life:

> Wenn es keine Kioske gäbe, wo man täglich den grossen
> Überblick kaufen kann, ich weiss es wirklich nicht, wie
> unsereiner sich diese Welt vorstellen würde. (VI 84)

The meretricious nature of the delusion is demonstrated clearly in the
figure of Gottlieb Biedermann, the self-important, successful business-
man. Significantly, when Biedermann und die Brandstifter opens, he is
reading a newspaper. The unconnected facts which he imagines that he
is meaningfully assimilating, in fact rob him of any sense of direction
and paralyse his volition. By the time that the intruders are installed
in Biedermann's attic with the drums of petrol, the nature of the
contents of which has been withheld from the policeman with the
connivance of Biedermann himself, the chorus is in a position to
comment on the incapacity of this 'Modell eines von Informationen
gesteuerten Menschen' [6]:

> Schwerlich durchschaut er, was eben geschieht
> Unter dem eigenen Dach. (IV 356)

Since Biedermann is constantly adrift in the world of vicarious
experience noted by the narrator of Bin, perception has in his case
become passive, and is no longer related to analysis and action.

Biedermann's inability to act stems from his dissociation from
reality, and this dissociation manifests itself in his use of language.
His language has no relationship to lived experience, but consists of
the clichés which he has absorbed from the mass media. Since he is
dependent on these mass media for his means of expression, he is open

to manipulation by the content of what they purvey to him. The mall-
eability of Biedermann, the representative Bürger, points to the very
close links in the modern world between Reproduktion and political
power. These links are fully appreciated by Hwang Ti, the tyrant in
Die Chinesische Mauer. Addressing the audience, he mocks them for
imagining that they will profit from the play which they are watching,
since he controls the much more important newspaper which they will
buy after the performance (II 175). The language of Faber, the
technologist who might be thought to be more conscious of the nature
of the modern world and more party to its functioning, demonstrates
that he too is adrift in a universe which he thinks he understands.
In the novel, technical jargon, trade-names, the language of advertising
and the confusing admixture of languages other than German all combine
to demonstrate his personal dislocation. This impoverished language is
not only an exposure of the shallowness of outlook of its user, but is
also a parody [7]. The language of Stiller, a third representative figure,
is equally revealing of his outlook. In a sense, the language of the
seven 'Hefte' which Stiller writes in prison is devoted to denial.
From the first rejection, 'Ich bin nicht Stiller!', to his final account
of the court's decision that he is the person whom he has claimed that
he is not, Stiller is engaged in rejecting some aspect of his past
behaviour or his present environment. Stiller betrays himself through
his language which reveals him, not as an artist who affirms because he
is impressed nor as an artist who accuses because he is outraged, but
as an artist who rejects because his character and the nature of the
modern world combine to sap him of the vigour necessary for the other
two attitudes. His language reveals Stiller as the artist of the world
of Reproduktion. In that it is self-revelatory in this manner, the
the language of Stiller's 'Hefte' is similar to that of Faber's
'Bericht'. Both the 'Hefte' and the 'Bericht' are personal diaries
which reveal, through the imperfect and subjective medium of their
language, the mentality of the writers and of the world which they
inhabit [8]. Thus, by employing the language of the attitude which he
wishes to expose and criticise, Frisch shows, in the figures of Stiller
and Faber, and to a lesser extent in that of Biedermann also, not only
the dire consequences of the individual's failure to make a commitment
to his own experience, but also the sheer difficulty of making such a
commitment in the world of Reproduktion.

Reproduktion and Stiller

It is appropriate that an artist, traditionally a figure credited
with greater perception than his fellows, should comment most fully on
the way in which perception is influenced by the world of Reproduktion.
Stiller, despairing of convincing his defence lawyer that he has in fact
been to the United States, nonetheless concedes to himself that Dr.
Bohnenblust's scepticism is justified. For in the age of Reproduktion
the individual is exposed to so much visual material drawn from all
parts of the world that his description of a given place is by no means
proof that he has been there:

> Wir leben in einem Zeitalter der Reproduktion. Das aller-
> meiste in unserem persönlichen Weltbild haben wir nie mit
> eigenen Augen erfahren, genauer: wohl mit eigenen Augen,
> doch nicht an Ort und Stelle; wir sind Fernseher, Fern-
> hörer, Fernwisser. (III 535)

For Stiller, the disjunction extends beyond the visual sphere to that
of the emotions. Literature, assimilated to the world of Reproduktion
in that it affords a means of vicarious experience, comes between the
individual and his emotions (III 535-536). By relating the themes
which recur in the course of his seven 'Hefte' to the received and
stereotyped interpretations of popular modern authors, some of whose
books are to be found in Stiller's studio [9], Stiller calls in question
the authenticity of the emotions from which the themes derive. Just as
the newspaper-reader can extract no coherent account from the ceaseless
and unconnected flow of news-items, so the individual who concerns himself with literature in the age of Reproduktion is incapable of
classifying, assessing and possibly benefitting from the variegated
literary stimuli to which he is subjected. Stiller ironically suggests
that, in this maelstrom of conflicting influences, a commitment to only
one form of inauthenticity represents an achievement (III 536). The
nature of the modern world thus obliges Stiller to call in question the
entire undertaking of the 'Hefte':

> Wozu also die Erzählerei! Es heisst nicht, dass einer
> dabei gewesen ist. (III 536)

Because the nature of experience has itself become tainted and question-
able, story-telling, traditionally the manner in which individual
experience is rendered apprehensible to others, is open to charges of
inauthenticity.

It is ironic that literature should have lost its reality only with
the coming of the age of Reproduktion, for literature has for long been
disseminated and made available by the mechanical process of printing.

It has also always had an innate tendency to create states of consciousness and expectation which are not in accord with reality. The bawd
Celestina, for example, sees in the existence of literature the permanent
guarantee of her business since her brothel offers distraction from the
burden of false emotions which literature can generate (III 110). It
is only in the age of Reproduktion, however, that literature has become
severed from its connection with reality because it has become part of
the ceaseless, machine-created spectacle of Reproduktion, and as a
consequence acquires the attributes of that spectacle, triviality and
speciousness. It is degraded to being a mere point of reference for a
cliché. Thus, the Verfasser in the Hörspiel Herr Biedermann und die
Brandstifter refers the listeners to 'Seldwyla, das Sie vermutlich aus
der Literatur kennen' (IV 277-278). The constant use of such literary
references as a form of shorthand for the evocation of stereotypes tends
to blur the distinction in the mind of the individual between what is
real and what is not. Indeed, the literary reference tends to acquire
greater authority than the counterpart in reality for which it is
serving as a notation. Just as the tourist's experience of a particular
place is devalued by his having seen before his arrival there so many
reproductions of that place, the individual's experience of life in the
age of Reproduktion, because it lags behind his experience of literature,
lacks directness and participatory intensity. Thus, Stiller conveys to
Julika in Davos his deep feeling for her and also his anguished foreboding that their relationship is not going to succeed. The intensity
of these conflicting emotions is expressed by him clasping her round
the waist and twice shouting 'Du' despairingly (III 473). Julika, the
ballet dancer accustomed to the simulated emotions of the stage, cannot
react to Stiller's emotion: for her, his embrace has the faintly
ridiculous air of a character in a classical play, 'Mortimer oder
Clavigo oder so, der Richtige fiel ihr nicht gerade ein' (III 474).
Literature is the point of reference for the orientation of Julika in
this situation [10]. The individual inhabits a world in which the
demoted status of literature contributes to his impression that his
behaviour has been anticipated to such an extent that his own
experience becomes a surrogate to which it is difficult, if not
impossible, to commit himself.

It is appropriate to consider at this point a passage from Tagebuch
1946-1949 since it contains an assertion of individuality in the age of
Reproduktion which contrasts with the attitude of Julika, and with the
fate which latterly befalls Stiller. Frisch relates how he arrived in

Paris in 1948 for that quintessentially Parisian event, the 'Quatorze
Juillet'. As in the case of any other modern tourist, images have
anticipated Frisch's actual experience of the city: 'Man denkt immer
an Maler, so, als hätte Paris sich den Farben berühmter Paletten ange-
passt' (II 582). In the park at Versailles, Frisch feels that so
many verbal and visual representations of Paris and its surroundings
have been made, and have been disseminated by technological processes,
that it is quite pointless for him to attempt a description of his
own: 'So, auf mich selbst verwiesen, schreibe ich heute über mich
selbst' (II 584) [11]. This introduces 'Autobiographie' (II 584-590),
which recounts the facts of Frisch's life up to that point. In the
city which the phenomenon of Reproduktion has made its own, the
individual feels that he has no source of authentic experience other
than himself. As a conscious gesture of self-assertion against the
manner in which his environment has been rendered amorphous, the writer
sets about giving shape and order to the fact of his individuality.
Human activities have been devalued by techniques of Reproduktion, and
thus it is not possible for Paris to be authentic, since authenticity
and Reproduktion are contrary principles [12]. In this sense Paris
becomes the symbol of the challenge which this world offers to the
individual.

It is a challenge which Julika signally fails to meet. Her
capitulation to the world of Reproduktion is total, and indicates the
dangers of this world for a weak and withdrawing person such as she
is. The symbol of this capitulation is the appearance of her photograph on the cover of a Swiss illustrated magazine (III 477). The
unreality of the photograph of her in ballet costume is increased by
her seeing it on the magazine while she is in Davos suffering from
tuberculosis which will prevent her ever appearing on the stage again.
That she appears alone on the cover of the magazine is an ironic comment
on the fact that she is a person who has withdrawn into 'ein Dickicht
einsamer Nöte' (III 450). There is a further irony contained in the
photograph in that it is a reproduction of what is already a stereotyped image of a ballet dancer: it is 'eine tolle Aufnahme..., die
fast an Degas erinnerte' (III 477). Julika professes intellectual
contempt for the magazine in her reaction to the caption of the
photograph. This contempt is shown as pretence when it is replaced by
her respect for the sheer numbers implied by the large circulation of
the magazine. The extent of its dissemination, the hallmark of success
for such a publication, is for Julika also a source for her phantasy
about the places her photograph will reach. Her last phantasy about

her photograph in lonely bedrooms unwittingly reflects her own position.
For her relationship to the appearance on the cover of the magazine,
like her relationship to the ballet where she appears on the stage free
'von allen menschlichen Zudringlichkeiten' (III 478), is essentially
a surrogate one. Julika's shortcomings as a person, especially her
sexual inadequacy, vanish in a phantasy of effortless success and
adulation. In so far as her phantasy world is supported and reinforced
by the 'Illustrierte', Julika is a classic example of the interaction
between it and the life of its readers [13]. In addition, Julika's husband
Stiller is identified from a photograph in a magazine, an identification
which he refuses. But this refusal is set in perspective by Sibylle,
whose outright rejection of the world of Reproduktion is ironically made
explicit in relation to Stiller and his art. She expresses horror at
the poster for the planned exhibition of his sculpture, and her reaction
demonstrates that the apparent difference in attitude to the 'Illustrierte'
between Stiller and his wife masks a deeper similarity. For Stiller,
incensed at what he feels to be the impositions of others upon his
identity, rejects identification by the 'Illustrierte', yet has not
hesitated to surrender the symbol of that identity, his signature, to
the processes of Reproduktion:

> Es war ein regelrechtes.Plakat wie für Furtwängler oder
> Persil, sie fand es schrecklich: A. Stiller, seine
> geliebte Handschrift an jeder Plakatsäule. (III 630)

Julika is able to enjoy vicarious fulfilment through the 'Illustrierte'
'eine ganze Woche lang' (III 477). Stiller's exhibition, which he
consigns to the same world as that of the 'Illustrierte', never takes
place because of his disappearance.

The fact that the magazine, on the cover of which Julika appears,
is Swiss, links Switzerland to the world of Reproduktion in the 'Zweites
Heft' of the novel. In the 'Drittes Heft', the mosaic structure of the
novel establishes a further link. Stiller's diatribe against Reproduktion, (III 535-536), is followed by two related passages. The first
describes his admiring relationship to the mulatto Florence in the
United States (III 536-544), whose direct and spontaneous response to
life is symbolised, in contrast to Julika, by the vigorous energy of
her dancing. This account, with its emphasis on a vitality foreign to
Stiller, is followed by one of Stiller's lengthiest attacks on
Switzerland (III 544-548), delivered, like the definition of Reproduktion, to the defence lawyer. For Stiller, Switzerland is characterised
by the presence of 'geistiger Unfreiheit', by 'Verlogenheit', and by
'Angst'. But Frisch is careful not to make the contrast between what

Stiller holds to be the defects of Switzerland and the zestful vigour
of Florence too stark. In Florence's immediate environment there are
Negresses who, attracted by the glossy illusions of cosmetics
advertising, long to be white (III 542). Two conclusions emerge from
the fact that the definition of Reproduktion, the account of Florence,
and the attack on Switzerland form a sequence. Firstly, it is individual
decisiveness of character, and not the conditions of the environment,
which determines the response to life, since the vital Florence is as
little representative of her environment as Sibylle is of hers, and
the unassertive Stiller is successful neither in the environment of the
United States nor of his native Switzerland. Secondly, Reproduktion is
linked to Switzerland, the small country becoming 'durch den Lauf der
Welt immer noch kleiner' (III 544), which has the characteristics of
Reproduktion. This is no less true of the plastic arts in Switzerland,
of which Stiller is a practitioner, than for the country as a whole.
The Swiss artist's traditional period abroad to enable him to establish
his own style from the contrasts to be found there has been rendered
superfluous by Reproduktion [14]. The plastic arts are ceasing to be a
form of self-expression. Frisch draws attention to the way in which
modern technology is rendering the environment uniform and blurring
national distinctions (V 393) [15]. Technology is causing the
authenticity which derives from a direct and unambiguous relationship
to a specific environment to vanish. Modern Switzerland, belonging as
it does to the world of Reproduktion, becomes in the novel Stiller a
symbol of the inauthenticity of that world.

The structure of the episode between Stiller and Sibylle in
Pontestrina, the Swiss ski-resort which is depicted as the epitome of
the false facade of the world of Reproduktion, serves to show that the
individual need not succumb to inauthenticity in his own life. It also
shows that resistance to inauthenticity requires decisiveness. Sibylle,
back in Zürich from having the child which she was expecting by Stiller
aborted, pays a last visit to the flat where she and Rolf have spent
their married life. It is empty, as the contents have been transferred
to the new house which Rolf has had built, and it seems to Sibylle that
the desolate and deserted rooms symbolise her lack of achievement in
life (III 637). But the description of the scene in the new house, to
which she then goes, reflects the disharmony of her personal relationships: the interior of the house is 'ein einziges Durcheinander,...ein
Haufen zum Anzünden' (III 637). Her feeling of emptiness, and her
deep unhappiness about the lack of contact in her marriage - both
reflected in the immediate environment - are heightened by the immobility

of Rolf's attitude in their interview in his office (III 636-641).
There, she answers Rolf's question as to where she is going from her
memory of a poster which she has seen on the way to the interview:
'Nach Pontestrina' (III 638). In her defeated state, the stimuli
provided by the world of Reproduktion influence her decisions.

The reality of the resort is contrary to the expectations aroused
by the poster, however (III 642). The poster has rendered meaningless
the specificity of the time and place of the resort which it purports
to depict. Similarly, the language of those visiting the resort is not
concerned with expressing reality. It consists of words devoid of
significance such as 'toll', 'süss', 'maximal' and 'goldig' (III 643) [16].
Sibylle talks with Stiller 'vor dem kitschigen Portal ihres Hotels'
(III 647), and is helped into her coat by 'ein sogenannter Boy, ein
Bündnerbub in Zirkus-Livree' (III 648). Sibylle's ski-instructor has
a 'Plakatlachen' (III 645), and the restaurant where she takes Stiller
is 'eine Orgie von Heimattümelei' in which the menu is printed 'im Stil
der Gutenberg-Bibel' (III 645). Her reaction to Stiller's misery in
these surroundings is to pretend pleasure and delight at all that is
offending him, and is described in terms which associate it with the
machinery which has produced the environment: 'Es muss wie eine Mecha-
nik gewesen sein' (III 643). It is nonetheless against this highly
unpromising background that Sibylle demonstrates the firmness of her
hold on the essentials of life, and shows how she permits her environment to affect her only superficially. For it is in Pontestrina that
she reveals to Stiller the reason why they must part. She has perceived
that his vacillation will persist, that he is not prepared to change his
attitude to life (III 647). Their relationship belongs now for her as
much to the past as the child which she no longer carries. Yet, by a
further irony, it is also in Pontestrina that the conditions for the
possibility of change in Stiller are set forth. Two days after what
he imagines to be his final interview with Julika, Stiller returns to
Pontestrina, where he and Sibylle sit 'in einer Wirtschaft mit Einhei-
mischen, mit Eisenbahnern, die feierabendlich jassten' (III 649).
Here they are served by 'eine dicke Wirtin', and the wine-list is 'auf
einer schwarzen Tafel an der Wand', near which is also hanging a
'Bildnis von General Guisan'. In this atmosphere, which even down to
the card-game, bears the hallmarks of a specific locality, Stiller
appears 'hastlos, eins mit sich selbst' (III 649). When he corrects
the railway-workers on a matter of fact regarding an avalanche in the
area, Sibylle is

überrascht und irgendwie entzückt, erleichtert...

Sibylle fühlte sich beschützt. (III 650)

Exceptionally, Switzerland is, in the depiction of the inn, shown as
capable of generating an atmosphere unostentatiously yet firmly redolent
of identity. Stiller, normally irresolute and indecisive, has thus,
exceptionally, the opportunity to establish himself emotionally, and
this demonstrates the extent to which his insecurity is influenced by
his environment. Lacking a firm commitment to himself, 'einen festen
Punkt', Stiller is largely at the mercy of his environment, and so can
find a brief spell of peace in the genuineness of the inn. But the inn
represents only a tiny island in the wider world of Reproduktion, and
Sibylle's decision to go to the United States, taken by her in the
hotel which represents the Pontestrina of the tourists, and hence also
inauthenticity, is one which in contrast reveals again the decisiveness
which renders the environment so much less important to her than to
Stiller. Sibylle's decision, taken at this point, is overt and
committed, and contrasts with Stiller's furtive disappearance which,
officially registered in January 1946 (III 392), occurs at approximately
the same time. Whereas the kind of character represented by Sibylle
retains the ability deliberately to choose, the kind of character
represented by Stiller finds himself unable to make the commitment to
choose in the world of Reproduktion.

The symbol of Stiller's inability to choose in this world is the
'ferme vaudoise'. The first indication of the kind of area to which
Stiller and his wife go is given by Rolf at the start of the 'Nachwort',
when he describes the surroundings of Territet, where the couple have
taken temporary refuge in a hotel, as consisting of 'lauter Hotels,
Tennisplätzen, Seilbähnchen und Chalets mit Türmchen und Gartenzwergen'
(III 731). It is in this area of artificiality that Stiller later
announces by letter that he has found 'das Haus unseres Lebens' (III
733), which becomes 'das Haus meines Lebens' (III 735), and which for
Rolf is the 'Haus seines Lebens' (III 739), prior to Rolf providing
the only accurate description of it. For it is difficult to establish
exactly what the place looks like until Rolf's first visit, despite
Stiller's assertion that 'alles ist hier echt' (III 735). His
apprehensions have not fully prepared Rolf for the reality of the
'ferme vaudoise', however. The garden, with its damaged dwarves and
statues, broken steps and balustrades, the defects of which show 'dass
alles nur Zement ist' (III 739), is so much at odds with even his
darkest expectations of Stiller's house that Rolf considers it 'einen
Durchgang zu seiner eigenen Liegenschaft' (III 739). But it is not,
and Rolf's lengthy description of the 'Kitschigkeit' (III 740) of the

house itself makes it, in the structure of the novel, the symbol of
Stiller's failure to establish his identity. With its imitation
materials and its horrendous style it is 'ein Schwyzerhüsli, teilweise
mit einer schottischen Burg fern verwandt' (III 740). Even Rolf, the
sympathetic friend, must conclude that the place reflects Stiller's
curious attitude to reality. His feeling that the house is an entirely
inappropriate reflection of any genuine human reality which might take
place in it, is heightened and affirmed by his second visit to it.
Unaware that Julika has gone into hospital for her fatal operation and
that Stiller has gone to visit her, Rolf and his wife arrive at 'MON
REPOS' (III 754) to find it empty, and the emptiness of the unreal
house communicates to them the feeling that somehow Stiller and Julika
are in their turn unreal. Rolf has

> das Gefühl, als wären Stiller und seine Frau überhaupt
> nicht mehr da, nicht mehr in Glion, nicht mehr auf der
> Erde, verschwunden unter Hinterlassung dieser skurrilen
> Kitschigkeit, die nie zu ihnen gehört hatte. (III 754)

The house and the area are a reflection of the hollowness and inauthenticity of Stiller's life. In past ages it was possible to cultivate
individuality on the margins of society. The 'ferme vaudoise', the
counterfeit idyll, shows that there is no such retreat from the world
of Reproduktion [17].

The stations of Stiller's career have charted a regression from a
life as an artist to an existence as a pawn of the world of Reproduktion.
This retrograde movement has taken place in the full knowledge and
awareness of the individual concerned. Stiller's capitulation as a man
is also his capitulation as an artist. He has abandoned the responsibility to himself of which his sculpture was an expression. But the
'Hefte' written in prison also constitute a protest against the world
of Reproduktion which is so insidious and all-pervading that it saps
the vitality of those who do not cultivate the inner resources and
moral courage to assert against it the primacy of the individual
personality. The insecure Stiller passes from active assertion of
individuality symbolised by his sculpture, to the protest of the
'Hefte' - for which others were the instigation -, to his final submission, symbolised by his 'Swiss pottery'. Stiller is a 'Künstlerroman
im Zeitalter der Reproduktion' [18], because it shows the forces of the
age which are successfully militating against individuality, as
symbolised in the fate of Stiller, the sculptor of limited talent.

The world of technology

The novels Stiller and Homo Faber are related to the extent that
Stiller is a consideration of the artist in the world of Reproduktion,
and Homo Faber is a consideration of the engineer in the world of
technology which has made Reproduktion possible. Having established
that, in the conditions of the modern world, the artist can become a
discredited figure, Frisch turns from him to consider the status of the
engineer, the creator and monitor of these conditions. A consideration
of the figure of the technologist is all the more relevant, as his
discoveries and adaptations have in a relatively short space of time
radically altered the nature of individual experience. This has been
done primarily by the introduction into human life of the dimensions of
speed and mobility, made possible by the adaptation of natural resources
to power machines. But this adaptation of the forces of nature by man
has brought with it conditions of life which are unnatural in the sense
that the human faculty for experience cannot keep pace with them.
Frisch sets forth his view of this development in a passage in Tagebuch
1946-1949, in which he draws a distinction between the harnessing of
natural resources and their adaptation as fuels. The speed generated
by these fuels creates a void in the traveller

> weil unser Erleben, wenn ein gewisses Tempo überschritten
> wird, nicht mehr folgen kann; es wird dünner und dünner.
> (II 392)

Technology thus poses a threat to the quality of experience, for the
conditions which it creates give rise to a dichotomy between the
apparently unlimited capacity of technology and the relatively constant
nature of human emotions. The dichotomy between intellect and emotions
is a feature of 'Selbstüberforderung' in the world of Reproduktion
depicted in Stiller. In Homo Faber, it is the chief characteristic of
the engineer [19]. Man's relationship to the machines of his creation
offers the prism through which this discrepancy can be examined.

The perfectability of the machine is insidious because it tempts
man ever further from the dimensions of the natural with which he can
cope. The natural, which is not subject to human control, can be
accepted as immutable, but the machine, which is capable of being
developed by human agency, cannot be so accepted. The omnipresence of
the machine in modern life is therefore a constant incitement to man
to disregard and abuse the framework of the natural which contains him,
by demanding an ever-increasing performance from his machines. For
Frisch the futility of this situation is symbolised by the motorist
who increases the speed of his car because he has been overtaken by

another motorist. Since he relates his own emotion of annoyance to
the performance of his vehicle, the motorist feels that he can restore
the balance of his emotions by improving the performance of the car,
by accelerating. In his reaction to this - 'das luziferische Verspre-
chen' (II 392) - the motorist becomes a representative figure. The
dangerous discrepancy between emotions and the perfectability of
machines is made apparent in Die Chinesische Mauer. In a world where,
technically, 'die Sintflut ist herstellbar' (II 149), Der Heutige
tries to demonstrate to the unchanged mentality of the oppressor and
tyrant the folly of maintaining a traditional attitude to conquest and
war. His failure to do this symbolises that in fact man has lost
control of the machines, including the machines of war, which he has
created. The capabilities of the machine have outstripped man's ability
to deal with it emotionally. In addition, a traditional shortcoming of
man, his disinclination radically to question his own behaviour, has
been exacerbated by the age of technology. To the activity surrounding
the creation and functioning of machines a purpose is attributed which
is not necessarily there. Indeed this activity may be a device to mask
lack of purpose. In 1784, long before the age of technology, disquiet
was expressed at the dangers inherent in the contrivances of man:

> A provision of endless apparatus, a bustle of infinite
> enquiry and research...may be employed, to evade and
> shuffle off real labour, - the real labour of thinking. [20]

The opportunity for thus shirking the responsibility of thought has
been enormously increased by the prevalence of the machine in the
modern world, and by the activities which surround the machine. The
machine provides a welcome distraction for the many people whom Frisch
sees as being characterised by a compulsion 'der Lebensangst beizu-
kommen durch pausenlose Beschäftigung' (II 406). The irony is that
the ceaseless activity of a technological age reflects a situation
where time becomes available for which adequate use cannot be found.
The speed and mobility of the modern age, in addition to dissociating
man from his natural framework, creates, as Don Juan complains to
Columbus, 'Zeit, die uns nichts nützt' (II 184), which man is obliged
to fill with action relating to nothing else than consuming time. In
this he finds the machine, the use and development of which has brought
about the situation, a welcome distraction.

The manner in which the machine, especially the vehicle of transport,
offers distraction from reflection is indicated by Stiller in his
recollections of his visit to the Mexican desert of Chihuahua. He
drives through the imposing scenery, and it is not until he stops at

a small oasis and sees a group of Indians that it occurs to him that
humans exist there as well as in civilisation. He is glad of the claims
his car makes upon him to distract him from further reflection which
could become uncomfortable (III 379). Since he is driving his own
vehicle, Stiller is able to counter the lack of movement which the
stop causes by activity relating to his vehicle. For lack of movement
introduces a hiatus into distraction which must be filled. Faber,
journeying by train and therefore not in charge of its functioning, is
pleased when the train restarts after a stop, although he is being
carried forward into the unknown dangers of the South American jungle:
'Immerhin war man zufrieden, dass es weiterging' (IV 35). The fact
that machinery functions and carries him forward is constantly
deflecting the attention of the individual from a consideration of
matters of wider import. Enderlin, disturbed by the conjunction of a
remark overheard at a party and a particular train of thought of his
own, leaves the party feeling that he is on the verge of an insight
which might relate aspects of life (V 41). But the manipulation of his
car distracts him and he abandons reflection. Svoboda, travelling in
southern Europe in order to allow Lila and himself time for reflection
about the deteriorating state of their marriage, receives a letter
from her poste restante in Barcelona, in which she informs him that
she is seriously considering leaving him. He reads the letter twice,
and then abandons himself quite consciously to the distraction offered
by driving. The narrator closes the scene with the reflection:

> Ist es nicht stets eine Ermunterung, wenn es scheint,
> dass das Leben vorwärtsgeht? (V 241)

Just as the product of the machine, the newspaper, provides distraction
from reality, so the machine offers a means for the individual to shirk
his responsibilities to himself. The obtrusion of the machine into the
life of the individual represents a permanent deflection from any
commitment to himself.

At times it appears as if machines, because of the way in which man
adulates them and organises his life in accordance with their needs, do
acquire an existence which is independent of man. At one level, this
can express itself in the apparent mockery on the part of the machine
at the extent to which man has become dependent on his creation. In
the Mexican desert, as he drives along far from any sign of civilisation,
Stiller falls to reflecting how man, and more especially Stiller and
his immediate companions, form the centre of the universe in that they
give reality to the desert, and to the sun and the moon, through their
eyes (III 380). These things would not exist without a human

consciousness of their existence. Stiller's grandiose speculations are
interrupted by a puncture, a reminder that it is really the machine
which has enabled him to see the desert which is giving rise to these
speculations. At another level, the machine appears to demonstrate
that its independence of the organic laws which control man render it
superior to these laws. The narrator in Gantenbein imagines Enderlin's
death occurring as he is about to drive away from a party. The other
guests later find him dead in a vehicle which has its engine running
and its indicator functioning (V 7). At a third level, the machines
with which he is surrounded seem malevolently to remind man that he has
added through them a dimension to his life which is sapping his natural
vitality and preventing him from penetrating to any real experience of
himself. Ironically, the airport, the epitome of modern technology,
demonstrates most clearly the inability of the individual to make a
commitment to himself in the modern age. It is at the airport, with
its multiplicity of machines, that an appreciation of the nature of
choice, and hence of commitment, is most fully shown to be distorted.
Commitment to a choice involves accepting that within the dimension of
time all is not possible for the individual, that one realisation of
the individual personality excludes other forms of realisation.
Enderlin's indecision at the airport, and his weariness at his own
indecision, demonstrate how the machine age has disrupted the individual's
relationship to commitment:

> Ich kann mir beides vorstellen:
> Enderlin fliegt.
> Enderlin bleibt.
> Langsam habe ich es satt, dieses Spiel, das ich nun kenne:
> handeln oder unterlassen, und in jedem Fall, ich weiss, ist
> es nur ein Teil meines Lebens, und den andern Teil muss ich
> mir vorstellen; Handlung oder Unterlassung sind vertauschbar.
> (V 129)

The airport, the symbol of modern man's technological achievement, is
thus also the symbol of his 'Weltlosigkeit' (IV 169), his inability to
experience reality through himself. Hanna suggests to Faber that the
attraction of technology resides in the fact that it creates a barrier
between the individual and his experience of reality. Technology
represents the ultimate distraction from a commitment to the real
nature of life: 'Technik (laut Hanna) als Kniff, die Welt so einzu-
richten, dass wir sie nicht erleben müssen' (IV 169). The terrible
vengeance which the forces of nature wreak on the technologist Faber
is the retribution exacted for his deification of technology.

Technology and <u>Homo</u> <u>Faber</u>

Faber clings to technology because it offers him the illusion of
order and explicableness in a world with which, owing to his dependence
on this illusion, he becomes increasingly unable to cope. Faber has
reached the point where he requires the barrier to experience which
technology offers. For Faber there are two constituent elements to
this barrier: functioning machinery which he can manipulate, and a
mechanistic pattern of routine to his life. He is aware of being at
risk, as it were, when these two elements are not present, as is the
case, when, for the first time in his life, he crosses the Atlantic by
ship (IV 75-76). His grounds for concern are justified, for it is on
board ship that he will start the destructive relationship with his
own daughter. Yet it is precisely one element of his normal life, the
necessity that he should be psychologically bolstered on all sides by
functioning machinery, which has led him into this abnormal situation.
For it was his insistence on repairing a broken electric razor which
caused him to be in his New York apartment when the shipping company
telephoned to advise him of a cancellation which required to be taken
up immediately. He admits that he had a spare functioning razor, and
that he did not even require to shave before going out with Ivy (IV
63), but the restoration of the explicable facade to his life takes
precedence over all else. Far from offering him existential protection,
however, his obsession with machines brings about his downfall. The
other element which he requires in his normal life, a mechanistic
pattern of routine, is no less dangerous, since it devalues and finally
causes to atrophy those faculties by which the individual reacts to
external reality. Thus, although the novel opens with a demonstration
of the supremacy of the natural over the technical in the snowstorm
which delays take-off to Mexico City, and which Faber admits to be
unique in his experience, he is able later to discount this, to
assimilate the flight which leads to incest and destruction, into the
meaninglessness of mechanistic routine simply because the engines of
the plane are functioning normally (IV 9). Since, for his psychological
security, everything must fit a pattern, he has become blind to everything which does not, and so has lost the discriminative adaptability
of behaviour which openness to experience brings with it. The limitedness of his response to his daughter Sabeth is indicative of the extent
to which his insistence and dependence on a pattern of routine excludes
him from contact with his fellow-men. Faber's belief that a pattern
offers safety is wholly illusory. The deprivation of faculties which

206.

it causes, isolates and eventually destroys.

The fact that human intercourse is increasingly assuming a machine-
like pattern is already apparent to the artist Stiller, and he
registers his deep unease that this pattern prevents any real contact
between people. He is most forcefully struck by this sense of
deprivation when he is visited in prison by the architect Sturzenegger.
For Stiller their interview is representative of

> eine Mechanik in den menschlichen Beziehungen, die...
> alles Lebendige sofort verunmöglicht, alles Gegenwärtige
> ausschliesst...Es funktioniert alles wie ein Automat:
> oben fällt der Name hinein...und unten kommt schon die
> dazugehörige Umgangsart heraus, fix und fertig, ready
> for use, das Klischee einer menschlichen Beziehung.
> (III 591)

Yet it is this deprivation in human intercourse which the engineer
Faber elevates into a way of life. He can respond only to the machine
because it makes no demands on him to deploy his emotions in any way.
Contact with his fellow-humans, on the other hand, is demanding:
'Menschen sind anstrengend' (IV 8). His morbid fear of emotional
involvement manifests itself most clearly in his relationships with
women. He finds it impossible to live with any woman for longer than
three weeks: 'Nach drei Wochen (spätestens) sehne ich mich nach Turbi-
nen' (IV 91). It is ironic that, when his emotions do break down the
barriers which he has erected against them, they should direct him
towards an incestuous relationship with Sabeth, daughter of his union
with Hanna, the only woman with whom he has not felt that the sexual
act is 'absurd' (IV 100). The disasters which he causes are the
inevitable outcome of his denial of all that is natural. Faber's
destructiveness is symbolic of the impoverishing effect on human experience which the ever-increasing role of the machine brings with it in
the modern world. For contact with machines generates no experience
since the machine is wholly circumscribed by its function, and hence
manipulation of the machine becomes part of that function and can be
related to nothing else [21]. The machine represents a threat to a
dimension of human experience without which, as the fate of Faber shows,
the individual cannot exist.

However impoverished he may be through his contact with the machine,
Faber is not so bereft of the ability to react that he cannot discern
the nature of the technological world of which he is a part, and, very
much more dimly, sense the deleterious effect which this world is
having upon him. This awareness finds expression in the passage 'Mein
Zorn auf Amerika!' (IV 175-177), which occurs during his brief stay on

the island of Cuba, and which forms a parallel to Stiller's attack on
Reproduktion. It is an attack by the engineer Faber on a mechanistic
attitude to life which Faber at this point sees represented most
strongly in aspects of American life. Faber, having destroyed his
daughter and having discovered that his new-found friend Herbert has
given himself wholly to the rhythms of life of the South American
jungle where he has decided to live, is returning to Athens to die.
The vehemence of his attack stems in part from his awareness of these
assertions of the natural impinging on his life, in part from the fact
that the mechanistic attitude is one which, up until the time of the
attack, he himself has fully endorsed. 'The American Way of Life' [22]
is the epitome of all that is unnatural: their food is unnatural,
their sexual insecurity is characterised as 'ihr Vakuum zwischen den
Lenden' (IV 176), and they organise the mechanised destruction of their
environment. Finally, the man who has caused his own daughter's death,
denounces the Americans' 'pornografisches Verhältnis zum Tod' (IV 177)
as the culmination of their unnatural attitude to life. Yet, despite
the intensity of his attack on the mechanistic view of life, it does
not represent a radical expunging of this attitude from his own outlook. In the first place, the whole of the Cuba episode, of which the
attack forms a part, is relativised by Faber's marginal situation when
it occurs. Secondly, if the attack on the mechanistic view is
paralleled by Stiller's attack on Reproduktion, then Faber's subsequent
behaviour has a further parallel with Stiller's identification with the
'ferme vaudoise'. For on Faber's return to Athens, his conversation
with Hanna 'shows that in plain contradiction to his prior insights
Faber has resumed his mechanistic outlook' [23]. The strength of the
insights garnered on Cuba, the hiatus in his normal life, has not been
sufficient to change Faber, even although these insights took place
against the knowledge of Sabeth's death and of his own involvement in
that death. Thus, if Faber is aware that his emotions had a contributory
role to play in the establishment of these insights, he is still,
despite all that has happened, unable or unwilling to accept that an
insight so established should influence behaviour.

The chief feature of Faber's conduct of his life is that he must
at all times seek to deny his experience. Experience is yielded by
the unpredictability of life, and assessement and assimilation of this
experience enable the individual to cope with, and to realise himself
in conjunction with, this unpredictability. Psychologically dependent
on the explicable nature of machines, Faber cannot tolerate the incal-
culable in life because he does not possess the resilience to deal with

it. His dislike and his deep-seated fear of the sexual urge stem from
this inability. Yet, fearful of the natural and its manifestations as
he is, Faber nonetheless places himself by virtue of his limited
response to women in a position which exclusively emphasises their
reproductive function: he can contemplate them only in terms of the
sexual act. The monstrous relationship to his own daughter is thus a
direct consequence of his mechanistic attitude. From the moment of
their first meeting on board ship, when he dismisses as fortuitous
Sabeth's resemblance to Hanna (IV 78), he persists in regarding her as
an object of sexual attention in face of the rapidly mounting evidence
that she might not only be Hanna's daughter, but also his own. If he
disregards, as is his wont, intuitive warnings, he also disregards,
exceptionally, the warnings provided by calculations as to dates and
periods of time because of the strength of his emotion for the girl.
Emotion suppresses his fragile and illusory control of life. The
destruction of his daughter is the terrible price which he has to pay
for previously ignoring his emotions.

Faber is, however, determined to prove to himself that the death
of his daughter is the consequence of his own views and wishes having
been flouted. His imperviousness to experience is demonstrated by the
fact that he asserts that the whole episode with his daughter need
never have taken place if his wish to have Hanna's pregnancy terminated
had been followed (IV 105). For Faber, man is superior to the animals
in the matter of limitation of reproduction. Control of this aspect of
human life is consonant with the dignity of man: 'Würde des Menschen,
vernünftig zu handeln und selbst zu entscheiden...Der Mensch plant'
(IV 106). What is striking about his assertions as to the correctness
of his own views after the death of his daughter is not so much that he
is seeking to justify himself for his own behaviour, but that he is
capable of trying to expunge the past in this way, that he is so
isolated from contact with reality that experience, even the destruction
of his daughter, does not penetrate to him in a formulative fashion.
Faber's tragedy is that he cannot learn from experience because he has
deadened himself to it. In contrast, the agony of felt experience
suffered by Yvonne in Die Schwierigen after the abortion of Hinkelmann's
child, shows that the perspectives provided by emotional awareness are
essential to the formation of attitudes to life (I 430). Of course,
Yvonne's emotions are directly linked to the physical fact that she has
carried the child, but this does not invalidate the contrast between
herself and Faber. The horrible reality of these emotions helps to

purge her of her guilt and provides her with a fresh dimension of
knowledge for the future. Such knowledge becomes the more inaccessible
for Faber the more wilfully he distances himself from it.

The whole course of Faber's destructive relationship with his
daughter is characterised by his rejection of the evidence with which
life presents him, and his reflections after her death demonstrate his
incorrigibility. It is only in relation to his own death that the
reality of life succeeds in asserting itself on his consciousness. It
is true that even in hospital in Athens he still seeks refuge in his
statistical illusions (IV 164). But on the night immediately preceding the operation, his intuition causes him to admit to himself that he
is dying (IV 198). Only the imminence of his own death causes him
fully and consciously to realise that life is not subject to the kind
of control which he thought he was exerting. Since he erases death from
his consciousness, Faber not only fails to affirm the nature of life,
but paradoxically ensures that the course of his life is spent in the
service of that which he denies. In Blätter aus dem Brotsack, Frisch
describes Ares as the god 'all jener, die zerstören müssen, zerstampfen,
zerreissen, um ihre Leere auszufüllen' (I 150). Homo Faber is the
portrayal of such an empty figure.

Faber, the representative of the technological world, mutilates
himself as a sentient being. Instead of developing all the facets of
his human identity, he strives, since the explicableness of the machine
offers him psychological support in an inexplicable world, to develop
that aspect of himself which he feels relates most closely to the
machine. This leads to his having neither the mechanical efficiency
of the machine nor the awareness of the human [24]. The flight from the
difficulties of life leads to disaster, since it is in a confrontation
with, and a resolution of, these difficulties that the balance of life
is maintained. Yet it is against the background of his daughter's
death that Faber affirms the necessity for a lack of balance, for the
devotion to the machine which has brought about the destruction of his
natural offspring. The use of the first person plural in Faber's
declamation of his auto da fe indicates his representative status:

> Was wir ablehnen: Natur als Götze! Dann müsste man
> schon konsequent sein: dann auch kein Penicillin, keine
> Blitzableiter, keine Brille, kein DDT, kein Radar und so
> weiter...dann los in den Dschungel! (IV 107)

Like other Frisch characters, the technologist Faber is incapable of
maintaining a middle position. He also imagines that technology has
conferred upon him a dimension which earlier generations did not

possess, namely, the ability to control life. Dazzled by his vision
of himself as a ruler of the universe, and contemptuous of the warnings
of his intuition, he remains blind to the ironic anomaly of his
position. Technological man, as represented by Faber, has been brought
back full circle by his attitudes to the level of his jungle ancestors
whom he so despises. The irrationality of Faber precludes all notions
of personal freedom contained in the concept of commitment.

In Stiller the artist and Faber the technologist, Frisch examines
aspects of the modern world. The fates which they encounter reflect
Frisch's pessimism at the nature of this world. Inseparable from the
professional failure of both is their failure as men, Stiller principally
as a husband, Faber principally as a father. The artist cannot achieve
proper communication inside his marriage, the creator of machines
destroys his daughter. Yet it is important to note that neither man
has significant stature or dimensions, either in his personal or his
professional capacity. Stiller's public recognition as a sculptor
extends to the municipality of Zürich once having purchased a statue by
him (III 431), and Faber's recognition as an engineer is indicated by
his working for the international agency UNESCO (IV 10). It is by
virtue of the fact that they are of limited talent in their respective
fields that their representative nature acquires an additional dimension.
For the extraordinary talent or ability will always assert itself regardless of circumstances, and although coloured by the age in which it
flourishes, it is in a sense independent of that age by virtue of its
energy. The mediocre talent or ability, on the other hand, does not
have the driving self-confidence of the great talent; to the extent that
it is dependent solely on the ethos of its age, its fate reflects more
accurately the temper of the age. The modern age silences the talent
of Stiller, and the ability of Faber has lent itself to developments in
that age which are incompatible with the forces of nature which control
human life.

Stiller, unable to face and to come to terms with the pressures
which have built up against him, flees to the United States. These
pressures emanate chiefly from his unsuccessful marriage, which becomes
for Stiller the symbol of what he considers to be his failures in other
fields. For it cannot be said that, up until the time of his flight,
he has lived up to his expectations of himself. His art does not
sustain him in the sense that he feels he is realising himself through
it, and it is significant that in the United States there is no mention

of an attempt to return to it. Associated with failure in Switzerland, his art is not re-invigorated by his experiences in America for two reasons, one arising from his personal shortcomings, the other deriving from the nature of the age in which he lives. Firstly, he has imagined that the United States will offer him a fresh start, free from the taint of failure, and this is an expectation which is beyond realisation. That his expectations are excessive is not altogether divorced from the second reason for the failure of the period in the United States. In the age of Reproduktion he has anticipated his experience of America and Mexico through the images of these places to which he has been exposed before he arrives there. His suicide attempt is an indication of his failure to authenticate to himself his actual experience there. In the same way, his accounts of incidents there are not accepted on his return to Switzerland as proof that he has actually been in America and Mexico. If Stiller's excessive hopes about these places were partly inspired by what the products of Reproduktion put before him prior to his arrival there, so the scepticism of his listeners on his return derives from the same source. The indeterminate nature of experience in the world of Reproduktion thus affects both Stiller and those to whom he returns. It affects the sculptor of minor talent and his public in such a manner that the possibility of communication is diminished. Julika, on first meeting Stiller at a party in his studio, thinks that the name is a nickname, because he is so quiet (III 490). If this is an erroneous supposition at the time, it is nonetheless prophetic about the eventual fate of Stiller. For the minor artist, self-expression in the age of Reproduktion is no longer possible, and since Stiller is not a Swiss name (V 323), it would appear that the fate of the introspective sculptor, although firmly linked to his Swiss background, has wider significance.

The term homo faber, derived from the ancient world where it designated the man who created tools and utilised them for the benefit of his fellow-man, acquires in the modern world an ironic dimension in view of the destruction which he wreaks. Instead of seeking, as his counterpart in the ancient world did, to adapt aspects of reality for the better enjoyment of its totality, homo faber in the modern world wishes to eliminate reality, with all its imponderables, as the basis for his life, and to replace it with the technology with which he feels emotionally secure because he believes that he can control it. In the face of the silence of homo ludens, the traditional interpreter of reality, it might seem reasonable to suppose that the outlook on life evolved by the technologist could replace an interpretation of reality established intuitively. But it emerges that it is the attempt to exclude from the technologist's viewpoint the intuitive element which renders it an incomplete and invalid basis for the conduct of life. If, in the figure of Stiller, Frisch demonstrates that the conditions of the modern world are largely inimical to the artist of moderate talent, in the figure of Walter Faber he shows that the engineer who resolutely attempts to adapt his life to these conditions evolves an attitude which denies life. For the safety of the technological world is an illusion which merely exposes those who believe in it even more to the unpredictable dangers which they are fleeing.

If it is true that both Stiller and Faber are unassertive and irresolute, and of limited talent and ability, it is also true that their experience of the modern world does not contribute in any way to their overcoming their defects. By nature men who are dependent for their stability on the influence of the environment, as the episodes in Pontestrina and Cuba show, they do not possess the moral stature to set before themselves the attainment of self-realisation, irrespective of the nature of this influence. Their inability to commit themselves to an identity is thus partly a consequence of their character, and partly a consequence of the environment of the second half of the twentieth century. The world of Reproduktion is depicted through what Frisch calls the 'Tagebuch eines Gefangenen' [25], which records the self-encapsulation of the artist in that world. The world of technology is depicted through the 'Tagebuch eines Moribunden' [26], which records the self-destruction of the creator of machines. In tracing the failure of these two representative figures, Frisch describes the forces in the modern world which work against the individual in his attempts to come to terms with himself.

3.   The Nature of Commitment

Identity, as exemplified in the story of the ambassador in
Gantenbein, is primarily the relationship of the individual to himself.
Commitment, as depicted in the relationships which Stiller and Julika,
and Rolf and Sibylle have to one another in Stiller, is shown primarily
to concern itself with the relationship of the individual to others.
Clearly, the concepts of identity and commitment overlap, but these
are the main areas of definition. Commitment can be manifested in the
sphere of friendship and trust, but in the works of Frisch it manifests
itself, directly or indirectly, in the relationships between men and
women. The contractual and semi-contractual relationships upon which
men and women enter contain a spectrum of the problems which the
individual faces both within himself and with the environment. Reinhart
in Die Schwierigen thus envisages marriage and its consequences as being
the supreme test of an individual:

> Das grösste Abenteuer aber, das es einzugehen gibt, schien
> ihm die Ehe, das Wagnis einer ganzen Bindung, Verpflichtung
> an ein Rätsel, das uns überdauert. (I 500)

The fact that Reinhart is incapable of contracting marriage, let alone
making a success of his other, less formal relationships with women,
does not invalidate the vision which he has of such a union, nor does
it lessen the extent of the claims which it makes on the contracting
parties. The ability to measure up to the demands made by the relationship of marriage can be inborn, as in the case of Sibylle, whose
behaviour also demonstrates that commitment to a relationship with a
particular person is not a blind act of faith. The maturity for
commitment can also be acquired, as in the case of Rolf, who is guided
by his experience to a position where he can realise what commitment
involves and is able to act on this realisation. Committed behaviour,
both inborn and acquired, contrasts with the indeterminate behaviour
of Stiller, who is impervious both to the power of example provided by
others and to the educative nature of his own experience. If he finally
fails, it is because he has not gone towards the possibilities which
experience has shown to him. He has been incapable of generating the
moral energy which commitment first of all requires of the individual,
and then, once commitment is established, sustains in him.

Commitment and experience

Since commitment is dependent on the nature of the individual's
relationship to his own experience, it is necessary to examine two

conditions, fulfilment of which Frisch holds to be necessary for
commitment: the ability constantly to adjust to the flow of experience,
and the maturity to accept the limited framework in which the individual
encounters his experience.

Every individual must contend with the essentially incommunicable
nature of his experience. But the urge to communicate this experience
cannot be denied, and the attempt to render it through language will
constitute the means by which experience is not only made partially
available to others, but to the individual himself [1]. This rendition,
since the experience itself resists language, is an invention which
attempts to convey the essence of the original. Frisch relates this
invention to the flow of time. The relationship of the individual to
his past experience, to his memory of himself, is not only an
approximation of that which is expressible, but is a constantly
adjusting approximation, since events in the past are always re-
created from the stand-point of the present: 'Erinnerung ist immer
ein Arrangement von jetzt aus' (V 332). Whilst one aspect of the
individual's account of his experience relates to the past, another
aspect relates to the future. Since the individual is constantly
seeking a means of expression for his experience, experience constantly
points forward to its own changing formulation:

> Sie (die Menschen) entwerfen, sie erfinden, was ihre
> Erfahrung lesbar macht. Die Erfahrung ist nicht ein
> Schluss, sondern eine Eröffnung; ihr Bezirk ist die
> Zukunft. (IV 264)

Experience provides the constantly adapting, ever richer framework of
reference against which fresh experience can be confronted, and which
in its turn can contribute to the process of re-adjustment. An open,
constantly evolving attitude to experience is the first condition of
commitment.

The continuing process of re-adjustment to experience takes place
within the confines of the personality of the individual. For Frisch
the fact that the structure of personality imposes a certain pattern
on the assimilation of experience is first discernible in the recurring
themes of the stories of other people which are the expression of their
experience. The longer one listens to a person 'umso erkennbarer wird
das Erlebnismuster, das er umschreibt' (V 332). The term 'Erlebnismuster' is Frisch's designation for the confines of experience which
indicate the contours of the individual personality. The immutability
of individuation is reflected in similarities in the pattern of
experience. Karl, the figure who pleads for the sanctity of life

amidst the senseless ravages of war in <u>Nun singen sie wieder</u>, gives
expression to the irrevocable nature of individuation by describing
its concomitant responsibility: the restrictions imposed by individuation are only tolerable if they are accepted as the conditions of
life. Personal freedom consists in accepting responsibility for what
is inalienably and ineradicably the individual personality:

> Man kann nicht seine Verantwortung einem anderen geben,
> damit er sie verwalte. Man kann die Last der persönlichen
> Freiheit nicht abtreten. (II 104)

Frisch's well-known statement in <u>Tagebuch 1946-1949</u> about the
individual's relationship to time has a direct bearing on the nature
of experience and of individuation:

> Die Zeit verwandelt uns nicht.
> Sie entfaltet uns nur. (II 361)

The personality can never be altered. It can only be enriched by
openness to the experience which time brings. Full acceptance of the
inalterable framework of the individual personality as the only means
properly to experience life is the second condition of commitment.

The major Frisch characters, and many of the minor ones, have
great difficulty in maintaining an open attitude to experience and in
accepting individuation. The most forceful exemplification of the
irrevocability of individuation is provided in <u>Biografie</u>. Kürmann,
the hero, is permitted by the conditions of stage presentation to do
what he cannot do in real life: to live his life over again. But
even within the framework of theatrical licence, the ineluctable in
life is represented to Kürmann by the <u>Registrator</u>, who tells him that
he is free to choose differently in the course of his life only within
the limits of the intelligence which he has always had (V 503). The
interplay between the immutable basis to the individual life and the
flux of experience which offers possibilities of action is what for
Frisch constitutes the movement of life [2]. It is precisely because
the individual has an immutable basis to his life that he is so much
more independent of environment and circumstance than the Frisch
characters imagine. Because they cannot accept the central paradox
that freedom consists in accepting limitation, they render themselves
much more dependent on the variable elements in life, the importance
of which they greatly over-emphasise. Thus the limitless freedom of
which they constantly dream is a much more tyrannical form of bondage
than the commitment which they so much fear. The Frisch characters
are unaware of the real freedom from the environment which they can
establish by accepting that the personality remains constant in any

216.

environment.

In _Stiller_ the hero rejects the freedom contained in the acceptance
of the confines of individuation, and this is contrasted with a parallel
depiction of commitment in Rolf. In the figure of Stiller are described
most fully the mental convolutions which the individual who cannot
accept himself is obliged to perform. These convolutions are doubly
dangerous, for they represent not merely the mental and emotional dishonesty of the individual circling round the question of self-acceptance.
Insensibly, these convolutions also develop a momentum of their own.
Like a swimmer caught on the edge of a whirlpool who, if he does not
free himself, is sucked ever more relentlessly from the calm water to
the vortex, the individual who does not accept himself is doomed to
destruction. For failure to accept oneself is not a stationary condition,
but develops into outright denial of the personality:

> Ich hoffe eigentlich nur, dass Gott (wenn ich ihm entgegen-
> komme) mich zu einer anderen, nämlich zu einer reicheren,
> tieferen, wertvolleren, bedeutenderen Persönlichkeit machen
> werde - und genau das ist es vermutlich, was Gott hindert,
> mir gegenüber wirklich eine Existenz anzutreten, das heisst
> erfahrbar zu werden. Meine condition sine qua non: dass er
> mich, sein Geschöpf, widerrufe. (III 671)

Thus, shortly before he is condemned by society to be Anatol Ludwig
Stiller, he abjures any attempt to commit himself to what he is, and so
prepares the way for the collapse described in the 'Nachwort'. This is
the point to which failure to accept the confines of the personality
must bring the individual, and since this is also the point where the
hold on the vital urge to seek self-realisation is finally relinquished,
it follows that Stiller's subsequent decline is described by a third
party. It is Stiller's tragedy that, despite the fact that he both
perceives intellectually and senses instinctively that self-acceptance
is the only path to salvation, he cannot muster the energy to set himself
in that direction. His example shows that self-acceptance is at the
centre of moral behaviour since it alone avoids self-destruction.

If the Frisch character cannot accept his internal reality, he also
has difficulty in coping with external reality. He is constantly upset
by that with which experience presents him. For him, experience is a
constant denial of expectation: 'Es ist immer etwas geschehen, aber
anders' (V 313), might well be the plaintive motto of all those for
whom reality proves such a disappointment. The Frisch character cannot
envisage that experience might have a formative role to play. It is
because he cannot adapt his views in the light of his experience that
he can evolve no flexible response to the unexpected. In _Nun singen sie_

wieder, the <u>Funker</u> points to the necessity of tempering views about
what the world should be like with experience of what it is like:

> Es ist keine Einsicht, was unserem Erlebnis nicht stand-
> hält! Es ist ein Wunsch, eine Träumerei, ein grosses
> Wort. (II 98)

But the intractability of reality is normally for the Frisch character
a source of affront, and, far from suggesting that the original expectation might require adjustment, serves merely to promote notions of the
injustice of the world. In this respect the <u>Senora</u>'s reaction in
<u>Andorra</u> to the destruction of her youthful dreams is typical. As a
young woman, in order to further her idea of what the world should be
like, she joined forces with her like-minded contemporaries in an attempt
to realise their conception of the world. Their disillusion when the
world continued as before vented itself on one another (IV 522). Denial
of experience, in the sense that what it offers is rejected and not
incorporated into the individual's outlook, is a characteristic of
these figures.

   Language offers a means of escape from the responsibilities imposed
by experience, since its inordinate use prevents any move towards active
commitment. Three related examples of this kind of retreat from commitment occur in <u>Stiller</u>. Firstly, Rolf, in an attempt to justify his own
extra-marital affairs and in order to obviate a commitment to his wife,
has developed a theory about freedom in marriage based, as he claims,
on his experience as a lawyer: 'Rolf hatte viel darüber zu sagen;
Sibylle nannte es seine 'Vorträge'' (III 558). Sibylle's description
shows her to be aware of the obfuscatory function of Rolf's words.
His verbose abuse of experience here contrasts with the simplicity of
the proposal made to Sibylle in New York later about their future,
where the directness of the language derives from an awareness of how
commitment clarifies issues and promotes decisions.

   The second example of retreat from action also offers a direct
parallel to Rolf's proposal to Sibylle in New York, as well as to his
earlier 'Vorträge'. In the juridical confrontation in Stiller's former
studio, Stiller feels that it is unnecessary that he should have to
admit explicitly to Julika that he is her missing husband. In a
complicated situation which has been rendered more difficult by
language, Stiller senses that the only possibility for Julika and himself to have a future together is to accept one another in the present
with as little overt reference to the past as possible. But he fails
to carry out what he senses to be true and necessary:

> Mir erscheint es so einfach, so klar. Trotzdem rede ich

> ziemlich lang, viel zu lang und mit der Zeit, wie immer,
> auch verworren' (III 713).

He cannot relate his behaviour to his perception, and thus fails to
present Julika with the clarity of alternatives as Rolf does in New
York. Stiller relates this particular failure to similar examples in
the past — he knows that words 'nur zersetzen, was eine Einsicht
gewesen ist' (III 713). Stiller cannot bring himself directly to
confront the clear alternatives which an 'Einsicht' contains, and which
would resolve the situation if acted upon. Now, suddenly, at this
point, he senses intuitively that such a moment for action is upon him:
'wie unter einer Lähmung meines Bewusstseins' (III 715), he sees that
he could now make a gesture of reconciliation to Julika. But he allows
the irrevocable moment to slip past, and returns to questioning his
wife in detail about her feelings. By means of language, he shies away
from the implications of commitment.

The third example of the dissociation of language and experience
is provided by the defence lawyer Dr. Bohnenblust later in the same
scene in the former studio. Bohnenblust is as much a one-dimensional
character as Knobel the warder. He is seen exclusively through the
eyes of Stiller, and in such a fashion as to suggest that a view from
one perspective does sufficient justice to him. It is thus ironic
that, immediately after Stiller himself has dissipated the possibilities
of action by his own futile talk, Bohnenblust should embark on a long
speech (III 716-720) designed to promote a reconciliation between
Stiller and Julika, a speech which, although dismissed contemptuously
by Stiller as a 'Wortschwall', cannot be very different in its dis-
connectedness from his own to Julika. Amongst the clichés of the
reserve officer — 'eine positivere Haltung...vonnöten' —, of the right-
wing politician — 'Franco wichtig für Europa' —, and of the Swiss
patriot — 'alles mit gesundem Schweizersinn' —, clichés which represent
views totally antipathetic to those held by Stiller, there are contained
remarks which penetrate to the heart of Stiller's situation: Stiller
is 'kein grosser Künstler'; Bohnenblust is of the opinion that 'Flucht'
is 'nie eine wahre Lösung', and that freedom is possible 'nur in der
Bindung'; and his closing exhortation is for Stiller to believe 'an
das Gute in mir selbst'. But Bohnenblust is largely the passive
creature of received opinions. Thus Stiller's contempt for Bohnenblust's
performance derives from his knowledge that none of the speech relates
to Bohnenblust's own experience and behaviour. What Stiller does not
appreciate is that his reaction to Bohnenblust's speech furnishes an
insight into Julika's reaction to his own. The one-dimensional Bohnen-

blust is here likened ironically to the many-facetted Stiller.

The sequence in which these three examples are presented is significant: Rolf's 'Vorträge' on freedom in marriage give way to the clarity
of his New York proposal, and Stiller's failure to verbalise a similar
proposal to Julika is followed by the long speech of Bohnenblust. The
sequence presents a movement in Rolf from dishonesty towards experience
to commitment to it, an awareness of dishonesty towards experience in
Stiller, and a depiction of unrelatedness to experience in Bohnenblust.
Stiller records Rolf's dishonest attitude in the 'Viertes Heft' and the
vanquishing of this attitude in the 'Sechstes Heft'. In the 'Siebentes
Heft', having recorded his own failure to trust his 'Einsicht', Stiller
presages his own decline in the 'Nachwort' - written by another - in
his record of the empty posturings of Bohnenblust. Stiller cannot be
ignorant of the consequences which failure to commit himself to
experience entails.

Commitment in relationships

The modern age places a special burden on the individual as he
seeks to understand himself and his relationships with others. This
has been brought about by the absence of an ontological framework for
human life in modern times. A direct consequence of this lack of
transcendental values is noted by the figure of Bin. Modern man is
obliged, since there no longer exist standards outside his world by
which he can measure himself, to seek for approval of himself in his
fellows, and this distorts the relationships between individuals:

> Nirgends aufgehoben, sehnt jeder sich nach der sicheren
> Achtung von seiten der Menschen - so sehr, so dringlich
> und aufdringlich, dass er alles darüber vergisst, sogar
> seine natürliche und vorhandene Liebe zu ihnen, das, was
> ihn allein von seinem dürren Geiz befreite. Ehrgeiz ist
> ja auch nur ein Geiz, und nichts...macht uns so einsam
> von einander wie unser Ehrgeiz. (I 633)

Formal relationships occur within the public structure of society,
where conventions and considerations of social propriety influence
the individual's behaviour. Such checks and balances are not always
an effective restraint on behaviour, as the parallel cases of the bank
clerk and the Staatsanwalt in Graf Öderland show. In general terms,
however, it is in his less formal relationships, where the role of the
individual is less clearly defined, that strains are most clearly
detected. This is above all true of the close relationships between
men and women. Hence observation of the individual's behaviour within
these relationships, where the individual is largely left to work out

his own salvation without the support of a formal social structure,
indicates the extent to which the individual can draw on himself and
his experience in sustaining the relationship and to what extent he
misuses the relationship to sustain himself.

The chief strain in these relationships is caused by one, or both
partners seeking in the relationship something which it is not the
function of the relationship to impart. In the case of the male
partner, it is frequently his attitudes, dictated by the 'Ehrgeiz' of
which Bin speaks, which are a root cause of the extravagant demands
made on the behaviour of the other partner. Since Rolf is able, through
time, to adjust his attitudes towards his wife Sibylle and thus
establish their relationship on a new basis, it is appropriate to examne
his attitudes at the point where he himself is gaining an insight into
their destructive consequences. This takes place during his stay in
Genoa, a period which represents the beginning of a change in his outlook. That Genoa is a turning-point is indicated by a list of insights
into himself, beginning: 'Er lernte kennen:...' (III 559), which his
enforced idleness in the Italian port enables him to make. Chief
amongst these insights is his realisation that he is incapable of feeling love for a woman unless he believes himself to be the centre of her
universe. The process of acquiring self-knowledge is a painful one.
At the end of the catalogue of insights, Rolf retains an unpleasant
memory of the painfulness of the confrontation: 'Es war eine Strapaze'
(III 560). He had arrived in Genoa evolving 'Pläne von knäbischer
Rachsucht' (III 551), a measure of the immaturity of his response to
the crisis in his marriage and the resulting limitedness of his
intentions about surmounting it. Such negative emotions, the outcome
of an attitude of mind maintained over many years, are not to be dispelled, however, by a few brief moments of insight, however painful and
revealing. Rolf resolves to return home, and to pretend by his demeanour
that the crisis has left him unaffected: 'Seine Haltung sollte sie
(Sibylle) vernichten' (III 566). 'Haltung' is a concept which is
discussed by Reinhart in Die Schwierigen while he is painting a portrait
of young Ammann. 'Haltung' designates the bearing of a person fully
conscious of himself and is an outer expression of inner balance (I 453);
Reinhart has been prompted to comment by the stiff and unnatural attitude
adopted by Ammann, which Reinhart dismisses as a 'Pose' (I 454). It is
with such an assumed false bearing, which is quite at odds with the
real state of his emotions, that Rolf decides to return from Genoa to
Zürich. Such a resolution, taken at this point, reflects the resilience

of immature self-esteem in the face of insight, and Rolf is not unaware
of the limited and ridiculous nature of his decision: 'Was aber...wenn
Rolf allein in der Wohnung blieb, allein mit seiner Haltung?' (III 566).
On his return to Zürich, the difficulties which his 'Haltung' impose
upon him are highlighted by the ludicrous interview with Sturzenegger,
the architect. Since he is convinced that the younger man is his wife's
lover, Rolf's vanity will not allow him not to display this assumed
knowledge to Sturzenegger (III 574). Devoid of a basis of confidence
in himself, he observes his performance as he imagines it will strike
Sturzenegger, namely as one of dignity and poise. As always, reality
does not correspond to preconceptions: 'Das Gespräch, in Würde begonnen,
schien auszurutschen' (III 575). Even when the nature of the interchange between himself and the younger man causes him to realise that
Sturzenegger is not in fact his wife's lover, Rolf still feels obliged
to behave in the manner which he has prescribed for himself. Yet when
Sturzenegger has left, he admits to himself the futility of the interview in relation to the unresolved crisis with Sibylle: 'Nichts war
überwunden, überhaupt nichts!' (III 576).

Two other depictions of the same self-centred obduracy appear after
Stiller. The hero in Die grosse Wut des Philipp Hotz is obsessed by
the injury done to his vanity by the fact that his wife is suing for
divorce. In this state of mind, he imagines that the audience are
defending his wife's action (IV 419). He further assumes that an
elderly woman who arrives at his flat is his wife's aunt who has come
to champion the cause of her niece. Accordingly, he delivers lengthy
speeches of self-justification, only to discover that the woman has come
from a department store to arrange a vacuum cleaner demonstration (IV
420-424). Gantenbein, who has been accumulating evidence to support his
theory that Lila is conducting an affair, opens the door one morning to
a young man whom he shows straight into the bedroom where Lila is still
asleep, and locks the bedroom door. Despite the fact that he is 'lang-
sam entsetzt, dass ich das wirklich getan habe, nicht bloss gedacht,
sondern getan' (V 197), he takes no steps to rectify the situation,
and leaves the flat. He returns to discover that the young man was a
student seeking advice from Lila on becoming an actor, and that Gantenbein's behaviour is causing Lila to leave him. The behaviour of the
three men - Rolf, Hotz, and Gantenbein - arises from their relationships
with women, and from resentment that these women may have transferred
their affections to another. But their behaviour also acts as a
general indication of the dangers of an inflexible attitude to reality.

222.

These situations show the manner in which insecurity renders the
individual unresponsive to reality by causing him to behave in a rigid
and arbitrary fashion.

It is in the nature of the characters who are mature, and hence
capable of commitment, that their response to life is adaptable. They
are aware that any commitment must take place within an ever-changing
framework of experience. Other characters are not aware of this, and
stake their continuing welfare on maintaining an unchanged pattern of
life. The weak and dessicated Hinkelmann, Yvonne's first husband in
Die Schwierigen, is thunderstruck when his wife announces that she is
leaving him. He is sure that he cannot live without her, and thus
cannot adapt his life to her departure from it (I 402). His subsequent
suicide confirms this. In the case of the vacillating Kürmann, the
final collapse of his illusions about the extent to which he can
determine the pattern of his life is symbolised by the purchase of a
revolver with which to coerce Antoinette. The Registrator comments on
her involvement in the situation which has led to the purchase:

> Sie will ihr eigenes Leben, sie sucht keinen Mann, der
> meint, dass sie ohne ihn nicht leben kann, und der einen
> Revolver kauft, wenn er eines Tages sieht, dass sie ohne
> ihn leben kann. (V 498)

The Dame in Don Juan goes further. By offering a commitment to him
through her love, yet firmly within the framework of her independence
of him, she sees an opportunity for Don Juan to break with his
egoistical treatment of women which, contrary to his intention, has
devoured his life: 'Ich bin die Frau, die frei ist vom Wahn, ohne dich
nicht leben zu können' (III 145). It is interesting to note that Don
Juan, the man whom life rescues from himself by causing him to become
a father, was created by Frisch at approximately the same time as the
figure of Rolf, the man who finally gathers the strength to be guided
by life [3]. Rolf's wife Sibylle has this strength in that she is 'frei
vom Wahn, ohne Rolf nicht leben zu können' (III 620). She demonstrates
this during her two-year stay in New York, and it is in New York that
Rolf demonstrates that he has attained her attitude, for it is there
that he proposes to her that they divorce or that they live together,
'aber endgültig' (III 661). Rolf's achievement is that his response
to life, has, within a framework of commitment, become adaptable.

The figure of Rolf assumes a unique position among the male
characters in the work of Frisch in that he adapts his behaviour in
the light of his experience. This distinguishes him even from Don Juan,
for Don Juan, although the figure closest to Rolf in that he too adapts

his behaviour, does so as the result of an accident of nature – he
makes Miranda pregnant – and not as a result of conscious decisions
after reflection on the experience with which life has presented him.
Frisch shows how the process of reflection on experience occurs in
his depiction of the Genoa episode and its aftermath, which convinces
Rolf of the disparity between life as it is and life as he imagines it
should be. Instead of entrenching himself further in his vain expectations of life, as so many Frisch characters do, Rolf is guided by the
reality of life. This is clear from the adjustment of his behaviour
in his relationship with Sibylle. He has regarded his sudden departure
for Genoa as a dramatic gesture on his part which will make his wife
conform to his way of thinking, and he expects, and also desperately
hopes, that she will contact him in Italy. But as he haunts the main
post office in Genoa and as she fails to contact him, he is forced to
admit the preposterous nature of his expectations, to realise 'wie un-
fähig er war, seine eigenen Theorien zu leben!' (III 560). Although
he does not alter his behaviour immediately, Rolf's honesty eventually
prompts him to bridge the gap, which features so prominently in Frisch's
work, between experience and intelligence.

Gantenbein, himself not a person to be guided by experience,
attributes the unsympathetic attitude of his imaginary daughter
Beatrice towards him to the fact that she is intelligent but has no
experience of life (V 308). Yvonne, on her return to Switzerland,
sees the same disparity in the socially prominent people with whom she
comes in contact. Their upbringing has not prepared them to draw
conclusions from life, and as a result they behave like lost children
(I 432). Don Juan, by accepting the fact that he is going to become a
father, bridges the gap which he had widened by seeking refuge in
geometry [4]. In the coalescence of all his faculties, he ceases to be
the traditional one-sided figure of Don Juan, as Frisch points out:
acceptance of fatherhood is 'seine Kapitulation' (III 171). It is
significant that this progression, depicted in terms of capitulation,
should find identical expression in the case of Rolf. That his case is
different, that his honesty towards his perceptions will cause him to
move to an acceptance of life rather than have such an acceptance thrust
upon him, is indicated by the fact that Rolf uses the same word about
himself as Frisch, the commentator, about Don Juan. Aware that the
insights which he has gained during his stay in Genoa are irreversible,
and that he must carry the knowledge of these insights with him even
if he does not immediately act upon them, Rolf senses the eventual
significance of a return to Zürich, and delays it as long as possible:

224.

'Die Kapitulation (so nennt er es) hatte er bis zur letzten Minute ver-
schoben' (III 565). By boarding the train for Zürich in Genoa, Rolf
embarks on the first stage of the long journey which will lead to his
statement of commitment in New York.

The nature of commitment, as explored in the relationship between
Rolf and Sibylle, is examined by Frisch in Die Schwierigen. If the
later novel depicts the eventual achievement of commitment in a relationship, the earlier one concerns itself with the manner in which an already
established relationship can be put to the test. Yvonne, after her
failed marriage to the immature Hinkelmann, her inconclusive affairs
on her return to Switzerland, and, above all, after her emotionally
exhausting liaison with Reinhart, meets her former employer Hauswirt
socially for the first time. What strikes her most is his lack of self-
importance, his awareness that he is not the centre of the world (I 473).
She accepts his offer of marriage, and their life together is seen through
the eyes of Yvonne:

> Es gibt reizende Abende. Er liest. Man zerstört sich nicht,
> das ist der Grund, worauf man geht, man ist nicht verliebt,
> man ist sich gewogen, man verträgt den Geruch des andern,
> und das ist viel. Ohne die schwärmerische Anmassung, man
> müsse verstanden sein und das andere verstehen, öffnet sich
> ein Gefilde voll schöner Erträglichkeit. (I 551) [5]

This passage, which is followed by general reflections on the true
possibilities of marriage as opposed to romanticised expectations about
it, is redolent of a tolerance which for Yvonne is especially valuable
after the extravagant and self-centred posturings of Reinhart [6]. The
subsequent crisis concerns Hauswirt's commitment to his marriage, and
is chiefly described through Yvonne's reaction to her husband as he
copes with it. The narrative thus provides an example of the indirect
presentation later much more fully developed in Stiller. It is the
news of Reinhart's suicide which prompts Yvonne to recall the crisis
in her marriage with Hauswirt, and this provides the contrastive framework against which the achievement of Hauswirt is assessed. The suicide
reminds Yvonne of the manner in which Hauswirt discovered that Hanswalter, the child Yvonne was carrying at the time of her marriage, is
not his son, but Reinhart's. In her recollection it seems to Yvonne
that by her attitude in refusing to influence Hauswirt, she enabled
him to take the decision to stay with her. One of the cardinal points
about Hauswirt's decision is that it is attended by silence on both
sides. Yvonne's original assessment of Hauswirt as a man who is
prepared to stand by his decisions has proved correct. Certainly, the
surmounting of the crisis deepens her respect for her husband:

> Yvonne empfand eine neue, eine unwiderstehliche Achtung
> vor dem Mann, der neben ihr blieb, vor allem, dass er
> ohne jedes innere Auskneifen vermochte, ohne die übliche
> Art der Enttäuschten, die sich am weiterlaufenden Leben
> durch spöttische Bitterkeit rächen, sich im Genusse
> boshafter Ansichten entschädigen. Es waren oft lange
> Abende, die sie seither nebeneinander vor dem Kamin
> sassen; Hauswirt hatte kein einziges Wort mehr davon
> gesprochen. Fand er nicht auch, man war sich näher
> gekommen, immer wieder ein ganz wenig näher? Er sass
> und las, er trank sein Glas voll Wein, und Yvonne rauchte,
> manchmal legte sie eine Patience. (I 597)

Although their life reverts to its pattern, it is enriched by increased
knowledge and respect. The harmonious sharing of life by two different
people with different experiences, yet bound by an acceptance of life,
is presented as a sterling achievement. Yet the framework of irony in
respect of both characters' previous expectations, and in respect of
previous depictions in the novel of _bürgerlich_ society, prevents the
close from becoming an endorsement of _bürgerlich_ values [7].

In the relationship between Hauswirt and Yvonne, and above all in
the crisis in that relationship, Frisch examines the working of commitment in a concrete situation. Yvonne, in that she has come to adapt her
expectations of life to her observations of the way in which life has
behaved in the past, is a precursor of Rolf. Hauswirt, in that he has
an inborn sense of how to react to life, a sense which never deserts
him, is something of a forerunner of Sibylle. The portrayal of the
relationship between Hauswirt and Yvonne points forward to the greater
complexities and the more sophisticated presentation of the concrete
situations in which commitment is examined in _Stiller_.

Commitment in _Stiller_

It has been indicated that the main characters in Frisch's novels
have a tangential relationship with characters and episodes involving
commitment [8]. These characters and episodes, by offering contrastive
behaviour to that of the main characters, provide a moral perspective
to the works as a whole. In _Homo Faber_, it is the hero himself who,
by the fleeting insights which he garners in Cuba, offers a commentary
on his normal behaviour. In _Die Schwierigen_, the minor character of
Hauswirt, and in _Gantenbein_, the even more minor character of the
ambassador, provide, through their attitudes and actions in situations
parallel to those in which the heroes find themselves, alternative
modes of behaviour which are based on responsibility and commitment to
the actuality of life. _Stiller_, however, in the situations of which

the main embodiment of the theme of commitment in the works of Frisch
is contained, presents these moral contrasts in a much more differentiated fashion and in a much more successful artistic form.

In the first place, Stiller, the most articulate of the major
characters, is most fully aware of his own shortcomings and of those
of the world in which he lives. His exposition of the problems arising
from both sets of shortcomings thus contains in its clarity of
definition a pointer towards possible behaviour through which he might
counter these difficulties. In this sense, awareness contains a moral
dimension. In the second place, Stiller, of all the major characters,
is the one most involved with the secondary characters in whose behaviour
Frisch embodies commitment. The minor characters in Die Schwierigen
and in Gantenbein, although they may provide contrasts to the main
character, are not directly involved with them. Indeed, in Gantenbein
there is no involvement at all, merely the contrastive anecdote. By
contrast Rolf and Sibylle are deeply involved with the main figure.
The difference in moral behaviour of these characters becomes more
convincing in its portrayal from the fact that Stiller's life runs
parallel to the lives of those who behave differently from him in
similar situations. By displaying this difference within a framework
of similarity of background and situation, Frisch most effectively
shows moral behaviour at work in the confusing flux of reality.

The technique by which Frisch displays this involvement has an
affinity to one employed in the visual arts, in which the artist
depicts his subject from a number of different vantage points in an
attempt to seize its elusive essence [9]. In presenting his characters
through 'eine Skala möglicher Betrachtungsweisen' [10], Frisch bears out
his belief that each individual is 'unfassbar' (II 369), for the
indefinable and inexpressible core of personality can acquire shape
only by surrounding it from all sides with what is capable of expression
and definition. In the novels of Frisch, the technique is most obviously
at work in the 'composite portrait' [11] of Gantenbein, in which the
narrator attempts to give form to himself through his 'Umschreibungen' [12].
But the 'vorsichtiges Sich-Herantasten an die Wirklichkeit' [13] of this
novel is apparent to some extent in the other novels. The complexities
of the sequence of incident in Homo Faber represent an attempt to show
that experience cannot be presented chronologically, and it has already
been mentioned that in Die Schwierigen, the earliest of the four major
novels, the technique of indirect presentation is employed. Indirectness
of presentation is central to the structure of Stiller. Frisch maintains

that the novel is traditional in that it invites the reader's credence
in the reality of the depicted events [14]. This minimises the fact,
however, that character and incident are presented in such a fashion
that the various viewpoints relativise one another so that the reader
is presented with something approaching the confusing density of reality.
The clearly delineated motivation of events which one tradition of
authorial omniscience presents to the reader is thus absent from Stiller.
The reports of the four main protagonists in the novel supplement,
contradict and adjust one another [15]. The effect on the reader is to
render uncertain preconceived notions and one-sided judgements. In
doing this, the novel also presents an approximation of the conditions
in which, in real life, decisions are taken and commitments made.

The formal structure of the novel, with the seven 'Hefte' written
by Stiller largely from statements made by others, and the 'Nachwort'
written by Rolf alone, offers the most obvious example of the fact that
its material is not presented from one consistent, single point of
view. Irony, 'the creative principle' [16] of the novel, is the basis
for the contrast between the formal and the actual relationship between
the two writers. For it is ironic that the man whom society charges
with the prosecution of Stiller for the misdemeanours arising from the
latter's disappearance, should be the only person who takes the trouble
to concern himself with the welfare of Stiller after his release from
prison [17]. Yet the irony is further deepened by the fact that Rolf's
friendship with the accused is also the main feature of Stiller's
complex and unexpected relationship to the juridical authorities. For
not only does Stiller's only friendship link him with an employee of
the legal machinery of the state, it is the state which has compelled
Stiller to try to come to terms with himself. On the other hand,
Stiller's relationship with his official defence lawyer, who asks him
to commit his life to paper, is, in contrast to that with Rolf, his
official prosecutor, fraught with misunderstandings arising from Bohnenblust's barely concealed apathy to his client. Bohnenblust's narrow
conception of his function is a reflection of the narrowness and lack
of warmth of the Swiss society which he represents, whereas Rolf's
attitude to Stiller - who was after all Sibylle's lover - is based on
humanity and forgiveness. Yet by a final irony, Rolf finds that the
description of Julika given by Stiller in the 'Aufzeichnungen' on her
first visit to his cell fits her exactly as she lies dead. Rolf
concludes that Stiller has seen her 'von allem Anfang an nur als Tote',
and, as he stands in the mortuary of the clinic, he is penetrated by

an overwhelming consciousness of Stiller's 'Verstündigung' (III 779)
towards his wife. Ironically, the words of Stiller's description of
Julika, especially its close (III 412), were intended to convey the
vibrancy of his response to her as a woman, a direct and liberating
response such as is depicted at no other point in the novel. Rolf, no
mere casual acquaintance, but a man deeply involved with Stiller, and
who, by exhortation and example, pointed to the path which Stiller
might have taken, here fundamentally misinterprets an important aspect
of the 'Aufzeichnungen'. One of the final acts of involvement of Rolf,
the sympathetic friend, stresses his distance from Stiller and so
emphasises the problem with which Stiller fails to come to terms: the
isolation of individuation.

Sibylle's involvement with both Rolf and Stiller provides a prism
through which a direct comparison of the two men can be made. This
comparison occurs at the height of her affair with Stiller, before both
men are put to the test, to which they react in different ways, of
having to take a decision in respect of her. Significantly, it is at
a time when she herself is shrinking from taking a decision about her
position, that she makes the direct comparison between them. She is
out sailing with Stiller, and as she reflects, firstly, on the fact
that she is probably pregnant by him, and secondly, on the professional
success of her husband, she feels inclined, as the boat drifts through
the water, herself to drift in a limbo of indecision, the opposite of
her normal self (III 631). Like Rolf, until such time as he has
learned the lesson of the Genoa episode, and like Stiller prior to his
incarceration and then on his release, Sibylle is here allowing her life
to escape her moral control. On the lake she gives way to a phantasy
about the impossible in respect of the two men: 'Beide zusammen in
einer Person, das wäre es gewesen!' (III 631). Yet even in her
indecisive state, her use of the past conditional tense implies an
acceptance of what can never be.

Rolf eventually makes an offer of commitment to Sibylle in New York
which she accepts. His commitment is given an ironic framework of
reference in that one of the subsequent manifestations of its
application is recounted and commented on by Stiller, who proves himself to be incapable of such a commitment in his own life. This occurs
when Rolf, for the purposes of the juridical confrontation, visits for
the first time Stiller's former studio, the scene of Sibylle's adultery
with the artist. Stiller observes that the Staatsanwalt is betraying
his nervousness by smoking 'ziemlich hastig' (III 710), and goes on

to ask himself what the purpose of Rolf's visit can possibly be in his
role as a husband, as opposed to that of an official. Sibylle had
already realised, ironically during her first visit to the same studio
at the start of their affair, that Stiller has a lively memory of at
least one case where he felt humiliated in the presence of a woman. He
had recounted at length the inglorious incident in the Spanish Civil
War after which Anja, the young Polish interpreter with whom Stiller
imagined he was in love, refused to take him seriously. Sibylle
recognised that this experience had affected him deeply, more: 'Er wollte nicht damit fertig werden' (III 617). Stiller's faculty for clearly
recalling humiliation, real or imagined, is too highly developed not to
militate against the more stable perspective which the curative effects
of time can permit the individual to achieve. Thus at the juridical
confrontation he attributes to Rolf the feelings which he, Stiller,
would experience in a similar situation, and the morbidity of these
feelings offers an explanation for the moral inertia of Stiller's own
life. Firstly, Stiller discounts the fact that part of the lesson of
the Genoa episode was for Rolf the realisation that 'Vorstellungen von
quälerischer Präzision' (III 710) - which Stiller imagines are now
plaguing Rolf in the studio - are utterly disruptive. Rolf did torture
himself in Genoa 'mit schamlos-genauen Vorstellungen' (III 560) of his
wife's involvement with another man, and the fact that he sought a
reconciliation with his wife is an indication of his decision to put
such 'Vorstellungen' aside. Secondly, there is a double irony in
Stiller's reaction. It must reflect the reality of Rolf's attitude,
since the fact that he is present at the studio, albeit in a nervous
state, indicates that he accepts that the place and its decaying
furniture has in fact nothing more to do 'mit seiner lebendigen Sibylle'
(III 710). Stiller's reaction also reflects his own position: he can
derive the energy for action to overcome his own past neither from his
intellectual perceptions of the extent to which the past can be
destructive, nor from the power of example of Rolf. The account of
this part of the juridical confrontation indicates differences in the
two figures in respect of the same phenomenon, coming to terms with
the past. One of the many ironies of this confrontation is that the
accused clings to a fixed view of what was, whereas the demeanour of
the official prosecutor demonstrates his commitment to what is.

   The attitude of Rolf at the juridical confrontation contrasts with
the false pose which he maintained during the interview in his office
with Sibylle. If the confrontation shows the extent to which Rolf has

changed, that interview had shown his similarity to Stiller. Rolf's
account of the interview presents him perfectly in control of himself,
but although given seven years after the event and recorded by Stiller
in the 'Viertes Heft' (III 580-581), it does not imply a justification
of his behaviour during the interview, but represents his present
recollection of the foolish action to which his false attitude at the
time forced him. For he describes the interview as he allowed it to
develop as a 'Farce', and the later behaviour of himself and Sibylle as
a 'kindische Farce'. But at no point, from the start, where his wife
sits on the other side of his desk 'wie eine Klientin', to the eventual
close of the interview and the ensuing separation, does he intervene to
alter the course of events. Like so many Frisch characters in situations
which are open to mediation by reason and action, he observes the
progress of the interview in horrified impotence: 'Er glaubte es
nicht'. Yet he is fully aware of the gesture which is required of him
to resolve the situation, or at least, of the contribution required of
him towards any resolution of the problem. But his false idea of
'Haltung' prevents him from making any gesture. In the inflexibility
of his weak and immature response to the situation, Rolf has never
seemed more like Stiller. The later reversal of his behaviour in New
York provides, on the other hand, the clearest contrast to the artist.

Rolf's version of the Zürich interview in the 'Viertes Heft' is
relativised by the version in the 'Sechstes Heft' (III 636-641)
provided by Sibylle. The two versions have in common that they are
recorded by Stiller, who comments, not without a hint of malice, that
the interview 'wurde von seiner Frau natürlich etwas anders erlebt'.
But in the reprise of certain words, Sibylle's version recreates the
sense of intense emotional frustration suggested by Rolf's. She feels
'wie eine Klientin', and her impression that the interview is a 'Farce'
finds expression in her remark that they are both behaving immaturely
– 'kindisch' –, precisely the sensation which had assailed Rolf. But
the vital difference between the two versions consists in the fact that
in hers Sibylle reports that she broached the topic of freedom in
marriage, which she later widens into the theme of commitment in human
relations in general. This topic had already exercised Rolf a month
earlier, when the transfer of furniture and household goods from the
old flat to the new villa built by Rolf started. As he stands in the
villa, amidst a confusion of packing cases, he becomes acutely aware
of the irrelevance of all these goods to the reality of his marriage,
to the significance of his relationship to his wife and to his son.
The transfer from the flat to the villa makes Rolf aware that emotional

commitment cannot be transferred in the same way in the name of freedom
in marriage (III 578). Now, in his office, Sibylle bitterly relates
the false concept of freedom in marriage - an aspect entirely omitted
from Rolf's version - to the parlous situation in which they both find
themselves: 'Du bist frei, ich bin frei, und dabei ist alles so jämmer-
lich'. The bondage of such misery contrasts with the real freedom of
commitment. Sibylle's statement on the nature of commitment in human
relationships provides a further stage in the education of Rolf, which,
starting in Genoa, progresses gradually and painfully until it is
translated into action in New York. Sibylle, although fully aware of
her moral responsibility to others, is no less aware of their
responsibility to her. A relationship can only be sustained by mutual
commitment to the specific nature of the partners. Sibylle claims that
Rolf has failed in such a commitment, that he is 'ein verheirateter
Junggeselle'. Without such a commitment, marriage is a futile undertaking:

> Entweder ist die Ehe ein Schicksal, meine ich, oder sie
> hat überhaupt keinen Sinn, sie ist ein Unfug.

Commitment is undertaken in the full knowledge of the necessary limitations of the partner as an individual, as Sibylle explains to Rolf by
reference to an incident in Cairo from their common past. Sibylle
extends the notion of committed choice to the network of relationships
which surrounds every individual:

> Spielraum in der Ehe, was heisst das? Ich will keinen
> Spielraum, ich will, dass ich für meinen Mann nicht 'irgend-
> eine' Frau bin. Warum verstehst du das nicht? Auch mein
> Vater ist nicht 'irgendein' Mann für mich. Und Hannes ist
> nicht 'irgendein' Kind, das wir nun gerade liebhaben,
> weil's uns gefällt.

In this sense the problem of commitment in marriage relates directly
to the manner in which the individual copes with this wider framework
of relationships. Commitment implies an acceptance of the personalities
in this framework, and in the case of the relationship of the couple,
the partnership where choice is involved, this acceptance implies in
turn a readiness to deepen one's awareness of the other's personality.
This full response can only be realised, however, if there is a counter-
response from the partner. At the close of the interview in Rolf's
office, Sibylle senses that Rolf is still immured in his false notions
of 'Haltung', which she knows it must be his responsibility to discard.

The 'Viertes Heft' of Stiller's 'Aufzeichnungen', which is in fact
the 'Protokoll' given by Rolf of his flight to Genoa and the continuing
crisis in his marriage on his return to Zürich, closes with the partners

separating from one another. The 'Sechstes Heft', on the other hand, which contains the 'Protokoll' given by Sibylle of her affair with Stiller and her marital crisis, closes with an account of the reconcil- iation between Rolf and Sibylle in New York. It is fitting that the account of the partner more resilient and more balanced by nature should close on this positive note, although it must be noted that the eventual successful outcome of the crisis is anticipated by Stiller recording the birth of a second child to Sibylle and Rolf in the course of Rolf's 'Protokoll' (III 566). Whereas the birth offers a contrast to the barrenness of Rolf's attitude to his wife in the 'Viertes Heft', the fact that he travels to New York in the 'Sechstes Heft' emphasises symbolically the distance which he has travelled since the Genoa episode and its aftermath, and the extent to which he has succeeded in coming to terms with himself. The journey to New York constitutes the 'Geste der Versöhnung' (III 581) which he had found impossible to make in his office, and in that it is a courageous acceptance of the demands made by life, has a parallel in the ambassador's reaction to the discovery about his identity in Gantenbein [18]. For the proposition which he makes to Sibylle in New York is not only devoid of his former posturing and equivocation, but it also accords Sibylle her right to freedom of choice by envisaging the possibility that she might not wish for a reconciliation, and is thus in stark contrast to the previous 'Vorträge' on his spurious notion of freedom in marriage. Rolf has achieved the maturity and flexibility of response to life to know that he can cope with either acceptance or refusal. The ability to make a decision and to accept the consequences of that decision are held by Ammann's father in Die Schwierigen to be rare qualities: 'Eine Wahl treffen und eine Verantwortung übernehmen wollen die allerwenig- sten' (I 508). Rolf's decision must be seen against the background of indecision as a theme in Frisch's work, as well as against the pattern of Rolf's earlier attitudes.

The figure of Sibylle also demonstrates that commitment does not entail inflexibility to the circumstances of life. She had previously withdrawn her commitment to Rolf and was prepared to place it else- where, was prepared to involve herself on a permanent basis with Stiller. In the latter relationship, commitment is also examined in relation to a journey. Shortly after the beginning of her affair with Stiller, she suggests to him that they go to Paris together, a trip which she will finance. The suggestion serves to highlight the chronic indecision of Stiller. When, in July 1945, five months before Sibylle sails for New York, they go to the station in Zürich to take the Paris train,

Stiller's irresolution over the step which he is about to take is
manifest (III 625). His display of decisiveness is an empty posture,
as Sibylle perceives, and this stifles her own desire to go to Paris.
Thus they sit on a station bench in a moral limbo, which is resolved
finally by the departure of the train. This incident is followed by
Stiller's telephone call to Sibylle at the end of September, in which
he suggests that they go to Paris. Sibylle's reaction takes place
against the density of incident and pre-occupation which constitute
daily life, and which not only makes a claim on the individual, but
also provides an excuse for not making any decision at all, for allowing life to decide, just as the train took the decision about the
original trip to Paris. Amongst other concerns, Rolf is pressing
Sibylle for a decision on whether the furniture should be moved to the
new villa, and she has promised to take her son Hannes to the circus.
Paradoxically, the plethora of her concerns crystallises the matter
for Sibylle, and her indecisive state, which was symbolised by her
drifting in a boat on the Zürichsee, evaporates. It is important to
note, however, that her thoughts at this point range over the entire
spectrum of considerations arising from her situation, that her decision
to go to Paris is taken in the full awareness of its implications (III
633). It transpires, however, when Sibylle goes to his studio, that
Stiller requires to travel to Paris in any case on business connected
with his forthcoming exhibition. In addition, the fact that the trip
to Paris is connected with the exhibition enables him to justify it to
Julika, who is still in the sanatorium in Davos. Sibylle's reaction
on learning this is as decisive as her previous resolution had been:
'Sibylle begriff. Sie sagte ganz einfach: 'Nein!'' (III 635). Her
rejection of Stiller also encompasses the rejection of his child which
she is carrying. She immediately takes the decision to have an
abortion (III 635-636), and her subsequent silence about the abortion
indicates that she has accepted a responsibility which she recognises
as being hers alone. She returns from having had the abortion to the
disastrous interview with Rolf, then goes to Pontestrina for the final
encounter with Stiller, where she takes the decision to break with her
present life, and to re-establish her relationship to herself in the
United States. Her sense of commitment adapts to the movement of life:
she can accept the past, and thus, after a period alone, she is able
to resume her relationship with Rolf. Stiller, unable to accept his
past, goes to the United States in order to escape from it, and
discovers that it pursues him and eventually destroys him, for he
cannot come to terms, as Sibylle does, with the constantly changing

circumstances of life.

The culmination of Sibylle's stay in the United States is her
reconciliation with Rolf in New York. The interview at the top of the
'Rockefeller-Turm' (III 660) forms the counterpart to the disastrous
interview in Zürich, and demonstrates, firstly, that Sibylle has re-
established the balance which is natural to her and which finds its
full expression in commitment, and secondly, that Rolf has allowed
himself to be guided by experience into a position where he realises
that decisive commitment in personal relationships is the only viable
mode of behaviour. Rolf's proposal is made against the panorama of the
multi-coloured lights of New York at night. The view is described in
ambiguous terms as being both attractive and repellent, and, in that
the visual attraction is likened to the aural attraction of the song
of the sirens, the suggestion is made that to yield too much to the
force of the attraction is to incur danger (III 662). At this point
the full extent of the technique of indirect presentation employed by
Frisch becomes apparent. It is not simply that Stiller is recording
Sibylle's account of the meeting with Rolf, a meeting which results in
the kind of commitment of which Stiller himself is eventually incapable,
but in addition, the description of the dangerous fascination exercised
by the lights of New York is made by Stiller himself [19], drawing on his
own recollections of the spectacle. Stiller's description bears witness to his ambivalent attitude to the essentially sterile nature of
the spectacle, and constitutes a commentary on Stiller's inability to
create in his life a scale of priorities which would enable him to
establish balanced relationships with those about him. Rolf, on the
other hand, distances himself from any possible involvement in the
scene by according it the traditional designation for tumultuous and
meaningless urban confusion: ''Babylon!', meinte Rolf' (III 661).
Later in the 'Nachwort', Rolf's judgement on the 'ferme vaudoise' is
equally uncompromising when he speaks of 'dieser skurrilen Kitschigkeit' (III 754). Stiller's description of New York acquires a further
justificatory note, however. The lights form a 'Sintflut von Neon-
Limonade, von Süssigkeit, von Kitsch, der ins Grandiose übergeht'
(III 662). The superficial brilliance of the scene is a tourist
attraction typical of the 'Zeitalter der Reproduktion'. The
technologically produced panorama offers as little possibility for
personal involvement as the artificial 'ferme vaudoise'. Yet Stiller's
'ferme vaudoise' is described as being the 'Haus seines Lebens'. The
measure of Stiller's failure in his personal relationships is symbolised, not merely in an object, a building, but by a building devoid

of individuality, by an object which is endlessly reproducible.
Against a technological sight known world wide, the lights of New York,
on the other hand, Rolf can preserve his individuality in his response
to the personality of another human being, Sibylle. Against this background, he establishes fully for the first time his relationship with
'die Frau seines Lebens' (III 661). The description of the New York
reconciliation between Rolf and Sibylle therefore records not only the
manner of this reconciliation, but also provides further indications
of Stiller's inability to make a similar kind of commitment. The final
indications of this inability are recorded by Rolf in the 'Nachwort'.
As Rolf, together with Sibylle on his second visit to the 'ferme
vaudoise' in Glion, awaits Stiller's return, he looks down on the
lights of Montreux which remind him of those in New York (III 754-755).
The passage, by linking New York and Montreux, points to the meretricious
background against which decisions must be taken in the modern world,
and offers a contrast in the behaviour of Stiller and Rolf.

It is important to emphasise the achievement of Rolf and of Sibylle,
and more particularly that of Rolf in gradually compelling himself to
draw conclusions from the Genoa episode and to alter his behaviour in
the light of these conclusions. For Rolf and Sibylle, as a couple,
form the contrast to Stiller and Julika, and Rolf as an individual is
a contrastive figure to Stiller. The two contrasts are essential for
the artistic balance of the novel. Rolf resolves his personal crisis,
and part of this solution consists of concessions to the social framework. These concessions do not detract from Rolf's accomplishment in
coming to terms with himself. Stiller, on the other hand, is, in his
self-centred weakness, incapable of making concessions to anyone, least
of all to the generality of society, and as a consequence the end of
the novel shows him, not merely alone, but also unlikely ever again to
establish viable human relationships. The portrayal of Stiller's
decline to this condition of moral apathy is rendered more credible by
being counterpointed by the accomplishment of Rolf, since the case of
Rolf demonstrates that the downfall of Stiller might have been avoided.
Stiller's inadequate attempts to come to terms with himself and his
environment are the more harrowing because of the parallel presentations
of Rolf's establishment of an equilibrium which might not have been
beyond the reach of Stiller. This equilibrium represents a form of
self-fulfilment possible within the sphere of close personal relationships, more specifically within the relationships between men and
women [20]. The constraints of society place limits on self-fulfilment

in the social sphere. Full self-fulfilment is possible only in the free choice of a partner and in a commitment to that partner. The novel Stiller owes its stature not least to the device whereby Stiller, in the course of the seven 'Hefte', charts the progress of Rolf towards self-realisation, as he himself fails to translate the self-knowledge which his incarceration brings him. Once outside the prison walls, his surrogate moral support, Stiller, having failed to change his behaviour, must collapse. The collapse is recorded by Rolf, whose sympathy for Stiller is the stronger for having trod much of the same stony path himself. The fate of Stiller who has lost forever the chance to realise himself through commitment, is depicted by Rolf, the man who knows the difficulty of attaining commitment, and who is also aware that the attainment of commitment is essential if the vital forces are not to ebb and run dry. A consideration of Stiller, and of Stiller and Julika, is incomplete without a complementary consideration of Rolf, and of Rolf and Sibylle. These complex relationships present the moral attitude of the novel, Frisch's major artistic accomplishment, and depict achievement and failure from the standpoint of personal commitment.

Stiller's account of the commitment of Rolf and Sibylle to one another in New York, by depicting his uneasy fascination for the technological world of Reproduktion symbolised in the lights of the city offers an insight into his own inability to make a commitment to his wife Julika. Indeed, the entire course of the seven 'Hefte' demonstrates his failure to make use of his experience, whether direct or indirect. Since he conceives his own direct experience uniquely in terms of failure as measured against an impossible ideal of himself, he rejects that experience, not only as being unworthy of his ideal, but also as being bereft of any guidance for the future. This emerges partly from the accounts of his behaviour given by Julika and Sibylle, in the 'Zweites Heft' and in the 'Sechstes Heft' respectively, and partly from his own general reflections in the first, third, fifth and seventh of the 'Hefte'. Parallel to this runs the record of Stiller's indirect experience in prison, which consists of Stiller's 'Protokoll' of the travails of Rolf and Sibylle. The situations which provoke Rolf's unreasonable behaviour, and that behaviour itself, are both sufficiently similar to Stiller's reactions to the circumstances of his own life to enable Stiller to feel at least some identification with Rolf's problems, and with Rolf as an example, as the latter succeeds in surmounting these problems. It is true that in his relationship with Sibylle, Stiller cannot establish the same parallels of behaviour and

situation. However, his committal to paper of Sibylle's 'Protokoll'
must cause him to face up to his experience with her. But the re-
awakening of his memory of both the positive side of that experience –
her offer of herself – and the negative side – the abrupt rupture which
also includes, unbeknown to Stiller at the time, the abortion of their
child – fail to make an impression on Stiller. It is not that he is
unaware of the fact that the opportunities of life are unique and do
not recur. He knows of the precarious and ephemeral framework to life
as he sits in his cell and reflects on the Mexican desert:

> Wieviel Wüste gibt es auf diesem Gestirn, dessen Gäste
> wir sind, ich habe es nie vorher gewusst, nur gelesen;
> nie erfahren, wie sehr doch alles, wovon wir leben,
> Geschenk einer schmalen Oase ist, unwahrscheinlich wie
> die Gnade. (III 379) 21

Stiller cannot cultivate the directness of approach necessary to
exploit this ephemerality and uniqueness, a quality which Sibylle
possesses instinctively and which Rolf acquires from his experience.
Stiller cannot surmount the difficulties which circumstances or he
himself place in his path in his relationship with Julika. The difficulties created by circumstances are symbolised in his first encounter
with Julika in prison, where the uncomplicated strength of his sexual
response to her arouses Julika, but the meeting is interrupted by
Knobel the warder. The difficulties created by himself are symbolised
later in the juridical confrontation in his former studio, where he is
aware of the straightforward gesture of commitment which is required
of him, and which his futile verbosity prevents him from making. He
is even aware of the elements in life which are central to the idea of
commitment: he conveys to himself the ideas of faith and trust through
the image of flying, of launching himself from the window-sill of a
building and trusting that the empty air will support and carry him
(III 436). Fully aware of the realities and demands of life, nudged
towards them by his own direct experience and with the example of
others to guide him, he fails, despite all, to muster the resolution
which life requires. In the most important character he has created,
Frisch demonstrates not only the difficulty of attaining a sense of
commitment, but also, in Stiller's inglorious end, the high price
exacted for failure.

In the entire corpus of Frisch's work, only three couples achieve
a relationship based on acceptance of the individual personality and
on commitment to the partner: the Rittmeister and Elvira in Santa Cruz,
Hauswirt and Yvonne in Die Schwierigen, and Rolf and Sibylle in Stiller.

238.

In all three cases the establishment of a stable relationship is the
consequence of a crisis overcome. In Santa Cruz, the appearance of
Pelegrin, symbol of the harmful longing which has undermined their
marriage for seventeen years, enables the Rittmeister and Elvira to
see for the first time that Pelegrin is a tawdry and puerile figure.
Hence, his potentially disruptive visit becomes the catalyst which
brings the couple together, once they have drawn the conclusions from
Pelegrin's appearance, in a new understanding of themselves and of one
another. In the case of Hauswirt and Yvonne, the crisis is brought
about by Hauswirt's discovery that Hanswalter is not his son. Hauswirt's
acceptance of the situation, as a fact of life which cannot be changed,
deepens and strengthens the relationship with Yvonne. With Rolf and
Sibylle, the crisis arises from Sibylle's affair with Stiller. Rolf
obstinately refuses to accept that life should have permitted this to
happen to him. Slowly and painfully he extricates himself from his
obstinacy to an attitude of forgiveness, as he comes to realise that
compliance with life represents the only possibility for self-fulfilment.
Of these three relationships, this last is the most sensitively and
fully drawn, and the one which, because of its development, highlights
most subtly the themes embodied in the main figure of the hero. The
Rittmeister is, from the outset, because of his strong sense of duty,
a contrastive figure to the irresponsible Pelegrin. In Die Schwierigen,
the robust self-confidence of Hauswirt forms an even clearer contrast
to the vacillating self-absorption of Reinhart. In Stiller, Rolf also
forms a contrastive figure with the difference that he becomes this,
only after abandoning an initial position very similar to that of
Stiller. As a consequence, the character of Rolf not only has a much
more complex depiction than that of the Rittmeister and Hauswirt, but
his role within the novel as a whole is considerably more important.
Moreover, the unmistakable warmth and richness of his restored relationship with Sibylle bear witness to a considerable increase in Frisch's
ability to present a positive relationship from the schematic portrayal
of the Rittmeister and Elvira. If Rolf, and the relationship with his
wife, thus represent an artistic highpoint in Frisch's writing up to
1954, the year Stiller was published, this relationship also represents
a watershed in Frisch's work [22]. For the only subsequent figure to
achieve a measure of dignity in coping with the problems of life, the
ambassador in Gantenbein, is not even a secondary character, but appears
in a contrapuntal anecdote. The relationship between Rolf and Sibylle
is the main direct portrayal of the theme which Frisch has since
presented by implication. After Stiller, the value of commitment becomes

indirectly apparent from the portrayal of relationships from which it
is absent.

The contrasting figures and episodes in the four main novels,
despite their varying importance in each individual work and in
Frisch's work as a whole, offer a yardstick against which the inauthentic lives and humiliating ends of the main figures can be
measured. It is to this yardstick that the novelist Christa Wolf
refers when she claims that Frisch considers his 'Auftrag' as a writer
to consist in

> Gegenbilder aufstellen gegen die ungeheuerlichen
> Deformationen von Menschen in dieser Zeit. [23]

Frisch's presentation is at all times noted for its sobriety, and
hence his 'Gegenbilder', precisely because of their restraint, are all
the more convincing. In an age of disabling conformity, Frisch's work
owes its stature not least to its relentless insistence on the importance
of the individual and his concerns. This insistence achieves its
fullest expression in the positive and negative portrayal of commitment
in his novels.

240.

CONCLUSION

The concern of Max Frisch with a specific locality and his interest
in the behaviour of the individual in that locality place him in a
Swiss tradition of men of letters whose involvement in public matters
is regarded by them as an indivisible part of their duty as writers.
Despite his grave reservations about many Swiss attitudes, Frisch's
deeply personal interest in his country has continued since its situation
in 1940 gave rise to the reflections in Blätter aus dem Brotsack. It is
understandable that the zest of many affirmations made there about
Switzerland should have abated, and that some of the relatively
unexamined opinions displayed should have undergone, through time,
qualification, and even radical revision. It is a mark of Frisch's
determination that his view of his country should evolve that in 1974,
in Dienstbüchlein, he re-assessed the earlier period of his life which
was so important for his relationship to Switzerland. In the later
work, the frame of reference is denser, the arguments more complex,
and, while the enthusiasm of the earlier book has slackened, the
strength of commitment remains undiminished. Frisch's Swiss background
is an ineradicable part of his identity. Much of the interest and
importance of Frisch lies in the fact that, in coming to terms with the
complexities of his position as a German-Swiss writer, he extracts
from a confrontation with problems deriving from a relationship to a
specific locality considerations which have universal validity.

The intrusion of technology into everyday life, a phenomenon
present prior to the Second World War but immeasurably accelerated by
it, manifests itself not merely in the standardisation of life, but
produces an inauthenticity in experience which tends to dissociate the
individual from himself and from his environment. For Frisch, the
function of the writer is to promote awareness of individuality.
Literature cannot change the course of the world, but it can contribute
to alter the individual's perception of reality. If the individual is
thus helped towards self-awareness, he can move towards the moral freedom to commit his identity to appropriate action. But in a world which
is becoming increasingly harmful and hostile to the individual, this
is becoming increasingly difficult. The personal dislocation caused
by the influence of technology forms a major theme in Frisch's work,
in which he depicts the extent to which Switzerland is subject to the
developments affecting the wider world.

In all his writing Frisch has proclaimed his fascination with the

theatre. Certainly, his fame rests principally - in the English-
speaking world, exclusively - on his achievements as a dramatist.
There must be set against this lifelong interest, however, an increasingly ambiguous relationship to the theatre in respect of his own
plays. It is not going too far to speak of his disillusion at what he
feels to be the discrepancy between his aims and his attainments. He
has recorded his dissatisfaction with 'Parabelstücke' [1] - the genre in
which he gained world-wide success with Biedermann und die Brandstifter
and Andorra -, and with the 'Theater der Permutation' [2], which sought
to move to new things. Most recently, in 1978, he published Triptychon,
the play which he will not allow to be performed, and in connection
with which he has given fullest expression to his doubts about his
dramatic works and about his relationship to the theatre [3]. In 1954,
Emil Staiger, reviewing the plays performed to date, had voiced
reservations about their artistic quality, and had gone on to contrast
what he held to be their deficiencies with the masterly achievement of
the newly published Stiller:

> Es ist, als hätte sich das durch die Anforderungen der
> Bühne beirrte Talent nun plötzlich Bahn gebrochen und
> ströme in unaufhaltsamer Fülle dahin. [4]

It is not appropriate at this stage to maintain firmly that Staiger's
judgement of 1954 holds good for the entire oeuvre, but three factors,
all relating in some degree to Frisch's Swiss background, can be put
forward which lend weight to the view that Frisch's ultimate importance
will be judged to lie in his prose-writing.

In the first place, historical circumstances created for Frisch a
situation which was short-lived, and unique in Switzerland. The concen-
tration of talent in the Zürich Schauspielhaus, and the atmosphere
which it generated, offered Frisch, towards the end of the Second
World War, an opportunity to write for the theatre at a point where he
was not unknown as a writer of prose. When Nun singen sie wieder was
first performed in 1945, Frisch had published, apart from his journal-
istic sketches and literary reviews, three novels and a diary, and was
about to publish Bin. In the Schauspielhaus there was thus a forcing
ground available to Frisch capable of adding a fresh dimension to his
career as a writer. In the event, the plays which resulted from him
taking this opportunity have posed for him artistic problems which
have no parallel in his prose-writing, and which derive from something
more than the scrupulous determination of the artist to seek improvement on his previous presentations. The fact that Triptychon is not
to be performed, at least for the present, could represent a culmination

of personal doubt. Certainly, in terms of chronology, Frisch's plays
bulk less in his career than his prose-writing: the twenty-three years
between the first productions of Nun singen sie wieder and of Biografie
represent almost exactly half the span of time between the publication
of Jürg Reinhart and that of Der Mensch erscheint im Holozän. Thus,
if there is not sufficient distance from Frisch's work to be able wholly
to accept that Frisch's involvement with the theatre has misapplied his
abilities, there is sufficient evidence for this view to form a not
insignificant element in a provisional assessment of Frisch today.

A second factor which must be taken into account in attempting in
1979 to set Frisch against his Swiss background relates to the changes
in the wider German culture during his lifetime. The Second World War
coloured Frisch's personal view of the traditional problem of the
German-Swiss, and more particularly, of the German-Swiss writer, in
defining his attitude to Germany. In addition, Switzerland's non-
involvement in the War assured the maintenance of an uninterrupted
creative tradition which enabled Frisch in 1945, the year in which the
rest of the German-speaking world was first able to begin to assimilate
the influences from which it had been excluded since 1933, to present
his first play. Speedy change, which the disruption of the War had
brought about, affected the theatre more than narrative writing. It
is possible that Frisch did not keep pace, either formally or thematic-
ally, with the change in the theatre. He could claim in 1978, for
example, partly in explanation of his own difficulties with the theatre,
that his career there had taken place in an 'Endepoche' which had
brought with it 'das Ende des literarischen Theaters' [5]. Moreover,
Frisch's best-known plays, Biedermann of 1958 and Andorra of 1961,
were successes to the extent that they were interpreted, whatever
Frisch's intentions, in terms of the past, namely, in terms of the
prelude to, and the aftermath of, the War. It is also possible that
Frisch has always been too unsure of his own intentions in the theatre
to find in the end of an era the driving force and support necessary
to express himself in a dramatic form appropriate to set against what
he felt to be the shortcomings of the traditional theatre. In prose-
writing, on the other hand, the pace of change was much slower. The
end of an era — proclaimed since the beginning of the century — found
Frisch well enough equipped in ideas and ability to be able to forge a
viable route of his own. Indeed, his self-confidence in the medium
could cause Stiller to be hailed as 'den Anfang einer neuen Entwicklung,
welche die Tradition nicht mehr als Ballast, sondern als Stimulans für
die eigene Produktion empfindet' [6]. His subsequent prose publications,

if they did not fully emulate the accomplishment of <u>Stiller</u>, were nonetheless to maintain this creative momentum.

Thirdly, the narrative mode, which is after all Frisch's heritage
from the German-Swiss literary tradition, is arguably more suited to
the expression of his concerns. For Frisch, literature has to do with
the depiction of the individual consciousness as it reacts to the world
around it and as it is in turn affected by that world. Literature
explores both that indefinable part of the individual which is not
accessible to scientific enquiry and measurement, but which is aware
of its relationship to the framework of life which can be so investigated,
and also that part of the individual which transcends any political
situation, but which is aware that its daily life is encompassed by
such a situation. Narrative lends itself to a depiction of such a
state of consciousness more than drama. The portrayal of the debilitating interaction between awareness of social helplessness and increasing
inability to express private reality, which figures so strongly in
Frisch's work, requires the discursive mode of the novel. Translation
to the stage of aspects of these concerns demonstrates that they are
incapable of generating and sustaining the tension essential to drama.
The qualifications and relativisations of the manner in which Frisch
approaches and describes reality can find their proper deployment only
in the cumulative effect which narrative can produce. Here, the mosaic
principle of Frisch's writing creates the complex inter-relatedness of
shifting perspectives which permits tentative and provisional stand-
points. The 'Sukzessivität' of stage presentation creates, on the
other hand, as Frisch admits, a situation in which 'Assoziation', the
key process of his narrative mode, is simply unable to work [7]. Frisch
regards the novel as offering, as a <u>genre</u>, a greater possibility of
exploring the problems of human relationships because the novel permits
greater use of the first person [8]. The individual, the speaker in the
first person, has always been at the centre of Frisch's interest.
Appropriately, it is in the last major novel <u>Gantenbein</u> that Frisch's
credo finds its expression when the narrator reflects:

> Manchmal scheint auch mir, dass jedes Buch, so es sich
> nicht befasst mit der Verhinderung des Kriegs, mit der
> Schaffung einer besseren Gesellschaft und so weiter,
> sinnlos ist, müssig, unverantwortlich, langweilig, nicht
> wert, dass man es liest, unstatthaft. Es ist nicht die
> Zeit für Ich-Geschichten. Und doch vollzieht sich das
> menschliche Leben oder verfehlt sich am einzelnen Ich,
> nirgends sonst. (V 68)

The 'remarkable thematic unity' [9] of Frisch's novels depict this modern
paradox.

As a German-Swiss with his particular experience of recent history, Frisch is acutely aware of the cardinal importance of committed identity in a world which, although it has possibly always been hostile to the individual, has at no previous time been so implacably inimical to him as now. The humiliations and unworthy ends of Frisch's heroes reflect the nature of the dangers to which the individual is exposed, and the irresolution of these heroes represents the opposite pole to the moral freedom of commitment in which they could realise themselves. Against the bleak modern landscapes which Frisch creates must be set his unremitting exhortations that men should concern themselves with both the local and the wider community in which they live, for they are all affected by the quality of life of their environment. His works portray defeats which warn of the consequences of passivity in the face of modern life. They are not wholly pessimistic, however, for they owe their artistic coherence to firm indications of moral attainment against which the failures of the heroes are measured. Max Frisch comes of a German-Swiss literary tradition in which the writer is defined as a 'Rater, Ermahner, Warner'. Less sanguine than his predecessors, he develops and modifies that tradition in the very changed circumstances of the second half of the twentieth century by proclaiming, and demonstrating, that the value and efficacy of the modern writer lies in 'die Arbeit jedes einzelnen an seinem Ort'.

REFERENCES   and   BIBLIOGRAPHY

245.

REFERENCES

I   THE SWISS SITUATION AND MAX FRISCH

1. The Swiss Situation

a. Introduction

1. Karl Schmid Aufsätze und Reden, Zürich/Stuttgart 1957, pp.12-13;
    Manfred Gsteiger Literatur des Übergangs, Bern/München 1963,
    p.151.

2. Fritz Ernst Helvetia Mediatrix, Zürich 1939, p.7.

3. Kurt Guggenheim Heimat oder Domizil? Die Stellung des deutsch-
    schweizerischen Schriftstellers in der Gegenwart, Zürich 1961,
    p.18.
    Thorbjörn Lengborn Schriftsteller und Gesellschaft in der
    Schweiz. Eine Studie zur Behandlung der Gesellschaftsproblematik
    bei Zollinger, Frisch und Dürrenmatt, Frankfurt 1972, p.29.

b. The Swiss situation and its definition

1. Hermann Weilenmann Pax Helvetica oder Die Demokratie der
    kleinen Gruppen, Erlenbach-Zürich 1951, pp.12-13.

2. Georg Thürer Free and Swiss. The Story of Switzerland,
    London 1970, p.111.

3. Quoted by William Rappard La Constitution Fédérale de la Suisse.
    Ses origines, son élaboration, son évolution, Neuchâtel 1948,
    p.22.

4. Werner Näf Die Schweiz in Europa. Die Entwicklung des schweize-
    rischen Staates im Rahmen der europäischen Geschichte, Bern
    1930, p.56.

5. Rappard op.cit., pp.32, 35.

6. Cf. Frisch's comments on the distortions caused by oral
    tradition, even in relation to the Second World War (VI 424-5)
    (References are to the six-volume Max Frisch – Gesammelte
    Werke in zeitlicher Folge, Frankfurt 1976).

7. Carl Spitteler Gesammelte Werke, Zürich 1945, vol. VIII p.586.

8. Edgar Bonjour Swiss Neutrality. Its History and Meaning,
    London 1948, pp.124-125.

9. Schmid op.cit., p.10.

10. George Soloveytchik Switzerland in Perspective, London 1954, p.22.

11. Hermann Weilenmann Die vielsprachige Schweiz. Eine Lösung des Nationalitätenproblems, Basel/Leipzig 1925, p.139.

12. Cf. Meinrad Inglin's novel Schweizerspiegel, Leipzig 1938, for the First World War, and Alice Meyer Anpassung oder Widerstand. Die Schweiz zur Zeit des deutschen Nationalsozialismus, Frauenfeld 1965, for the Second.

13. Gottfried Keller Sämtliche Werke, Bern 1947, vol. 21 p.102

14. J. R. von Salis Schwierige Schweiz, Zürich 1968, p.156.

15. Eudo C. Mason 'Switzerland and Germanistic Studies Today', German Life and Letters, 1 1947-48, p.65.

16. C-F. Ramuz Oeuvres complètes, Genève 1941, vol. 19 p.41.

17. Albin Zollinger Gesammelte Werke, Zürich 1961, vol. III p.252.

18. Felix Moeschlin Wachtmeister Vögeli, Zürich/Leipzig 1932, p.51.

19. Inglin Schweizerspiegel, p.772.

20. Spitteler Gesammelte Werke, vol. VIII p.592.

21. Walter Muschg Pamphlet und Bekenntnis Olten/Freiburg i.B. 1968, p.350.

22. Jörg Steiner Der schwarze Kasten, Olten/Freiburg i.B. 1965, p.23.

23. Zollinger Gesammelte Werke, vol. I p.404

24. Schmid op.cit., p.87.

25. Weilenmann Die vielsprachige Schweiz, p.227.

26. Muschg op.cit., pp.347-348.

27. Emil Brunner 'Der christliche Staat' in Geisteserbe der Schweiz Schriften von Albrecht von Haller bis zur Gegenwart (ed. Eduard Korrodi) Erlenbach-Zürich 1943, p.421.

28. Emil Ermatinger Dichtung und Geistesleben der deutschen Schweiz, München 1933, p.19.

29. Schmid op.cit., p.17.

30. Inglin Schweizerspiegel, p.1058.

31. Spitteler Gesammelte Werke, vol. VIII p.581.

32. Ramuz Oeuvres complètes, vol. 19 p.127.

33. Gsteiger op.cit., p.153.

34. Karl Schmid Zeitspuren - Reden und Aufsätze, Zürich/Stuttgart 1967, p.18.

35. Hans Bänziger Heimat und Fremde. Ein Kapitel 'Tragische Literatur-geschichte' in der Schweiz: Jakob Schaffner, Robert Walser, Albin Zollinger, Bern 1958, p.9.

36. Schmid Aufsätze und Reden, p.100.

37. Näf op.cit., p.15.

38. Weilenmann Pax Helvetica, p.12.

39. Schmid Aufsätze und Reden, p.101; Hans Bänziger sees the 'Ehe-dramen und Eheromane' of Frisch and Dürrenmatt as 'Beispiele der Gegenläufigkeit' because they 'gehören...trotz ihrer Modernität zum Unzeitgemässen'. Frisch und Dürrenmatt, 5. neu bearb. Aufl. Bern/München 1967, p.18.

40. Schmid Aufsätze und Reden, p.91.

41. Fritz Ernst Europäische Schweiz, Zürich 1961, p.53.

42. Ernst Helvetia Mediatrix, p.7.

43. Zollinger Gesammelte Werke, vol. I p.404.

c. The predicament of the Swiss writer

1. F. R. Leavis The Great Tradition, London 1955, p.9.

2. Frisch sees institutions encouraging this tendency: they are 'das Bestehende, das sich für die Antwort hält'. 'Die grosse Devotion' Die Weltwoche 12. Juli 1968

3. Zollinger Gesammelte Werke, vol. I p.366

4. Guggenheim op.cit., p.13.

5. Gsteiger op.cit., p.146.

6. Max Wehrli 'Gegenwartsdichtung der deutschen Schweiz' in Deutsche Literatur in unserer Zeit, Göttingen 1959, p.108.

7. Gsteiger op.cit., p.143; Kurt Marti Die Schweiz und ihre Schriftsteller - Die Schriftsteller und ihre Schweiz, Zürich 1966, pp.16-17.

8. Guido Calgari Die vier Literaturen der Schweiz, Olten/Freiburg i.B. 1966, p. 12.

9. Dora Gerber Studien zum Problem des Künstlers in der modernen deutschschweizerischen Literatur, Bern 1948, p.14.

10. Peter Bichsel Des Schweizers Schweiz, Zürich 1969, p.25.

11. Gerber op.cit., p.19.

12. Ramuz Oeuvres complètes, vol. 19 p.47.

13. Spitteler Gesammelte Werke, vol. VII p.456.

14. Ludwig Hohl 'Notizen' in Bestand und Versuch - Schweizer Schrifttum der Gegenwart (ed. Bruno Mariacher/Friedrich Witz), Zürich 1964, p.380.

15. Jean Moser Le roman contemporain en Suisse allemande de Carl Spitteler à Jakob Schaffner, Lausanne 1934, p.255.

16. Ermatinger op.cit., p.24.

17. Gsteiger op.cit., p.144.

18. Alfred Zäch Die Dichtung der deutschen Schweiz, Zürich 1951, p.8.

19. Martin Kraft 'Schweizerhaus' Das Haus-Motiv im Deutschschweizer Roman des 20. Jahrhunderts, Bern/Frankfurt 1971, p.24.

20. Elsbeth Pulver 'Die deutschsprachige Literatur der Schweiz seit 1945' in Die zeitgenössischen Literaturen der Schweiz (ed. Manfred Gsteiger) Zürich/München 1974, p.196.

21. Spitteler Gesammelte Werke, vol. VII p.499.

22. Bichsel op.cit., p.20. A fascinating example of such a translation was undertaken by the novelist Martin Walser; he attempted to render into Mundart a sentence of the then West German Bundeskanzler Kiesinger 'Bemerkungen über unseren Dialekt' Neue Zürcher Zeitung 25. Juni 1967.

23. Zollinger Gesammelte Werke, vol. III p.166.

24. Calgari op.cit., p.40; Bänziger Heimat und Fremde, p.15.

25. Schmid Zeitspuren, p.21.

26. Muschg op.cit., pp.238, 350.

27. Gerber op.cit., p.14.

28. Spitteler Gesammelte Werke, vol. VIII p.582.

29. Keller Sämtliche Werke, vol. 22 p.300.

30. Eduard Korrodi Schweizerische Literaturbriefe, Frauenfeld/Leipzig 1918, p.17.

31. Marti op.cit., p.69.

32. Moser op.cit., pp.242-243.

33. Gsteiger op.cit., p.138.

34. Kraft op.cit., p.7.

35. Keller Sämtliche Werke, vol. 21 pp.107-108.

36. Gottfried Keller Gesammelte Briefe, Bern 1951, vol. 2 p.357.

37. Ermatinger op.cit., p.27.

38. Zäch op.cit., p.8.

39. Ermatinger op.cit., p.vi; Guggenheim op.cit., pp.17-18; Heinz-Peter Linder Die schweizerische Gegenwart im modernen Roman der deutschen Schweiz, Worb 1957, p.119.

40. Bänziger Frisch und Dürrenmatt, p.11; cf. also 'Die Schweiz ist ein Land ohne Utopie' (IV 258-9).

41. Friedrich Dürrenmatt Dramaturgisches und Kritisches, Zürich 1972, p.240.

42. 'Notizen aus Berlin und Wien II' Neue Zürcher Zeitung 6. März 1948.

43. Gerber op.cit., p.23.

44. Zäch op.cit., p.9.

45. Manfred Gsteiger 'Eine Einführung' Die zeitgenössischen Literaturen der Schweiz, p.58.

46. Marti op.cit., p.70.

47. ibid, pp.71-72.

48. ibid, p.18. In this category Marti places, amongst others, the novels of Zollinger and Frisch's work 'von 'Stiller' bis 'Mein Name sei Gantenbein''.

49. Hugo Leber Texte - Prosa junger Schweizer Autoren, Zürich 1964, p.16.

50. Manfred Gsteiger 'La génération de Frisch et Dürrenmatt' Le Monde Hebdomadaire 12 mai 1969.

2. Max Frisch as a Swiss Citizen

a. The influence of the Second World War on Frisch's attitude to Switzerland

1. Dürrenmatt Dramatisches und Kritisches, p.232.

2. Thirty years after the end of the war Frisch is still referring in public to the effect his travels in devastated Europe had on him: Max Frisch, Hartmut von Hentig Zwei Reden zum Friedenspreis des Deutschen Buchhandels 1976, Frankfurt 1976, pp.104-105.

3. Cf. also V 371, and Heinz Ludwig Arnold Gespräche mit Schriftstellern, München 1975, pp.22-23.

4. Manfred Jurgensen comments on the play (first performed 29th March 1945): 'Der Position des Schweizers im Weltkriege gleich übersieht Frisch beide Lager, ohne als Betrachtender in das Geschehen eingreifen zu können oder zu wollen'. Max Frisch - Die Dramen, Bern 1968, p.92.

5. Frisch disclaims any inflated status, however, for what he wrote during the war, cf. Arnold op.cit., p.23.

6. Lengborn op.cit., p. 215.

7. Speaking about Italian 'Gastarbeiter' in Switzerland, Frisch describes them as 'ein Menschenschlag, der höflich ist noch in der Beschwerde' and concludes of the ethos in which they are raised: 'Kultur kommt nicht als Bildung, sondern als praktisches Erbe' (V 376).

b. **False perspectives of Switzerland**

1. Frisch also sees the opprobrium attracted by criticism of one's country as a consequence of the division of the world into ideological blocs, Zwei Reden zum Friedenspreis, p.93.

2. Interview with Gerardo Zanetti 'Soll der Onkel auf die Barri- kade steigen?' Die Woche 19. August 1964

3. Karl August Horst 'Notizen zu Max Frisch und Friedrich Dürren- matt' Merkur Juni 1954, p.595; Lengborn op.cit., p.156.

4. Rolf Kieser 'An Interview with Max Frisch' Contemporary Literature 13, 1972, p.11.

5. 'Gespräch mit Max Frisch' Der Schriftsteller in unserer Zeit. Schweizer Autoren bestimmen ihre Rolle in der Gesellschaft (ed. Peter André Bloch, Edwin Hubacher), Bern 1972, p.29; else- where Frisch comments ironically: 'Diese Wilhelm-Tell-Legende – das ist nicht meine Entdeckung – ist eine Import-Sage, Tell ist also eigentlich ein Gastarbeiter-Held'. Arnold op.cit., p.57.

6. Cf. also VI 75-76, and Der Schriftsteller in unserer Zeit, p.28.

7. 'Blätter aus dem Brotsack. Neue Folge' Neue Zürcher Zeitung 29. Dezember 1940.

8. Arnold op.cit., pp. 52-53.

9. 'Und die Schweiz? Interview mit Max Frisch' Neutralität, August 1964, p.2.

10. Just as he depicts the political misuse of 'Bestand' in Die Chinesische Mauer, so Frisch sees 'Angst' motivating virulent anti-Communism: 'Antikommunismus ist vielleicht nicht Hass, aber Angst: aber man kann auch die Angst politisch missbrauchen'. 'Wir müssen unsere Welt anders einrichten' Die Tat 9. Dezember 1967.

11. 'Planung tut not' Die Weltwoche 29. April 1955.

12. 'Wir müssen unsere Welt anders einrichten' loc.cit.

c. **The nature of Frisch's commitment to Switzerland**

1. 'Die grosse Devotion' Die Weltwoche 12. Juli 1968.

2. 'Vorwort' to Markus Kutter, Lucius Burckhardt Wir selber bauen unsere Stadt, Basel 1953, p.9.

3. Die neue Stadt (in conjunction with Markus Kutter and Lucius Burckhardt), Basel 1956, p.57.

4. Frisch was subsequently to take a less ecstatic view of the 1939 'Landesausstellung' in Dienstbüchlein (VI 571-572).

5. 'Und die Schweiz?' loc.cit., p.3.

6. Zwei Reden zum Friedenspreis, p.109.

7. Cf. also Horst Bienek Werkstattgespräche mit Schriftstellern, München 1962, p.27.

8. Cf. also Der Schriftsteller in unserer Zeit, p.18.

9. Quoted by Willi Fehse in Von Goethe bis Grass - Biografische Porträts zur Literatur, Bielefeld 1963, p.208.

10. Arnold op.cit., pp.59-60.

3. Max Frisch as a Contemporary Swiss Writer

a. The relationship to a Swiss tradition

1. Frisch pays tribute to the influence on him of Der grüne Heinrich (II 587); for comparisons between the two writers cf. Karl Schmid Unbehagen im Kleinstaat, Zürich/Stuttgart 1963, p.170, Mary Cock''Countries of the Mind': Max Frisch's Narrative Technique' Modern Language Review, 65 1970, p.825 footnote 1, and Hans Rudolf Hilthy 'Ein Buch aktiver Erinnerung' Über Max Frisch II (ed. Walter Schmitz), Frankfurt 1976, p.400.

2. Keller Sämtliche Werke, vol. 21 p.98.

3. ibid, vol. 21 p.98.

4. C. F. Meyer 'Erinnerungen an Gottfried Keller' Geisteserbe der Schweiz, p.305.

5. Cf. Manfred Jurgensen Max Frisch - Die Romane, Bern/München 1972, p.231.

6. Cf. Carol Petersen Max Frisch, Berlin 1966, p.11.

7. Cf. Rolf Kieser Max Frisch - Das literarische Tagebuch, Frauenfeld/Stuttgart 1975, p.150.

8. Gsteiger Literatur des Übergangs, p.141.

9. Cf. Frisch's own comment: 'Es ist unser künstlerisches Versagen, wenn sie (unsere Meinungen) sich nicht in Darstellung auflösen' (IV 247).

10. In his speech 'Die Schweiz als Heimat?' Frisch indicates his positive reactions to prominent figures in German-Swiss literature who have avoided presenting an uncritical picture of Switzerland (VI 512-513).

11. Walter Weideli 'Stiller or Le Malaise Helvétique' Adam, XXVII no. 275 1959, p.67.

12. Bänziger Heimat und Fremde, p.118.

13. Lengborn op.cit., p.215.

14. Wehrli loc.cit., p.116.

15. Frisch uses the same image to describe the frustrated attempts
    of the 'andorranische Jude' to communicate with those about
    him: 'Er redete in ein Schweigen hinein, wie in Watte' (II 373).

16. Frisch admits to having been himself at times 'schreierisch
    polemisch', Arnold op.cit. p.62, because of a lack of response
    to his writing.

17. Frisch dedicated the book edition of Andorra to the Zürcher
    Schauspielhaus (IV 579); cf. VI 512, and Arnold op.cit. p. 61
    for his characterisation of his relationship to the Schauspiel-
    haus, and VI 289-290 for his later disillusion.

18. E. Brock-Sulzer 'Das deutschschweizerische Theater der Gegen-
    wart' German Life and Letters, 12 1958-59, p.18.

19. Peter André Bloch (ed.) Der Schriftsteller und sein Verhältnis
    zur Sprache dargestellt am Problem der Tempuswahl Eine Dokumen-
    tation zur Sprache und Literatur der Gegenwart, Bern/München
    1971, p.97.

20. Cf. Greta Rau 'Max Frisch, dramaturge et romancier' Preuves,
    août 1958, p.44, and Marianne Biedermann Das politische Theater
    von Max Frisch, Lampertheim 1974, p.1.

21. Bienek op.cit., p.29.

22. The figure of Zola and his relationship to the Dreyfus affair
    is mentioned much more ironically in the 'Version für Paris,
    1972' of Die Chinesische Mauer (II 197).

23. Cf. Josef Nadler Literaturgeschichte der deutschen Schweiz,
    Leipzig/Zürich 1932, p.499 for the general point, and Kurt
    Guggenheim Das Ende von Seldwyla, Zürich/Stuttgart 1965, p.34
    for the difficulties encountered by Keller on his return to
    Zürich.

24. Cf. Muschg op.cit., pp.201-202, Walter Muschg 'Zur Lage des
    Schrifttums in der deutschen Schweiz' Die Schweiz Ein nationales
    Jahrbuch, n.p. 1930, p.177, and Pulver Die zeitgenössischen
    Literaturen der Schweiz, p.165.

25. Bienek op.cit., p.31.

26. Guggenheim Heimat oder Domizil?, p.32; the most sustained
    polemic against the attitude defined by Guggenheim, and against
    Frisch, is conducted by Hans Jürg Lüthi in his 1975 'Rektorats-
    rede' to the University of Bern Schweizer Schriftsteller und
    die Schweiz, Bern 1975.

27. Zanetti loc.cit.

28. Cf. Dieter-E. Zimmer 'Über die Aufführung in Zürich' Max Frisch -
    Beiträge zu einer Wirkungsgeschichte (ed. Albrecht Schau)
    Freiburg i.B. 1971, p.314.

29. Dramaturgisches Ein Briefwechsel mit Walter Höllerer, Berlin 1969, p.33.

30. Max Frisch 'Die andere Welt' Atlantis, 1945 Heft 1/2, p.3.

31. Der Schriftsteller in unserer Zeit, p.35; cf. also Arnold op.cit., pp.16-17.

b. The contribution to a Swiss tradition

1. The reflections and sketches of Tagebuch 1946-1949 are interspersed with comments on the progress of the building of a public swimming-pool, Letzigraben, in Zürich - for which Frisch's design won a competition - from the start of the work in August 1947 until the opening of the completed pool on 18 June 1949.

2. 'Nachwort' by Max Frisch to J. C. Trewin and H. Hearson Euer Gnaden haben geschossen? Eine Geschichte aus Merry Old England, Zürich 1954, p.92.

3. Cf. Bienek, op.cit. p.29, where Frisch refers to his work on the later play Andorra in terminology associated with building.

4. Friedrich Dürrenmatt 'Schriftstellerei als Beruf' Theater-Schriften und Reden, Zürich 1966, p.54.

5. Jacob Steiner 'Zur Schweizer Literatur der Gegenwart' Der Schweizer Buchhandel, Heft 4 1967, p.113.

6. Frisch discusses this gratitude elsewhere: VI 511, and Der Schriftsteller und sein Verhältnis zur Sprache, p.75.

7. Der Schriftsteller und sein Verhältnis zur Sprache, p.68.

8. Walter Schenker Die Sprache Max Frischs in der Spannung zwischen Mundart und Schriftsprache, Berlin 1969, p.106; Schenker's study is an invaluable source for this aspect of Frisch.

9. Der Schriftsteller und sein Verhältnis zur Sprache, p.79.

10. Schenker op.cit., p.102.

11. ibid p.83.

12. Cf. Spitteler Gesammelte Werke, vol. VII p.500.

13. Quoted by Schenker op.cit., p.11.

14. ibid p.57.

15. E. Brock-Sulzer 'Uberlegungen zur schweizerischen Dramatik von heute' Akzente, 3 1956, p.46.

16. Schenker op.cit., pp.11-12.

17. 'Andorra ist der Name für ein Modell' (IV 462).

18. Cf. also the 'Vorspiel' to Die Chinesische Mauer (II 145), and a note to the book edition of Biografie (V 579).

19. Schenker op.cit., p.117.

20. ibid p.131; cf., however, Frisch's subsequent qualification of the Tagebuch statement in Kieser op.cit., p.59.

21. Cf. S.P. Hoefert 'Zur Sprachauffassung Max Frischs' Muttersprache, 73 1963, p.259.

22. Cf. also II 513.

23. Werner Weber 'Zu Frischs 'Biedermann und die Brandstifter'' Max Frisch - Beiträge zu einer Wirkungsgeschichte, p.247.

24. Dramaturgisches, p.39.

25. Reinhart Baumgart 'Othello als Hamlet' Über Max Frisch (ed. Thomas Beckermann), Frankfurt 1971, p.194.

26. Cf. Jürgen H. Petersen Max Frisch, Stuttgart 1978, pp.91-98, for a discussion of the anticipation of this in Tagebuch 1966-1971.

27. Cf. Oskar Holl Der Roman als Funktion und Überwindung der Zeit, Bonn 1968, p.168 for this point in respect of Stiller.

28. For Biedermann und die Brandstifter cf. Bänziger Frisch und Dürrenmatt, p.93, Ulrich Weisstein Max Frisch, New York 1967, p.143, and Eduard Stäuble Max Frisch, St. Gallen 1967, pp.110-111; for Andorra cf. Weisstein op.cit., p.155 and Stäuble op.cit., p.210.

29. Weisstein mentions the meeting but only because it was 'disappointing' for Frisch, op.cit., p.22.

c. A Swiss tradition and the modern world

1. Muschg Pamphlet und Bekenntnis, p.288.

2. Bienek op.cit., p.30.

3. Cf. also VI 635-636, and Arnold op.cit., p.44.

4. Der Schriftsteller in unserer Zeit, p.22.

5. Adelheid Weise Untersuchungen zur Thematik und Struktur der Dramen von Max Frisch, Göppingen 1969, p.187.

6. Dramaturgisches, pp.38-39. A Swiss example of the ineffective-ness of literature on personal decision-making is noted by Kurt Marti: Dürrenmatt's Die Physiker was first produced in 1962, the year in which the Swiss, in a referendum, refused to renounce nuclear weapons: 'Man klatschte der Komödie Beifall und legte danach ein 'Nein' zum Atomverzicht in die Urne, so das Spiel der verrückt gewordenen Irrenärztin seelenruhig weiterspielend', op.cit., p.54.

7. Der Schriftsteller in unserer Zeit, p.25; in Tagebuch 1946-1949, in the section 'Zum Theater' (II 401-403), Frisch sets very clear limits to art: the power of the theatre lies in its aesthetic effect, and this can only be achieved by excluding all that militates against the creation of such an effect.

8. Der Schriftsteller in unserer Zeit, p.23.

9. Dieter-E. Zimmer 'Noch einmal anfangen können. Ein Gespräch mit Max Frisch' Die Zeit 22. Dezember 1967; cf. also Dramaturgisches, pp.39-40.

10. Der Schriftsteller in unserer Zeit, p.18.

11. ibid p.23.

12. Dramaturgisches, p.34; cf. also Mein Name sei Gantenbein (V 68).

13. Dramaturgisches, p.42.

14. Bienek op.cit., p.120.

15. J. R. von Salis asks the rhetorical question: 'Wird nach Frisch und nach Dürrenmatt nicht doch in der Schweiz ein wenig anders diskutiert als vor ihnen?' op.cit., p.154.

16. Der Schriftsteller in unserer Zeit, p.19; cf. also Arnold op.cit., p.48.

II THEMES IN THE WORK OF MAX FRISCH WHICH RELATE TO HIS SWISS BACKGROUND

Introduction

1. Cf. Carol Petersen op.cit., p.60; Hans Mayer Dürrenmatt und Frisch – Anmerkungen, Pfullingen 1963, p.52; Christoph Burgauner 'Versuch über Max Frisch' Merkur, Mai 1974, p.445.

A. IDENTITY

1. Identity and the Impact of Time

1. Cf. V 362-363; Der Schriftsteller in unserer Zeit, p.27 ff.; Arnold op.cit., p.57.

2. Arnold op.cit., p.58.

3. ibid pp.56-57.

4. Jurgensen rightly emphasises the integration of the sections containing this depiction into the novel Max Frisch – Die Romane p.81; much Frisch criticism, notably Karl Schmid's frequently quoted essay 'Max Frisch: Andorra und die Entscheidung', Unbehagen im Kleinstaat pp.169-200, tends to excise these sections for the purposes of discussion.

5. Cf. Werner Zimmermann 'Max Frisch: Stiller' Prosadichtungen unseres Jahrhunderts, Düsseldorf 1969, vol. 2 p.124.

6. Carol Petersen op.cit., p.23.

256.

In this Weisstein links him to two earlier heroes: Jürg in
Jürg Reinhart and Balz Leuthold in Antwort aus der Stille,
op.cit., p.37.

Cf. Hans-Jürgen Baden Der Mensch ohne Partner Das Menschenbild
in den Romanen von Max Frisch, Wuppertal-Barmen 1966, p.14.

This passage is repeated almost word for word in Stiller
(III 696-697), as Stiller, lunching with Rolf in a country
restaurant shortly before the final disastrous confrontation
with his failed past life in his studio, reflects nostalgically
on what once was.

10. Frisch elsewhere describes the sense of a full relationship
to time, and hence to work (II 445).

11. There is a most striking resemblance between Reinhart's
reaction to his office in Die Schwierigen, the whole tenor of
Graf Öderland and a passage in Robert Walser's novel
Geschwister Tanner (1907), Genf und Hamburg 1967, pp.42-43;
Frisch names Walser as a major influence on him, cf. 'Materialien zu Max Frisch 'Stiller' (ed. Walter Schmitz), Frankfurt
1978, p.342.

12. One of the qualities which Frisch envisages as flowing from a
'friedensfähige Gesellschaft' is the restoration of a meaningful relationship to work, Zwei Reden zum Friedenspreis, p.107.

13. Over thirty years later Frisch examines the individual's
relations to the dead more fully in Triptychon (1978).

14. The theme which Rip van Winkle represents occurs also in
Die Schwierigen (I 559) and in Nun singen sie wieder (II 95-96).

15. Karlheinz Braun Die epische Technik in Max Frischs Roman
'Stiller' als Beitrag zur Formfrage des modernen Romans,
Diss.phil. Frankfurt 1959, p.56.

16. Hedin's version, 'Ein nordamerikanisches Märchen', is reprinted
in Materialien zu Stiller, pp.144-152; cf. Linda J. Stine
'Chinesische Träumerei - amerikanisches Märchen: Märchenelemente
in Bin und Stiller' Max Frisch - Aspekte des Prosawerks (ed.
Gerhard P. Knapp), Bern 1978, pp.37-51, for an excellent
discussion of the function of this story in Stiller.

17. The dreams of Rip and the Staatsanwalt in Graf Öderland
(III 89) are reinforcements of their everyday situations.

18. Cf. Michael Butler The Novels of Max Frisch, London 1976,
pp.63-64.

19. He later refers to this task as 'eine Sisyphos-Arbeit' (III 666).

20. Cf. Werner Stauffacher 'Langage et mystère - A propos des
derniers romans de Max Frisch' Etudes Germaniques, 20 1965,
p.335.

21. Numa-F. Tétaz 'Préface' 'Le désert des miroirs (Mein Name sei
Gantenbein), Lausanne 1969, p.14.

22. Paradoxically it is the instrument for measuring time which can help towards avoiding responsibility towards time: 'Die Uhren zeigen immer jetzt. Ein Schutz vor der Erinnerung und ihren Schlünden' (V 43).

23. The importance of the 'Erste Heft' for Stiller's clear appreciation of his own predicament must be stressed: as he acknowledges the incommunicable nature of identity (III 412), so, immediately after giving expression to his fear of 'Wiederholung', he recognises its necessity (III 421).

24. Jurgensen op.cit., p.117.

25. Doris Merrifield implies limitations to Sabeth's responses also, Das Bild der Frau bei Max Frisch, Freiburg i.B. 1971, p.83.

26. Brigitte Bradley comments on the relationship between technology and incest in this passage, 'Max Frisch's Homo Faber: Theme and Structural Devices' Germanic Review, 41 1966, p.288.

27. Faber strenuously rejects all manifestations of 'Traum' and 'Dichtung' which could re-create the 'Urganzes' of time: he dismisses dreams (IV 15), novels (IV 15, 79) and folklore (IV 45).

28. There is here a strong similarity to Salamo's psalm to the astronauts in Dürrenmatt's Die Physiker, Zürich 1962, pp.35-36.

29. Ehrismann's sensation of limitless time presages the existential anarchy of his life without an identity; the same sensation in the Staatsanwalt in Graf Öderland (III 27) is the precursor to the political anarchy in which he becomes involved.

30. Heide-Lore Schaefer 'Max Frisch: Santa Cruz Eine Interpretation' Germanisch-Romanische Monatsschrift Neue Folge 20 1970, p.82.

31. Hans Geulen Max Frischs 'Homo Faber', Berlin 1965, p.82.

2. Identity and the Forces of the Environment

1. 'Ein Mensch geht weg' Neue Zürcher Zeitung 26. Juni 1932.

2. Stiller perceives in a dream the self-destructive nature of his relationship to Julika - they both walk bearing stigmata (III 415); later he dreams about 'crucifying' a photograph of his wife (III 680); in a dream Faber senses his progress towards death (IV 15-16); the Registrator comments on Kürmann's recurring dream of physical decay (V 556-557).

3. Cf. Annemarie Schnetzler-Suter Max Frisch-Dramaturgische Fragen, Bern 1974, p.26 for Frisch's reservations in 1970 about Santa Cruz; Roland Links rightly points out, however, that these reservations do not negate the clear relationship of the play to Frisch's 'Gesamtwerk', 'Stiller' Materialien zu Stiller, p.325.

4. Cf. Karl Schmid 'Versuch über Max Frisch' Schweizer Annalen, 3 1946/47, pp.329-330.

258.

5. <u>Antwort aus der Stille</u>, Stuttgart/Berlin 1937, pp.89-90.

6. 'Neue Unternehmungen jüngerer Schweizer Autoren - Konfrontation
    mit Julika', <u>Neue Zürcher Zeitung</u> 29. September 1954, reprinted
    in <u>Materialien zu Stiller</u>, p.35.

7. <u>Bin</u>, written in 1944, was published in 1945 (I 667); <u>Santa Cruz</u>,
    written in 1944, was first performed in 1946 (II 759).

8. Reinhart comments in <u>Die Schwierigen</u>: 'Jugendfreunde glänzen
    so unermesslich in ihrem Vorzug, dass sie ledig bleiben von
    jeder enttäuschenden Verwirklichung' (I 585).

9. Cf. Gertrud B. Pickar 'The Narrative Time-sense in the Dramatic
    Works of Max Frisch' <u>German Life and Letters</u> 28 1974/75 p.1.

10. Cf. Jurgensen <u>Max Frisch - Die Romane</u>, p.173 for a comment on
    Frisch's treatment of light.

11. Weise <u>op.cit.</u>, p.69.

12. Jurgensen <u>Max Frisch - Die Romane</u>, p.33.

13. Mayer <u>op.cit.</u>, p.35.

14. <u>ibid</u> p.36.

15. Hawai is merely 'ein Wort' (II 51); 'Am Ende ist es ein Wort,
    nichts weiter, eine goldene Ahnung' (I 643), says the
    narrator of Peking.

16. The bond of sympathy between the <u>Staatsanwalt</u> and the bank
    clerk has parallels in the relationship between the <u>Staatsan-
    walt</u> and <u>Der Fremdling</u> in <u>Rip van Winkle</u>, and above all in
    that between Rolf and Stiller.

17. Arnold <u>op.cit.</u>, p.49.

18. Rainer Zoll <u>Der absurde Mord in der modernen deutschen und
    französischen Literatur</u> Diss.phil., Frankfurt 1962, p.23.

19. Friedrich Dürrenmatt claims not merely local Swiss, but
    universal, significance for the figure of Öderland <u>Theater-
    Schriften und Reden</u>, p.260.

20. Cf. Weise <u>op.cit.</u>, p.71.

21. There are two parallel scenes on the Zürichsee in <u>Stiller</u>,
    firstly between Stiller and Julika (III 522-523), the one
    point in the novel where Julika reveals herself, both literally
    and metaphorically, to Stiller; and secondly, between Stiller
    and Sibylle (III 630-632), where Sibylle contrasts her lover
    Stiller with her husband Rolf.

22. Cf. Max Gassmann <u>Max Frisch - Leitmotive der Jugend</u> Diss.phil.,
    Zürich 1966, p.100; Jautrite Salins <u>Zur Wirklichkeitsdarstel-
    lung in Max Frischs Werken</u> Ph.D., Rutgers State University
    1968, p.12.

23. Weise designates the passion for geometry and for chess as
    'Symbole einer 'utopischen Identitätssuche'' op.cit., p.113.

24. Yet, as he waits 'eine lange und öde Stunde' for the interview
    with the 'Amtsarzt', which will grant him his yellow arm-band,
    Gantenbein is disturbed, not at the deception which he is about
    to perpetrate, but at the minimal social role to which his
    impersonation commits him: 'Auch ein Blinder, hatte er ein-
    sehen müssen, ist ein Glied der Gesellschaft' (V 42).

25. Three times Faber has telephoned his apartment in New York to
    be told each time that no-one of his name is known there
    (IV 163-164).

26. Arnold op.cit., pp.49-50.

27. Cf. Helmut Naumann Der Fall Stiller Antwort auf eine Heraus-
    forderung – Zu Max Frischs 'Stiller', Rheinfelden 1978,
    pp.128-133, for the most useful summary of the chronology of
    the novel.

28. Cock loc.cit., p.827.

29. The only other dream which he can recall from his spell in
    hospital involves his mother; earlier he had written, as he
    looked at his mother's grave: 'Meine Mutter war überzeugt,
    dass ich mit diesem Leben schon fertig werde.' (III 672).

30. The passage immediately following the reflections on Mexico
    contains Rolf's statement on the nature of 'Selbstüberforderung'
    (III 668-670), thus providing a further example of the mosaic
    structure of the novel.

31. Hildegard Emmel Das Gericht in der deutschen Literatur des
    20. Jahrhunderts, Bern 1963, p.144 gives an incorrect picture
    of brisk resolution in Rolf immediately on his return to
    Zürich which does not accord with the evidence (III 570 ff.).

32. Weise characterises, in Santa Cruz and Don Juan, a child as the
    'Symbol für eine 'wirkliche Identitätssuche'' op.cit., p.113;
    the same holds good for the novels.

33. Cf. Joachim Müller 'Das Prosawerk Max Frischs – Dichtung unserer
    Zeit' Max Frisch – Beiträge zu einer Wirkungsgeschichte, p.24.

34. Cf. Biedermann op.cit., p.42.

35. Cf. Monika Wintsch-Spiess Zum Problem der Identität im Werk
    Max Frischs, Zürich 1965, p.99.

36. Arnold op.cit., p.18.

3. Identity and its Limitations

1. Frisch uses a similar image to describe the political dangers
   of language in his 'Büchnerpreisrede' of 1958 (IV 236).

2. A consequence of the constant difficulty for the writer to give
   expression to experience is that, over the years, 'der Schriftsteller...erlebt ungern, was er keinesfalls in Worte bringen
   kann' (VI 627).

3. Cf. the statement of the <u>Staatsanwalt</u> in <u>Rip van Winkle</u>:
   'Niemand, und wenn man ihn foltern würde, ist imstande, die
   Wahrheit zu sagen – es sei denn, er erfinde sie' (III 813);
   cf. also the forthcoming article in <u>Quinquereme</u> by Malcolm
   Pender: ''Das erfundene Beispiel': Max Frisch's Sketch 'Glück'.'

4. Stauffacher <u>loc.cit.</u>, p.333.

5. Walter Schmitz 'Nachwort' <u>Über Max Frisch II</u>, p.558.

6. Bienek <u>op.cit.</u>, p.25.

7. Heinrich von Kleist <u>Sämtliche Werke und Briefe</u>, München 1961,
   pp.319-324, esp. p.320.

8. Rolf's description of Julika shortly before her fatal operation
   is an instance of facial expression indicating impossibility of
   communication (III 748); on the other hand, Rolf's smile holds
   out encouragement to Stiller for the latter to attempt to
   establish his identity in the warmth of human contact (III 535);
   the painful lesson of Genoa has been transformed into this
   expressive and receptive smile, unique in Frisch's male
   characters.

9. The figures from the past which appear at the end of <u>Santa Cruz</u>
   (II 74-75), in the course of <u>Biografie</u>, and in 'Das zweite Bild'
   of <u>Triptychon</u>, represent partial realisations of this thought.

10. Markus Werner <u>Bilder des Endgültigen – Entwürfe des Möglichen</u>
    Zum Werk von Max Frisch, Bern/Frankfurt 1975, p.28.

11. The failure of the film as a repository of human experience
    becomes apparent to Walter Faber, watching in horror as a film
    on which the dead Sabeth appears is run through for him in
    error (IV 185-192).

12. <u>Stücke 1</u>, Frankfurt 1962, p.156; in the 1972 Paris version this
    line is altered to 'Ich spiele darin die Rolle eines Heutigen'
    (II 145).

13. <u>Stücke 1</u>, p.223; this speech is missing entirely from the Paris
    version.

14. Cf. Tildy Hanhart <u>Max Frisch: Zufall, Rolle und literarische
    Form</u> Kronberg/Ts 1976, p.72.

15. Hans Egon Holthusen 'Deutsche Literatur nach dem zweiten Welt-
    krieg' <u>Der unbehauste Mensch</u>, 3te. Aufl. München 1955, p.290;
    Holthusen later characterises <u>Gantenbein</u> as a depiction of 'der
    moderne Intellektuelle am Ende seines Lateins', 'Ein Mann von
    fünfzig Jahren' <u>Merkur</u> 18 1964, p.1076.

16. 'Er (Stiller) inszeniert sein Leben. Seine Beziehungen zu ande-
    ren Menschen bleiben ichbezogen. Sie werden Teil seines Ich-
    Theaters'. Jurgensen <u>Max Frisch – Die Romane</u>, p.66.

17. Cf. Hanhart <u>op.cit.</u>, p.24, Kieser <u>op.cit.</u>, p.89, Zimmermann
    <u>op.cit.</u>, p.153.

18. Bienek <u>op.cit.</u>, p.25.

261.

19. Howard S. Babb <u>Jane Austen's Novels: The Fabric of Dialogue</u>,
Hamden Connecticut 1967, pp.132-133.

20. Cf. C. W. Hoffmann's assessment of Faber: 'Afraid of chance
or accident, he has avoided situations or relationships that
might have called for an unforeseen response', 'The Search for
Self, Inner Freedom and Relatedness in the Novels of Max Frisch'
<u>The Contemporary Novel in German - A Symposium</u> (ed. R.R. Heitner),
Texas 1967, p.107.

21. The distancing of the individual from his performance, and the
subsequent effect on the performance, is described by Edward
Bullough <u>Aesthetics</u> (ed. E. M. Wilkinson), London 1957, p.66.

22. Cf. Doris Fulda-Merrifield 'Max Frischs 'Mein Name sei Gantenbein'' <u>Max Frisch - Beiträge zu einer Wirkungsgeschichte</u>, p.167.

23. Salins <u>op.cit.</u>, p.26.

24. Bruno Schärer 'Geschichten und Geschichte - Zu Max Frischs
Prosa' <u>Neue Zürcher Zeitung</u> 30. Oktober 1966.

25. Hoffmann <u>loc.cit.</u>, pp.95-96.

26. Cf. Baden <u>op.cit.</u>, p.16.

27. Werner <u>op.cit.</u>, p.26.

28. It is significant that Hauswirt's decision, like that of the
ambassador, is attended by silence (I 596).

29. Cf. Malcolm Pender 'The Role of Rolf the <u>Staatsanwalt</u> in Max
Frisch's <u>Stiller</u>' <u>German Life and Letters</u> 32 1979, pp.332-342.

30. Cf. Salins <u>op.cit.</u>, p.176.

B.   COMMITMENT

1. <u>Fear of Commitment and its Consequences</u>

1. In the first published version of the play, a similar statement
by the <u>Registrator</u> opens the action, <u>Biografie - Ein Spiel</u>,
Frankfurt 1967, p.7.

2. Another version of this envy is displayed by Faber when he
reflects: 'Der Roboter braucht keine Ahnungen' (IV 75).

3. 'Über naive und sentimentalische Dichtung' <u>Schillers Werke</u>
Nationalausgabe, Weimar 1962, vol. 20 p.428.

4. It is interesting to speculate to what extent Frisch's sympathy
and liking for Albin Zollinger relate to the fact that Zollinger's enclosed position in Switzerland during the latter part
of his life so closely resembles the existential position of
the Frisch hero.

5. The falsity of Kürmann's attitude to Antoinette is of the same
order: 'Ich werde glauben, dass ich ohne Antoinette Stein
nicht leben kann. Ich werde ein Schicksal daraus machen' (V 488).

6. The feelings of Viktor, the hero of Spitteler's novel Imago, offer a striking similarity to those of Stiller in Glion; after a variety of reverses following his return to Switzerland, Viktor displays the same kind of spiritual impotence, Gesammelte Werke, vol. IV p.331.

7. Hans-Joachim Pruszak Menschliche Existenz unter der Eigengesetzlichkeit der Lebensbereiche in Max Frischs Dramen, Diss.phil. Berlin 1965, p.107.

8. 'Als habe nicht jeder Mensch sein eigenes Schicksal, das ihm gehört, ihm allein, und als sei er nur für uns geboren, als lebte er nur uns zur Freude und litte nur uns zum Schmerz, als stürbe er nur uns zur Trauer'. Antwort aus der Stille, p.120.

9. At the close of his 'Aufzeichnungen', composed in prison in the autumn of 1952, Stiller describes his suicide attempt in Oakland, and concludes: 'Das war vor etwa zwei Jahren...und ich war bereits achtunddreissig' (III 727).

10. Hans Bänziger Zwischen Protest und Traditionsbewusstsein Arbeiten zum Werk und zur gesellschaftlichen Stellung Max Frischs, Bern/München 1975, p.67, p.69.

11. Jurgensen Max Frisch - Die Romane, p.89.

12. Erich Franzen 'Über Max Frisch' Über Max Frisch, p.75.

13. Dieter-E. Zimmer 'Über die Uraufführung in Zürich' Max Frisch - Beiträge zu einer Wirkungsgeschichte, p.314.

14. Jürgen Petersen op.cit., pp.126-129, gives a most succint account of Stiller's spiritual dislocation.

15. Cf. Hoffmann loc.cit., p.98.

16. Quoted by Stäuble op.cit., p.51.

17. The extent to which the individual, instead of making use of his experience, can become a prisoner of the narration of that experience, is noted by Frisch when he recalls how he recounted a visit he made to Hungary, 'Die andere Welt' loc.cit., p.2.

18. Helmut Pfanner, in 'Stiller und das 'Faustische'' Max Frisch - Beiträge zu einer Wirkungsgeschichte, pp.47-58, disregards the clear distinctions drawn in the report of this conversation between Rolf and Stiller; thus, despite interesting insights, Pfanner is led to conclusions about the close of the novel which are at odds with the evidence.

19. Tagebuch 1946-1949 anticipates Rolf's statement: 'Es ist leicht, etwas Wahres zu sagen, ein sogenanntes Apercu, das im Raum des Unbedingten hängt; es ist schwierig, fast unmöglich, dieses Wahre anzuwenden, einzusehen, wieweit eine Wahrheit gilt. (Wirklich zu sein!)' (II 545).

20. Cf. Kurt Marti 'Das zweite Gebot im 'Stiller' von Max Frisch' Materialien zu Stiller, p.212.

21. Baden op.cit., p.18.

22. Biedermann op.cit., p.31.

23. Weise op.cit., p.63.

24. Lengborn op.cit., p.132.

25. Max Frisch 'Neue Unternehmungen jüngerer Schweizer Autoren' Materialien zu Stiller, pp.35-36.

26. As Faber talks with Hanna in her flat in Athens on the eve of their daughter's death, she says to him: 'Es wird alles so klein, wenn du darüber redest!' (IV 148).

27. This is an expansion of a much shorter passage (III 685), in which Stiller, reflecting that he has never cultivated his inner resources in any of the stations of his life, recalls his time in New York.

2. Commitment, Reproduktion and Technology

1. Gerhard Kaiser 'Max Frischs Homo Faber', Über Max Frisch II, p.275.

2. Walter Benjamin 'Das Kunstwerk im Zeitalter seiner technischen Reproduzierbarkeit' (Zweite Fassung) Gesammelte Schriften (ed. Rolf Teidemann/Hermann Schweppenhäuer), Frankfurt 1974, vol. I.2, p.479.

3. Hans Magnus Enzensberger 'Eine Theorie des Tourismus' Einzelheiten I - Bewusstseins-Industrie, Frankfurt 1965, p.199.

4. ibid, p.203.

5. Braun op.cit., pp.6-7.

6. Biedermann op.cit., p.22.

7. Geulen op.cit., p.91.

8. Franzen loc.cit., pp.73-74.

9. In the collection of books in the studio ('eine Bibliothek kann man es wohl nicht nennen' (III 705)), are works by Hemingway, Jung, Mann and Proust (III 705-706), all mentioned ironically in the speech to Bohnenblust.

10. Cf. Mayer op.cit., p.39

11. Tagebuch 1966-1971 also contains a short sketch of Paris, which is referred to as 'die Allerweltsgeliebte und voll Literatur' (VI 118).

12. Benjamin op.cit., p.476.

13. Mayer op.cit., p.42.

14. Paul Nizon Diskurs in der Enge Aufsätze zur Schweizer Kunst, Bern 1970, p.27.

264.

15. Der Heutige in Die Chinesische Mauer explains his dress to Mee Lán, the daughter of the dictator of the China of two thousand years ago: 'Warum starren Sie mich so an...Ich trage das Kostüm unserer Zeit: Konfektion' (II 160); the Andorrans, for all their chauvinism, wear 'heutige Konfektion' (IV 561).

16. The fashionable language of the jet-set is as unreal as the political slogans which Der Heutige commends to the tyrant in Die Chinesische Mauer: 'Terroristen, Elemente, Agitatoren. Sehr nützliche Worte, Majestät; sie ersticken die Wahrheit im Keime' (II 182).

17. Cf. Mayer op.cit., p.50.

18. ibid, p.48.

19. Hoffmann loc.cit., p.108.

20. Sir Joshua Reynolds Discourses on Art, London 1966, pp.185-186.

21. Theodor Adorno 'Nicht Anklopfen' Minima Moralia, Frankfurt 1975, p.43.

22. This phrase is accusingly declaimed three times; Faber looks at himself in the mirror at three strategic points in the novel; Ivy and Faber make love three times in his apartment, so contributing to the situation which causes Faber to be there when the call comes from the shipping company; on his final visit to New York, Faber unsuccessfully telephones his apartment three times; thus a threefold occurrence, adumbrated by the threefold mention of the word 'Haus' which firmly links Stiller's life to the 'ferme vaudoise', is in Homo Faber developed into a thematic device indicative of vengeful and malevolent pursuit.

23. Bradley loc.cit., p.290.

24. ibid, p.283.

25. Bienek op.cit., p.24.

26. ibid, p.24.

3. The Nature of Commitment

1. The point is made at the beginning of Gantenbein: 'Ein Mann hat eine Erfahrung gemacht, jetzt sucht er die Geschichte dazu' (V 11); the novel constitutes a description of this search.

2. Cf. Jiri Stromsik 'Das Verhältnis von Weltanschauung und Erzählmethode bei Max Frisch' Über Max Frisch II, pp.138-139.

3. The first version of Don Juan was performed in 1953, Stiller was published in 1954.

4. The Dame points out to him that he must incorporate geometry into life, if both life and geometry are not to be impoverished: 'Warum glaubst du nicht an eine Frau, Juan, ein einziges Mal? Es ist der einzige Weg zu deiner Geometrie' (III 145).

5. Cf. Elvira in Santa Cruz: 'Man muss sich kennenlernen...ohne dass man verliebt ist' (II 64).

6. To call the marriage 'a toneless living death', Butler op.cit., p.39, seems to be judging it without relation to the fabric of the novel.

7. Cf. Jürgen Petersen op.cit., p.37.

8. Cf. above p.154.

9. Stromsik loc.cit., p.140.

10. Ursula Roisch 'Max Frischs Auffassung vom Einfluss der Technik auf den Menschen – nachgewiesen am Roman Homo Faber' Über Max Frisch, p.86.

11. Hoffmann loc.cit., p.110.

12. Hanhart op.cit., p.27.

13. Heinrich Geisser Die Entstehung von Max Frischs Dramaturgie der Permutation, Bern/Stuttgart 1973, p.53.

14. Arnold op.cit., p.43.

15. Cf. Gertrud Pickar ''Kann man schreiben, ohne eine Rolle zu spielen?' Zur Problematik des fingierten Erzählens in Stiller' Max Frisch – Aspekte des Prosawerks, pp.77-102.

16. Butler op.cit., p.54.

17. Critics tend to take a rather negative view of Rolf: cf. esp. Butler op.cit., pp.83-86, and Pickar loc.cit., pp.84-86; only Hildegard Emmel op.cit., pp.120-150, goes a considerable way towards establishing the Staatsanwalt as a positive figure.

18. Horst Steinmetz Max Frisch: Tagebuch, Drama, Roman, Göttingen 1973, p.77.

19. Cf. Braun op.cit., p.151.

20. Cf. Weise op.cit., p.60.

21. Similar thoughts occur to Faber as he looks down from the plane which is taking him to Athens and death: 'Zone des Lebens, wie dünn sie eigentlich ist, ein paar hundert Meter...eine Oase eigentlich' (IV 195); the most radical formulation of the fragile basis to human life is contained in Frisch's latest publication: 'Romane eignen sich in diesen Tagen überhaupt nicht, da geht es um Menschen in ihrem Verhältnis zu sich und zu andern, um Väter und Mütter und Töchter beziehungsweise um Söhne und Geliebte usw., um Seelen, hauptsächlich unglückliche, und um Gesellschaft usw., als sei das Gelände dafür gesichert, die Erde ein für allemal Erde, die Höhe des Meeresspiegels geregelt ein für allemal' Der Mensch erscheint im Holozän, Frankfurt 1979, p.16.

22. Cf. Hoffmann loc.cit., pp.100-101.

266.

23. Christa Wolf 'Max Frisch, beim Wiederlesen oder: Vom
     Schreiben in Ich-Form' Max Frisch Text & Kritik 47/48, p.11.

                              CONCLUSION

1.   Cf. Dramaturgisches, pp.18-19, Arnold op.cit., pp.35-36.

2.   Cf. Dramaturgisches, pp.27-33.

3.   Peter Ruedi 'Die lange Ewigkeit des Gewesenen' Gespräch mit Max
     Frisch' Deutsche Zeitung 21 April 1978.

4.   Emil Staiger ''Stiller' - Zu dem neuen Roman von Max Frisch'
     Neue Zürcher Zeitung 17. November 1954, reprinted in Max Frisch -
     Beiträge zu einer Wirkungsgeschichte, pp.59-62, and in Materialien
     zu Stiller, pp.391-395, here p.391.

5.   Ruedi loc.cit.

6.   Wolfgang Frühwald 'Parodie der Tradition. Das Problem literarischer
     Originalität in Max Frischs Roman 'Stiller'' Materialien zu Stiller,
     p.260.

7.   Dramaturgisches, p.29.

8.   Arnold op.cit., p.40.

9.   Butler op.cit., p.9.

BIBLIOGRAPHY

Primary Literature

1. Publications

Gesammelte Werke in zeitlicher Folge (ed. Hans Mayer, with Walter
    Schmitz) 6 vols., Frankfurt 1976 (The text is identical to
    Werkausgabe Edition Suhrkamp, 1976)

Triptychon Drei szenische Bilder, Frankfurt 1978

Der Mensch erscheint im Holozän Eine Erzählung, Frankfurt 1979

2. Speeches

'Wir hoffen' in Max Frisch/Hartmut von Hentig Zwei Reden zum Friedens-
    preis des Deutschen Buchhandels 1976, Frankfurt 1976

'Haben wir eine demokratische Öffentlichkeit?' Rede vor dem Parteitag
    der Sozialdemokratischen Partei der Schweiz 1976, in Literatur aus
    der Schweiz Texte und Materialien (ed. Egon Ammann, Eugen Faes),
    Zürich 1978

'Die Schuld der Biedermänner' Rede beim SPD-Parteitag Frankfurter
    Rundschau 17. November 1977

3. Interviews, etc.

Arnold, Heinz Ludwig 'Gespräch mit Max Frisch' in Gespräche mit Schrift-
    stellern, München 1975

Bienek, Horst 'Max Frisch' in Werkstattgespräche mit Schriftstellern,
    München 1962

Bloch, Peter André and Bruno Schoch 'Gespräch mit Max Frisch' in
    Der Schriftsteller und sein Verhältnis zur Sprache dargestellt am
    Problem der Tempuswahl, Bern 1971

----- and Edwin Hubacher 'Gespräch mit Max Frisch' in Der Schriftsteller
    in unserer Zeit Schweizer Autoren bestimmen ihre Rolle in der
    Gesellschaft, Bern 1972

Frisch, Max Dramaturgisches Ein Briefwechsel mit Walter Höllerer,
    Berlin 1969

Häsler, Alfred 'Wir müssen unsere Welt anders einrichten. Gespräch mit
    Max Frisch' Die Tat 9. Dezember 1967

Kieser, Rolf 'An Interview with Max Frisch' Contemporary Literature
    1972, pp.1-14

Ruedi, Peter 'Die lange Ewigkeit des Gewesenen. Ein Gespräch mit
    Max Frisch' Deutsche Zeitung 21. April 1978

Vogel, Paul 'Und die Schweiz? Ein Interview mit Max Frisch'
    Neutralität 2 1964, pp.2-6

Zanetti, Gerardo 'Soll der Onkel auf die Barrikade steigen? Ein Gespräch
    mit dem Schriftsteller' Die Woche 19. August 1964

Zimmer, Dieter-E. 'Noch einmal anfangen können. Ein Gespräch mit Max
    Frisch' Die Zeit 22. Dezember 1967

Secondary Literature

1. On Max Frisch

Arnold, Heinz Ludwig (ed.) Max Frisch Text & Kritik 47/48 München 1975

Baden, Hans-Jürgen Der Mensch ohne Partner Das Menschenbild in den
    Romanen von Max Frisch, Wuppertal-Barmen 1966

Bänziger, Hans Frisch und Dürrenmatt 5.Aufl., Bern/München 1967

-------- Zwischen Protest und Traditionsbewusstsein Arbeiten zum Werk
    und zur gesellschaftlichen Stellung Max Frischs, Bern/München 1975

Barlow, Derrick ''Ordnung' and 'Das wirkliche Leben' in the Work of
    Max Frisch' German Life and Letters 19 1965/66, pp.52-60

Beckermann, Thomas (ed.) Über Max Frisch, Frankfurt 1971

Bicknese, Günther 'Zur Rolle Amerikas in Max Frischs Homo Faber'
    German Quarterly 42 1969, pp.52-64

Biedermann, Marianne Das politische Theater von Max Frisch,
    Lampertheim 1974

Blöcker, Günther 'Max Frisch: Mein Name sei Gantenbein' in Literatur
    als Teilhabe, Berlin 1966

Bonnin, Gunther 'Stiller - Swiss Don Quichotte' Aufsätze zur Schweizer
    Literatur Queensland Studies in German Language and Literature
    vol. II, Brisbane 1971, pp.103-106

Boveri, Margret 'Max Frisch - Tagebuch 1966-1971' Neue Rundschau 83
    1972, pp.540-548

Bradley, Brigitte 'Max Frisch's Homo Faber: Theme and Structural
    Devices' Germanic Review 41 1966, pp.279-290

Braun, Karlheinz Die epische Technik in Max Frischs Roman 'Stiller' als
    Beitrag zur Formfrage des modernen Romans Diss.phil., Frankfurt 1959

Burckhardt, Lukas 'Vortrag über Max Frisch'. Delivered in the Swiss Embassy, Washington, on 17 January 1963. Typescript in Zentralbibliothek, Zürich

Burgauner, Christoph 'Zwei Interessen und Zwei Instanzen - Max Frisch: 'Tagebuch 1966-1971'' Frankfurter Hefte 1972, pp.911-913

--------- 'Versuch über Max Frisch' Merkur 1974, pp.444-463

Butler, Michael The Novels of Max Frisch, London 1976

Cock, Mary ''Countries of the Mind': Max Frisch's Narrative Technique' Modern Language Review 65 1970, pp.820-828

Dahms, Erna M. Zeit und Zeiterlebnis in den Werken Max Frischs Bedeutung und technische Darstellung, Berlin 1976

Deschner, Karlheinz 'Max Frisch - Stiller und andere Prosa' in Talente Dichter Dilettanten Überschätzte und unterschätzte Werke in der deutschen Literatur der Gegenwart, Wiesbaden 1964

Dürrenmatt, Friedrich 'Eine Vision und ihr dramatisches Schicksal: Zu 'Graf Öderland' von Max Frisch' in Theater-Schriften und Reden, Zürich 1966

Eckart, Rolf Max Frisch: Andorra, München 1965

Emmel, Hildegrad 'Max Frisch: Parodie und Konvention' in Das Gericht in der deutschen Literatur des 20. Jahrhunderts, Bern 1963

Esslin, Martin 'Max Frisch' in German Men of Letters (ed. Alex Natan) vol. III, London 1964

Federico, Joseph A. 'The Hero as Playwright in Dramas by Frisch, Dürren-matt and Handke' German Life and Letters 32 1978/79, pp.166-176

Frank, Claudia 'Will nicht Stiller sein' Frankfurter Hefte 1956, pp. 750-752

Frühwald, Wolfgang and Walter Schmitz Max Frisch - 'Andorra', 'Wilhelm Tell' Materialien, Kommentare, München 1977

Gassmann, Max Max Frisch - Leitmotive der Jugend, Diss.phil., Zürich 1966

Geisser, Heinrich Die Entstehung von Max Frischs Dramaturgie der Permutation, Bern/Stuttgart 1973

Geissler, Rolf 'Max Frisch: Homo Faber' in Möglichkeiten des modernen deutschen Romans 2.Aufl., Frankfurt 1965

Geulen, Hans Max Frischs 'Homo Faber' Studien und Interpretationen, Berlin 1965

Gockel, Heinz Max Frisch - Gantenbein: Das offen-artistische Erzählen, Bonn 1976

Gontrum, Peter 'Max Frisch's Don Juan: A New Look at a Traditional Hero' Comparative Literature Studies 2 1965, pp.117-123

270.

Haberkamm, Klaus 'Max Frisch' in Deutsche Literatur seit 1945 in Einzeldarstellungen (ed. Dietrich Weber), Stuttgart 1968

Hammer, J. C. 'The Humanism of Max Frisch – An Examination of Three of the Plays' German Quarterly 42 1968, pp.718-726

Hanhart, Tildy Max Frisch: Zufall, Rolle und literarische Form, Kronberg/Ts 1976

Hartung, Rudolf 'Max Frisch – Mein Name sei Gantenbein' Neue Rundschau 1964, pp.682-686

Henningsen, Jürgen 'Jeder Mensch erfindet sich eine Geschichte – Max Frisch und die Autobiographie' Literatur in Wissenschaft und Unterricht 1971, pp.167-176

Hill, Philip 'A Reading of The Firebugs' Modern Drama 13 1970-71, pp.184-191

Hillen, Gerd 'Reisemotive in den Romanen von Max Frisch' Wirkendes Wort 19 1969, pp.126-133

Hoefert, Siegfried 'Zur Sprachauffassung Max Frischs' Muttersprache 1963, pp.257-259

vom Hofe, Gerhard 'Zauber ohne Zukunft. Zur autobiographischen Korrektur in Max Frischs Erzählung Montauk' Euphorion 70 1976, pp.374-396

Hoffmann, Charles W. 'The Search for Self, Inner Freedom and Relatedness in the Novels of Max Frisch' in The Contemporary Novel in German A Symposium (ed. R. R. Heitner), Austin, Texas 1967

Horst, Karl August 'Notizen zu Max Frisch und Friedrich Dürrenmatt' Merkur 1954, pp.593-596

––––– 'Andorra mit anderen Augen' Merkur 1962, pp.396-399

Iden, Peter 'Das gestörte Empfinden. Todesbilder der Liebe in Max Frischs 'Triptychon' and Francois Truffaut's 'La chambre verte' Theater 1978 Sonderheft der Zeitschrift Theater heute, 1979, pp.62-66

Johnson, Uwe Max Frisch – Stichworte, Frankfurt 1975

Jurgensen, Manfred Max Frisch – Die Dramen, Bern 1968

––––––– Max Frisch – Die Romane, Bern/München 1972

––––––– (ed.) Frisch: Kritik – Thesen – Analysen Queensland Studies in German Language and Literature vol. VI, Bern/München 1977

Kaiser, Joachim 'Öderländische Meditationen' Frankfurter Hefte 1956, pp.388-396

Karasek, Hellmuth Frisch, 5te Aufl. Velber bei Hannover 1974

Kieser, Rolf 'Man as his own Novel: Max Frisch and the Literary Diary' Germanic Review 47 1972, pp.109-117

––––– Max Frisch – Das literarische Tagebuch, Frauenfeld/Stuttgart 1975

Kjoer, Joergen 'Max Frisch, Theorie und Praxis' Orbis Litterarum 27
    1972, pp.264-295

Knapp, Gerhard P. (ed.) Max Frisch - Aspekte des Prosawerks, Bern 1978

Kraft, Martin Studien zur Thematik von Max Frischs Roman 'Mein Name
    sei Gantenbein', Bern 1969

Mayer, Hans Dürrenmatt und Frisch Anmerkungen, Pfullingen 1963

----- 'Die Schuld der Schuldlosen' Der Spiegel Nr.25 1972, pp.124-125

Meinert, Dietrich 'Objektivität und Subjektivität des Existenzbewusst-
    seins in Max Frischs 'Andorra'' Acta Germanica 2 1968, pp.117-124

Merrifield, Doris Das Bild der Frau bei Max Frisch, Freiburg i.B. 1971

Müller, Joachim 'Max Frisch und Friedrich Dürrenmatt als Dramatiker
    der Gegenwart' Universitas 17 1962, pp.725-738

Müller-Salget, Klaus 'Max Frischs 'Montauk' - Eine 'Erzählung?''
    Zeitschrift für deutsche Philologie 97 Sonderheft September 1978,
    pp.108-120

Naumann, Helmut Der Fall Stiller Antwort auf eine Herausforderung. Zu
    Max Frischs 'Stiller', Rheinfelden 1978

Pender, Malcolm 'The Role of Rolf the 'Staatsanwalt' in Max Frisch's
    Stiller' German Life and Letters 32 1978/79, pp.332-342

Petersen, Carol Max Frisch, Berlin 1966

Petersen, Jürgen H. Max Frisch, Stuttgart 1978

Pickar, Gertrud 'The Narrative Time Sense in the Dramatic Works of
    Max Frisch' German Life and Letters 28 1974/75, pp.1-13

Pruszak, Hans-Joachim Menschliche Existenz unter der Eigengesetzlichkeit
    der Lebensbereiche in Max Frischs Dramen Diss.phil., Berlin 1965

Rau, Greta 'Max Frisch, dramaturge et romancier' Preuves août 1958,
    pp.44-49

Reich-Ranicki, Marcel 'Über den Romancier Max Frisch' Neue Rundschau
    1963, pp.272-284

--------------- 'Max Frisch: 'Mein Name sei Gantenbein'' in Literatur
    der kleinen Schritte Deutsche Schriftsteller heute, München 1967

Salins, Jautrite Zur Wirklichkeitsdarstellung in Max Frischs Werken
    Ph.D., Rutgers State University 1968

Schärer, Bruno 'Geschichten und Geschichte - Zu Max Frischs Prosa'
    Neue Zürcher Zeitung 30. Oktober 1966

Schau, Albrecht (ed.) Max Frisch - Beiträge zu einer Wirkungsgeschichte
    Freiburg i.B. 1971

----- 'Modell und Skizze als Darbietungsformen der Frisch'schen
    Dichtung - dargestellt an 'Der andorranische Jude'' Aufsätze zur
    Schweizer Literatur Queensland Studies in German Language and
    Literature vol. II Brisbane 1971, pp.107-123

272.

Schenker, Walter Die Sprache Max Frischs in der Spannung zwischen
    Mundart und Schriftsprache, Berlin 1969

Schmid, Karl 'Versuch über Max Frisch' Schweizer Annalen 3 1946/47,
    pp.327-333

------ 'Notizen zu 'Graf Öderland'' Programmhefte des Schauspielhauses
    Zürich 1950/51, pp.1-5

------ 'Max Frisch: Andorra und die Entscheidung' in Unbehagen im
    Kleinstaat, Zürich/Stuttgart 1963

Schmitz, Walter (ed.) Über Max Frisch II, Frankfurt 1976

------ Max Frisch - 'Homo Faber' Materialien, Kommentar, München 1977

------ Materialien zu Max Frisch 'Stiller' 2 vols., Frankfurt 1978

Schnetzler-Suter, Annemarie Max Frisch - Dramaturgische Fragen, Bern
    1974

Schürer, Ernst 'Zur Interpretation von Max Frischs 'Homo Faber''
    Monatshefte 59 1967, pp.330-343

Stäuble, Eduard Max Frisch Gesamtdarstellung seines Werkes, St. Gallen
    1967

Steinmetz, Horst Max Frisch: Tagebuch, Drama, Roman, Göttingen 1973

Suter, Gody 'Als Glosse: Die Schweiz und Max Frisch' Du August 1967,
    pp.654-655

Tétaz, Numa-F. 'Préface' to Le désert des miroirs (Mein Name sei
    Gantenbein) (trs. A. Coeuroy), Lausanne 1969

Völker-Hezel, Barbara 'Fron und Erfüllung - Zum Problem der Arbeit bei
    Max Frisch' Revue des langues vivantes 37 1971, pp.7-43

Vormweg, Heinrich 'Othello als Mannequin' Der Monat, Dezember 1964,
    pp.76-83

Wailes, Stephen L. 'The Inward Journey: Homo Faber and Heart of
    Darkness' New German Studies 6 1978, pp.31-44

Weber, Werner 'Max Frisch 1958' in Zeit ohne Zeit Aufsätze zur Literatur
    Zürich 1959

Weise, Adelheid Untersuchungen zur Thematik und Struktur der Dramen
    von Max Frisch, Göppingen 1969

Weisstein, Ulrich Max Frisch, New York 1967

Wellwarth, George 'Friedrich Dürrenmatt and Max Frisch: Two Views of
    the Drama' Tulane Drama Review March 1962, pp.14-42

-------- 'Max Frisch: The Drama of Despair' in The Theater of
    Protest and Paradox, New York 1964

Werner, Markus Bilder des Endgültigen - Entwürfe des Möglichen Zum
    Werk von Max Frisch, Bern/Frankfurt 1975

Westphal, Gundel Das Verhältnis von Sprechtext und Regieanweisung bei Frisch, Dürrenmatt, Ionescu und Beckett Diss.phil., Würzburg 1964

Wintsch-Spiess, Monika Zum Problem der Identität im Werk Max Frischs, Zürich 1965

Zimmermann, Werner 'Max Frisch: Stiller' in Deutsche Prosadichtungen unseres Jahrhunderts vol. 2, Düsseldorf 1969

Ziolkowski, Theodore 'Max Frisch: Moralist without a Moral' Yale French Studies 29 1962, pp.132-141

2. On the Swiss Background

Amman, Egon and Eugen Faes (ed.) Literatur aus der Schweiz Texte und Materialien, Zürich 1978

Bachman, Dieter 'Eine weitläufige Literaturprovinz?' Merian Januar 1975, pp.88-91

Bänziger, Hans Heimat und Fremde Ein Kapitel 'Tragische Literatur-geschichte' in der Schweiz: Jakob Schaffner, Robert Walser, Albin Zollinger, Bern 1958

Bergmann, Karl Hans Die Bewegung 'Freies Deutschland' in der Schweiz 1943-1945, München 1974

Bettex, Albert Spiegelungen der Schweiz in der deutschen Literatur 1870-1950, Zürich 1954

Bichsel, Peter Des Schweizers Schweiz, Zürich 1969

Boeschenstein, Hermann Deutsche Gefühlskultur - Studien zu ihrer dichterischen Gestaltung, Bern 1954

--------------- 'Contemporary German-Swiss Fiction' German Life and Letters 12 1958/59, pp.24-33

Bonjour, Edgar Swiss Neutrality Its History and Meaning, London 1946

-------, H. S. Offler and G. R. Potter A Short History of Switzerland Oxford 1952

Brock-Sulzer, Elisabeth 'Überlegungen zur schweizerischen Dramatik von heute' Akzente 1956, pp.43-48

--------------- 'Das deutschschweizerische Theater der Gegenwart' German Life and Letters 12 1958/59, pp.12-23

Bucher, Werner and Georges Ammann (ed.) Schweizer Schriftsteller im Gespräch 2 vols., Basel 1970/71

Calgari, Guido Die vier Literaturen der Schweiz, Olten/Freiburg i.B., 1966

274.

Chapuisat, Edouard L'influence de la Révolution Francaise sur la Suisse, Paris 1934

Dürrenmatt, Friedrich Theater-Schriften und Reden, Zürich 1966

---------- Monstervortrag über Gerechtigkeit und Recht Nebst einem kleinem helvetischen Zwischenspiel, Zürich 1969

---------- Dramaturgisches und Kritisches, Zürich 1972

Ermatinger, Emil Dichtung und Geistesleben der deutschen Schweiz, München 1933

Ernst, Fritz Die Schweiz als geistige Mittlerin Von Muralt bis Jakob Burckhardt, Zürich 1932

----- Helvetia Mediatrix, Zürich 1939

----- Gibt es eine schweizerische Nationalliteratur?, St. Gallen 1955

----- Europäische Schweiz, Zürich 1961

Fehr, Karl Der Realismus in der schweizerischen Literatur, Bern/München 1965

Fringeli, Dieter Gut zum Druck Literatur der deutschen Schweiz seit 1964, Zürich/München 1974

-------- Dichter im Abseits Schweizer Autoren von Glauser bis Hohl, Zürich/München 1974

-------- Von Spitteler zu Muschg Literatur der deutschen Schweiz seit 1900, Basel 1975

Gasser, Adolf 'Der Irrweg der Helvetik' Schweizerische Geschichte 17 1947, pp.425-455

Gerber, Dora Studien zum Problem des Künstlers in der modernen deutsch-schweizerischen Literatur, Bern 1948

Gsteiger, Manfred 'Schweizerische Literatur? Variationen zu einem Thema' in Literatur des Übergangs Essays, Bern/München 1974

-------- (ed.) Die zeitgenössischen Literaturen der Schweiz Kindlers Literaturgeschichte der Gegenwart, Zürich/München 1974

Guggenheim, Kurt Heimat oder Domizil? Die Stellung des deutschschweizerischen Schriftstellers in der Gegenwart, Zürich 1961

---------- Das Ende von Seldwyla, Zürich/Stuttgart 1965

Günther, Werner Dichter der neueren Schweiz 2 vols., Bern/München 1963/1967

Holthusen, Hans 'Kritische Perspektiven der deutschen Schweiz' in Kritisches Verstehen Neue Aufsätze zur Literatur, München 1961

Jung, C. J. 'Die Bedeutung der schweizerischen Linie im Spektrum Europas' Neue Schweizer Rundschau 21 1928, pp.469-479

Keller, Gottfried Sämtliche Werke, Bern 1931-1948

------ Gesammelte Briefe, Bern 1950-1954

Kohlschmidt, Werner (ed.) Bürgerlichkeit und Unbürgerlichkeit in der Literatur der Deutschen Schweiz, Bern/München 1978

Kohn, Hans Nationalism and Liberty The Swiss Example, London 1956

Korrodi, Eduard Schweizerische Literaturbriefe, Frauenfeld/Leipzig, 1918

------ Schweizerdichtung der Gegenwart, Leipzig 1924

------ (ed.) Geisteserbe der Schweiz Schriften von Albrecht von Haller bis zur Gegenwart, Erlenbach-Zürich 1943

Kraft, Martin 'Schweizerhaus': Das Haus-Motiv im Deutschschweizer Roman des 20. Jahrhunderts, Bern/Frankfurt 1971

Leber, Hugo (ed.) Texte Prosa junger Schweizer Autoren, Zürich/Köln 1964

Lengborn, Thorbjörn Schriftsteller und Gesellschaft in der Schweiz Eine Studie zur Behandlung der Gesellschaftsproblematik bei Zollinger, Frisch und Dürrenmatt, Frankfurt 1972

Linder, Heinz-Peter Die schweizerische Gegenwart im modernen Roman der deutschen Schweiz, Worb 1957

Lüthi, Hans Jörg Schweizer Schriftsteller und die Schweiz, Bern 1975

Mariacher, Bruno und Friedrich Witz (ed.) Bestand und Versuch Schweizer Schrifttum der Gegenwart, Zürich 1964

Marti, Kurt Die Schweiz und ihre Schriftsteller - Die Schriftsteller und ihre Schweiz, Zürich 1966

Mason, Eudo 'Switzerland and Germanistic Studies Today' German Life and Letters 1947/48, pp.60-71

Meyer, Alice Anpassung oder Widerstand Die Schweiz zur Zeit des deutschen Nationalsozialismus, Frauenfeld 1965

Moser, Jean Le Roman Contemporain en Suisse Allemande de Carl Spitteler à Jakob Schaffner, Lausanne 1934

Muschg, Walter 'Zur Lage des Schrifttums in der deutschen Schweiz' in Die Schweiz Ein nationales Jahrbuch, n.p. 1930, pp.173-187

------ Tragische Literaturgeschichte, Bern 1948

------ Pamphlet und Bekenntnis Aufsätze und Reden, Olten/Freiburg i.B. 1968

Nadler, Josef Literaturgeschichte der deutschen Schweiz, Leipzig/Zürich 1932

Näf, Werner Die Schweiz in Europa Die Entwicklung des schweizerischen Staates im Rahmen der europäischen Geschichte, Bern 1938

Neue Helvetische Gesellschaft Unser Schweizer Standpunkt 1914-1954, Zürich 1955

Nizon, Paul Diskurs in der Enge Aufsätze zur Schweizer Kunst, Bern 1970

Ramuz, C.-F. 'Besoin de grandeur' Oeuvres complètes Genève 1941, vol. 19

Rappard, William La Constitution Fédérale de la Suisse Ses origines, son élaboration, son évolution, Neuchâtel 1948

——— Collective Security in Swiss Experience 1291-1948, London 1948

de Reynold, Gonzague Défense et Illustration de l'Esprit Suisse, Neuchâtel 1939

von Salis, J. R. Schwierige Schweiz, Zürich 1968

Schmid, Karl Vom Geist der neueren Schweizer Dichtung, Stuttgart 1949

——— Aufsätze und Reden, Zürich/Stuttgart 1957

——— Unbehagen im Kleinstaat, Zürich/Stuttgart 1963

——— Zeitspuren Aufsätze und Reden II, Zürich/Stuttgart 1967

Siegrist, Christoph 'Der engagierte Zeitroman in der neueren Schweizer Literatur' Schweizer Monatshefte 53 1974, pp.700-713

Soloveytchik, George Switzerland in Perspective, Oxford 1954

Spitteler, Carl Gesammelte Werke, Zürich 1945

Stamm, Alice Die Gestalt des deutschschweizerischen Dichters um die Mitte des 19. Jahrhunderts, Frauenfeld/Leipzig 1936

Steiner, Jacob 'Zur Schweizer Literatur der Gegenwart' Der Schweizer Buchhandel Heft 4 1967, pp.113-121

Thürer, Georg Free and Swiss - The Story of Switzerland Adapted and translated from the German by R. P. Heller and E. Long, London 1970

Van Abbé, Derek 'The Swiss in German Literary History' German Life and Letters 9 1955/56, pp.100-108

Wehrli, Max 'Gegenwartsdichtung der deutschen Schweiz' in Deutsche Literatur in unserer Zeit (ed. Wolfgang Kayser), Göttingen 1959

Weilenmann, Hermann Die vielsprachige Schweiz Eine Lösung des Nationalitätenproblems, Basel/Leipzig 1925

——— Pax Helvetica oder Die Demokratie der kleinen Gruppen, Erlenbach-Zürich 1951

Whitton, Kenneth 'The 'Zürcher Literaturstreit'' German Life and Letters 27 1973/74, pp.142-150

Wiechert, Ernst Rede an die Schweizer Freunde 1947, Zürich 1947

Wilbert-Collins, Ely A Bibliography of Four Contemporary German-Swiss Authors: Friedrich Dürrenmatt, Max Frisch, Robert Walser, Albin Zollinger, Bern 1967

Wildi, M. 'Contemporary German-Swiss Literature' German Life and Letters 12 1958/59, pp.1-11

277.

Zäch, Alfred <u>Die Dichtung der deutschen Schweiz</u>, Zürich 1951

Zbinden, Hans <u>Welt im Zwielicht</u> Vier kulturhistorische Essays, Zürich/Stuttgart 1951

------- <u>Schweizer Literatur in europäischer Sicht</u>, Zürich/Stuttgart 1964

Zollinger, Albin <u>Gesammelte Werke</u>, Zürich 1961

STUTTGARTER ARBEITEN ZUR GERMANISTIK
herausgegeben von
ULRICH MÜLLER, FRANZ HUNDSNURSCHER UND CORNELIUS SOMMER

SAG 1: **Christian Hörburger,** Das Hörspiel der Weimarer Republik. Versuch einer kritischen Analyse. 1975, 512 Seiten, kart., ISBN 3-88099-002-6   DM 75.—

SAG 2: **Jürgen Friedmann,** Frank Wedekinds Dramen nach 1900. Eine Untersuchung zur Erkenntnisfunktion seiner Dramen. 1975, 192 Seiten, kart., ISBN 3-88099-00-X   DM 32.—

SAG 3: **Knud Willenberg,** Tat und Reflexion. Zur Konstitution des bürgerlichen Helden im deutschen Trauerspiel des 18. Jahrhunderts, 1975, 304 Seiten, kart., ISBN 3-88099-001-8   DM 42.—

SAG 4: **Festschrift für Adalbert Schmidt zum 70. Geburtstag.** Herausgegeben von Gerd Stein und Gerlinde Weiss. 1976, 568 Seiten, 12 Abb., kart., ISBN 3-88099-033-4   DM 78.—

SAG 5: **David Bathrick,** The Dialectic and the Early Brecht: An Interpretive Study of „Trommeln in der Nacht". 1975, 152 Seiten, kart., ISBN 3-88099-004-3   DM 30.—

SAG 6: **Klaus-Peter Ewald,** Engagierte Dichtung im 17. Jahrhundert. Versuch einer Erklärung des Psalmendichtungsphänomens dargestellt am Beispiel der Psalmen 23 und 130. 1975, 390 Seiten, kart., ISBN 3-88099-005-0   DM 55.—

SAG 7: **Erika Haas,** Ideologie und Mythos. Studien zur Erzählstruktur und Sprache im Werk Anna Seghers. 1975, 260 Seiten, kart., ISBN 3-88099-006-9   DM 34.—

SAG 8: **Josemaria Taberner Prat,** Über den „Marat/Sade" von Peter Weiss: Artistische Kreation und rezeptive Mißverständnisse. 1976. 438 Seiten, kart., ISBN 3-88099-007-5   DM 54.—

SAG 9: **Hans Ternes,** Das Groteske in den Werken Thomas Manns. 1975, 142 Seiten, kart., ISBN 3-88099-008-5   DM 23.—

SAG 10: **Peter Nasse,** Die Frauenzimmer-Bibliothek des Hamburger „Patrioten" von 1724. Zur weiblichen Bildung in der Frühaufklärung. 1976, 775 Seiten, kart., ISBN 3-88099-009-3   DM 88.—

SAG 11: **Angelika Steets,** Die Prosawerke Ödön von Horvaths. Versuch einer Bedeutungsanalyse. 1975, 292 Seiten, kart., ISBN 3-88099-010-7   DM 38.—

SAG 12: **Albert J. Camigliano,** Friedrich Schiller and Christian Gottfried Körner, A critical Relationship. 1976, 220 Seiten, kart., ISBN 3-88099-011-5 DM 32.—

SAG 13: **Frederick George Thomas Bridgham,** Rainer Maria Rilke: Urbild and Verzicht. 1975, 250 Seiten, kart., ISBN 3-88099-013-1   DM 32.—

SAG 14: **Isolde Vöpel,** Der Satzduktus in Schillers dramatischer Versrede. 1976, 182 Seiten, kart., ISBN 3-88099-013-1   DM 32.—

SAG 15: **Gunda Lusser-Mertelsmann,** Max Frisch. Die Identitätsproblematik in seinem Werk aus psychoanalytischer Sicht. 1976, 352 Seiten, kart., ISBN 3-88099-014-X   DM 48.—

SAG 16: Leoni Müller-Loreck, Die erzählende Dichtung Lou Andrea-Salomes. Ihr Zusammenhang mit der Literatur um 1900. 1976. 256 Seiten, kart., ISBN 3-88099-015-8   DM 32.—

SAG 17: Philip A. Mellen, Gerhart Hauptmann and Utopia. 1976, 124 Seiten, kart., ISBN 3-88099-016-6   DM 24.—

SAG 18: Richard D. Hacken, The Religious Thought of Martin Opitz as the Determinant of his Poetic Theory and Practice. 1976, 124 Seiten, kart., ISBN 3-88099-017-4   DM 21.—

SAG 19: Ute Schneider, Der moralische Charakter. Versuch einer Gattungsbestimmung anhand der frühen Moralischen Wochenschriften. 1976, 265 Seiten, kart., ISBN 3-88099-018-2   DM 42.—

SAG 20: Fritz Rüdiger Sammern-Frankenegg, Perspektivische Strukturen einer Erinnerungsdichtung. Studien zur Deutung von Storms ,,Immensee''. 1976, 240 Seiten, kart., ISBN 3-88099-019-0   DM 33.—

SAG 21: Judith Popovich Aikin, The Mission of Rome in the Dramas of Daniel Caspar von Lohenstein, Historical Tragedy as Prophecy and Polemic. 1976, 348 Seiten, kart., ISBN 3-88099-020-4   DM 46.—

SAG 22: Günter Scholdt, Der Fall Norbert Jacques. Über Rang und Niedergang eines Erzählers (1880—1954). 1976, 532 Seiten, kart., ISBN 3-88099-021-2   DM 69.—

SAG 23: Wolfgang Minaty, Paul Boldt und die 'Jungen Pferde' des Expressionismus. 1976, 122 Seiten, kart., ISBN 3-88099-022-0   DM 18.—

SAG 24: George Wallis Field, Hermann Hesse. Kommentar zu seinen sämtlichen Werken. 1976, 145 Seiten, kart., ISBN 3-88099-023-9   DM 38.—

SAG 25: Käte Hamburger, Kleine Schriften 1976, 282 Seiten, kart., ISBN 3-88099-024-7   DM 50.—

SAG 26: Edward McInnes, The Development of German Social Drama 1840—1900. 1976, 300 Seiten, kart., ISBN 3-88099-025-5   DM 44.—

SAG 27: Rolf-Werner Nolle, Das Motiv der Verführung. Verführer und ,,Verführte'' als dramatische Entwürfe moralischer Wertordnung in den Trauerspielen von Gryphius, Lohenstein und Lessing. 1976, 408 Seiten, kart., ISBN 3-88099-026-3   DM 45.—

SAG 28: Karl Müller, Das Dekadenz-Problem in der österreichischen Literatur um die Jahrhundertwende, dargelegt an Texten von Hermann Bahr, Richard von Schaukal, Hugo von Hofmannsthal und Leopold von Andrian. 1976, 164 Seiten, kart., ISBN 3-88099-027-1   DM 35.—

SAG 29: Jaikyung Hahn, Helfrich Peter Sturz (1736—1799): Der Essayist, der Künstler, der Weltmann. Leben und Werke. Mit einer Edition des vollständigen Briefwechsels. 1976, 532 Seiten, 32 Abb., kart., ISBN 3-88099-028-X   DM 75.—

SAG 30: Manfred Michael, Friedrich Hebbels Herodes und Mariamne: Literarhistorische Studien zur gesellschaftlichen Funktion und Klassenbedingtheit von Werk und Wirkung. 1977, 742 Seiten, kart., ISBN 3-88099-029-8   DM 80.—

SAG 31: **Glen A. Dolberg,** The Reception of Johann Joachim Winckelmann in Modern German Prose Fiction. 1977, 165 Seiten, kart.,
ISBN 3-88099-030-1   DM 28.—

SAG 32: **Anthony J. Harper,** „David Schirmer — a Poet of the German Baroque"
1977, 262 Seiten, kart., ISBN 3-88099-031-X   DM 40.—

SAG 33: **Martin Hüttel,** Marxistisch-leninistische Literaturtheorie: Die theoretische Bedeutung der Literaturkritik von Marx, Engels und Lenin. 1977, 164 Seiten, kart., ISBN 3-88099-032-8   DM 20.—

SAG 34: **Jens Rieckmann,** Der Zauberberg: Eine geistige Autobiographie Thomas Manns. 1977, 186 Seiten, kart., ISBN 3-88099-033-6   DM 29.—

SAG 35: **Beth Bjorklund,** A Study in Comparative Prosody: English and German Iambic Pentameter. 1978, 494 Seiten, kart.,ISBN 3-88099-034-4   DM 68.—

SAG 36: **Karl-Heinz Köhler,** Poetische Sprache und Sprachbewußtsein um 1900: Untersuchungen zum frühen Werk Hermann Hesses, Paul Ernsts und Ricarda Huchs. 1977, 302 Seiten, kart.,ISBN 3-88099-035-2   DM 42.—

SAG 37: **Nancy Lukens,** Büchner's Valerio and the Theatrical Fool Tradition. 1978, 232 Seiten, kart., ISBN 3-88099-035-0   DM 25.—

SAG 38: **Alan Corkhill,** The Motif of „Fate" in the Works of Ludwig Tieck. 1978, 240 Seiten, kart., ISBN 3-88099-039-5   DM 42.—

SAG 39: **Vicki Hill,** Bertolt Brecht and the Post-War French Drama
1978, 350 Seiten, kart., ISBN 3-88099-040-9   DM 42.—

SAG 40: **Sibylle Mulot,** Der junge Musil. Seine Beziehung zur Literatur und Kunst der Jahrhundertwende. 1977, 284 Seiten, kart.,
ISBN 3-88099-041-7   DM 38.—

SAG 41: **Giuseppe Dolei,** L'arte come espiazione imperfetta: Saggio su Trakl. 1978, 186 Seiten, kart., ISBN 3-88099-042-5   DM 22.—

SAG 42: **Naomi Ritter,** House and Individual: The House Motif in German Literature of the 19th Century. 1978, 210 Seiten, kart.,
ISBN 3-88099-043-3   DM 34.—

SAG 43: **William H. Wilkening,** Otto Julius Bierbaum: The Tragedy of a Poet. A Biography, 1978, 216 Seiten, kart.,ISBN 3-88099-044-1   DM 45.—

SAG 44: **Michael Wulff,** Konkrete Poesie und sprachimmanente Lüge. Von Ernst Jandl zu Ansätzen einer Sprachästhetik. 1978, 650 Seiten, kart.,
ISBN 3-88099-045-X   DM 85.—

SAG 45: **Werner Brändle,** Die dramatischen Stücke Martin Walsers. Variationen über das Elend des bürgerlichen Subjekts. 1978, 250 Seiten, kart.
ISBN 3-88099-046-8   DM 34.—

SAG 46: **Wolfgang Lechner,** Mechanismen der Literaturrezeption in Österreich am Beispiel Ödön von Horvaths. 1978, 568 Seiten, kart.,
ISBN 3-88099-047-6   DM 78.—

SAG 47: Theodor Mechtenberg, Utopie als ästhetische Kategorie. Eine Untersuchung der Lyrik Ingeborg Bachmanns. 1978, 140 Seiten, kart.,
ISBN 3-88099-048-4 DM 18.—

SAG 48: Ekkehard Gühne, Gottscheds Literaturkritik in den „Vernünfftigen Tadlerinnen" (1725/1726). 1978, 470 Seiten, kart.,
ISBN 3-88099-049-2 DM 65.—

SAG 49: Carolyn Thomas Dussere, The Image of the Primitive Giant in the Works of Gerhart Hauptmann. 1978, 263 Seiten, kart.,
ISBN 3-88099-050-6 ca. DM 35.—

SAG 50: Hans Höller, Kritik einer literarischen Form: Versuch über Thomas Bernhard. 1979, ca. 140 Seiten, kart.,
ISBN 3-88099-051-4 in Vorbereitung

SAG 51: Manfred Lefevre, Von der proletarisch-revolutionären zur antifaschistisch-sozialistischen Literatur. Die Entwicklung der Literaturkonzeption deutscher kommunistischer Schriftsteller von der End-Phase der Weimarer Republik bis zum Jahr 1935. 1979, ca. 450 Seiten, kart.,
ISBN 3-88099-052-2 ca. DM 62.—

SAG 52: Erhard Jöst, Agitation durch Kriegslyrik. Ein Unterrichtsmodell für den Deutschunterricht auf der Sekundarstufe II. 1978, 117 Seiten, kart.,
ISBN 3-88099-053-0 DM 10.—

SAG 53: Maria-Eva Jahn, Techniken der fiktiven Bildkomposition in Heinrich Heines Reisebildern. 1978, 80 Seiten, 8 Abb.,
ISBN 3-88099-054-9 DM 26.—

SAG 54: Mary Gerhart-Weber, The Question of Belief in Literary Criticism: An Introduction of the Hermeneutical Theory of Paul Ricoeur. 1979, ca. 250 S., kart., ISBN 3-88099-055-7 ca. DM 40.—

SAG 55: Heike Mück, Unterrichtseinheit Lustspiel: Gerhart Hauptmann. Der Biberpelz. 1979, ca. 100 Seiten, kart., ISBN 3-88099-056-5 ca. DM 10.—

SAG 56: Gordon Browning, Tristan Tzara: The Genesis of the Dada Poem or from Dada to AA. 1979, 200 Seiten, kart., ISBN 3-88099-057-3 DM 35.—

SAG 57: Sabine D. Jordan, Ludwig Ferdinand Huber (1764—1804). His Life and Works. 1979, 307 Seiten, kart., ISBN 3-88099-058-1 DM 48.—

SAG 58: Erich Mayser, Heinrich Heines „Buch der Lieder" im 19. Jahrhundert. 1979, 286 Seiten, kart., ISBN 3-88099-059-X DM 40.—

SAG 59: Günther Gottschalk, Dichter und ihre Handschriften: Betrachtungen zu Autographen des jungen Hermann Hesse im Marbacher Archiv. 1979, ca. 100 Seiten, kart., ISBN 3-88099-060-3 ca. DM 20.—

SAG 60: Elisabeth Welzig, Literatur und journalistische Literaturkritik: Untersucht an den steirischen Tageszeitungen 1945—1955. 1979, 232 Seiten, kart., ISBN 3-88099-061-1 DM 38.—

SAG 61: W. B. Mullan, Grillparzer's Aesthetic Theory: A Study with Special Reference to his Conception of the Drama as "eine Gegenwart". 1979, 200 Seiten, kart., ISBN 3-88099-062-X DM 32.—